Delivering Home-Based Services

Delivering Home-Based Services

A SOCIAL WORK PERSPECTIVE

Edited by Susan F. Allen
and Elizabeth M. Tracy

Columbia University Press   New York

Columbia University Press
Publishers Since 1893
New York   Chichester, West Sussex
Copyright © 2009 Columbia University Press
All rights reserved

Library of Congress Cataloging-in-Publication Data
Delivering home-based services : a social work perspective /
edited by Susan F. Allen and Elizabeth M. Tracy.
p. cm.
Includes bibliographical references and index.
ISBN 978-0231-14146-8 (cloth : alk paper) —
ISBN 978-0-231-14147-5 (pbk. : alk. paper) —
ISBN 978-0-231-52030-0 (e-book)
1. Home-based family services. 2. Home care services. 3. Social work with children.
I. Allen, Susan F., 1951– II. Tracy, Elizabeth M. III. Title.

HV697.D45   2009
362.82'53—dc22   2008054884

Columbia University Press books are printed on permanent and durable acid-free paper.
This book is printed on paper with recycled content.
Printed in the United States of America

c 10 9 8 7 6 5 4 3 2 1
p 10 9 8 7 6 5 4 3 2 1

References to Internet Web sites (URLs) were accurate at the time of writing.
Neither the author nor Columbia University Press is responsible for URLs
that may have expired or changed since the manuscript was prepared.

Contents

Preface

This book builds upon social work's legacy of home visiting, which has reasserted itself in the current emphasis on community-based social work practice. The renewed emphasis on home-based rather than agency-based services stems in part from changes in funding streams and increased efforts to serve clients directly in their ecological contexts. Service delivery in the home is now common to forms of practice as diverse as home health visits with older adults, case-management services with paroled offenders, and placement-prevention and family-reunification services in child welfare.

The contributors to this volume, national experts in their respective fields, view the home as more than just a setting where social workers deliver services. The home provides the ecological context for human development and family interaction. As such, it can have a dynamic effect on service delivery. Chapters in this book present rationales for and overviews of evidence-based models for delivering home-based services across different client populations and social work fields of practice.

The purpose of this book is to enhance and enrich the social work profession's understanding of approaches to delivering home-based services. Readers will become familiar with a variety of models for the delivery of home-based services and will be able to identify key factors and issues crucial to effective home-based practice with the range of clients served in social work fields of practice. Our hope is that by examining home-based services in a variety of contexts, we can add to the knowledge base, elucidate and integrate key practice issues that emerge, and conclude with a conceptual framework for home-based services across social work settings.

Too often, the literature on home-based practices is fragmented and lacks a unified approach to the topic. However, there is much that unifies home-based services across social work settings. For example, many chapters in this text discuss the complex issues of hard-to-reach clients and their families, who might not receive services if they are not delivered in the home environment. Consumers' health and disability issues are discussed frequently in this book, as this topic cuts across all social work settings for home-based services. Regarding interventions, delivering home visits usually involves multiple social work roles, including those of broker, advocate, and educator/psychoeducator. As a comprehensive overview of home-based services usable both as a scholarly resource and a course text, this book fills a significant gap in the social work literature. It is time for social workers to revitalize and reclaim this practice arena, and we hope that this volume will serve as a resource in that endeavor.

This book is divided into three parts. The first part discusses the historical context, contemporary applications, ethical complexities, and administrative and social-policy context for home-based services. The chapters concern the historical and current context for home-based services (Susan F. Allen and Elizabeth M. Tracy), the array of ethical issues that confront home-based workers (Kimberly Strom-Gottfried), administrative and supervision issues unique to agencies that provide home-based services (Kristine Nelson, Mindy Holliday, and Katharine Cahn), and the social-policy contexts (Cathleen A. Lewandowski and Katharine Briar Lawson) that inform and shape service delivery.

The middle section, the heart of the book, comprises eight chapters on home-based practice in social work fields of practice. These are early childhood programs (Susan F. Allen), school-based services (Cynthia Franklin and Christine Lagana-Riordan), child welfare (Cathleen A. Lewandowski and Katharine Briar-Lawson), child mental health (Mary Armstrong, Roger Boothroyd, Mary E. Evans, and Anne Kuppinger), criminal justice (José B. Ashford, Katherine O. Sternbach, and Maureen Balaam), adult mental health (Patrick Sullivan), older adult services (Kathryn Betts Adams), and hospice and end-of-life care (Ellen Csikai). To ensure that the coverage was comprehensive and uniform for the reader, the authors for each chapter in this middle section followed a common outline:

1. The population
2. Policy and agency context

3. Purposes and goals of social work home-based services
4. Theoretical framework
5. Empirical base
6. Practice guidelines
7. Issues of diversity and practice with populations at risk
8. Implications for home-based practice

The concluding section of the book consists of the final chapter, which synthesizes a framework for understanding home-based services, building on commonalities from the practice-setting chapters, and comments on future directions for home-based social work (Elizabeth M. Tracy and Susan F. Allen). An appendix contains addresses and Web sites for organizations associated with home-based programs, research, or policies.

This volume grew out of a longstanding working collaboration between Susan Allen and Elizabeth Tracy. We have learned much from each other about home-based services as we planned training workshops and wrote journal articles on the role of home-based services in school social work and on preparing social work students for home-based practice. We have benefited from the tradition of home-based services in social work and from the work of others in the field. Susan Allen would like to thank the many clients who welcomed her into their homes over the years, leading her to appreciate the value and importance of home-based services. Elizabeth Tracy is indebted to Dr. James Whittaker, the Charles O. Cressey Endowed Professor Emeritus at the University of Washington School of Social Work, for introducing her to the topic of home-based services and for mentoring her early and continued work in family-preservation services. We have each found much that is lasting in home-based services and that is true to the mission and focus of social work. It is our hope that this volume will introduce the reader to the range of home-based services in the social work profession and will form the foundation for further research into the effectiveness and expansion of these services.

Delivering Home-Based Services

PART I

Introduction

One

_____

Historical and Current Context

SUSAN F. ALLEN AND ELIZABETH M. TRACY

Chapter Overview

Despite the different terms used and the different reasons for delivering services in homes, the unifying thread across social work fields of practice for the service models described in this book is the dynamic of providing help in the ecological context of the home. This chapter introduces the historical and current context for home-based social work practice and discusses the rationales for delivering services in the home. This chapter also discusses the skills needed for delivering home-based services, as the home environment can affect each step of the social work intervention process. The chapter concludes with comments on the dimensions of social work in-home practice that are considered in the following chapters.

Definition of Home-Based Services

There are a number of different perspectives to consider when defining social work practice that occurs in recipients' homes. Sometimes the home is viewed as just another setting where social work assessment and interventions take place. In this view, the work of assessment and intervention is not affected to any significant degree by the setting in which it occurs. At other times, the home environment is considered to have an influence on social work assessment and intervention practices, either by facilitating the work or presenting challenges to the work at hand. In this book, we approach this topic from the latter perspective: the home environment should be seen as a dynamic force with a substantial effect on the content and method of service delivery.

This book is concerned with a service-delivery model that takes place across a variety of social work practice settings and may be referred to as home-based/in-home services, home-based practice, home-based programs, or home visiting/visitation. The commonality across these various terms is that they all involve working with people in their "natural environments." Some practice orientations, such as family-centered practice and some forms of case-management services, value and support the use of home visiting as a major or primary means of service delivery. In other settings, a visit to the home may occur just once, in the context of other types of services delivered or in situations where eligibility for a service must be determined. One-time or time-limited home visits may be used in the context of early intervention or prevention services, such as in home visits to mothers soon after the birth of a child (e.g., Daro et al. 2005). Likewise, the home may be the vehicle to deliver intensive services to families, and thus visits are made as often and as long as needed during a defined time period (e.g., Henggeler et al. 1998; Kinney, Haapala, and Booth 1991).

In addition to variations in the duration and intensity of home visiting, home-visit services differ in their overall objective or focus. Masten and Coatsworth (1998) identify three primary objectives: "process focused," "resource focused," or "risk focused." Process-focused home-based practice emphasizes fostering connections between the practice setting and the people served by that setting. Resource-focused home visits involve enhancing access to needed community resources and services, both formal and informal. Risk-focused home visits deal with eliminating or ameliorating risk factors. Risk-focused home visits are typically initiated by a referral to community or agency services due to physical, social, or emotional problems or difficulties. Of course, the primary purpose of home visits may change over time with the needs of the client and as the social worker–client relationship develops.

Rationales for delivering home-based services include ensuring continuity of care, improving access to difficult-to-reach clients, minimizing barriers to care, facilitating generalization of new skills to the natural environment, and minimizing the power imbalance by meeting people on their own turf (Gomby, Culross, and Behrman 1999; Lindblad-Goldberg, Dore, and Stern 1998; Wasik and Bryant 2001). Social workers who assess clients in their homes may be able to observe directly the resources and challenges in the client's environment. This can lead to a more accurate assessment of client needs. While being cognizant of confidentiality issues, home visitors may be able to engage with family members who would not otherwise attend family sessions and intervene to strengthen crucial client informal-support networks. Resourceful social workers can take advantage of the home environment to build on the strengths of family interactions and resources. Proponents of home-based work also note the compatibility of this form of practice with core social work values, such as client self-determination and involvement in the service-delivery process (Beder 1998; Weiss 1993).

History of Home-Based Services in Social Work

Home visiting has a long legacy in social work and, in many ways, the use of home visits parallels major changes in social work practice and policy (see table 1). Home visiting was originally termed "friendly visiting" when it was organized in the late 1800s as a volunteer service by charity-aid organizations (Richmond 1899/1906). One of the basic tenets of friendly visiting was to explore all possible sources for self-help and to seek naturally occurring sources of help for the family. The home visit was essential to assessing what resources within the family and surrounding community could provide assistance, thereby reducing the need for formal charitable services. In *Friendly Visiting Among the Poor*, Richmond describes the manner in which relatives, friends, and others known to the family would be contacted regarding "their theory as to the best method of aiding, together with some definite promise as to what they themselves will do" (188) to help. The home visit was the window into both establishing and securing these resources for the family.

In the first half of the 1900s, the use of home visiting expanded to schools and hospitals, as well as to child welfare and social services. One of the first volumes of the National Association of Social Workers' journal *Social Work* contains a description of a comprehensive home-service approach with multi-problem families, the St. Paul Family-Centered Project (Birt 1956), which in many ways foreshadows the delivery of current intensive family-preservation services. While early home-visit work was essentially viewed as the medium of help, this view shifted as social workers adopted more psychologically based approaches to intervention, and the home and social environment of clients increasingly became an adjunct to treatment. In this view, the home visit was important because family members and key informal helpers could be more involved in treatment planning and in the maintenance of treatment gains. However, as Beder (1998) and Hancock and Pelton (1989) point out, with time, as part of the trend of social workers seeking a more professional status, home-based work fell into disregard and became a neglected area in practice and professional training. Home visits were also criticized for invading clients' privacy, particularly prior to the 1970s, when financial and social services were linked. The home did not again become a respected site for prevention and intervention services until the 1980s and beyond (Adnopoz 2006). Home visiting returned to favor following the passage of the Adoption Assistance and Child Welfare Act of 1980 and the formation of a national resource center and organization devoted to home-based services (Nelson and Landsman 1992).

As part of the current emphasis on community-based services, Lightburn and Schamess (2002) view home-based practices as an antidote to past practices that were unsuccessful due to "fragmentation, inaccessibility, unresponsiveness to cultural differences, and isolation from integral family and community systems that support development" (820). Today, social workers in many practice settings work with clients in their homes. For example, in the field of mental health, community-based systems of care have been promoted by federal, state, and foundation initiatives over traditional institutional care (Lightburn and Sessions 2006). The President's New Freedom Commission on Mental Health (2003) is consistent with a move toward more home-based services; the report set forth the need for community-based services with the goal to make mental health care consumer and family driven.

The NASW Center for Workforce Studies' 2004 survey of a nationwide random sample of ten thousand licensed social workers provides some information on the extent of home visiting. Their sample of 4,436 respondents was stratified by region and yielded a response rate of 49.4 percent. Eighty-one percent of the respondents were actively employed as social workers, 79 percent held an MSW, 12 percent held a BSW, 2 percent held doctorates, and 8 percent had no social work degree. Survey participants worked in the following practice specialty areas: 37 percent in mental health and addictions, 13 percent in child/family welfare, 13 percent in health care, 9 percent in aging, 8 percent in school social work, 6 percent in services for adolescents, and 14 percent in all other areas of social work. Based on an analysis of data from the NASW Workforce Study, over one-third (36.5 percent) reported that some portion of their time was currently spent conducting home visits. Amounts of time spent on home visits varied as follows: 17.2 percent reported spending 1 to 10 percent of their time conducting home visits, 12.3 percent reported 11 to 50 percent, and 6.9 percent reported from 51 to 100 percent of their time. Some, but not all, felt prepared to provide home-based services to children and families. When asked to rate their ability to provide home visits on a scale from 1 (low) to 5 (high), 9.4 percent ranked their ability as 1, 11.8 percent ranked their ability at 2 or 3,

TABLE 1.1

Highlights in the History of Home Visiting in Social Work

1890s	Friendly visiting of charitable organization societies; *Friendly Visiting Among the Poor* (Richmond 1899/1906)
1900s	Emergence of home-visiting teachers and school liaisons; Massachusetts General Hospital begins a home-visiting program
1949	St. Paul's Family-Centered Project—early home-based service approach
1960s	Home visits for social-welfare practice
1970s	Social services separates from income assistance; First National Clearinghouse for Home-Based Services established
1980s	Family Preservation and Support Services Program (PL103-66)—reasonable efforts to prevent placement, home-based family-preservation programs; Education of the Handicapped Act Amendments, Part H (PL 99-457, 1986)—intervention with young children who are disabled or at risk and their families in their natural environment; National Resource Center for Family Based Services established
1990s	Growth in home-based services: home health care, hospice, early childhood, intervention, multisystemic treatment for youth and families; Adoption and Safe Families Act (PL 105-89)
2000s	Promoting Safe and Stable Families Amendment (PL 107-133) focuses on child safety, well-being, and permanency; President's New Freedom Commission on Mental Health

Source: Reprinted, with permission, from Allen and Tracy (2008).

9.1 percent ranked their ability at 4, and 24 percent ranked their ability at 5. It should be noted that the focus of this survey was current practice experiences and may underrepresent social workers' experiences conducting home visits during the course of their career.*

Skills for Delivering Home-Based Services

Home- and community-based services provide an opportunity to define and work with client problems in conceptually different ways than in an office setting. Work in homes, neighborhoods, and other natural settings hold tremendous promise for the development of collaborative, working partner-

---

* One of the chapter authors (SA) took an informal poll of home-visiting experience in a master's-level family-therapy class. Of eighteen students, all but two were currently conducting home visits in their field placement or at work or had conducted home visits in past social-service jobs.

ships between social workers and clients. However, meeting clients in their homes rather than in a more controlled office environment can also lead to challenging situations and present ethical dilemmas (see chapter 2). When delivering home-based services, social workers must possess well-developed skills for keeping interviews focused despite distractions (Lindblad-Goldberg et al. 1998), setting appropriate boundaries with clients, maintaining client confidentiality, ensuring social worker and client safety, and making use of supervision (Allen and Tracy 2008). Delivering effective services to clients in their home environment requires certain interview skills and involves each step of the intervention process: engagement, assessment, goal planning and implementation, and evaluation and termination.

Although basic interviewing skills used for all types of social work practice are needed for in-home work, the development of certain skills can be particularly important. Social workers meeting with clients in the home need to be particularly aware of the rich nonverbal aspects of communication both on their parts and the parts of clients and their families. For example, how a social worker dresses and her body language as she sits in a cluttered kitchen may be more crucial to her interaction with the client than what she says. Reading the nonverbal cues of clients may alert the worker to an escalating confrontation despite the words being said. Home environments are full of distractions, such as televisions blaring and extended family dropping by, and these can derail the helpful focus of an interview. Other times, they can present opportunities to deal with vital issues. Therefore, home-visitation social workers need to develop both keen abilities to structure and redirect the interview process and to assess events for their therapeutic potential as they are unfolding. In addition, social workers have opportunities to revise consumers' own views of their home environment and their interaction patterns with family members through reframing, another especially valuable interview skill. For example, a social worker may reframe an elder's embarrassment over a messy kitchen as her commitment to continue to make home-cooked meals for her family despite the elder's physical challenges. Interview skills such as these are valuable at every phase of the intervention process. In addition, each step of social work home-based practice presents unique challenges and opportunities.

Engaging with clients and their families enrolled in home-based programs can be particularly challenging, as these programs often target families who have been unable or unwilling to access office-based services and may have difficulty trusting and developing relationships with helping professionals (See, e.g., LeCroy and Whitaker 2005; Lindblad-Goldberg et al. 1998; McCurdy and Jones 2000). Nevertheless, the neighborhood and home environments offer tools that may help the engagement process. Social workers' observational skills become crucial as they look for strengths to acknowledge, such as safety equipment in a house with a young child or a frail elder, which may enhance the development of a therapeutic alliance. An asset of providing in-home services, as well as a challenge in regards to confidentiality and limit setting, is that contact can be established with all those who live in the home and not just those who would attend office sessions.

Social workers' observations of clients' living situations can have a particularly important influence on the assessment process. This awareness of the neighborhood and home environments may lead more rapidly to a holistic understanding of the client's environmental strengths and challenges compared to assessments in an office setting, where much of the information provided by the client is verbal. Aspects of the neighborhood and home environment can be observed to evaluate the assets and challenges for the client (Allen and Tracy 2008). For example, social workers may observe strengths of the neighborhood, such as proximity to community resources, and challenges such as safety concerns. A strength of the home environment can be the presence of and supportive communication with extended family members; a challenge, the lack of physical space for privacy needs. When social workers use formal tools to help structure the assessment process, tools can be selected that will help evaluate the resources and challenges reflected in the consumer's natural environment. For example, the Home Observation for Measurement of the Environment (Caldwell and Bradley 1984) may be used in initial assessments of families with children; the Social Work Assessment Tool (Reese et al. 2006) can be used for on-going assessment of hospice services. Eco-maps that chart consumers' interactions with their environment, genograms to map the history of family relationships, and family timelines to list the sequence of important events can be very useful in a wide range of home-based practice settings (Lindblad-Goldberg et al. 1998).

Specific social work practice skills, including observation, collaboration, and facilitation of role plays, are particularly important when setting goals and implementing interventions in the home environment. Consumers and their families partner with social workers to develop goals within the environmental context that provides the resources for implementation. Social workers use their awareness of the client's environment to support goals that build on client strengths. In addition, specific family members who are crucial to setting goals and implementing interventions are more likely to be present during home visits than at office sessions. Because home-visitation programs tend to serve consumers who deal with particularly daunting life challenges, it can be vital to develop small, obtainable goals in incremental steps so that consumers and their families can early on experience some success in making changes

(Lindblad-Goldberg et al. 1998). Social work interventions may involve modeling, role plays, and reinforcement of new behaviors with the client and family members in the home environment, where they will be implemented. Observations of family interactions and resource deficits in the consumer's natural environment may also provide crucial clues to roadblocks in the therapeutic process.

Delivering services in the home environment can benefit the evaluation and termination phases of social work practice. Meeting with consumers in their homes enhances the evaluation and reinforcement of behavioral changes. Social workers may be able to observe and comment on progress in the home environment that would not be visible during office visits, supplementing the consumer's verbal reports of goal attainment. Family members crucial for the earlier phases of treatment may also provide helpful input as goals are evaluated and services terminated.

Dimensions of Home-Based Practice

Home-based practice can be thought of as having four dimensions: who, what, when, and where. Each dimension is described below.

Who

Programs that deliver home-based services take different approaches to the focal problem in terms of whom they serve. Those that take a universal approach make an effort to reach all of those in a given population, in order to prevent problems from developing. Other programs take a selected approach, serving those assessed as specifically at risk for developing a problem. Programs that only serve those identified as having developed the problem take a targeted approach.

What

Home-based programs also vary in the objectives of the services provided. As previously mentioned, they may be process, resource, or risk focused (Masten and Coatsworth 1998). These objectives relate to the types of services delivered (Allen and Tracy 2004). A thorough assessment of client resources and needs provides the basis for goal setting and is a key component of home-based practice. Services provided in home-based practice run the gamut of social work interventions, including, for example, all types of case-management interventions (e.g., instrumental, informational, and material support), crisis-intervention strategies, advocacy, social support, enhancing problem-solving skills, and promoting informal social support systems.

When

Home-based services may target clients during any lifespan period, from birth, as in early childhood home visiting, to death, as with hospice care. Since the focus is on intervening in the client's environmental context, home-based practice often involves work with the client's extended family and personal social network. Therefore, although a program may target clients at a particular point in their lifespan, home-based social workers in any given agency routinely work with clients in a wider range of lifespan periods. The life-stage tasks of the focal client group can influence the client needs and type of services delivered.

Where

Home-based services emanate from agencies that cover the range of social work settings of practice. Those covered in this book include schools, child welfare, mental health, criminal justice, and hospice. As such, home-based services derive from many policy and agency contexts. Depending on the field of practice, social policies may either facilitate or impede the delivery of home-based services (see chapter 4). In addition, there are administrative challenges inherent in delivering home-based services that cut across agency settings and fields of practice (see chapter 3).

Summary

Home visiting, with its lengthy tradition in social work, is an essential component of current social work practices that focus on working with clients in their natural environmental context to deliver accessible services that build on client strengths. This book provides a comprehensive view of the "who, what, when, and where" of social work home-based services in diverse practice settings and with social work clients throughout the lifespan. In addition, it addresses the special challenges in terms of ethical dilemmas and administrative practices for practitioners and agencies that deliver services to clients in their homes and discusses how social policies provide an influential context for service delivery and evaluation.

REFERENCES

Adnopoz, J. A. 2006. Working with high-risk children and families in their own homes: An integrative approach to the treatment of vulnerable children. In *Handbook of community-based clinical practice*, ed. A. Lightburn and P. Sessions, 364–378. New York: Oxford University Press.

Allen, S. F., and Tracy, E. M. 2004. Revitalizing the role of home visiting by school social workers. *Children and Schools* 26 (4): 197–208.

——. 2008. Developing student knowledge and skills for home-based social work practice. *Journal of Social Work Education* 44 (1): 125–143.

Beder, J. 1998. The home visit, revisited. *Families in Society: The Journal of Contemporary Human Services* 79: 514–522.

Birt, C. 1956. Family-centered project of St. Paul. *Social Work* 2: 41–47.

Caldwell, B., and Bradley, R. 1984. *Home Observation for the Home Environment (HOME)*. Rev. ed. Little Rock: University of Arkansas.

Daro, D., Howard, E., Tobin, J., and Harden, A. 2005. *Welcome home and early start: An assessment of program quality and outcomes*. Chicago: Chapin Hall Center for Children.

Gomby, D. S., Culross, P. L., and Behrman, R. E. 1999. Home visiting: Recent program evaluations: Analysis and recommendations. *The Future of Children* 9 (1): 4–26.

Hancock, B. L., and Pelton, L. H. 1989. Home visits: History and functions. *Social Casework: The Journal of Contemporary Social Work* 70 (1): 21–27.

Henggeler, S. W., Schoenwald, S. K., Borduin, C. M., Rowland, M. D., and Cunningham, P. B. 1998. *Multisystemic treatment of antisocial children and adolescents*. New York: Guilford.

Kinney, J. D., Haapala, D., and Booth, C. 1991. *Keeping families together: The Homebuilders model*. New York: Aldine de Gruyter.

LeCroy, C. W., and Whitaker, K. 2005. Improving the quality of home visitation: An exploratory study of difficult situations. *Child Abuse and Neglect* 29: 1003–1013.

Lightburn, A., and Schamess, G. 2002. The generativity and intergenerational nature of social work practice. In *Social workers' desk reference*, ed. A. R. Roberts and G. J. Greene, 817–821. New York: Oxford University Press.

Lightburn, A., and Sessions, P., eds. 2006. *Handbook of community-based clinical practice.* New York: Oxford University Press.

Lindblad-Goldberg, M., Dore, M. M., and Stern, L. 1998. *Creating competence from chaos: A comprehensive guide to home-based services.* New York: W. W. Norton & Company.

Masten, A. S., and Coatsworth, J. D. 1998. The development of competence in favorable and unfavorable environments: Lessons from research on successful children. *American Psychologist* 53: 205–220.

McCurdy, K., and Jones, E. D. 2000. *Supporting families: Lessons from the field.* Thousand Oaks, Calif.: Sage.

NASW Center for Workforce Studies. 2004. *A study of the roles and use of licensed social workers in the United States.* Washington, D.C.: National Association of Social Workers.

Nelson, K. E., and Landsman, M. J. 1992. *Alternative models of family-based services in context.* Springfield, Ill.: Charles C. Thomas.

New Freedom Commission on Mental Health. 2003. Available online at http://www.mentalhealthcommission.gov/reports/FinalReport/toc.html.

Reese, D. J., Raymer, M., Orloff, S. F., Gerbino, S., Valade, R., and Dawson, S. 2006. The social work assessment tool (SWAT). *Journal of Social Work in End-of-Life and Palliative Care* 2 (1): 65–95.

Richmond, M. E. 1899/1906. *Friendly visiting among the poor: A handbook for charity workers.* New York: The Macmillan Company.

Wasik, B. H., and Bryant, D. M. 2001. *Home visiting: Procedures for helping families.* 2nd ed. Newbury Park, Calif.: Sage.

Weiss, H. B. 1993. Home visits: Necessary but not sufficient. *The Future of Children* 3 (3): 113–128.

Two

Ethical Issues and Guidelines

KIMBERLY STROM-GOTTFRIED

I went to a family's apartment to meet with them about their son's truancy and it seemed the entire neighborhood was there as well as some extended family. They had put on this elaborate meal and expected me to sit down and join them. Was it inappropriate to do so? How was I supposed to handle confidentiality with all those people around? What about setting boundaries?

I was doing court-ordered in-home family counseling with a family, and during the first meeting all three adults and a teenage son smoked. The son's girl-friend watched a talk show on TV and occasionally participated in the conversation. An infant child in the home cried constantly and a four-year-old noisily chased the family's cats with a toy car. I wanted the racket and the smoking to stop but I worried about alienating the family and violating their self-determination. Was I putting my needs ahead of theirs? Was I being disrespectful?

I am a case worker for frail elders residing in an urban high-rise apartment building. My clients there often offer me food and drinks, but their housing is so decrepit I can't bear the thought of accepting, for hygiene reasons alone. But I feel bad declining; I can't be honest about my reasons . . . after all they have to live in these conditions. It would be like I thought I was better than them. I have another client who wants to read Bible passages for each visit and another who shows me pictures of her grandson and hints that she should introduce us. I commented on one woman's quilt and she offered to sew one for me! I'm sure workers who see clients in the office never have to worry about these things!

As these accounts illustrate, social workers in home-based services must apply recognized ethical principles to novel and occasionally unpredictable circumstances. Given the isolation and autonomy that characterize in-home services, it is especially important that workers possess broad knowledge of ethics and sound decision-making skills. This chapter examines some elements of home-based services that give rise to ethical dilemmas and describes the application of principles such as self-determination, competence, and confidentiality to in-home practice. An ethical decision-making model is introduced and applied to a case to illustrate the critical thinking required for effective, ethical in-home practice.

Ethics in the Context of Home-Based Services

The term "ethics" refers to the knowledge and guidance used to distinguish right from wrong in a given situation. Ethical dilemmas arise when it is difficult to discern which action is the "right" one because two values or goods are in conflict with each other. In the introductory vignettes, we see this as the social worker balances respect for the clients' choices (to smoke, watch TV, have extended family present) with other rights and considerations (the worker's right to be free of second-hand smoke, her responsibility to manage the session in an efficient and effective manner, protecting client privacy). Sometimes, social workers can find compromise in these competing tensions. At other times, it seems impossible, and sound, purposeful decision making is required to choose the greater good among various options. In addition to the ethical dilemmas common to all practice settings, home-based work is characterized by three features that complicate ethical decision making: increased exposure to information, greater autonomy, and diminished control.

Exposure to Information

A clear benefit of home-based services is that it allows the worker to more readily and viscerally envision the client's reality. Experiencing the curiosity and concern of neighbors in an apartment building, the physical conditions of a public housing project, or the isolation of a rural locale helps put the worker in the client's shoes. These encounters should positively influence rapport, insight, case planning, and other features of the working relationship. Immersion in the client's home life also presents challenges. The worker has an opportunity to observe the client's surroundings and must use his or her clinical and ethical acumen to decide which of the things observed are relevant to the helping process and which are not. For example, a worker who finds an immigrant family using a barbecue grill indoors may intervene to educate the clients about the risks of carbon monoxide poisoning and fire, regardless of the purposes of the visit. But what if the same worker observes all adults in the household smoking or spreading lard on bread? If unhealthy activities are observed, where should the worker draw the line in acting on his or her observations? Do clients, in opening their homes to professionals, open themselves up to all manner of critiques about how they choose to live their lives? Can workers effectively carry out their responsibilities if they selectively attend to troubling data? On what basis should workers act on their observations or choose restraint?

Immersion in the client's lived experience also means access to the sights, sounds, and smells that accompany that environment. Reading in a file that three adults and seven children live in a small apartment is one thing, but seeing it is quite another. The advantage, of course, is an increased appreciation for the clients' living conditions. The downside may be that the worker is left with intense feelings and images that are difficult to shake. Such powerful impressions and experiences may make it difficult for the worker to maintain appropriate boundaries, to focus on professional purposes, and to avoid burnout and vicarious trauma (Naturale 2007). Home-based work can provide a potent introduction into the client's lived experience, and, as such, it can both enhance the professional encounter and complicate it.

Autonomy

Another source of ethical complexity arises from the autonomy inherent in in-home services. Workers in these settings are often working without a safety net. Because there is less accessible backup and consultation, workers must have the maturity and confidence to approach novel situations, the ability to determine when assistance is needed, and the competence to seek out help when situations dictate. In-home workers must demonstrate integrity and trustworthiness, eschewing the temptations that can accompany freedom from oversight and office protocols. Organizations must be able to trust that home-based workers are carrying out their visits competently and reliably, allotting the appropriate amount of time to each case, and making sound judgments in the absence of ready oversight. Workers must be able to trust that their employers have the proper policies and precautions in place to assure safe and effectual service delivery. Proper training, orientation, supervision, and administration are some of the organizational imperatives for competent services outside of traditional office settings (see chapter 3).

The enhanced autonomy of in-home care can also lead to role ambiguity for the worker and the client. Is the worker a friendly visitor, a clinician, an investigator, or a friend? Clients without a history of receiving in-home services may be uncertain about the protocols for hosting such a visit. Unless they are properly informed prior to the visit, this confusion can lead to resentment, apprehensions, and heightened anxiety. It can also lead to complications in the session, such as the presence of other guests in the home, offers of food, or lack of preparation for the visit, if, for example, the child client is not home. Workers who are not clear about their roles, responsibilities, and objectives for the session may have difficulty staying on task, structuring the meeting, and setting appropriate boundaries. Without comfort in the mission and the authority they possess as professionals, these workers may defer to the "host"/client's wishes and behaviors and cede control of the session. As with the abundance of observations in a home visit, the abundance of freedom also requires clarity of purpose and clearly communicated expectations in order to be managed effectively.

Diminished Control

A third defining feature of home-based services is that the environment is largely out of the worker's control. Moving the interaction from the professional's office to the client's "turf" has both tangible and subtle implications. The client's home may be remote and isolated or teeming with activity. The time allotted to the interview may be punctuated with intrusions from neighbors, family, and pets. Clients may feel more secure in the home environment and engage in behaviors they might not otherwise do in an office setting— slapping a child, lying on the sofa, using the bathroom with the door open, playing video games, preparing a snack. As with the other dynamics in home-based care, a fluid environment and client comfort can enhance the worker's capacity to understand and engage with the client system. It can also create dilemmas, as workers determine where and how to draw limits on requests, behaviors, or activities.

Safety and hygiene are particular concerns stemming from the diminished worker control in home-based services. The risk of worker injury or harm stems from three primary factors: the surroundings, the client, and the worker's demeanor. Clients' home environments can produce both safety and security concerns from such elements as neighborhood violence, unleashed animals, precarious stairs or furniture, vermin, and access to weapons. The risk from clients themselves is heightened by a past history of violence against persons, property, or pets; alcohol or drug intoxication; physical impairments; other conditions that produce feelings of powerlessness; and problems with impulse control, information processing, or emotional regulation. Case situations in which the client may experience intense emotions such as extreme frustration, a sense of injustice or oppression, fear, embarrassment, or grief can escalate risk. So too does access to weaponry, particularly firearms.

A social worker's own actions and attitudes have a bearing on the risk of violence. Workers who approach the client in an overtly authoritative, dismissive, confrontational, or demanding fashion may provoke client ire or fail to respond to the signs of escalating tension. Behaving in a way that does not respect the client's rights, wishes, and personal space may also increase the risk of physical or verbal aggression.

Addressing Health and Safety Risks

While these various health and safety risks are obviously unsettling, workers can take steps before and during visits to reduce the chance that they will experience harm. All staff providing home-based services should be familiar with agency policies and protocols for safety, including location logs, cellphone use, available backup, and procedures for paired visits accompanied by other staff or law-enforcement personnel. Workers should review available information about the client system, geographic location, and presenting problems in order to anticipate possible areas of risk. For example, is the home in a neighborhood noted for its crime rate or in a region populated by methamphetamine labs or other illegal activity? Is the proximity of neighbors a sign of safety or a potential risk? Is the nature of the visit likely to evoke strong emotion (a child protective investigation) or to be well-received by the client (a child development evaluation)?

During contacts prior to the visit, the worker may solicit the client's advice, for example: "Is there anything I should know in terms of safety when I'm visiting?" Such an open-ended question can helpfully alert the worker to anything from a rotted porch to gang activity or a surly neighbor.

Respectfulness is an important tool in mitigating risk. The worker should negotiate an appointment time with the client in advance and contact him or her promptly if it needs to be postponed or rescheduled. Inform the client about the duration and purpose of the session so that he or she can be prepared and use the time wisely. Upon arrival, the worker should introduce himself or herself and request permission to enter the home. The worker should be mindful of body posture and vocal tone, using both to present a calm, caring, and competent demeanor. Being respectful does not mean being careless. Respect does not compel the worker to accept a piece of cake from a counter covered with roaches. It does mean that in declining, the worker thanks the client for the kind gesture. Some workers offer excuses: "I'm not hungry," "I just ate," or "I'll be eating lunch soon." Others will simply say "no, thank you." Whether assessing safety or responding to hygiene concerns, efforts to preserve the client's dignity will both help diminish risk and enhance the helping relationship.

During the visit itself, workers should be dressed in comfortable and non-restrictive clothing, lock valuables in the car trunk, park facing out and near the building, observe exit routes from the home itself and the area in general, and be alert to hazards or other signs of danger. Workers should avoid placing themselves in situations where either they or the clients are trapped without an egress. Therefore, workers should stand to the side when knocking on the door and, once inside, try to be positioned in such a fashion that both parties can safely reach a door. Keen observation will give clues to the client's state of mind and to the availability of weapons or objects that may be used as weapons: kitchen knives, crowbars, or ashtrays.

During the session, workers should have car keys and a cellphone readily accessible, should emergency assistance be needed. If the environment or the client raises concerns for safety, the worker should end the session and depart promptly. Research supports the notion that well-trained workers' instincts are reliable indicators of impending risk (Smith 2006; Spencer and Munch 2003). If violence occurs in the home (e.g., a fight or partner assault), the worker should not try to intercede but should call 911 or another emergency number for assistance. As tempting as it may be to intervene, social workers are not well equipped to assist in such a matter, and in doing so may run the risk of turning the attention of the aggressors on themselves.

In the event of a physical confrontation from which escape is impossible, the worker should defend himself or herself with available resources; blocking blows with a briefcase or sofa cushion, dropping to the floor with feet directed at the assailant, or verbally defusing threats with weapons by encouraging the assailant to talk and set aside the weapon, focusing attention on the individual rather than the weapon itself. Ultimately, anticipation and rehearsal are the best preparations for the threat of physical violence. Staff development sessions should address self-defense, physical restraint, and verbal deescalation techniques and equip workers to determine which situations are amenable to which measures.

The unpredictability of the home environment can be a significant source of distress for new or occasional home-based workers. Increased confidence and safety come from understanding the various risks, preparing appropriately, and conducting visits in a watchful and respectful manner. These efforts free the worker to engage with the client unencumbered by apprehensions that can cloud judgment and professional acumen.

Ethical Decision Making

Professionals delivering services outside a traditional office setting must be alert to the unique dynamics of in-home practice in order to fulfill their ethical responsibilities. Familiarity with the values and ethical standards of the social work profession is, of course, a prerequisite for all practitioners, as is the ability to use a decision-making framework to resolve complex dilemmas. Effective ethical decision making, particularly in settings as challenging as home-based services, requires more than an instinctual, gut-response process. Social workers who employ a comprehensive decision-making framework assure that they have generated and weighed an array of appropriate options and accurately applied ethical standards, policies, and laws in reaching a decision. Thoughtful resolution of ethical dilemmas also facilitates the resolution of future dilemmas, as workers use the framework to reflect on their choices and adjust future actions accordingly. The six-part framework employed in this chapter is memorable and easy to use (Strom-Gottfried 2007). In responding to six questions (who, what, when, where, why, how), workers are encouraged to seek consultation in generating and weighing options and use self-knowledge and social work practice skills to effectively determine and carry out a course of action. Specifically, the worker faced with an ethical dilemma should ask:

- Who will be helpful?
- What are my choices?
- When have I faced a similar dilemma?
- Where do ethical, clinical, and legal guidelines lead me?
- Why am I selecting a particular course of action?
- How should I enact my decision?

Let's look at each in turn.

Who Will Be Helpful?

Competent, ethical practice requires that social workers seek out advice for problem solving and professional development. Common resources include supervisors, colleagues, and consultants with expertise in a particular area (child development, law enforcement, mental health, etc.). Ideally, consultation takes place before the worker takes actions. In these instances, the individuals consulted can help generate alternatives, bring fresh perspectives to existing options, help anticipate advantages and disadvantages of various steps, and prepare the worker to carry out the decision. When workers have ongoing, trusting relationships with colleagues, mentors, or supervisors, consultation also plays an important role in enhancing a worker's self-awareness and growth, as vulnerabilities and repetitive patterns can be explored and addressed.

Workers who are seeking input on ethical dilemmas must, of course, be mindful of the privacy concerns in a given case. Supervisors and other agency personnel whose role is to provide staff guidance and backup are generally entitled to full case information. In the absence of explicit permission from the client, other professionals in and out of the agency may still be able to comment on the concepts imbedded in a case if it is presented without identifying information. For example, "What should I do if a client reports committing a crime thirteen years ago?" frames the problem without unnecessary information, in contrast to "a middle-aged woman I've been seeing for agoraphobia reports killing an infant thirteen years ago." Some details, such as the nature of the crime in this case, need to be divulged because they are relevant to the decision-making process, but the abiding guidelines should be to share information only for professional purposes and to share as little information as necessary to meet that goal. Social workers and other professionals are under ethical obligations to respect the privacy of information shared with them in the course of consultation (American Counseling Association 2005; American Psychological Association 2002; NASW 1999). Friends and family members, of course, have no such responsibility and are thus inappropriate resources for assistance in solving ethical dilemmas.

Even when social workers must make instantaneous ethical decisions, consultation is called for after the fact. Raising an ethical dilemma and processing it with an informed and experienced colleague helps evaluate the wisdom of the decision made in the moment and generates other considerations and options that might be employed in the future. In reflecting on a case, the worker should ask: "Did the decision turn out the way I anticipated?" "Did it have a positive outcome?" "If the impact was not positive, is there anything I can do now to rectify the situation?" "Would I make the same decision in the future?" "What might I do differently?"

In home-based services, where many ethical struggles take place outside the watchful eye of colleagues or supervisory personnel, it is imperative that workers have the capacity to identify ethical dilemmas and the comfort to discuss them with other professionals. Shame, ego, and hubris can block workers from seeking input in the face of dilemmas or following a decision. Yet the failure to seek assistance closes the door on creative, sound, and shared solutions, contributes to professional isolation, and creates risk should poor, rash, or ill-considered decisions result.

What Are My Choices?

By their nature, dilemmas arise because two unappealing or flawed options present themselves. The key to resolving dilemmas is to expand the
options, in the hope that a clearly superior choice emerges. In the absence
of that, specifying options will be the first step in weighing them out and
articulating, ultimately, which is a preferable course for action. This step
is explicitly included in the decision-making model to compel workers to
think creatively and in doing so finding "a third way" out of the problem
(Kidder 1995, 167).

When Have I Faced a Similar Dilemma?

This question requires the worker to consider past actions that may have
bearing on the current situation. Over the course of a career, problems arise
that are not novel but are simply variations on past challenges. Social workers who employ a decision-making model can capitalize on their attention
to and evaluation of past dilemmas in order to determine what features of
the "new" dilemma distinguish it from the old one. For example, a common
dilemma in all practice settings is whether to accept gifts from clients. Sometimes gifts create conflicts of interest for workers, are a strategy for manipu-
lation, or blur professional boundaries. But gifts may be also be pure acts of
kindness (the child who paints the worker a birdhouse), a demonstration of
strengths and dignity (a client who gives the worker extra tomatoes from his
garden), or a culturally significant overture (a Southeast Asian family that
gives the worker a ceramic butterfly to commence the helping relationship).
Individual workers develop personal policies on gifts or adopt those of their
employers. But in the moment with clients, they must rely on their professional judgment in evaluating a situation and the particular considerations
of that case. Thus, the home-based worker whose client wants to make her a
quilt responds not simply to that offer but also within the context of her own
history of handling offers of gifts.

Where Do Ethical, Clinical, and Legal Guidelines Lead Me?

This step in the decision-making process requires the worker to weigh the
advantages and disadvantages of various options in light of ethical principles,

social work values and ethics, laws and regulations, organizational policies, and practice guidelines. This step requires the worker to possess a considerable amount of information about these various concepts and to have the capacity for critical thinking in applying and weighing the concepts. It also demands a high tolerance for ambiguity, as the various considerations seldom lead to a clear, singular solution. Rather, the benefit of this step is in identifying the risks and benefits of various choices, enabling the worker to consciously anticipate outcomes and prioritize options. If the analysis reveals a negative aspect to a particular choice but the choice is otherwise the most desirable, the worker presses forward with this full knowledge and may additionally be able to take steps to mitigate potential harms.

The ethical principles to be weighed in this step include *beneficence* (which choice creates the greatest good or averts harms?), *veracity* (which choice upholds truthfulness?), *fidelity* (which choice promotes promise keeping and trustworthiness?), and *justice* (which choice more fairly distributes any potential harms and benefits?).

The social work values and ethical standards are derived from the NASW Code (1999). Prominent values of the profession include *service* to others, prized over self-interest; action on behalf of *social justice*, particularly in issues such as poverty, discrimination, and other social or structural inequalities; respect for individuals' inherent *dignity and worth* and the abiding importance of healthy *human relationships*; and individual and organizational *integrity* and professional *competence*. The 155 standards embodied in the NASW Code of Ethics operationalize these values into guidelines that professionals must employ in their interactions with clients, colleagues, employers, and society at large. While some standards are explicit and unambiguous ("1.03F, Social workers should obtain clients' informed consent before audiotaping or videotaping clients or permitting observation of services to clients by a third party"), others use relative language that must be interpreted given the context of a particular situation ("1.14, When social workers act on behalf of clients who lack the capacity to make informed decisions, social workers should take reasonable steps to safeguard the interests and rights of those clients"). Clearly, implementation of the latter standard requires both a substantive knowledge about client competence and a normative sense of what steps are reasonable to represent that client's interests. This highlights once again the significance of consultations. Social workers cannot develop the required expertise in a vacuum. Similarly, only through conversations with others can they benchmark their own appraisal of what is "reasonable" against that of other professionals.

ETHICAL STANDARDS: CORE CONTENT AREAS

Self-determination	Privacy and confidentiality
Informed consent	Supervision
Competence	Nondiscrimination
Conflicts of interest	Professionalism
Dual and sexual relationships	

While many resources offer a comprehensive review of the NASW Code and an explication of the standards (Reamer 1998; Strom-Gottfried 2007), attention to nine core content areas serves as a foundation for ethical decision making. *Self-determination* refers to the client's rights to make life decisions without undue interference or restraint. Intervention is, however, allowed in instances where clients' choices may put them or others at risk of "serious, imminent and foreseeable harm" (NASW 1999, 1.01). *Informed consent* refers to the client's right to know the purpose of the services, risks, limits, costs, and alternatives, as well as the right to refuse service and the consequences of doing so. Standards on *competence* require social workers to practice only in those areas where they have established expertise, to represent accurately their credentials and abilities, to assure that personal problems do not impair their delivery of services, and to seek assistance in learning and adopting novel approaches.

Conflicts of interest arise any time a worker's interests diverge from those of the client, as when a worker who is preoccupied by discomfort in a client's filthy home conditions shortens the visit and thus shortchanges her attention to the client's needs. Conflicts of interest also emerge in those instances where interests diverge within a client system. For example, in home visits to evaluate parenting skills, the worker might determine that the teen child's interests are best served by emancipation from his parents, despite their protestations.

Dual and sexual relationships are particularly pernicious and troubling subsets of conflicts of interest. In these cases, workers' relationships with clients outside the helping relationship (business arrangements, friendships, intimate contact, etc.) have troubling effects on their ability to carry out their professional responsibilities. Beyond the damage accruing from the loss of therapeutic focus, dual and sexual relationships can be exploitive and harmful, as the trust required for a helping relationship is breached.

Privacy and confidentiality form the foundation of social work encounters, as they allow clients to share their most personal concerns and experiences.

Professionals are expected to exercise discretion, sharing information only with client consent, to avert impending harms, to comply with laws and policies such as mandated reported statutes, or for other "compelling professional reasons" (NASW 1999, 1.07c). The NASW Code offers numerous standards about the proper use and conduct of *supervision*, to ensure that workers maintain proper levels of competence and that supervisors are equipped to provide knowledgeable oversight and fair evaluation of employees and student workers.

Provisions in the NASW Code on *nondiscrimination* set forth standards for relating to colleagues, clients, students, and others in a fair and unbiased manner, as well as requiring efforts to eradicate the systemic causes of oppression and marginalization. An array of standards speak to fundamental issues of *professionalism*, cautioning workers to act with honesty and trustworthiness, resolve conflicts respectfully, put clients' needs before their own, and recognize their roles as representatives of their agencies and the field of social work. In addition to adherence to the NASW Code, social workers who are licensed or credentialed must be familiar with any affiliated codes of conduct promulgated by state authorities or professional organizations. Like the NASW Code, the standards in these documents serve as a resource in selecting ethical actions.

Properly resolving an ethical dilemma also requires an understanding of the relevant laws and policies in a given situation. Consider, for example, a social worker providing in-home hospice services who observes child maltreatment during a visit. Irrespective of other clinical or ethical considerations, the law clearly requires the worker to report the observation of child abuse to child welfare authorities. Workers who are familiar with their legal obligations can structure their activities accordingly. For example, informing clients about the limits on confidentiality at the outset of service can help avoid shock and betrayal if a child abuse report is necessary. While few ethical dilemmas are solved with laws and policies, familiarity with these responsibilities is essential for the social worker to properly evaluate his or her choices.

The consideration of practice guidelines is relevant for ethical decisions in that they help the worker analyze the competing goods (or "bads") in dilemmas, anticipate the effects of various actions, and strategize on the most effective ways to approach the decision. For example, is the client who mentions her "eligible bachelor grandson" simply making conversation, or is she trying to blur boundaries and derail the interview? What accommodations in the chaotic household are necessary to have an effective session and which are simply pet peeves of the particular worker? When a family has friends gathered and a meal prepared for the worker's visit, is it indicative of a misunderstanding about the role and purpose of the session, an effort to ingratiate themselves with the worker, an attempt to keep the interview at a superficial level, or an act of hospitality amid a gathering of all who care about the client? Accurate and insightful interpretation of case scenarios provides guidance for action. Boundary-blurring behaviors that stem from unfamiliarity with the helping process can be resolved by education. Those indicative of cultural preferences may be accommodated or altered through information and compromise. Similar behaviors that are intended to distract may be addressed though interpretation, confrontation, and firm boundaries.

Complex dilemmas and their resolutions rest at the intersection of ethical and clinical decision making. Therefore, a well-developed knowledge base, carefully applied, is necessary to generate and appraise choices.

Why Am I Selecting a Particular Course of Action?

As alluded to earlier, the worker's self-awareness and sensitivity to self-interest are key components in ethical decision making. Workers who reflect on their motivation in selecting a course of action have a benchmark by which to evaluate the wisdom of their decisions. Justifying a decision, if only to oneself, identifies biases and blind spots and requires articulation of the primacy of a particular choice over the others. For example, the worker who allows a client to read Bible passages during home visits because he "didn't want to hurt her feelings" is on much shakier ethical ground than the one who allows it in order to better understand the client's perspective and resources. Similarly, the worker who declines to take a case because she has insufficient experience with developmental disabilities is taking an ethical stance, in contrast to a worker rejecting the same case because "that part of town gives me the creeps." In the end, the impetus for a decision matters as much as the decision itself.

How Should I Enact My Decision?

Sometimes, the basis for successful resolution to an ethical dilemma rests in how the decision itself was carried out. The worker who declines the client's offer of dinner, a quilt, or a date with the grandson must effectively employ communication skills and social work knowledge in order to preserve the relationship while setting appropriate limits. Sensitivity, empathy, and respect are crucial elements in acting on an ethical decision. This is another area in which consultation is crucial, as supervisors and colleagues can ably assist the worker in preparing for the session and conveying the intended message. Retrospective evaluation of dilemmas in consultation may also reveal what aspects of the process of carrying out the decision led to its ultimate success or failure.

The use of an ethical decision-making model may seem cumbersome and fruitless, particularly at first. As with all skills, it becomes a more natural process with repeated use and as sound decisions form a foundation for tackling future dilemmas. While the model assures that all workers make mindful decisions, it does not assure that they will all reach the same conclusion. As Reamer (1999) notes, reasonable people disagree, and thoughtful, ethical professionals may choose different paths when faced with the same dilemma. The differences do not suggest that one choice is more ethical than the other. Both can be ethical; both likely have particular benefits and drawbacks. The worker who feels he can ask for clients to limit visitors and cease smoking and watching TV during his visits without signaling disdain or judgment is not more ethical than the worker who sets limits on the TV but ignores the smoking and the intrusions. Each professional's personality, risk tolerance, experiences, and training guide him or her to draw the line in one place or another in balancing client wishes with worker prerogatives. This is not to say that anything goes or that any decision is acceptable. Rather, within a given situation, there may be a number of ethically sound options. The legitimacy of the decision derives from the basis on which it is made and the worker's capacity to carry it out effectively. Even amid differences in style and choices, social workers who are open to conversation and consultation can expand their capacity for ethical problem solving by sharing diverse perspectives and strategies, if unencumbered by fear, shame, or narrow right/wrong thinking.

Applying the Model

Ella received a referral for an assessment of an elder suspected of having Alzheimer's disease. The client resides with her son and his family. Although the son was informed in advance that he would be an important part of the initial interview, he was curt and cross during the intake visit at his home. Upon leaving, Ella observed many chained dogs and an "arena" in the backyard, which led her to wonder if dog fights are taking place on the premises.

Who will be helpful? Ella's first line of consultation after the visit should be with her supervisor and trusted colleagues. She will need assistance processing her assessment of the woman, the home environment, and the son's behavior. These conversations can help Ella evaluate the importance of her observations of the dogs and the relevance for her work with the family. If Ella is particularly distressed at the discovery of the dogs or annoyed with the son's demeanor, consultation can help her reflect on her countertransference and the ways that may affect her judgments in the case. Supervisory discussions may help expand her empathy and her thinking about the case. Perhaps the son was simply exhausted by care for his mother or skeptical that any genuine assistance would be forthcoming, rather than being guarded in light of illegal activity, as Ella surmised. Even if Ella's appraisals are entirely accurate, supervisory consultation helps assure that she is thinking critically about the case and what she observed, making certain that her actions are the result of sound knowledge rather than a rush to judgment in heightened emotion.

The consultation should also effectively map out Ella's next steps, including other resources she should pursue to better understand the case and her options. Perhaps law-enforcement or animal-control personnel can educate her about signs that indicate the presence of dog fighting and the implications for the client's safety if such activities are taking place at her place of residence. A review of statutes and policies or consultation with an agency attorney would inform Ella about her responsibilities and processes for reporting criminal activity if, in fact, dog fighting is taking place.

Consultation will also reveal whether Ella is capable of continuing to work autonomously with this client system, whether paired visits are needed for safety, or if outright transfer is called for given her strong distrust of the primary caregiver.

What are my choices? Consultation may reveal numerous options. Some of these could be pursued sequentially, while others might be approached simultaneously. Among the possibilities are:

- Moving the client immediately
- Continuing to work on the case while ignoring the dog-ring concerns
- Referring (anonymously?) the observation of the dog-ring to the proper authorities and allowing them to investigate and intervene if needed
- Broaching the question of the dogs with the son as part of the evaluation of the household and the client's safety

Each choice balances and privileges different values. Speaking with the son is respectful and opens the door for a legitimate explanation for Ella's observation in the backyard. However, it may put Ella and the elderly client at risk if it is the site of illegal activity and Ella's questions provoke the son's ire. A preliminary conversation with the son might prompt him to improve care for the dogs or move the operation, thereby avoiding apprehension.

Ignoring the observations may keep Ella's focus on the primary tasks of helping the client, but at the expense of tolerating reprehensible activities that may in fact expose the client to danger. Moving the client, even if it is possible to do so, fails to address distressing observations by either ruling out dog fighting or closing down the operation. Referring the concerns to the proper authorities keeps separate those concerns from Ella's mission, but a resulting investigation may still rebound harmfully on Ella and her client. It may also alienate the son (the client's primary caregiver), particularly if he feels unfairly targeted by the report.

When have I faced a similar dilemma? This is not the first time Ella has encountered illegal or uncomfortable information in the course of her evaluations of elderly clients. In one instance, she observed a daughter on total disability for back problems lifting her wheelchair-bound mother, raising the possibility of insurance fraud. In another case, Ella discovered marijuana plants under a grow light when she opened the wrong door to a client's bedroom. In both cases, she elected to focus exclusively on her clients and their needs. In the first case, she felt she had an insufficient basis to conclude that the daughter was defrauding the disability authorities and decided her role was not to serve as their investigative extension. Ella's decision to overlook the marijuana plants was also influenced by her mission and her role. Through consultation and reflection, she determined that the client was put at greater risk by alienating his otherwise caring and adept family than he was by the presence of an illegal pot-growing room. Ella was also uncomfortable about the manner in which she discovered the plants. Though her discovery was inadvertent, she feared the family might perceive that in-home workers were "snooping" and resist further intervention. She had forged a positive relationship with the family and had considered talking frankly with them about her discovery and the bind that it created, but she ultimately opted not to mention it, feeling it would detract from her primary responsibilities.

How is the current case different from these precedents? Depending on the client's level of incapacity, the presence of vicious dogs could pose a direct risk to her safety. In that alcohol, drugs, firearms, and gambling are commonly associated with dog fights, the client might also be at risk from crowds who gather for fights. If the things Ella observed are markers of a dog-fighting ring, they were certainly not hidden in the way the marijuana plants were, nor do they require her to undertake an investigative function to uncover relevant information. Two other differences distinguish this case: the son's behavior and the risk to animals. Ella must determine whether the son's churlish demeanor indicates increased risk for his mother or is simply off-putting. If it is the latter, Ella must ask herself if her observations at the home indicate a bias against the son or if she is holding him to a higher standard because he is uncooperative. Ella is also an unabashed pet lover, so she is particularly sensitive to the possibility of animal abuse. But in light of her previous decisions not to explore troubling information, is the illegal and inhumane treatment of animals more worthy of intervention than drug crimes or fraud?

Where do ethical and clinical guidelines lead me? The option of talking with the son prior to taking further action maximizes the principles of fidelity, justice, and veracity in that it is forthright, does not presume illegal activity or judgments, and is proper for the full assessment of the client's well-being. If the son is responsive and Ella's concerns are unfounded, the conversation may be also a beneficent choice. Reporting the observations to the authorities, whether dog fighting is founded or not, will be perceived as a breach of trust by the son and perhaps jeopardize the client. Ignoring it creates other possible harms for the elderly client. And, while ignoring the dog ring is not untruthful, unjust, or untrustworthy, it allows suspicions to stand unexamined and it may permit an array of illegal and socially unacceptable activities to continue unabated.

An exploration of Ella's choices in light of professional values yields similar pros and cons. If Ella were to start by talking with the son, she would certainly be acting in a competent, responsible, and trustworthy manner. That choice is clearly indicative of respect for the dignity and worth of others, which is valued in the profession of social work. Taking action, whether through meeting with the son or reporting to the authorities, puts the interests and needs of others (the client and her family) ahead of those of the worker, who may wish to stay out of it. Moving the client may be precipitous and jeopardize the mother-son and worker-family relationships unnecessarily, in the absence of other information about the danger conveyed by the dogs.

The NASW Code of Ethics has a number of standards to guide Ella's decision, most notably:

- Social workers respect and promote the right of clients to self-determination and assist clients in their efforts to identify and clarify their goals. Social workers may limit clients' right to self-determination when, in the social workers' professional judgment, clients' actions or potential actions pose a serious, foreseeable, and imminent risk to themselves or others (NASW 1999, 1.02).

■ Social workers' primary responsibility is to promote the well-being of clients. In general, clients' interests are primary. However, social workers' responsibility to the larger society or specific legal obligations may on limited occasions supersede the loyalty owed clients, and clients should be so advised (NASW 1999, 1.03).

■ Social workers should have a knowledge base of their clients' cultures and be able to demonstrate competence in the provision of services that are sensitive to clients' cultures and to differences among people and cultural groups (NASW 1999, 1.05b).

■ Social workers should protect the confidentiality of all information obtained in the course of professional service, except for compelling professional reasons. The general expectation that social workers will keep information confidential does not apply when disclosure is necessary to prevent serious, foreseeable, and imminent harm to a client or other identifiable person or when laws or regulations require disclosure without a client's consent. In all instances, social workers should disclose the least amount of confidential information necessary to achieve the desired purpose; only information that is directly relevant to the purpose for which the disclosure is made should be revealed (NASW 1999, 1.07b).

■ Social workers should inform clients, to the extent possible, about the disclosure of confidential information and the potential consequences, when feasible before the disclosure is made. This applies whether social workers disclose confidential information on the basis of a legal requirement or client consent (NASW 1999, 1.07d).

■ When social workers act on behalf of clients who lack the capacity to make informed decisions, social workers should take reasonable steps to safeguard the interests and rights of those clients (NASW 1999, 1.14).

The effect of these standards on Ella's decisions will rest on her assessment of the facts of the case and on the results of her consultations. For example, are her apprehensions about the dogs valid concerns about a dangerous activity or rash value judgments based on a lack of understanding of her clients' rural culture? Do the dogs present a serious, imminent, and foreseeable risk to health and safety, such that the client's right to privacy and self-determination in keeping them might be overruled? Is the mother competent to make decisions about her own well-being and keep herself safe, or must the social worker intervene on her behalf? Is it feasible for Ella to converse with the son about her plan to report her concerns for investigation by adult-protective or animal-control authorities, or would the very conversation create a safety risk? These questions demonstrate the interconnection between social work practice and social work ethics. Professionals must use their knowledge of human behavior, communications, cultural practices, social issues, and a host of other topics in order to effectively weigh, select, and implement their ethical responsibilities.

Social workers must also be mindful of relevant laws and policies. If Ella's state has laws on adult protection, she would be mandated to report relevant suspicions of harm to adult-protection authorities. The laws on animal cruelty and related reporting requirements would be relevant. Most likely, Ella will find that dog fighting is illegal but that she is not under legal compulsion to report it. Her agency's policies on referral to other agencies, reporting criminal activity, and relationships with clients' caregivers would further shape her decisions.

Why am I selecting a particular course of action? Because ethical decisions involve both personal and professional prerogatives, social workers must reflect on their choices and motivations to assure that their reasoning is sound. For example, Ella might choose not to act on her concerns about the dogs until she gets further information to confirm or refute the presence of risk to the client. This is a reasonable ethical decision. Contrast it with the decision not to act because "snitches get stitches." The decision not to act is ethically untenable in this instance, because Ella's rationale puts her own needs and fears above those of her client. Similarly, confronting the son with her observations and concerns is proper in light of Ella's role and responsibilities. Confronting him because she personally thinks dogs should not be chained and left outside is an improper basis for action.

How should I enact my decision? Some aspects of the "how" question are imbedded in Ella's choices, in that she is considering whether to speak with the son first, whether any report should be anonymous, and other process questions. She will need to be careful about the timing of her actions, especially if she perceives the potential for violence as a result of a report or removal of the client. She may decide to delay her decision, in order to gather more information and better understand her client and his family. If she is able to build a more trusting bond with the son, she may be able to more confidently and effectively approach him about her observations and apprehensions. Ella must place a priority on respectfulness and the mitigation of harms in whatever path she chooses to pursue.

Conclusion

There exists no specialized code of ethics to guide social work practice in home-based services. Rather, professionals who work in home settings must thoughtfully and readily apply existing concepts and standards to novel and complex scenarios. The use of a decision-making framework assures that in-home workers seek consultation to generate and evaluate alternatives, consider various aspects of the dilemma, and prepare to carry out the decision with skill and sensitivity. Workers who are proficient and comfortable in facing ethical dilemmas are prepared for safe and competent service delivery, even in unpredictable and intimidating circumstances.

REFERENCES

American Counseling Association. 2005. *ACA code of ethics.* Available online at http://www.counseling.org/Resources/CodeOfEthics/TP/Home/CT2.aspx.

American Psychological Association. 2002. *Ethical principles of psychologists and code of conduct.* Available online at http://www.apa.org/ethics/code.html.

Kidder, R. M. 1995. *How good people make tough choices: Resolving the dilemmas of ethical living.* New York: Simon and Schuster.

National Association of Social Workers (NASW). 1999. *Code of ethics.* Washington, D.C.: NASW Press.

Naturale, A. 2007. Secondary traumatic stress in social workers responding to disasters: Reports from the field. *Clinical Social Work Journal* 35 (3): 173–181.

Reamer, F. G. 1998. *Ethical standards in social work: A critical review of the NASW Code of Ethics.* Washington, D.C.: NASW Press.

———. 1999. *Social work values and ethics.* New York: Columbia University Press.

Smith, M. 2006. Too little fear can kill you: Staying alive as a social worker. *Journal of Social Work Practice* 20 (1): 69–31.

Spencer, P. C., and Munch, S. 2003. Client violence toward social workers: The role of management in community mental health programs. *Social Work* 48 (4): 532–544.

Strom-Gottfried, K. J. 2007. *Straight talk about professional ethics.* Chicago: Lyceum.

Three

Administrative Supports and Practices

KRISTINE NELSON, KATHARINE CAHN, AND MINDY HOLLIDAY

No matter whether located in a child welfare agency, a school, or a health clinic, home visiting requires different administrative supports than services provided in an office or clinic, and the role of the supervisor often must expand or deviate from the role of the supervisor in a traditional agency. In leaving the agency, the social worker gives up the familiarity, convenience, and safety of an office to practice in a constantly changing environment. This chapter will cover some of the additional support needed by these workers and the role of the supervisor in providing that support.

The first section of this chapter discusses the selection, training, and supervision of social workers to ensure their success. This includes the recruitment and retention of diverse staff and the importance of having a team of workers to share the practical and emotional challenges of home visiting. The second section describes the role of administrative staff in securing resources and referrals from community agencies, building a positive workgroup culture, and dealing with planned and unplanned change. A third section discusses technological support and program evaluation for continuous improvement. Final sections summarize tips for new supervisors and for home visitors and comment on current challenges and future directions for the administration of home-based programs.

Recruiting, Training, and Supporting Home Visiting Staff

Home-visiting programs that have maintained integrity and quality service have identified their social workers as central to program success. The personnel best suited for home-based services share characteristics such as dedication, commitment, an appropriate knowledge base, and experience. Programs may be designed to serve a wide range of practice areas, but all home-based programs rely heavily on these key staff characteristics (Kinney, Haapala, and Booth 1991).

The most satisfied and successful family workers are those who combine relevant education, experience, flexibility, emotional intelligence, and a worldview that supports nontraditional approaches to human-service work (Coleman and Clark 2003; McCroskey and Meezan 1997). The level of education and experience needed varies across programs, but having the most prepared staff to provide quality services is always a top priority (Carrilio 2007).

Recruitment Strategies

Clear, concise job descriptions of the unique aspects of in-home work are crucial, as individuals will self-select based on their views and availability for working in family homes, especially when working on a flexible, twenty-four-hour, seven-days-a-week schedule (Holliday and Cronin 1990). The reputation of a program or agency has a substantial effect on staff recruitment. Often, social workers are attracted to programs that are perceived as "cutting edge" or hold feminist/social-justice perspectives (Finn and Jacobsen 2007; Hyde 2003). Social workers have also reported that they will seek employment with a supervisor who has a solid reputation, even if the agency may not be as desirable. This is particularly true in communities of color, where informal alliances influence individuals to work in one program or another (Gutierrez and Lewis 1999).

Recruitment of individuals who are well suited for home-visiting programs also requires a multicultural, multiphased recruitment and interview process (Gutierrez and Lewis 1999; Kinney et al. 1991). Programs in Michigan such as the VESTA program, which served juveniles returning to the community from maximum-security training schools, recruited social workers that were a "good fit" by going beyond the traditional application process. The ethnicity, culture, and economic status of the families to be served were central to staff selection. When appropriate, it was helpful to have former consumers provide perspectives on what was most valuable in personnel. For some communities in Detroit, it was crucial to have European American social workers from working-class backgrounds, as they related more easily to youth and families of the working poor. In the city proper, it was important to have African American men who had grown up in the community, had intimate knowledge of the challenges facing the youth, and who could be positive role models to help instill hope and promote candor. Other flexible, nontraditional approaches can include a variety of strategies at the interview stage, such as videotaping spontaneous role plays of potential home-visiting situations or interviewing applicants in groups to observe interpersonal styles beyond the written application process.

Developing relationships with schools of social work and other human-service programs helps identify potential staff early in their career. Additionally, since many service providers in communities of color have developed programs of their own due to a lack of culturally sensitive practice, multicultural connections are critical for community building and recruitment of staff (Hyde 2003, 2004; Checkoway 1997).

A final consideration in recruitment is background screening for in-home workers who will be working with children and vulnerable or elderly adults. Many child welfare, health, and mental health programs already require background checks for employment. Frail elders and dependent adults may also be at risk of neglect and abuse. Screening should include checking the legitimacy of references, exploring gaps in employment, checking child abuse and criminal databases, and signed agreements of compliance with mandatory reporting laws (Loar 2007).

Service Teams

One common feature across home-visiting programs is the use of teams of workers from different disciplines or who perform different functions. Indeed, in home- and community-based social work in England, Smale (1995, 70) found that "the smallest unit of staff that can engage in community social work is a team of workers." This is true in other areas of practice as well. In psychiatric home visits with elderly patients, Roane, Teusink, and Wortham (2002) used a multidisciplinary team composed of social workers, nurses, attending psychiatrists, and nonpsychiatric physicians. Allen and Tracy (2004) recommend a team approach for in-home interventions in school social work for situations requiring specialists such as speech therapists, nurses, or learning specialists. A successful early childhood home-visiting program for low-income first-time mothers employed a multicultural, multilingual team composed of three masters-level professionals and five paraprofessionals, in order to respond to a variety of client needs (De la Rosa et al. 2005). Finally, in a study of hospice care, Reese and Raymer (2004) found that including a social worker in interdisciplinary teams significantly improved team functioning and led to better outcomes, including fewer hospitalizations, greater patient satisfaction, and reduced costs.

The ability to work in a team is important for a variety of reasons. Workers can share work, knowledge, and resources and build stable, collaborative relationships among agencies and organizations (Adams and Nelson 1997). Multidisciplinary teams help prevent burnout, provide continuity of care when workers leave, and allow for multiple perspectives on the situation. Weekly team meetings provide support and supervision as well as backup and creative approaches to difficult situations. Working in a team also enhances safety, which is essential for the well-being of social workers and service recipients across practice venues. Whether the issue being addressed is health, mental health, substance abuse, delinquent behavior, or familial violence, the ability to go in pairs or have backup reduces stress for everyone. This is particularly true for new home-visiting staff, who may have some anxiety about working in the community and in family homes. Team approaches also generate a shared sense of responsibility and often help establish the collaborative nature of services with consumers (Carrilio 2007; Finn and Jacobson 2007).

In one example of an interdisciplinary team that provided child welfare services, a housing inspector mobilized team and community services for an isolated young single parent, thus averting a referral for child neglect (Adams and Krauth 1995). In-home family-preservation services have also made extensive use of professional and paraprofessional teams to meet both the therapeutic and concrete needs of multiply stressed families (Nelson and Landsman 1992).

Training and Feedback Loops

Many programs have specific training expectations prior to providing services. For example, the Families First program, modeled after the HOMEBUILD-ERS program, required that staff attend forty hours of orientation to learn the philosophical and theoretical approaches that laid the foundation for services (Kinney et al. 1991). In the last two decades, this preparatory training has been recognized nationally as helping maintain model adherence and positive outcomes for consumers. State child welfare agencies have developed various "academies" to assure worker preparedness and certification in specialized areas such as child protection. After the initial training in the programs modeled after HOMEBUILDERS, such as Families First, the new social workers accompany more experienced staff, shadowing them throughout the first few months. Training continues until new employees demonstrate the competency and confidence needed to provide the services on their own, if ongoing teamwork is not feasible. This level of efficacy is based on self-report by the home-visiting social worker and is confirmed by the more experienced staff shadowing the new home visitor. In the mid-1990s, feedback loops were also formalized in the HOMEBUILDERS program, with feedback provided by supervisors to case-carrying staff and case-carrying staff providing feedback to the supervisor. This same process was utilized with supervisors and program administrators throughout the organization.

In addition, the Families First program in Wayne County, Michigan, maintained face-to-face support whenever requested by a team member. Catholic Service of Macomb's Families First program provided ongoing observation of team members, so that feedback would be experienced as part of the normal professional-development process. Forms, used primarily as talking points for the observer and the social worker to debrief following the home visit, highlighted the strengths of the specific social worker and identified areas for improvement. Additionally, the organizational culture was designed with the belief that continuous improvement was the standard and that learning was ongoing. Though this can be a bit more costly during a program's start-up phase, the value in retaining high-quality staff has been well documented (Bednar 2003; Levy-Zlotnik et al. 2005).

Safety Training

A particularly important aspect of training in home-visiting programs is preparing staff to deal with issues of personal safety. Home visits in unfamiliar, high-risk neighborhoods with families often involved in substance abuse and having a history of family violence require the development of special policies and procedures. Training in how to assess neighborhood and client risks, deescalate potentially violent situations, and identify exit strategies needs to be continually provided. In addition to training, safety protocols can help prevent dangerous situations. Safety protocols must include knowledge of where workers are and when they are to return, provisions for emergency communication (cellphones or two-way radios), availability of supervisory support after hours or on weekends, arrangements to pair workers for visits, and procedures for documenting and reviewing all instances of violence or threats of violence. If an incident should occur, treatment for any injuries and emotional and psychological support from supervisors and co-workers need to be provided. Training in nonviolent self-defense techniques may also increase worker confidence in areas that consistently present high risk (Spencer and Munch 2003; Perry-Burney 2001).

Supervision

Equally important to the effectiveness of home-based social work is the preparedness of the supervisory personnel. Many programs require social workers to be "on call," which in turn requires program policies and job descriptions that provide substantive backup support to the home-visiting staff (Holliday and Cronin 1990). Programs often promote from within, so that the supervisors remain current in their experience of the community and the consumers being served. Family-preservation, child welfare, and juvenile justice programs have been known to have supervisory staff provide some direct service, so that the supervisors do not become removed from daily operations (Kinney et al. 1991; Holliday and Cronin 1990).

Promoting from within has also proven to be an effective strategy for retaining a diverse workforce. As previously discussed, much emphasis is placed on building collaborative relationships among communities of color. The opportunity for continued professional growth and increased responsibilities encourages loyalty to the program by staffmembers that started as case-carrying social workers. It is important to stress that individual reputations are formed and become known throughout the community by word of mouth. Both rural communities and urban communities share this phenomenon, and it remains critical for home-visiting programs (Ginsberg 2005).

Administrative Aspects of Supervision

Managing Relationships with the External Environment

The effective delivery of home-based services depends on maintaining effective relationships with a range of community resources. The home-based services unit needs to work actively to maintain good relationships with the larger agency of which it forms a part. From the point of view of a home-based team and supervisor, both the external community and the larger agency make up the external environment.

The supervisor stands at a strategic and potentially very powerful inter-section between the unit and the external environment. Research shows that when relationships with the external environment are strong, the unit will survive, adapt, and serve clients more effectively (Alter and Hage 1993; Kraatz 1998; Provan and Sebastian 1998). A supervisor can get more resources from the environment to support staff and benefit clients. She can establish partnerships that make the worker's job easier and produce better outcomes for client families. He can send information up the line and out to the community to improve the quality of management decision making (Mulroy 2004). The supervisor is keenly aware of conditions in the field. The supervisor learns from staff how things are going with partner agencies and service providers, family and neighborhood supports, and upper management in the agency, and he hears from these agencies how staff are doing. This "in-the-middle" position imparts both pressure and power to the home-based supervisor (Alter and Hage 1993).

Pressure comes from the need to balance competing demands. In Kadushin's (1974) classic description of supervisory roles, the administrative role of supervisor includes the need to translate management intentions into worker practice. Pressure comes from above, as the supervisor must carry out management intentions. For example, the supervisor may be asked to work with staff to implement new practices, changes in workload, new paperwork, or other changes that may or may not make sense to the worker. Pressure can also come from the world external to the agency, for example if community partners or families complain about services or workers or if a much-needed resource is no longer available due to lack of funds. And, finally, pressure can come from within the unit. Workers convey their own needs for support and often the needs of their client families as well. Balancing competing demands from workers, on the one hand, and upper management and the community, on the other, can be a source of great pressure to the supervisor and requires constant communication. Said one new supervisor in training, "I never realized there would be so many meetings!"

While potentially producing a great deal of pressure, this intersection can, at the same time, be a position of real power for a supervisor. The skilled supervisor or administrator will be able to translate client and worker needs into new resources, helpful policy changes, and good interagency working relationships for the unit. Even the home-based practitioner can develop skills in managing the external environment to develop resources and form good working relationships. Some useful skills—advocacy, negotiation, collaboration, resource development, relationship and network building, and passion and vision—are described in the accompanying box.

SKILLS FOR MANAGING CONNECTIONS WITH THE ENVIRONMENT

(1) Advocacy: The ability to compile worker findings and client challenges into a well-reasoned and compelling case statement for community or agency change.

(2) Negotiation: Working with community agencies, interest groups, and management to identify the interests of each party and pathways to recognizing mutual concerns and building on one another's resources. This includes the ability to separate the personal from the problem and the ability to identify common measures of success (Fisher, Ury, and Patton 1991).

(3) Collaboration: Building common purpose and structures to mutual advantage is a challenge that is embedded in home-based practice. This requires basic negotiation and communication skills, as well as an understanding of the institutional drivers (motivating factors) and structures of all agencies involved. It calls for an ability to take risks and give up individual power to expand the power of the whole (Glisson and Hemmelgarn 1998; Kraatz 1998; Mattessich and Monsey 1992).

(4) Resource development: The formal skills of grant writing, contract development, and individual donor development, as well as the informal skills of trading, social marketing, and coalition building all help increase agency resources.

(5) Relationship and network building: Just as for the line practitioner, the most powerful aspect of the administrative practitioner in home-based services may be listening, establishing an experience of mutuality and empathy, and finding common ground. Only then can negotiation, advocacy, and resource development take root (Kraatz 1998; Provan and Sebastian 1998; Roberts-DeGennaro 1997).

(6) Passion and vision. The supervisor who can retain a clear passion for practice and awareness of the effects of every change on both workers and clients will be highly effective and powerful at negotiating the environment external to the unit, developing powerful collaborations, and securing resources for clients and staff (Kanter 1991; Kouzes and Posner 2002; Wheatley 1992).

The first step in transforming pressure into power is assessment. A supervisor can apply the familiar home-based services practice of ecomapping (Carrilio 2007; Hartman 1978) to the unit, instead of to a client or family. In this exercise, the supervisor draws a map on a sheet of paper or a flip chart, showing the unit in the center and surrounding it each external entity that might be a source of resources or stress. A line drawn between the unit and each outside player can show the nature of the relationship between them (Carrilio 2007). For example, if the relationship is a strong and resourceful one, the line can be strong and solid. If there is conflict, the line can be jagged. If the relationship is weak, the line can be dotted; nonexistent, if there is no relationship; or one-directional, if information flows up but not down. This can be an individual exercise or an excellent focus for a unit meeting or retreat, so that staff can direct the supervisor to relationships that most need improvement. (This exercise was developed by K. Cahn, based on an initial concept of Pamela Day in the "Supervising Family Centered Practice" and "Supervising for Excellence" training projects at the University of Washington, 1988–2001.)

Once assessment has identified the source of stress, the supervisor can design an improvement strategy using the skills of relationship building, advocacy, negotiation, and resource development listed above. For example, one supervisor set up a program of cross-training with other agencies in the community. At no cost to any agency, all were able to build staff knowledge of community resources and improve interagency collaboration with clients. Another started a regular coffee meeting with the local sheriff to assure good connections after hearing from several staff that the relationship with law enforcement was becoming a challenge for staff. A third developed a plan to more effectively communicate work conditions to upper management. (Examples drawn from training participants in supervisory training conducted by K. Cahn, 1988–2001.)

Building a Resilient Workgroup Culture

Just as the external environment plays a powerful role in the health of the unit, the health of the unit culture is a powerful predictor of unit effectiveness in any environment. A key aspect of the administrative and supportive role of supervision is the fashioning of a strong, resilient workgroup culture. Workgroup culture has been tied in the literature to a variety of positive outcomes. Earlier, this chapter discussed the value of a positive workgroup culture to recruitment of staff, which has been confirmed in research (Arthur 2001). Workgroup culture is also related in important ways to staff retention (Bednar 2003; Levy-Zlotnick et al. 2005) and to client outcomes (Glisson and Hemmelgarn 1998; Guterman and Bargal 1996). A home-based supervisor must understand and know how to promote a healthy work group culture.

Understanding what constitutes a healthy workplace culture is the first step. Aspects of workgroup culture associated with retention of workers include clarity of mission and vision (Rycraft 1994), an uplifting sense of meaning and purpose (Kouzes and Posner 2002), the presence of both rewards and punishment (Ryan and Oestreich 1998), and a balance of available resources and demands of the job.

Senge (2006) coined the term "learning organization" to describe a work environment where workers are able to try new things and sometimes even fail without punishment. Using systems theory, he asserts that this kind of organization is in the best position to adapt and grow in response to changes in community and client demographics. Another recent work on organizational culture has identified the need for organizations to shift from a top-down, fear-based management structure to one where staff is empowered and supportive, which parallels the way agencies work in supporting their clients. "Driving fear out of the workplace" is the path to high performance (Ryan and Oestreich 1998, 3).

The most cited aspect of a supportive workgroup culture is the presence of a supportive supervisor (Levy-Zlotnick et al. 2005; Rycraft 1994; Zischka and Fox 1983). Supervisors are crucial in the orientation, training, and development of staff. Supervisors provide emotional support as well as case and clinical consultation as case issues unfold. The supportive role of the supervisor is particularly important in home-based practice. Because so much time is spent in the field, home-based workers can feel isolated. Research shows that professional isolation is a primary source of stress, burnout, and turnover in social services (Sundet and Cowger 1994). Home-based supervisors can reduce the isolation and build a sense of team among their staff by staying in communication, promoting participatory decision making, and developing opportunities for training (Zischka and Fox 1983). Research on client empowerment has established that the best predictor of client empowerment is the degree to which a worker is empowered (Guterman and Bargal 1996). In light of this evidence, the supervisor of home visitors can expect that an investment in worker empowerment will improve client outcomes.

Creativity may be required in home-visiting programs that do not operate out of a common office space. When staff is mobile, working out of cars with cellphones and laptops, there is a risk of isolation and the absence of quality control. It will be important to establish a strong supervisor-to-worker connection and to build more formal opportunities for team gatherings. Regular all-team training, end-of-the-week team debriefs, or a weekly breakfast or coffee break are examples of solutions supervisors have implemented to respond to the challenge of forming a coherent culture when managing far-flung and mobile staff.

Managing Change

The pace of change has been accelerating in social services, as it has in the corporate sector. In one management book, Vaill (1996, 27) referred to the current pace of change as "permanent whitewater." New funding streams, practice approaches, and agency partnerships all impinge on the life of a home-based supervisor and the team he or she supervises. Funding cuts and management changes occur regularly and can suddenly affect and alter staffing patterns and the level of resources available to support clients. Often these changes are imposed externally and are not predictable. Such externally imposed change can leave the home-based team and supervisor feeling powerless and frustrated. Particularly in the world of home-based practice, where so much of the planning is customized to client needs and dependent on mobilizing a shifting world of natural and traditional supports, the supervisor must help staff adapt and grow in the face of change. The effective home-based services supervisor will help his or her unit become nimble and capable of growing, learning, and orienting constantly to new constellations of services and resources (Lipman-Blumen 1996).

Being ready and responsive to change calls for the ability to learn. Vaill (1996) says change happens so quickly that one must be constantly learning. He recommends helping the staff and unit develop a lifelong learning posture, drawing on nontraditional skills such as systems thinking, intuition, and spirituality, along with traditional skills more often associated with planned change. Strong ties with community coalitions, other agencies, client voice, and empowerment groups will help gain early information about emerging trends and cushion the blow of the unexpected (Glisson and Hemmelgarn 1998; Schmid 2004).

Sometimes change is planned, and the supervisor has the opportunity to participate and engage staff and client voices in shaping the change (Adams and Nelson 1997). For example, with the planned introduction of a new practice approach, the supervisor can work in a more methodical way to help staff come on board. With continual expansion of knowledge regarding what works with clients (evidence-based and promising practices), the home-visiting supervisor may play a role in developing and implementing new practices or other planned changes with the team. Velasquez (2004, 62–63) shows how the stages-of-change model, promoted as part of motivational interviewing, applies to organizations and systems. Organizations and communities also move from "pre-contemplation" to "contemplation," "preparation," "action," and "maintenance." Like people, organizations can experience relapse. Velasquez outlines the administrative skills useful at each stage of a change episode.

Change can be challenging, and part of a supervisor's role is to engage staff in the change process. Supervisory skills that can assist in staff engagement include providing a context of meaning that enrolls and engages workers (Smith and Peterson 1988) and helping workers understand whether it will benefit them and clients directly (the "what's in it for me" test; Gladwell 2000). Training can also play a part in introducing a change. Research shows that a small percentage of workers will adopt changes early, as a result of trainings and conferences, while nearly two-thirds are more likely to learn from peers or by direct observation and coaching (Rogers 1995). A supervisor can help workers learn the new skills or practices required by setting up opportunities to observe a peer or practice on one case at a time.

Workers will be most likely to engage in the change when they are active participants in planning the change. A supervisor will find the unit more adaptable and likely to learn if team members are engaged in customizing the practice to the unit, in planning how the practice will be implemented, in the selection of training or coaching approaches, and in designing any evaluation (Smale 1998). The active ownership of the change process can thus be transferred from management to the supervisor and then to the team members themselves (Smale 1998). Depending on the program, the supervisor may wish to develop a change team that includes client and client voices as well as workers. Incorporation of worker and client voices into the change process may seem time consuming at first, but if practiced it will be more effective and efficient in the long run by increasing engagement and ownership and producing a higher quality of planning (Adams and Nelson 1997).

Bridges (2004) cautions that the change process not be rushed. Noting how hard it is to tolerate the uncertainty of change, he advises allowing as much time as possible between the end of the old way of doing things and the design and implementation of new practices. Short-term structures and projects can support work during a neutral or transitional period and allow for the emergence of new practices and policies consistent with new values and principles.

Approaches to Continuous Program Improvement

Technological Support and Program Evaluation

Because of the complexities and coordination involved, technological support can mean the difference between a successful, cost-effective program and one that does not meet its goals. New software supports the careful scheduling needed to minimize travel time and maximize face-to-face contact with families (Bertels and Fahle 2006; Eveborn, Flisberg, and Ronnqvist 2006). In addition, records can be automatically kept for management and evaluation purposes through the use of up-to-date information systems (Carrilio 2007; Johnson, Hinterlong, and Sherraden 2001).

Cellphones with GPS location tracking are useful in assuring safety and for scheduling and rescheduling appointments. Missed appointments are costly, and a call to confirm that the person is home and expecting the social worker can result in substantial savings. Cellphones can aid in connecting families quickly to needed resources and in making referrals. Finally, supervision and feedback in a crisis situation may also be more readily available with the use of cellphones (Perry-Burney 2001; Spencer and Munch 2003).

Laptop computers are another asset for home visitors. In some situations, applications and other needed forms can be completed with clients on the spot. While it may not be advisable to take a laptop into all settings, having a laptop in the car can help the social worker productively fill downtime caused by missed appointments or a gap in scheduling with necessary case recording. Laptops can also be useful in program-evaluation efforts, as participants, if comfortable with technology, may be able to complete questionnaires and survey instruments directly on the computer.

Program Evaluation

Program evaluation is critical for a number of reasons: providing feedback on program operations, justifying expenses to funders, and finding out "what works with whom." While extensive, rigorous evaluation efforts require large budgets and knowledgeable evaluators, usually from outside the agency, other levels of evaluation can be done "in house." Jacobs (1988; cited in Pecora et al. 1995) identified five levels of program evaluation in family-support programs, according to their purpose: preimplementation, accountability, program clarification, tracking progress toward objectives, and measuring program impact. Each addresses a different audience, requires different tasks, and utilizes different types of data.

Preimplementation studies involve collecting data for program planning and establishing a pre-service baseline. Some type of needs assessment is usually required by funders using either existing data or community surveys. For example, in early childhood preventive interventions, establishing baseline conditions of immunizations, child abuse or neglect, or preventable diseases is necessary to subsequently document program effectiveness.

Studies done primarily for accountability may use agency data to describe program participants, services, and costs to report to funders and build community support. Several aspects of home-based programs require careful documentation because of their contribution to costs: frequency and length of visits, caseloads, supervisory and administrative costs, and staffing (Barnett 1993). In early childhood home-visiting programs, low-risk families may be visited once, while high-risk families may require daily visits at the outset and weekly or monthly visits for more than a year (Krugman 1993; Barnett 1993). In addition, transportation costs can vary widely. In home-based family-preservation programs, workers spent from 10 to 45 percent of their time traveling to families' homes, depending on whether they were located in urban or rural areas (Nelson et al. 1988).

Staffing, including experience, qualifications, training, and turnover, is another important variable in evaluations focused on accountability. In a study of eleven family-based programs, Nelson and Landsman (1992) found that in-home programs in private agencies hired staff with less experience and education and often had higher turnover than higher-paying programs in public agencies. Similarly, programs may use higher-paid professionals such as nurses or graduate-level social workers, paraprofessionals, or volunteers to deliver the majority of in-home services (Krugman 1993; Barnett, 1993). Reimbursement formulas under managed care or Medicare have created problems in funding costs in hospice, early childhood, and mental health programs because they do not reimburse different levels of staffing (Reese and Raymer 2004; Krugman 1993; Roane, Teusink, and Wortham 2002).

Program-clarification studies provide feedback for program improvement from program staff, agency data, and interviews with consumers. Qualitative and descriptive data can provide insights on what kinds of services work best with what type of client. Although useful for internal purposes, these studies rarely satisfy the needs of outside constituents and funders.

Studies that track progress toward objectives and measure program impact usually require more rigorous studies than the program-evaluation strategies described above. Ideally, they involve evaluators from the outset, to develop logic models that link the program's objectives, interventions, and outcomes (see Carrilio 2007, 23–25, for an example of logic modeling). In addition, interventions used and populations served should be tracked to identify shifts or document fidelity to the intended program model. It is often important to wait until the initial throes of program implementation have stabilized before undertaking such studies.

In addition to clarifying program objectives, one of the most important aspects of such studies is the measurement of program outcomes. The use of standardized instruments that have clinical benchmarks or norms requires expertise in matching measurement tools to expected outcomes and client populations. Many excellent research tools have been validated on limited populations and lack cultural responsiveness and sensitivity. Some are insensitive to the relatively modest changes achieved with high-risk populations in comparing pre-service and postservice testing (Pecora et al. 1995).

Establishing program impact, the goal for evidence-based practice, requires sophisticated research designs that both carefully track program implementation and measure outcomes and have a no-treatment or alternative-treatment comparison or control group. While these types of studies are most useful for advancing the knowledge base of practice and are more often being required in legislation and by funders, they are costly and take a longer time than most program budgets allow. They are most often funded by government grants and use outside evaluators from universities or consulting firms (Jacobs 1988; cited in Pecora et al. 1995).

Tips for New Supervisors

Mastering the administrative aspects of supervision is important to home-visiting programs. The supervisor who is promoted from a position as a home visitor may at first find the administrative aspects of the job daunting or unappealing. The good news is that the skills required for administration are based on skills most will have learned on the line while serving client families.

For example, building the coalitions and community relationships necessary to recruit staff or secure resources calls on the same relationship and networking skills used to build a team around a family or individual client. Assessing staff for goodness of fit and developing a diverse and culturally competent team will call on interpersonal connection and assessment skills needed in a home or community environment. Listening carefully and helping a worker or agency partner describe a complaint or community need employs the same keen (nonreactive) listening skill developed as a home visitor. Aggregating those complaints into a request for new services or a case statement to the agency or community is similar to the advocacy role played by a line social worker. Team-culture building—reaching out to reduce worker isolation and increase the experience of team connectedness and a positive workgroup culture—is familiar to the home-based worker who has helped a client restore natural helping networks or build safe and supportive family connections. Building a rewarding, strengths-based organizational culture draws on the same skills as building on strengths to promote family or client competence and learning. And, certainly, the skills of managing and planning change are the daily bread of the supervisor practiced in home visiting.

Even apparently new skills such as program evaluation or grant writing call on the same clear-outcomes thinking and goal setting practiced by many home-based workers who use goal-attainment scaling, miracle questions, or behavioral anchoring. The technological infrastructure of the work (phones, equipment, and the like) seems "hard," rather than "soft" or human, but, like concrete services in client lives, when technology works well it can be very empowering. Newer technologies are a wonderful fit with the flexibility of home-based work, allowing staff and supervisors to be related and connected even across distance and time.

Core practices generalize to supervision, and core values are consistent as well. The values of systems thinking, strengths-based learning, cultural competence, and the engagement of client and worker voices are all core aspects of administrative supervision and support, just as they are to home-based service delivery.

Tips for Home Visiting Staff

Just as new supervisors often feel overwhelmed, line workers are often unsure of what they can ask for or how to access supervisory support. Carrilio (2007) offers a number of suggestions: First, there needs to be clarity on what requires supervisory input or approval in addition to knowing and using the supervisor's expertise. Second, issues need to be addressed as they arise. "Do not wait or pretend the issue will fix itself" (116). Third, use supervisory feedback to become aware of personal problems and reactions and stay in touch with feelings as they arise. Fourth, be proactive in planning professional development and offer suggestions for trainings. Fifth, if available, use the team's expertise and experience. Finally, respect team and group dynamics: do not go behind someone's back, keep lines of communication open, be considerate of time constraints, and listen closely to feedback. Team leaders need to take responsibility for understanding the intervention models and assuring collaborative team functioning. Both team leaders and members need to be attuned to group dynamics and seek support and consultation to resolve issues.

Conclusions: Current Challenges and Future Directions

Home-based service delivery presents many administrative challenges, some of which have been discussed throughout this chapter and elsewhere in this volume. New models of administration are needed, because traditional practice models will not meet the challenges of home-based service delivery and will not suit practice in the future. As more service-delivery sectors move to home-based models of care, it will be important to research and share effective approaches to agency administration and to develop and test approaches that are a match for current challenges and future directions in practice.

The most central challenge is the defining characteristic of home-based services: that staffmembers work in the home and community, not in an office. Distance and dispersal of staff thwart the use of traditional supervisory and management practices. Classic administrative approaches to training, culture building, and accountability must be retooled. For example, basic practices such as the standard staff meeting, one-on-one supervisory consultations, team-building rituals, and even "management by walking around" must be redesigned when staff are not in the office most days—or at all. Greater connectivity with clients and their families does not have to mean the loss of engagement and connectivity with and among staff.

This chapter has presented some solutions to the logistical challenge of working beyond agency walls, but many more solutions will emerge over the coming years. As has been mentioned, the administrator or supervisor of home-based services must be more intentional about relationship building and communication because he or she can no longer rely on the spontaneous connection afforded by an office setting. Attention to a team's learning opportunities, promoting the development of a cohesive team culture, and providing sites to gather and recharge team energy will emerge as essential administrative approaches for reducing and counteracting worker isolation.

Technology will also be part of the solution to the challenge of connecting with workers, coordinating information, and providing quality control. Cellphones, e-mail, and laptops allow staff to communicate with one another and with supervisors and to enter data and case notes into a central registry. New technology allows connection across distances far more easily than in previous decades.

However useful as a solution, technology also poses its own challenges. Few home-based service agencies can afford the most sophisticated equipment, and the costs of providing technical support and training to all staff can be prohibitive. Laptops, cellphones, and Web technology may not yet be available to many staff. When they are, programs may not be adapted to Web access or to accommodate the simultaneous demands of access and the protection of client confidentiality. Security and personal safety considerations may make carrying a laptop inadvisable. Cellphones may not work and Internet access may be sporadic or slow in many rural areas. Workers with strong relational and cultural competence may not feel comfortable with technology.

A third challenge of home-based work is complexity. It is particularly true for the home-based services worker that services are not delivered in a silo (Carrilio 2007). The complexity of interagency connections has increased incrementally over time, and the need to manage information, stay current with practice, and form relationships across a variety of professional settings and cultures poses a challenge for administrator and worker alike. Managing complexity requires staff and administrators who can work beyond a checklist, think creatively and holistically, and adjust rapidly to new information. Complexity theory (Wheatley 1992) suggests that collaboration, an appreciation of interconnectivity, creativity, and a clear sense of purpose and vision are skills that lend themselves to operating successfully in this new environment. Fortunately, these are skills that have long marked the home-based services practitioner.

While the historic roots of social work practice involve home-based services, most core practices and theories of administration were articulated more recently during the last century, when agency-based professional practice was the dominant approach. As we circle back to rediscover, reinvent, and update our profession, we will need to develop and articulate administrative values and practices that fit with the world of home and community-based services.

REFERENCES

Adams, P., and Krauth, K. 1995. Working with families and communities. In *Reinventing human services: Community and family-centered practice*, ed. P. Adams and K. Nelson, 87–108. Hawthorne, N.Y.: Aldine de Gruyter.

Adams, P., and Nelson, K. 1997. Reclaiming community: An integrative approach to human services. *Administration in Social Work* 21 (3/4): 67–81.

Allen, S. F., and Tracy, E. M. 2004. Revitalizing the role of home visiting by school social workers. *Children and Schools* 26: 197–208.

Alter, C., and Hage, J. 1993. *Organizations working together*. Newbury Park, Calif.: Sage Publications.

Arthur, D. 2001. *The employee recruitment and retention handbook*. New York: Amacom.

Barnett, W. S. 1993. Economic evaluation of home visiting programs. *The Future of Children* 3 (3): 93–112.

Bednar, S. A. G. 2003. Elements of satisfying organizational climates in child welfare agencies. *Families in Society: The Journal of Contemporary Human Services* 84: 7–12.

Bertels, S., and Fahle, T. 2006. A hybrid setup for a hybrid scenario: Combining heuristics for the home health care problem. *Computers and Operations Research* 33: 2866–2890.

Bridges, W. 2004. *Transitions: Making sense of life's changes*. Cambridge, Mass.: Perseus Books.

Carrilio, T. 2007. *A case-management guide for caregivers*. Columbia: University of South Carolina Press.

Checkoway, B. 1997. Core concepts of community change. *Journal of Community Practice* 4: 11–29.

Coleman, D., and Clark, S. 2003. Preparing for child welfare practice: Themes, a cognitive-affective model, and implications from a qualitative study. *Journal of Human Behavior in the Social Environment* 7: 83–96.

De la Rosa, I. A., Perry, J., Dalton, L. E., and Johnson, V. 2005. Strengthening families with first-born children: Exploratory study of the outcomes of a home visiting intervention. *Research on Social Work Practice* 15: 323–338.

Eveborn, P., Flisberg, P., and Ronnqvist, M. 2006. LAPS CARE: An operational system for staff planning of home care. *European Journal of Operational Research* 171: 962–976.

Finn, J., and Jacobsen, M. 2007. *Just practice: A social justice approach to social work*. Peosta, Iowa: Eddie Bowers Publishing Co., Inc.

Fisher, R., Ury, W., and Patton, B. 1991. *Getting to yes: Negotiating agreement without giving in*. 2nd ed. New York: Penguin Books.

Ginsberg, L., ed. 2005. *Social work in rural communities*. Alexandria, Va.: Council on Social Work Education Press.

Gladwell, M. 2000. *The tipping point: Or how little things can make a big difference*. New York: Little, Brown and Co.

Glisson, C., and Hemmelgarn, A. 1998. The effects of organizational climate and interorganizational coordination on the quality and outcomes of children's service systems. *Child Abuse and Neglect* 22 (5): 401–421.

Guterman, N., and Bargal, D. 1996. Social workers' perceptions of their power and service outcomes. *Administration in Social Work* 20 (3): 1–20.

Gutierrez, L., and Lewis, A. 1999. *Empowering women of color*. New York: Columbia University Press.

Hartman, A. 1978. Diagrammatic assessment of family relationships. *Social Casework* 57: 465–476.

Holliday, M., and Cronin, R. 1990. Families first: A significant step toward family preservation. *Families in Society: The Journal of Contemporary Human Services* 71 (5): 303–306.

Hyde, C. 2003. More harm than good? Multicultural initiatives in human service agencies. *Social Thought* 8 (3): 23–43.

——. 2004. Multicultural development in human service agencies: Challenges and solutions. *Social Work* 49: 7–16.

Johnson, E., Hinterlong, J., and Sherraden, M. 2001. Strategies for creating MIS technology to improve social work practice and research. *Journal of Technology in the Human Services* 19 (3/4): 5–22.

Kadushin. A. 1974. *Supervision in social work.* New York: Columbia University Press.

Kanter, R. M. 1991. *Change master skills: What it takes to be creative.* In *Managing innovation,* ed. J. Henry and D. Walker. London: Sage for the Open University.

Kinney, J., Haapala, D., and Booth, C. 1991. *Keeping families together: The HOME-BUILDERS model.* New York: Aldine de Gruyter.

Kouzes, J., and Posner, B. 2002. *The leadership challenge.* 3rd ed. San Francisco: Jossey-Bass.

Kraatz, M. S. 1998. Learning by association? Interorganizational networks and adaptation to environmental change. *Academy of Management Journal* 41: 621–643.

Krugman, R. D. 1993. Universal home visiting: A recommendation from the U.S. Advisory Board on Child Abuse and Neglect. *The Future of Children* 3 (3): 184–191.

Levy-Zlotnick, J., DePanfilis, D., Daining, C., and Lane, M. 2005. Factors influencing retention of child welfare staff: A systematic review of research. Washington, D.C.: Institute for the Advancement of Social Work Research.

Lipman-Blumen, J. 1996. *Connective leadership: Managing in a changing world.* New York: Oxford University Press.

Loar, L. 2007. Increasing safety for at-risk adults: Screening in-home care providers. *Social Work* 52: 271–274.

Mattessich, P. W., and Monsey, B. R. 1992. *Collaboration: What makes it work: A review of research literature on factors influencing successful collaboration.* St. Paul, Minn.: Amherst Wilder Foundation.

McCroskey, J., and Meezan, W. 1997. *Family preservation and family functioning.* Washington, D.C.: Child Welfare League of America.

Mulroy, E. A. 2004. Theoretical perspectives on the social environment to guide management and community practice: An organization-in-environment approach. *Administration in Social Work* 28: 77–96.

Nelson, K. E., Emlen, A., Landsman, M., and Hutchinson, J. 1988. *Factors contributing to success and failure in family-based child welfare services.* Ames: The University of Iowa School of Social Work, National Resource Center on Family Based Services.

Nelson, K. E., and Landsman, M. J. 1992. *Alternative models of family preservation: Family-based services in context.* Springfield, Ill.: Charles C. Thomas.

Pecora, P. J., Fraser, M. W., Nelson, K. E., McCroskey, J., and Meezan, W. 1995. *Evaluating family-based services.* Hawthorne, N.Y.: Aldine de Gruyter.

Perry-Burney, G. D. 2001. Safety of intensive in-home family workers. *Family Preservation Journal* 5 (2): 44–52.

INTRODUCTION

Provan, K. G., and Sebastian, J. G. 1998. Networks within networks: Service link overlap, organizational cliques, and network effectiveness. *Academy of Management Journal* 41: 453–463.

Reese, D. J., and Raymer, M. 2004. Relationships between social work involvement and hospice outcomes: Results of the National Hospice Social Work Survey. *Social Work* 49: 415–422.

Roane, D. M., Teusink, J. P., and Wortham, J. A. 2002. Home visits in geropsychiatry fellowship training. *The Gerontologist* 42: 109–113.

Roberts-DeGennaro, M. 1997. Conceptual framework of coalitions in an organizational context. *Journal of Community Practice* 4: 91–107.

Rogers, E. M. 1995. *Diffusion of innovations*. New York: The Free Press.

Ryan, K. D., and Oestreich, D. K. 1998. *Driving fear out of the workplace: Creating the high-trust, high-performance organization*. San Francisco: Jossey-Bass.

Rycraft, J. R. 1994. The party isn't over: The agency role in the retention of public child welfare caseworkers. *Social Work* 39: 75–80.

Schmid, H. 2004. Organization-environment relationships: Theory for management practice in human service organizations. *Administration in Social Work* 28: 97–113.

Senge, P. 2006. *The fifth discipline*. Rev. ed. New York: Doubleday.

Smale, G. 1995. Integrating community and individual practice: A new paradigm for practice. In *Reinventing human services: Community and family-centered practice*, ed. P. Adams and K. Nelson, 59–80. Hawthorne, N.Y.: Aldine de Gruyter.

———. 1998. *Managing change through innovation*. London: The Stationery Office.

Smith, P. B., and Peterson, M. F. 1988. Leadership as the management of meaning. In *Leadership, organizations, and culture*. Newbury Park, Calif.: Sage.

Spencer, P. C., and Munch, S. 2003. Client violence toward social workers: The role of management in community mental health programs. *Social Work* 48: 532–544.

Sundet, P. A., and Cowger, C. D. 1994. The rural community environment as a stress factor for rural child welfare workers. *Administration in Social Work* 14: 97–110.

Vaill, J. 1996. *Learning as a way of being: Strategies for survival in a world of permanent whitewater*. San Francisco: Jossey-Bass.

Velasquez, M. M. 2004. *In the change book: A blueprint for technology transfer*. Available online at http://www.nattc.org/resPubs/changeBook.html.

Wheatley, M. 1992. *Leadership and the new sciences*. San Francisco: Berrett-Koehler.

Zischka, P. C., and Fox, R. 1983. Burnout and the catalytic role of the supervisor. *The Clinical Supervisor* 1 (2): 43–52.

Four

Social Policy Context

CATHLEEN A. LEWANDOWSKI AND KATHARINE BRIAR-LAWSON

Individuals must have basic needs met for both survival and functioning in society. Families have historically played the predominant role in providing for their care and overall well-being. In fact, families provide up to 90 percent of all the education, counseling, caregiving, and norm enforcement for their members (Briar-Lawson et al. 2001). Nonetheless, they rely on societal institutions to help with resources, services, and supports.

The twentieth century ushered in a number of social-service programs and policies in support of individuals and families. Whether provided by public, voluntary, or for-profit organizations and facilities, many key services have undergone pendulum-like swings over the decades (Burghardt and Fabricant 1992). Some programs have served individuals and families in their homes. Other services have been provided in centers and institutions. Many of these twentieth-century policies and practices have been refined or altered for twenty-first-century needs and realities. In a few service sectors, such as child welfare and early childhood prevention and intervention services, the use of home-based services has been more pronounced than in prior decades. In other sectors, such as in criminal justice, home-based services have increasingly been criticized as ineffective and are being used less frequently.

This chapter identifies the key policies relevant for home-based services in a range of fields of practice. Selected dynamics and dimensions of services are explored as they contextualize the use of home-based practices. By examining key public-sector policy domains, some of the factors that facilitate or impede home-based practices within different service systems are identified. Finally, the chapter examines critical policy issues and suggests future strategies and directions for advancing home-based services.

Early Childhood Programs

The most thoroughly researched home-visiting programs are those that focus on young children from infancy to preschool ages. Some well-known home-visiting programs include Parents as Teachers, Early Head Start, Home Instruction for Parents of Preschool Youngsters, Healthy Families America, Nurse-Family Partnership, Hawaii Healthy Start, and the Comprehensive Child Development Program (Gomby, Culross, and Behrman 1999; Wasik and Shaffer 2006).

Early Head Start (EHS) began with the 1994 reauthorization of the Head Start Act. The program was designed to "provide early, continuous, intensive, and comprehensive child development and family support services" to low-income families with children under age three (Administration for Children and Families 1994). EHS administrators could elect to deliver services via high-quality center-based care for infants and toddlers, home-based support for child and family development, or a "mixed" model in which some families receive center-based services, some receive home-based services, and some receive a combination of both. The Revised Head Start Performance Standards at that time prescribed weekly ninety-minute home visits for such programs (Brookes et al. 2006).

The 110th Congress reauthorized the Head Start for School Readiness Act to improve program quality and expand access to early-intervention programs. Of note, this reauthorization specifies that Head Start programs should conduct outreach to migrant and seasonal workers and remove barriers to enrollment and participation of homeless children. Head Start programs are also to coordinate their activities with existing home-based and family-support services (GovTrack.us 2008).

The Children's Health Act of 2000 expanded, intensified, and coordinated research, prevention, and treatment activities for children with disabilities. The act authorized the Healthy Start demonstration program, which is designed to reduce infant-mortality rates by expanding access to health-care services for pregnant women and infants. Healthy Families New York is one such demonstration project. To date, Healthy Families New York, through home-based services to pregnant women by paraprofessionals, has been shown to be effective in reducing the incidence of low-birth-weight infants and to reduce the number of women who have a subsequent child (DuMont et al. 2008).

Congress reauthorized the 1986 Education of the Handicapped Act Amendments, Part H (PL 99-457), as Part B, for special education for children three years and up, and Part C, for early intervention for children from birth to three years of age, in 1997 (PL 105-17, Individuals with Disabilities Education Act; IDEA) and again in 2004 (PL 108-446, Individuals with Disabilities Improvement Education Act; IDEA). The IDEA stipulates that states can provide federally funded services to families with at-risk children and to those with a developmental delay or disabling condition.

Some home-based and family-centered practices that have developed over the years in child welfare and mental health can be attributed in part to contextual reinforcements from the disabilities movements. Early on, some parents of children with disabilities found themselves interacting with the child welfare and mental health systems. Policy requirements such as the least restrictive and least intrusive practices took hold in child welfare and mental health as these programs intersected at the local levels.

Children with disabilities, required to be in the least restrictive settings, attend public schools and live in their family's homes. Thus it is unsurprising that family and home-based services developed as part of school-based social work services.

Schools and Educational Policies

Home visiting has a long history of use with children in schools as school social workers employ this method of intervention with elementary, middle, and high school students (Allen and Tracy 2004). Federal education policy created a context for home visits as early as the 1970s. The Elementary and Secondary Education Act of 1965 mandated parent participation in the education of their children beginning in 1971 (Constable 1992). In 1997, the U.S. Department of Education announced seven education priorities, and home-school communication was identified as a key strategy for achieving these priorities (US DOE 1997). The Council of Chief State School Officials went one step further by explicitly suggesting that schools secure parents as "partners in education." To do so, they recommended that schools hire school-family liaisons and provide social work services in the schools (Constable 1992).

The No Child Left Behind Act of 2001 (NCLB) promotes accountability-based school reform with the goal of helping all students experience academic achievement (Bryan 2005). In fact, NCLB mandates the development of school-family-community partnerships as a key to closing the achievement gap, but this clause is often overlooked (Bryan 2005). Home-visiting interventions present a unique way to establish school-family partnerships and have the potential to affect the academic achievement of students. School-based home visits may be a component of family-centered practice but also may be related to disciplinary practice, such as truancy interventions.

Child Welfare Policy

Child welfare programs, especially child-protection services, foster care, and adoption, are shaped in part by home-based practice expectations. The evidentiary nature of child welfare practice, especially in the area of child abuse and neglect, has warranted home-based assessment and interventions. Parents and other caregivers often contest allegations and charges filed against them. Since the home is where the child resides, and their care, developmental supports, and interactions occur in the home environment, home-based assessments and interventions dominate much of child welfare practice.

Ironically, home- and family-based practice has not been codified into law even though it has informed federal policy. This may largely be attributable to the nature of federal funding for child welfare. Authorized by the Social Security Act, Title IV-B funds constituted nearly $300 million in FY 2007 to states for family preservation and related services, with a 25 percent match requirement by the states (U.S. Department of Health and Human Services [US DHHS] 2008). This is compared to Title IV-E, in which nearly $5 billion was awarded in FY 2006 to states for out-of-home placements. Despite the availability of waivers to fund nationally significant demonstration projects, federal funds are primarily spent on foster care and not on home-based services.

The current funding streams for family preservation or Title IV-B funding and foster care or Title IV-E funding have certain implications for policy implementation. Title IV-B funding is an allocation to states and is based on the proportion of the state's population of children under twenty-one years of age multiplied by the state's average per capita income. In contrast, the Title IV-E foster care program is an entitlement program, which means it is available to anyone who meets the program's eligibility criteria (Child Welfare League of America [CWLA] 2008). This difference in funding mechanisms may have the unintended consequence of encouraging out-of-home placements and discouraging family preservation, simply because there is no cap or limit to the amount of Title IV-E funding that states may spend.

Prevention of out-of-home placement may invariably involve some home-based practices. Such practices ensure that caseworkers can see "in vivo" family-based interactions and the physical, social, and emotional conditions that surround the child or children. Based on PL 96-272, the Adoption Assistance and Child Welfare Act of 1980, states have been required to demonstrate "reasonable efforts" at placement prevention and in keeping the family intact. The Indian Child Welfare Act of 1978 set an even higher threshold for placement prevention and required "active efforts" at promoting family intactness and placement prevention. The family-preservation movement began in the 1970s and sought to prevent out-of-home placement by providing intensive services to families. These services were often home based.

The family-preservation movement ultimately led to the passage of the Family Preservation and Support Services of the Omnibus Reconciliation Act of 1993 (US DHHS 2008), which promoted family preservation and family supports. The language for this act targets children in families, including adoptive families at risk or in crisis, but does not mention home-based services. Furthermore, the definition of family-support services cites community-based rather than home-based services "to promote the well being of children" and to provide children with a stable family environment.

In summary, federal law does not mandate home-based services for families of children with abuse and neglect risk factors. Moreover, policy mandates for home-based services at the federal level are less clear than might be expected. Further, families who receive home-based services and the social workers who provide such services are affected by multiple and sometimes overlapping policies.

Mental Health

Home and community-based services for individuals with mental illness have their origins in the community mental health movement, which originated in events occurring after World War II. The movement was largely fueled by the revelation that there was a high incidence of psychiatric disorders from the war and that more men had been rejected from service for psychiatric disorders than the total number of those fighting at the peak period of the war (Foley and Sharfstein 1983).

The National Mental Health Act of 1946 established the National Institute of Mental Health (NIMH) to foster research, train personnel, and aid states in the prevention, diagnosis, and treatment of neuropsychiatric disorders. Previously, most mental health services were provided in institutions. The passage of this act marked the beginning of the mental health movement, which was supported by millions of like-minded citizens who banded together over a period of many years to advocate for community-based mental health services.

A final piece of legislation, the National Mental Health Study Act of 1965, set the stage for the community mental health movement. This act required NIMH to appoint a commission to Congress to plan and conduct a thoroughgoing reevaluation of the nation's approach to mental illness. By focusing on acute and chronic mental illness but ignoring mental health promotion, the commission overrode the desires of citizen groups and those of other mental health professionals who were advocating for prevention. Under President Kennedy, the concept of the Community Mental Health Center (CMHC) began to come together. In October 1963, Kennedy signed PL 88-164 into law, which only provided funds for facilities. In October 1965, President Johnson signed the CMHC Act Amendment into law, authorizing federal funds to assist in the initial staffing of the CMHC. To promote community- and home-based services, there were also a series of judicial decisions affirming the civil rights of those with mental illness and upholding the right to treatment in the least restrictive environment. In 1975, the services CMHCs were required to provide expanded from five to twelve, to include children, the elderly, screening, follow-up and transitional care for individuals with severe and persistent mental illness, and alcohol and drug treatment. Ultimately, the CMHC Act was subsumed under the Mental Health Systems Act of 1980.

The Community Support Program (CSP), advocated by NIMH in 1978, was a milestone in the anti-institutionalization movement, as it offered comprehensive community-support systems for severely mentally disabled adults. Soon after they were established, it quickly became apparent that CMHCs were being overtaken by the urgency of the needs of the severely mentally ill. CSPs were designed to address these needs, including the concrete needs for food, clothing, housing, and social services (Foley and Sharfstein 1983). However, critics of efforts to build such community supports emphasize the absence of cultural competence and family-centered approaches. In essence, practices have been critiqued for being individually focused and not responsive to the family or cultural context that might generate resources and strengths for the recovery process (Barrio 2000).

Following these mental health reforms, attention was increasingly paid to the mental health needs of children. It is estimated that 70 percent or more of children's mental health needs are provided in schools (Hoagwood 2002). This is reinforced by PL 94-142, the Education for All Handicapped

Children Act of 1975, now called the IDEA. This act helped to promote inno-vative practice models such as "wraparound services," allowing emotionally disturbed children to remain in their own homes and classrooms.

While significantly influential, these new laws and their concomitant pol-icy initiatives, such as wraparound services, are plagued by a lack of specifi-cally designated funding (Furman 2002). Congress partially addressed this lack of funding in 1989 by expanding the Early and Periodic Screening, Diag-nosis, and Treatment provision of Title XIX of the Social Security Act of 1935. As a result, many states began to use Medicaid funding for children's mental health services (Furman 2002), including wrap-around services.

The Comprehensive Community Mental Health Services for Children and Their Families Act of 1992 promoted "systems of care," comprehensive and individualized assessments, effective treatment plans, service integration, and family-centered and evidence-based practices. Even though studies of pilots have shown mixed results (Bickman, Noser, and Summerfelt 1999), the Pres-ident's New Freedom Commission on Mental Health report (2003) urged the expansion of the system-of-care model. Other concerns regarding wraparound models include the potential for disempowering families through overreliance on family partners or therapeutic assistants and the provision of services in a cookie-cutter approach, despite the model's emphasis on individualizing ser-vices (Furman 2002). Within this context, system-level integration and sup-ports and ancillary services can enhance or detract from the parent–service coordinator partnership. Home-based services are implied but not made ex-plicit (New Freedom Commission 2003). The vast patchwork of programs and funding and the differential and often competing views about practice may make home- and family-based strategies more difficult to coordinate.

Mental health reforms over the years have resulted in dramatic policy shifts, as institutional care has been replaced by home- and community-based supports. Consistent with the policy emphasis on noninstitutional care is the rise of community-based "systems of care." This implies that better outcomes for children will be achieved if systems, including mental health, juvenile justice, schools, and child welfare, work together (Knitzer 1982).

Criminal Justice

Adult Offenders

Home visiting in the criminal-justice field for adults largely occurs in the context of probation and parole. Probation is given in lieu of incarceration;

parole occurs after incarceration, when offenders reenter the community. Probation emerged at the beginning of the twentieth century and was legislated into law in a few states at that time. Home visiting by probation officers was a carryover from the Charity Organization Society movement, and many of the early probation officers were volunteers who, as in other fields of practice, would seek to bring about desired change by establishing an "enduring friendship" (Leiby 1978, 115). The carryover of friendly visiting was natural, because many of the early probation officers were recruited from social-service organizations. Unique to these early days of home visiting was the practice of some probation officers allowing homeless probationers to reside with them temporarily in their home (Lathrop 1905).

The stated purpose of probation is the dual function of safety of the community and rehabilitation of the offender. Personal contacts, either office or home based, with individuals on probation were viewed as essential. At the same time, such personal contacts have been the subject of deep concern and skepticism. Home visiting in particular has generally been perceived to be ineffective, underproductive, and impractical in light of limited resources (Lindner 1992). These concerns have been validated by research that consistently suggests that home visiting has been ineffective in both of its purposes of safety and rehabilitation (Rothman 1980). By 1980, home visiting had often been replaced by office visits, in an attempt to deal with safety and resource issues. Despite the criticisms and the research findings, home visits were firmly rooted in early probation and continue to be viewed as integral to modern probation.

Resource limitations and concerns for safety preclude probation officers from conducting home visits. Instead, the field of criminal justice is increasingly relying on technology. Global positioning (GPS) technology has paved the way for a new approach to managing probationers through electronic monitoring. While the stated or manifest function of home visiting in probation has been safety and rehabilitation, social control has consistently been its latent function. Home visiting was perceived as useful in deterring future criminal behavior by creating the impression that "big brother is watching" (Harris 1984, 23). Thus, in probation, the home visit, conducted initially by a "friendly visitor," is being replaced by an ankle bracelet.

Since 2001, frequent home and office visits have been identified as key components of intensive probation for domestic violence offenders (Johnson 2001). Nonetheless, intensive programs such as these require a great deal of staffing and may increasingly be replaced by technicians and electronic monitoring. In terms of recent policy, the Adam Walsh Protection and Safety Act of 2006 mandates the use of electronic monitoring as a condition of release for pretrial defendants for specific cases involving a victim who is a minor. Though states and probation agencies vary on which individuals are most suitable for electronic monitoring, typical types of clients include sex offenders, domestic-violence clients, clients with restraining orders, substance abusers, violent clients, and gang-related clients (Brown, McCabe, and Wellford 2007).

Parole has changed dramatically since the mid-1970s. At that time, most inmates served open-ended, indeterminate terms, and a parole board had wide discretion to either release them or keep them behind bars. In principle, offenders were only released if they had been rehabilitated. Monitoring their continued progress in the community through home and office visits, again, in principle, would be manageable. This made parole a privilege to be earned, and inmates knew they could be returned to prison if they violated parole. Today, indeterminate sentencing and discretionary release have been replaced in many states with determinate sentencing and automatic release. Offenders receive fixed prison terms and are released at the end of them. Once released, 80 percent of returning prisoners are assigned to a parole officer. The remaining 20 percent, including those who have committed the most serious crimes and have served their full sentence, leave prison with no postcustody supervision. Despite the essential work of parole officers, their numbers have not kept pace with demand, and caseloads have continued to increase. Under these conditions, there is little time for monitoring through home visits or for providing needed services. Thus, no-parole systems have undercut postrelease supervision, including home visits, as field supervision tends to be undervalued, underfunded, and understaffed (Petersilla 2000).

Juvenile Justice

Like child welfare and children in the mental health and disability-care systems, juvenile offenders are increasingly targeted for diversion services. This reduces the likelihood of institutional care and promotes more home- and community-based interventions. Many of these interventions have their origins in the juvenile justice reform movement that began in earnest during the 1950s. Since the beginnings of the juvenile court in the Progressive Era, there had always been a degree of skepticism regarding the role of the juvenile court in treating juvenile offenders as children in need of protection from the stigma and harm caused by criminal prosecution. However, it was not until the 1950s that the public and policymakers became increasingly concerned that the focus on rehabilitation in the juvenile court was not preventing the increase in the number of juvenile offenses (Manfredi 1998).

64

INTRODUCTION

In *Gault vs. the United States*, the Supreme Court ruled that juvenile offenders had a right to due process and liberty as afforded other citizens under the Bill of Rights and that these rights took precedence over the protective custody that often occurred when juvenile offenders were brought to the court. The Juvenile and Delinquency Prevention Act of 1974 was passed to reduce the number of status offenders in secure detention facilities and the number of juveniles in adult jails. It is based on a rehabilitation model, focusing on the treatment of the offender, rather than on a retribution model, which favors a punitive approach. The act narrowed the focus of what was considered a juvenile offense, expanded due process for juvenile offenders, placed an increased emphasis on offenses instead of offenders, and limited judicial discretion in juvenile cases (Manfredi 1998). The Juvenile Justice Delinquency and Prevention Act of 2002 sought to reduce the use of institutions by promoting graduated sanctions that were community based and preventive in nature. Unlike other social policies, this act prescribes home-based services. This is explicitly legislated in part because the home is both the site for services and for home-based detention.

Unlike the many delinquency-prevention programs that build parent and family capacity, the use of family-centered practices has been more limited in juvenile justice programs. Reframing of a youth's problems as a family issue requiring family-based interventions may also be seen as shifting the focus from the behavioral problems of the youth to other factors. This might divert attention away from the offense and related behavioral-change requirements expected of the youth. Despite this, many youth in the juvenile justice system may have mental health or substance abuse issues, educational problems, disabilities, and child welfare challenges. Thus, family-centered and home-based practice may be offered because of cross-systems involvement or inter-professional collaboration.

While few would argue for the unfettered discretion of parole boards in the 1960s, improved parole guidelines can create uniformity and be used to objectively weigh factors known to be associated with recidivism. Given the increasing human and financial costs of prison, along with all the collateral consequences to families and communities, investing in effective reentry programs may be a prudent strategy. Home visiting by qualified and well-trained parole officers can play a role in such reentry programs.

Older Adults

In 1965, President Johnson passed the Older Americans Act (PL 89-73), a key piece of legislation in providing supportive services to the elderly. In addition to creating the Administration on Aging, it authorized grants to states for community planning and services, as well as for research, demonstration, and training projects. Later amendments added grants to Area Agencies on Aging for local needs identification, planning, and funding of services, including but not limited to community- and home-based nutrition programs, health-promotion and disease-prevention activities, in-home services for frail elders, and services that protect the rights of elders (US DHHS 2007).

In 1975, Congress mandated a new program, Adult Protective Services (APS), under Title XX of the Social Security Act. APS workers are often the first responders to reports of elder abuse, neglect, or exploitation. Though a federally mandated program, there was little or no federal funding attached for APS programming. Thus APS programs have developed in accordance with the needs and constructs of each state (Teaster et al. 2006).

The Older Americans Act Amendments of 2000 contained a new program, the National Family Caregiver Support Program, which helps families who struggle to care for their ill or disabled loved ones. Under this program, organizations provide many community- and home-based support services, including information and assistance, counseling, support groups, and respite care (US DHHS 2007).

The federal government began providing reimbursement for home health services with the enactment of Medicare and Medicaid in 1965, as Titles XVIII and XIX of the Social Security Act. Home health care for elders is now a rapidly growing sector of government expenditures. At the same time, nursing homes expanded in the 1970s, and politicians began looking at home-based care as a more cost-effective alternative to nursing homes. In response, Congress passed the Channeling Demonstration project in 1979 to explore the viability of expanded service coverage for home-based care. This resulted in multisite projects with case-management services. Findings indicated that home-based care was not a cost-effective alternative to nursing-home care (Weissart 1990). Despite these findings, funding for home-based care continues, as policymakers tend to support it.

Recent research suggests that home-based health care may result in the shifting rather than the reduction of cost, and the real benefit may be in improving the quality of life of elders and their families (Yaggy et al. 2006). Home-based care for older adults was extended with the Omnibus Reconciliation Act of 1980, which eliminated prior hospitalization as an eligibility requirement for home-based care and did away with the previous limit of one hundred home health visits. Additional services, such as psychotherapy provided by MSW social workers for depression (Gellis et al. 2007), have recently been provided to elders in their homes.

Medicaid provides payment for persons who are eligible for skilled nursing and is not time limited. In contrast to the initial Medicare model, Medicaid was designed for long-term services to persons with chronic illness and disabilities (Binstock and Cluff 2000). Medicaid now includes home and community-based services as alternatives to institutional care. The Omnibus Reconciliation Act of 1981 authorized a special waiver program that extended Medicaid coverage to allow states to apply for federal Medicaid matching funds to provide a broader range of home- and community-based services. This waiver allows individuals to receive services that support activities of daily living (ADL). Eligibility for this waiver program involves individuals who would be in a nursing home if they did not receive assistance with their ADLs.

The United States has a long way to go to provide the array of home-based services and support needed to sustain older adults in their homes and communities. Innovations building around the country include the development of NNORCS (Neighborhood Naturally Occurring Retirement Communities). Even end-of-life care is often deemed more desirable when it is as homelike as possible. The hospice movement has spearheaded such rights and services.

Hospice

Hospice care began in the 1970s in the United States and was provided by volunteer groups offering nursing and supportive services, helping family members with any number of tasks, and providing emotional support. In 1979, the Health Care Financing Administration funded demonstration programs at twenty-six hospices across the United States to assess the cost effectiveness of hospice care and identify the services hospices should provide.

The first publicly funded hospice benefit was established by the Tax Equity and Fiscal Responsibility Act of 1982, through Part A of the Medicare health insurance program. The Medicare Hospice Benefit (MHB) created a payment system based on four levels of care: routine care, continuous care, respite care, and general inpatient care. In 1986, the MHB was enacted by Congress. States were given the option of including hospice care in their Medicaid programs, and hospice care was made available to terminally ill nursing home residents. Congress made the MHB permanent in 1986, and states could include hospice care as a covered benefit under Medicaid. In 1991, hospice care was also authorized in military hospitals under the Civilian Health and Medical Program of the Uniformed Services and added as a benefit for veterans in 1995 (National Hospice and Palliative Care Organization 2007).

Other Populations

This section addresses other populations that currently receive home-based services. These include persons with disabilities, veterans, individuals with HIV/AIDS, those with substance abuse issues, and the homeless. Though there is some overlap between these populations and those that have already been discussed, federal legislation addresses some of the unique needs of each of these groups, establishes policy, and provides separate funding streams.

Persons with Disabilities

One of the most profound influences on home- and family-based practices has come from the arenas of disability policy and practice. Federal laws such as the IDEA and, more recently, the Olmstead Act of 1999 requires those with disabilities, of all ages, to be integrated into the community using the least intrusive and restrictive practices. Nationally, the 1972 amendment to the 1965 Medicare legislation extended home-based care to persons younger than sixty-five years of age who were receiving Social Security disability insurance (SSDI) and who had end-stage renal disease (Binstock and Cluff 2000). The Olmstead Act will require more community- and home-based services for older persons with disabilities, moving away from nursing homes and related institutional service models.

Veterans

Currently, home-based services to veterans are not well developed. Social work practitioners may conduct outreach to homes and families, but many services for veterans are accessed through veterans' hospitals, vet centers, and related community-based rather than home-based programs. The VA may provide home visits to eligible veterans in response to their health-care needs. Both Veterans Affairs and the military are striving to respond to the emerging health-care needs of returning veterans wounded during recent conflicts in Iraq and Afghanistan. In 2007, there were more than fifty thousand veterans who had been wounded in hostile and nonhostile events since 2002 in Iraq and Afghanistan. As of July 2007, Army hospitals had treated 651 amputees, and 609 of them were from Iraq (Copeland 2007). The Community Based Health Care Organization, a recent initiative of the U.S. Army Medical Command to provide oversight of Army Reserve and National Guard soldiers undergoing medical treatment, has served more than four thousand soldiers. Though progress is being made, more needs to be done to support veterans and their families. Strengthening home-based services can be an important component in meeting these needs, especially for disabled veterans.

Health and HIV/AIDS

The Ryan White Comprehensive AIDS Resource Emergency (CARE) Act, enacted in 1990, provides federal funding for medical and supportive services for HIV-infected persons (Marconi et al. 1994). Funding is provided to metropolitan areas hardest hit by the AIDS epidemic. Children with HIV/AIDS may also benefit from home-based services that are integrated within a community context. Although awareness of the needs of HIV-affected children and their families has resulted in some increase in home-based and outreach services, funding and other constraints impede the long-term provision of such services (Gewirtz and Gossart-Walker 2000). By helping persons obtain home health care, case managers may help prevent costly institutionalization (London et al. 2001).

In summary, the Ryan White Act seeks to improve the quality and availability of care for low-income, uninsured, and underinsured individuals and families affected by HIV in the United States (Henry J. Kaiser Family Foundation 2007). Though Title IV of the act provides funding for family-centered services, it does not indicate whether services should be home based or center based. When home-based services are provided to persons living with HIV/AIDS, it is most likely to be a form of home health care.

Substance Abuse Recovery

Home-based services are less prominent in the field of addiction than agency-based and institutional methods of service delivery. Though the reasons for this are unknown, the traditional emphasis on the individual in recovery in twelve-step programs as well as professional modes of intervention may contribute to the dearth of home-based modes of service delivery. When home-based modes of intervention are developed, they tend to identify the family as the identified client. More importantly, harm-reduction rather than abstinence-only methods serves as the practice framework for home-based approaches in the field of addictions. Harm-reduction practices in addiction treatment may be more amenable to family involvement, because they emphasize more realistic goals of reduction than absolute abstinence (Marlatt, Blume, and Parks 2001).

Unlike other fields, where there is more likely to be an explicit focus on families, if not family and home-based services, the addictions arena is relatively new to such practices. Nonetheless, increasing evidence about the multiple benefits of family involvement in the recovery process may hasten the adoption of family- and home-based forms of service delivery.

Home-Based Services and the Homeless

One of the key assumptions of home-based services is that the services will be provided in a client's home. This assumption leads us to ask what it is we mean by "home," and whether some individuals are excluded from receiving services because their "home" or where they live is outside the parameters of what we traditionally consider to be a personal residence. Homelessness affects all ages and involves both individuals and families, such as single mothers with children. Families also differ from individuals in their pattern of shelter use and transitional housing. Families are more likely than individuals to stay in a shelter or transitional housing program. This may reflect the fact that living on the street or on someone's couch is more difficult for families. Moreover, many families are escaping domestic violence and spousal abuse (U.S. HUD 2007). Domestic-violence service providers are less likely to be enthusiastic about family preservation or family-centered practice, particularly if the homeless family is escaping from spousal abuse. Because of these circumstances, service providers who make home visits may expect to be making their "home visit" to a homeless shelter or other institutional setting.

Policy Issues and Dilemmas for Home-Based Services

From this brief inventory of selected policies and practices across a number of service sectors, it is clear that home-based services and home visiting, while deemed desirable if not a necessary condition for effective service, is yet to be codified as practice across all key service systems. Instead, language in federal legislation tends to be more generic, as seen in terms such as "community based" and "supportive services." Though the rationale for such language is not known, it may be that legislators are reluctant to use the term "home based," as it may imply a personalized form of services that may be available to some, but not all, citizens.

Nonetheless, the policy context is promising if not facilitating. Why should this finding emerge? As evident throughout the discussion in this chapter, the attention to families and support of their functions in federal policy is nascent, if not absent. The focus instead is usually on individuals. Family-capacity building, where the home environment is the strategic site for assessment and interventions, is far from being understood or used as a framework for public policy. On the other hand, movements led by consumers, parents, and professionals to advance more family- and often home-based services may provide a backdrop for more systematic attention to this critical component in care and services. As long as the individual and not the care system, such as the family, is considered to be the "client," systematic approaches to home- and family-based services may be impeded.

Who Is the Client: The Individual or the Family?

For many, a family focus is often a precondition for home-based services and practices. Whether the individual or the family is seen as the client depends on the practitioner and the service strategy. Some practitioners reframe individuals presenting problems and needs as family-system issues (Briar-Lawson et al. 2001). Others see the client as an individual family member, and the family is seen as a means to an end rather than an end in and of itself. In this context, some home-based social workers and related practitioners seek to empower the family to meet the needs of their individual family members. This can pose a dilemma for workers, as the unit of intervention is the family but the identified outcomes may be related to an individual family member. In such situations, the worker is faced with the competing needs of the individual and the needs of the family as a whole.

This ambiguity about who the client is adds to the difficulty in delineating policy for the delivery of home-based services. Most notably, the lack of clarity resulted in a 1971 Supreme Court case, *Wyman v. James* (400 U.S. 309), in which the Supreme Court considered whether a requirement that welfare recipients and applicants must allow home visits by caseworkers violated the Fourth Amendment's reasonable-search requirement. In order to issue a ruling, the Supreme Court found it necessary to specify the identified client. The court defined the purpose of the home visit as the welfare of the dependent child and held that the visit did not violate the Fourth Amendment. In their ruling, the Supreme Court made it clear that the needs of a dependent child are paramount and that the mother's claim to her right of privacy was secondary (Saltzman and Furman 1999). It is possible that the case would have been resolved differently had the family as a whole been named as the identified client. In that case, the mother might then have been able to assert her constitutional right to privacy and refuse services. Instead, the Supreme Court reinforced the idea that the child as an individual was the client and that the family was a means to an end rather than an end in and of itself.

Home-Based Services as Social Control

While the stated purpose or function of home-based services is often the well-being of the family or the individual family member, the unstated or latent purpose of home-based services may be social control. The notion that it is not only right but necessary for poor people to permit a stranger into the home to ask questions, make judgments, and give advice has become firmly entrenched across a range of settings and fields of practice (Hancock and Pelton 1989). Social workers as well as clients of home-visiting programs often have to confront the paradoxical or dual nature of the home visit, which has both an investigative and helping component. While home visits in child welfare may be most known for this dual function, there are other contexts where the purpose of the visit is less ambiguous. For example, social workers who conduct home visits for child-custody cases suggest that home visits can provide more accurate evaluations for decisions (Lytle-Viera 1987). The purpose of home visits for adoption may be less ambiguous for both social workers and families, as the investigative function of the home study is explicit. Beyond the home study, social workers usually do not provide services to potential adoptive families.

Given the wide range of opportunities and needs for home-based services, it may seem curious that there is a dearth in definitive policy and a patchwork rather than systematic set of approaches regarding the use and value of the home for service delivery, information gathering, and capacity building. This may be attributable to the nature of U.S. policy itself in relation to families.

Absence of Family Policy

It can be argued that one of the key barriers to developing policies for home-based services is the absence of coherent public policy in support of families (Maluccio 1991). Even though families provide cradle-to-grave service for their members, there is a profound absence of U.S. public-policy support for families and their multiple functions. This may be due to the fact that families are seen as private entities not to be burdened by governmental regulation or interventions unless absolutely warranted.

Few social-service policies mention the delivery of home-based services as an approach to service. An additional dilemma is that family-centered approaches to services, including home-based approaches, lack a theoretical base upon which to build (Cole 1995). A need for more of an evidence base for practice in many home-based social work practice settings further impedes policy reforms.

Medicaid Waivers: Preventing Institutional Care

Despite the availability of home-based services across some, although not all, fields of practice, gaps in services continue to be more pronounced when the explicit goal is one of diverting an individual from institutional care. The goal of providing home-based services in many fields of practice is to prevent an institutional placement. To address some of the gaps, several states have successfully received Medicaid waivers to provide home-based health care for other identified populations who are at risk of institutional care. Between 2003 and 2004, the reported number of Home and Community-Based Services (HCBS) waivers rose from 263 to 267. These groups included the aged, aged or disabled, individuals with physical disabilities, individuals with mental retardation and developmental disabilities, medically fragile or technology-dependent children, individuals with HIV/AIDS, and individuals with traumatic brain and spinal-cord injury. The aged and aged or disabled were the largest group receiving services through Medicaid HCBS waivers. Following the aged, those most served were persons with mental retardation/developmental disabilities, those with physical disabilities, individuals with HIV/AIDS, children with special needs, individuals with traumatic brain injury and spinal-cord injuries, and individuals with mental health needs. Children had the largest increase in HCBS waivers, at 22 percent, followed by traumatic brain injury (21 percent) and the physically disabled (10 percent). Declines were recorded in the aged/disabled waivers and the mental health waivers (1 percent and 5 percent, respectively) (Binstock and Cluff 2000).

Despite the additional individuals who receive home-based services through Medicaid waivers, there are many at-risk populations who are underserved and lack access to home-based services. For example, in child welfare, unless there is an allegation of abuse or neglect, postadoptive families and adolescents in independent living do not generally receive home-based services. As described in this chapter, persons with disabilities, veterans, children and families who are affected by HIV/AIDS, and individuals and families in recovery from substance abuse could also benefit from receiving services in the home.

The Influence of Technology

Technological advances will increasingly influence the provision of home-based services, including the use of telepsychiatry for long-distance assessment and treatment, the Internet for computer-assisted counseling to individuals who are confined to their home, and electronic monitoring. which is replacing home visits in the criminal-justice system. On the one hand, the increased reliance on technology suggests an increased emphasis on social control instead of growth and rehabilitation, especially in the field of criminal justice. On the other hand, it is entirely possible that technology can empower those who are homebound and who live great distances from office-based services. Given the growing use of technology in lieu of home-based services, it is imperative that social work maintain standards of practice for technologically enhanced service delivery.

Summary and Future Challenges

From this brief inventory of selected service sectors and related policies, it is clear that home-based services are prominent features of many systems. However, they are less frequently legislated or, if so, more likely to be found at the state or local level, though funding may be provided by the federal government through various funding mechanisms. All service sectors share the family context for serving individuals. However, not all are similarly robust in valuing family-centered or home-based care. Given the fact that most individuals and their families may have co-occurring needs, such as child abuse and mental health or elder abuse and addiction, it is more likely that one service system will be a gateway to another. Thus, if home-based and family-centered practices are crucial to one service sector and cross-sector collaboration occurs, then more home- and family-based practices might be advanced.

In prior years, efforts have been made to foster family-centered practices as the framework for public policy for all social services, across selected states. However, there has been little investment in sustaining such efforts (Briar-Lawson et al. 2001). The more recent federal focus on fatherhood initiatives suggests that home- and family-based services must address absent fathers and be more inclusive in their strategies for engagement. Despite such additive effects, such initiatives do little to foster an integrative family-centered or family-supportive policy for the United States. In the face of such policy deficits, it is thus both affirming and promising that family-centered and home-based services are as prevalent as we have suggested. Even in the absence of explicit legislation, it can be argued that with additional empirical evidence and cross-sector collaboration, more family-centered and home-based policy and practice may emerge. It is possible that what early social workers sought to foster over one hundred years ago might indeed offer a guidepost for more unified home-based policies and practices for the twenty-first century.

REFERENCES

Administration for Children and Families. 1994. *Head Start Act amendments of 1994: Summary of major provisions.* Available online at http://www.hhs.gov/news/press/pre1995pres/940501a.txt.

Allen, S. F., and Tracy, E. M. 2004. Revitalizing the role of home visiting by school social workers. *Children and Schools* 26 (4): 197–208.

American Psychological Association, Office on Aging. 2008. Elder abuse and neglect: In search of solutions. Available online at http://www.apa.org/pi/aging/eldabuse.html.

Barrio, C. 2000. The cultural relevance of community support programs. *Psychiatric Services* 51 (7): 879–884.

Bickman, L., Noser, K., and Summerfelt, W. T. 1999. Comparative outcomes of emotionally disturbed children and adolescents in a system of services and usually care. *Psychiatric Services* 48: 1543–1548.

Binstock, R. H., and Cluff, L. E. 2000. Issues and challenges in home care. In *Home care advances: Essential research and policy issues,* ed. R. H. Binstock and L. E. Cluff. New York: Springer.

Briar-Lawson, K., Lawson, H., Hennon, C., and Jones, A. 2001. Family centered policies and practices: International implications. New York: Columbia University Press.

Brookes, S. J., Summers, J. A., Thornburg, K. R., Ispa, J. M., and Lane, V. J. 2006. Building successful goals in two Early Head Start programs: A qualitative look at contributing factors. *Early Childhood Research Quarterly* 21: 25–45.

Brown, T. M. L., McCabe, S. A., and Wellford, C. 2007. *Global positioning system*

(GPS) technology for community supervision: Lessons learned. Washington, D.C.: National Center for Criminal Justice Technology, U.S. Department of Justice.

Bryan, J. 2005. Fostering educational resilience and achievement in urban schools through school-family-community partnerships. *Professional School Counseling* 8 (3): 219–227.

Burghardt, S., and Fabricant, M. B. 1992. *The welfare state crisis and the transformation of social service work.* Armonk, N.Y.: M. E. Sharpe.

Child Welfare League of America. 2008. Legislative alert, March 21, 2005: Action needed—No caps on kids! Available online at http://www.acf.hhs.gov/programs/olab/budget/2006/2006_appro_lang_109_149.htm.

Cole, E. 1995. Becoming family centered: Child welfare's challenge. *Families in Society: The Journal of Contemporary Human Services* 76 (3): 163–172.

Constable, R. T. 1992. The new school reform and the school social worker. *Social Work in Education* 14 (2): 106–113.

Copeland, L. 2007. Camp helps wounded Iraq war veterans get back on feet. *USA Today.* Available online at http://www.usatoday.com/news/nation/2007-09-30-Offroad_helpthetroops_N.htm.

DuMont, K., Mitchell-Herzfeld, S., Greene, R., Lee, E., Lowenfels, A., Rodriguez, M., et al. 2008. Healthy Family New York (HFNY) randomized trial: Effects on early child abuse and neglect. *Child Abuse and Neglect* 32: 295–315.

Foley, H. A., and Sharfstein, S. S. 1983. *Madness and Government: Who Cares for the Mentally Ill?* Washington, D.C.: American Psychiatric Press.

Furman, R. 2002. Wrap-around services: An analysis of community-based mental health services for children. *Journal of Child and Adolescent Psychiatric Nursing* (July–September): 124–131.

Gellis, Z. D., McGinty, J., Horowitz, A., Bruce, M. L., and Misener, E. 2007. Problem-solving therapy for late-depression in home care: A randomized field trial. *American Journal of Geriatric Psychiatry* 15: 968–978.

Gewirtz, A., and Gossart-Walker, S. 2000. Home-based treatment for children and families affected by HIV and AIDS. Dealing with stigma, secrecy, disclosure, and loss. *Child and Adolescent Psychiatric Clinics of North America* 9 (2): 313–330.

Gomby, D. S., Culross, P. L., and Behrman, R. E. 1999. Home visiting: Recent program evaluations: Analysis and recommendations. *The Future of Children* 9 (1): 4–26.

GovTrack.us. 2008. H.R. 1429: Improving Head Start for School Readiness Act of 2007. In *GovTrack.us: Tracking the 110th United States Congress.* Available online at http://www.govtrack.us/congress/bill.xpd?bill=h110–1429.

Hancock, B. L., and Pelton, L. H. 1989. Home visits: History and function. *Social Casework: The Journal of Contemporary Social Work* (January): 21–27.

Harris, M. K. 1984. Rethinking probation in the context of the justice model. In

Probation and justice: Reconsideration of mission, ed. P. D. McAnany, D. Tomson, and D. Fogel, 15–37. Cambridge, Mass.: Oelgeschlager, Gunn, and Hain.

Henry J. Kaiser Family Foundation. 2007. *HIV/AIDS policy fact sheet: The Ryan White program*. Menlo Park, Calif.: The Henry J. Kaiser Family Foundation. Available online at http://www.kff.org/hivaids/upload/7582_03.pdf.

Hoagwood, K. 2002. Overcoming barriers to reducing the burden of affective disorders. *Biological Psychiatry* 52 (6): 655–675.

Johnson, R. R. 2001. Intensive probation for domestic violence offenders. *Federal Probation* 65 (3): 36–39.

Knitzer, J. 1982. *Unclaimed children: The failure of public responsibility to children and adolescents in need of mental health services*. Washington, D.C.: Children's Defense Fund.

Lathrop, J. C. 1905. The development of the probation system in a large city. *Charities* (January): 344–349.

Leiby, J. 1978. *A history of social welfare and social work in the United States*. New York: Columbia University Press.

Lindner, C. 1992. The probation field visit and office report in New York State: Yesterday, today, and tomorrow. *Criminal Justice Review* 17 (1): 44–60.

London, A. S., Fleishman, J. A., Goldman, D. P., McCaffrey, D. F., Bossette, S. A., Shapiro, M. F., et al. 2001. Use of unpaid and paid home care services among people with HIV infection in the USA. *AIDS Care* 13 (1): 99–121.

Lytle-Vieira, J. E. 1987. Kramer vs. Kramer revisited: The social work role in child custody cases. *Social Work* 32 (1): 5–11.

Maluccio, A. N. 1991. The optimism of policy choices in child welfare. *American Journal of Orthopsychiatry* 6 (4): 606–609.

Manfredi, C. R. 1998. *The Supreme Court and juvenile justice*. Lawrence: The University of Kansas Press.

Marconi, K., Rundall, T., Gentry, D., Kwait, J., Celentano, D., and Stolley, P. 1994. The organization and availability of HIV-related services in Baltimore, Maryland, and Oakland, California. *Journal of AIDS and Public Policy* 9: 173–181.

Marlatt, G. A., Blume, A. W., and Parks, G. A. 2001. Integrating harm reduction therapy and traditional substance abuse treatment. *Journal of Psychoactive Drugs* 33 (1): 13–21.

National Hospice and Palliative Care Organization. 2007. 2007 in review. Available online at http://www.nhpco.org/templates/1/homepage.cfm.

New Freedom Commission on Mental Health. 2003. *Achieving the promise: Transforming mental health care in America. Final report*. Rockville, Md.: US DHHS (Pub. No. SMA-03- 3832).

Petersilla, J. 2000. Sentencing and corrections: Issues for the twenty-first century. *Papers from the Executive Sessions on Sentencing and Corrections* (November, no. 9). Washington, D.C.: U.S. Department of Justice.

Rothman, D. J. 1980. *Conscience and convenience: The asylum and its alternatives in progressive America*. Boston: Little, Brown and Company.

Saltzman, A., and Furman, D. M. 1999. *Law in social work practice*. Chicago: Nelson-Hall.

Teaster, P. B., Dugar, T. A., Mendionado, M. S., Abner, E. L., Cecil, K. A., and Otto, J. M. 2006. *The 2004 survey of state adult protective services: Abuse of adults 60 years and older*. Lexington: The National Committee for the Prevention of Elder Abuse and The National Adult Protective Services Association, The University of Kentucky. Available online at http://www.ncea.aoa.gov/NCEARoot/ Main_Site/ pdf/2-14 06%20FINAL%2060+REPORT.pdf.

U.S. Department of Education (US DOE). 1997. The seven priorities of the U.S. Department of Education: Working document, July 28, 1997. Available online at http://www.ed.gov/updates/7priorities/index.html.

U.S. Department of Health and Human Services, Administration on Aging. 2007. Older Americans Act. Available online at http://www.aoa.gov/about/legbudg/ oaa/legbudg_oaa.asp.

U.S. Department of Health and Human Services, Administration on Children Youth and Families. 2008. Child welfare services: Title IV-B, subpart of the Social Security Act. Available online at http://www.acf.hhs.gov/programs/cb/pro-grams_fund/state_tribal/ss_act.htm.

——. 2008b. Appropriation language: Excerpts from the Departments of Labor, Health and Human Services, and Education, and Related Agencies Appropriations Act, 2006—Public Law 109–149. Available online at http://www.acf.hhs. gov/programs/olab/budget/2006/2006_appro_lang_109_149.htm.

——. 2007. *Child maltreatment 2005*. Washington, D.C.: U.S. Government Printing Office.

U.S. Department of Housing and Urban Development, Office of Community Planning and Development (US HUD). 2007. *The annual homeless assessment report to Congress*. Washington, D.C.: U.S. Department of Housing and Urban Development. Available online at http://www.huduser.org/Publications/pdf/ahar.pdf.

Wasik, B. H., and Shaffer, G. L. 2006. Home visiting: Essential guidelines for home visits and engaging with families. In *The school services sourcebook*, ed. C. Franklin, M. B. Harris, and P. Allen-Meares, 745–752. New York: Oxford University Press.

Weissart, W. G. 1990. Strategies for reducing home-care expenditures. *Generations* 14 (2): 42–44.

Yaggy, S. D., Michener, J. L., Yaggy, D., Champagne, M. T., Silberberg, M., Lyn, M., et al. 2006. Just for us: An academic medical center community partnership to maintain the health of a low-income senior population. *The Gerontologist* 46 (2): 271–276.

PART II

Home-Based Services in Social Work Fields of Practice

Five

Early Childhood Programs

SUSAN F. ALLEN

Home-based programs for families with young children serve families during pregnancy and until their children are five years old and eligible for public-school kindergarten. Programs are usually divided into those that serve
families from pregnancy until the child turns three and those that serve preschoolers. These programs target two populations: families whose child has
been diagnosed with a disability and those whose child is assessed as having
factors that put them at risk for poor developmental outcomes. Despite programmatic differences, early childhood home-visiting programs share the
"same underlying assumption" that the years before children begin formal
education "is a unique developmental period that serves as a foundation for
behavior, well-being, and success later in life" (Karoly et al. 1998, 107).

In-home service delivery is particularly relevant to programs for families
with young children. Home visitors receive a view of families' ecological contexts in their homes and communities that can be crucial for individualizing
services to family needs (Gomby, Culross, and Behrman 1999; Wasik and Bryant 2001). Meeting on the family's home turf helps foster trust and supports
the family-centered approach to service delivery by emphasizing the importance of the family's role in the service provider–family relationship (Weiss
1993). It is more convenient for families and eliminates barriers to receiving
help, such as transportation and childcare issues (Wasik and Bryant 2001).
Furthermore, meeting in the home, a crucial setting for child development,

maximizes opportunities to observe and intervene in parent-child interactions (Wasik and Bryant 2001; Weiss 1993).

Early childhood home visitation has proliferated in the last couple of decades primarily in response to evidence that it may be a cost-effective measure to prevent, or at least ameliorate, such emotionally and financially costly societal ills as child abuse, delinquency, and academic failure (Heckman 2006; Karoly et al. 1998; Wasserman 2006). However, researchers have urged some caution regarding high expectations for the preventive effects of these programs (Daro 2006a; Gomby et al. 1999; Weiss 1993).

The Population

Demographics of Children at Risk

Children who receive home-based interventions due to at-risk status test within the normal range for development. Although they may develop normally early in life, these children are at risk of developing delays over time. The overriding environmental risk factor targeted by early childhood programs is socioeconomic status, usually operationalized as family income near or at the U.S. poverty level. Research indicates that children living in poverty are more likely than other children to experience maltreatment (Luthar 1999), poor health (Brooks-Gunn and Duncan 1997), aggression and behavior problems (Dodge, Pettit, and Bates 1994; Luthar 1999), and academic difficulties (Brooks-Gunn and Duncan 1997) .

Poverty rates for young children, which had declined in the 1990s, have rebounded since 2000 (Douglas-Hall, Chau, and Koball 2006). For children under the age of six, 20 percent—4.9 million—lived in poverty in 2005, and 42 percent—10.2 million—lived in low-income families. Young children continue to have higher rates of poverty and are experiencing a faster rate of increase than school-age children are. Children with parents who are immigrants, Latino, or African American are especially likely to have a low family income.

Many home-visiting programs for at-risk children have the specific goal of preventing child maltreatment (Geeraert et al. 2004). In 2005, 16.5 per thousand children under the age of three were victimized by abuse or neglect, and 54.5 percent of all child victims were seven years old or younger (Children's Bureau 2007). Young children have higher rates of especially serious consequences of physical abuse and neglect, including death, nonorganic failure to thrive, brain injuries, and impaired growth (Guterman and Taylor 2005).

With the high rates of poverty and maltreatment for young children, the demand for home-based preventive intervention is clear. Actual numbers of families enrolled in home-visiting programs is unknown. However, by combining information from the larger multistate programs, estimates are that 400,000 to 500,000 children who are at risk receive home-visiting services (Daro 2006a, 2006b). Thirty-seven states fund some kind of home-based services for these families beginning during pregnancy or shortly after birth (Daro 2006a, 2006b).

Demographics of Children with Disabilities

Federal legislation mandating services for children with disabilities identifies two categories: diagnosed physical or mental conditions that have a high probability of leading to developmental delay and a documented delay in one or more areas of development (Individuals with Disabilities Education Improvement Act [IDEA] 2004). The traditional term for services to these families is "early intervention" (EI).

Birth indicators such as prematurity and lack of prenatal care increase the risk of disability for an infant (Hebbeler et al. 2007). Some risk factors have improved while others have not. Birth rates for adolescents and women ages twenty to twenty-four are declining, as are rates of cigarette smoking during pregnancy (Division of Vital Statistics 2006). No improvement was seen in 2004 in the timely access to prenatal care. Rates of premature births (less than thirty-seven weeks gestation) and low birth weights (less than 2,500 grams) are increasing steadily. In 2004, 12.5 percent of births were premature, and 8.1 percent exhibited low birth weight (Division of Vital Statistics 2006).

All states provide EI services for young children with disabilities and their families. In the fall of 2005, 293,816 infants and toddlers received EI services (Hebbeler et al. 2007). The National Early Intervention Longitudinal Study (Hebbeler et al. 2007) provides a description of families enrolled in EI programs. NEILS data on reasons for eligibility for EI services are provided in table 5.1.

The two populations served by early childhood home-visiting programs overlap in terms of children with disabilities who also have environmental risk factors. Families receiving EI services are more likely than the general population to be African American and low income. This is attributed to the fact that "demographic factors such as low income or minority status are associated with more limited access to medical care and adequate nutrition, which in turn are associated with more compromised birth outcomes and poorer health and development" (Hebbeler et al. 2007, 2–6).

TABLE 5.1
Leading Reasons for Enrollment in EI Services (Percent)

REASON FOR ENROLLMENT	%
Speech/communication impairment or delay	41.1
Prenatal/perinatal abnormalities (e.g., very low birth weight)	18.9
Motor impairment or delay	17.5
Global delayed development (e.g., physical growth abnormality)	12.2
Congenital disorders (e.g., Down syndrome)	8.9
Central nervous system disorders (e.g., cerebral palsy)	6.5

Note: n = 5,293.
Source: Adapted from Hebbeler et al. (2007).

Policy and Agency Context

Growing awareness in the 1960s of poverty's effects on cognitive development led to implementation of home visiting as a preventive intervention for low-income families with preschool-age children (Wasik and Bryant 2001). The early programs, such as the Portage Project (Shearer 1992) and the High/Scope Perry Preschool study (Schweinhart and Weikart 1983), used parent education to enhance the learning environment in the home and affect the cognitive development of the child. Initial longitudinal studies of these programs showed mixed results, and interest turned to intervening at younger ages.

Models were developed for home visiting to families with children under the age of three. Some continued the trend of programs for families of preschoolers by emphasizing the enhancement of cognitive development (Shearer 1992). Others also focused on improving child physical health and preventing maltreatment (Daro and Harding 1999; Duggan et al. 1999). Supported by research on the effects of the environment—particularly interactions with principal caregivers—on infant/toddler development, these programs took a community-based approach (Guralnick 1997). Interventions focused on promoting formal and informal social supports to meet the complex array of family needs and on enhancing the quality of parent-child interactions.

Separate EI programs for families of young children with disabilities also focused primarily on enhancing the cognitive abilities of children to promote better long-term educational outcomes. In 1986, EI received federal support with the passage of PL 99-457, Education of the Handicapped Act Amendments, Part H. The goals of this legislation were:

- To enhance the development of infants and toddlers with disabilities
- To reduce educational costs by minimizing the need for subsequent special education
- To minimize the likelihood of institutionalization and maximize independent living
- To enhance the capacity of families to meet their children's needs (Hebbeler et al. 2007)

Congress reauthorized this legislation as Part B, for special education for children starting at three years old, and Part C, for EI for children from birth to three years of age, in 1997 (PL 105-17, Individuals with Disabilities Education Act [IDEA]) and again in 2004 (PL 108-446, Individuals with Disabilities Improvement Education Act [IDEA]). The IDEA stipulates that states can provide federally funded services to families with at-risk children as well as to those with a disability. However, the NEILS found that only 3.9 percent of the children enrolled in Part C programs qualified solely due to environmental risk factors (Hebbeler et al. 2007). This percentage may increase with the IDEA 2004 and CAPTA 2003 provisions for referral of neglected and abused children to Part C programs (Herman 2007). The IDEA (2004) also mandates Part C services for children who are homeless or experience trauma due to exposure to family violence.

With each reauthorization of IDEA, emphasis has been placed on an ecological perspective of serving families in their "natural environment" and on using family-directed approaches (IDEA 2004). For most programs, that translates to home-based services.

Features that vary across home-visiting programs, besides the targeted population, are services offered, goals, background and training of staff, and funding sources. Some programs, especially those that serve families with infants and toddlers, use home visiting as the primary mode of service delivery. Other programs, often those that serve families with preschool children or those for younger children that supplement cognitive stimulation in the home with group learning with peers, are more likely to be center-based, with home visiting as an adjunctive service. Professionals from a range of disciplines (for example, social work, early childhood education, or nursing) or paraprofessionals supervised by professionals make home visits. In-service training can be extensive or minimal. Federal, state, or local government provides the funding for many of these programs; others seek private grant support. It is common for these programs to have funding from a variety of sources: "Almost all state-based home visiting programs combine funding from several federal, state, local, and private sources. . . . This dependence on varied sources of funding is often a product of necessity. However, diversification of funding sources is also a strategy pursued by many home visitation programs to ensure sustainability" (Wasserman 2006, 3–4).

The IDEA (2004) stipulates that services in federally supported programs be based on peer-reviewed research. Funding sources for programs that are not supported through IDEA Part C and target children with environmental risk factors usually require empirical verification of effectiveness as well. Programs replicated as effective are often those with a carefully scripted curriculum, such as Home Instruction Program for Preschool Youngsters (HIPPY; Baker, Piotrkowski, and Brooks-Gunn 1999) and Parents as Teachers (PAT; Wagner and Clayton 1999). Other evidence-based programs use a treatment manual that emphasizes treatment fidelity but allow for some individualization of services, such as Nurse Family Partnerships (NFP; Kitzman et al. 1997) and Healthy Families America (HFA; Wasserman 2006). Regardless of whether programs use a specific replicated model or not, most monitor effectiveness with systemized data collection for program evaluation.

Descriptions of two different home-visiting programs are provided in the box.

Purpose and Goals of Social Work Home-Based Services

Social work has a definite role to play in early childhood home visiting. It was "one of sixteen disciplines specifically identified as a contributing profession" (Mahoney 2007, 3) in the IDEA. Although early-intervention models usually do not specify that social workers be hired as service coordinators, there has been a tendency in some programs to hire social workers, due to their preparation in dealing with the challenges presented by the families served (Olsen and DeBoise 2007). Social workers, trained to be culturally competent and to use empowerment and family-centered approaches in work with vulnerable populations, can be effective service coordinators in home visitation (Trivette, Dunst, and Hamby 1996). The services provided by these programs "are directly related to roles that are traditionally associated with social work, including parent education, case management, family support, and personal and family counseling" (Mahoney 2007, 3). Social workers, in the role of service coordinator for the family, provide social and emotional support for family members; developmental assessment and monitoring of infants, toddlers, and preschoolers; parent education; and case management/service coordination. Table 5.2 details these functions and provides examples of how they could be applied by social workers in early childhood home visitation.

Home Instructional Program for Preschool Youngsters (HIPPY, USA)
(Baker, Piotrkowski, and Brooks-Gunn 1999; Bradley and Gilkey 2002)

History—Originally developed in Israel for low-income and immigrant families; began in United States in 1984; programs located in a number of states, including Arkansas and New York

Target population—Low-income families with children from three to five years of age

Goals—School readiness; facilitate the transition to school for parents and children

Staff—Home-based educators are paraprofessionals often from same community as the client families; supervised by a coordinator who also meets with parents in groups

Structure of Program—Two-year program for each family; weekly contact through a combination of individualized home visits and center-based parent groups over a thirty-week period during the school year; uses a structured curriculum that focuses on enhancing child's cognitive abilities and uses role plays to teach skills; parents work with child about fifteen minutes daily on target skills

Early Head Start (EHS) **(Olsen and DeBoise 2007;**
Raikes and Love 2002)

History—Began in 1995 as result of the 1994 Head Start reauthorization legislation; funding authorized to support multistate expansion toward nationwide implementation

Target population—Pregnant women and children ages birth to three years in low-income families, including those with disabilities; 90 percent must be at or below poverty level

Goals—To extend the services of Head Start to families with younger children, enhancing child development and providing comprehensive support services to families

Staff—Interdisciplinary, some sites specifically employ social workers to do home visits

Structure of Program—Follow the Head Start Program Performance Standards with goals for child and family development, community development, and staff development; sites vary in offering services that include center-based child care, home visiting, or both; 85 percent of EHS families receive at least monthly home visits; most programs provide parent education and case management with targeted efforts to involve fathers as well as mothers

Social workers may take slightly different roles in center-based early childhood programs such as Head Start for children ages three to five (Zigler and Muenchow 1992) and some EI programs for children with disabilities (Mahoney and Wiggers 2007). Masters-trained social workers in Part C center-based programs can provide social support, case management, and promote child development with parents (Mahoney and Wiggers 2007). Home visits may be less frequent, and social workers may become a bridge between educators and the home, similar to the role of school social workers with families of older children (see chapter 6).

Social workers may take roles other than those of service coordinator or school social worker in early childhood programs. Olsen and DeBoise (2007, 48) discuss an EHS model for families of children ages birth to three years, in which teams of masters- and bachelors-level social workers "effectively deliver mental health services" in a manner that is "strengths-based, practical, and clinically and culturally sensitive." Other programs, which employ paraprofessionals or bachelors-level professionals as service coordinators, may use masters-trained social workers as consultants to work directly with families or consult with service coordinators in situations that require significant mental health expertise (Oser and Cheatham 2000). Social workers also function as supervisors and administrators both in programs for children with environmental risks (Olsen and DeBoise 2007) and for children with disabilities (Mahoney and Wiggers 2007).

Theoretical Framework

Theoretical literature focuses on the ecological perspective and the family-centered approach as the philosophical underpinnings of best practices for home-based services for families of young children. Although the ecological perspective and family-centered approach to helpgiving are frequently discussed for home-based services with a range of populations, these theoretical contexts have historical roots in early childhood services.

Ecological Perspective

Bronfenbrenner's (1974) conceptual model delineating the ecological factors affecting children's development grew from his involvement with Head Start program evaluations in the early 1970s. He concluded that the benefits of preschool interventions seemed to erode with time and that the best results came

TABLE 5.2
Home-Visiting Program Interventions with Parents

INTERVENTION	DESCRIPTION	EXAMPLE
	Service Coordination*	
Emotional support	Listening to and supporting family members as they discuss concerns and develop skills to meet their own needs	Listening to a parent's concerns about her toddler or about others who affect her toddler
Material support	Directly providing material goods to meet family needs	Providing used clothing for family members and diapers for the infant
Information support	Answering questions and providing written materials that help families make decisions about how to meet family needs	Providing written brochures on community services and answering questions about these agencies
Instrumental support	Linking families with formal services, including, e.g., investigating application procedures, supporting families during initial contacts, and monitoring services for adequacy	Helping a mother connect with a day-care center that meets her scheduling and service needs and monitoring this service for adequacy
Advocacy	Direct contact with agencies and/or guiding families through grievance processes when families are not receiving adequate services that they are entitled to	Contacting the public-welfare agency when a family fails to receive their monthly allotment of food stamps and helping them appeal the decision to cancel this benefit
Service integration	Communication and cooperation between professionals from different agencies to coordinate service delivery for a specific family	Calling a professional from a mental-health agency that is working with a parent in order to collaborate on goals
Promoting informal support networks	Helping establish or enhance a family's connection with informal social supports, such as extended family members, friends, neighbors, other families in similar situations, and informal community resources such as churches and support groups	Referring parents to a community support group for first-time parents or including a neighbor in a home visit to support a mother as she works out babysitting arrangements

continued

TABLE 5.2

Home-Visiting Program Interventions with Parents (*continued*)

INTERVENTION	DESCRIPTION	EXAMPLE
	Parent Education	
Parenting support and instruction	Providing parent instruction through written material, curriculum-based activities, and/or in response to parent questions; model activities with children; observe parent inter-actions and provide feedback	Demonstration of enhancing language development when reading a book to a toddler; having parent read to toddler and provide feedback to parent
Child development assessment and monitoring	Administering standardized developmental assessment and/or screening instruments to screen for developmental delays and monitor developmental progress	Administering a Denver II to an infant and discussing the results with parents

* Service Coordination interventions adapted from Moxley (1989).
   Source: Reprinted with permission (Allen 2007a).

when parents were involved and when interventions went beyond educating the child and focused on the child's total environmental context. He argued that for low-income Head Start children, "the critical forces of destruction lie neither within the child nor within his family but in the desperate circumstances in which the family is forced to live. What is called for is intervention at the *ecological level*, measures that will effect radical changes in the immediate environment of the family and the child" (54). Children are seen in the context of their families, which are seen in the context of the external environment. Interventions that target family needs could lead to improved family effectiveness and affect the child's development. The ecological perspective assumes that positive parent outcomes translate to positive outcomes for children.

Professional Approaches to Home-Based Services

The family-centered approach to helpgiving endorsed by the IDEA is one of four paradigms articulated by Dunst and colleagues (Dunst et al. 1991) and cited widely in the early childhood home-visiting literature (e.g., Mahoney and Filer 1999; Trivette et al. 1995). The four paradigms for approaches to work with families are professional centered, family allied, family focused, and family centered.

Approaches that are professional centered or family allied are child oriented, emphasizing child-development outcomes. Child-oriented approaches use help-giving processes that promote the family's reliance on the service provider as a child-development expert. Goals and interventions focus on children's learning needs and do not consider the child's family and community context (Mahoney and Filer 1999; Wasik and Bryant 2001). The role of the home visitor is to provide parents with child-development information and make recommendations to improve parenting skills.

Approaches that are family focused or family centered are family oriented, promoting changes in the child's environmental context. Interventions identify and support family competencies to enable independence through empowerment. Family-oriented approaches are rooted in the ecological perspective. Programs that espouse family-oriented approaches attempt to improve parents' life situations in addition to promoting positive child outcomes. With the continued trend in emphasizing the importance of the family's role in the family-professional partnership, additional terms used are "family directed" (IDEA 2004) and "family driven" (Osher and Osher 2002) (see also chapter 7).

However, Dunst (2000, 101) cautions that "comparisons and contrasts between family- centered/family-systems models and other child-focused, relationship-focused, and parent-child focused models" can be "artificial and divisive." The focus on the child must not get lost in the focus on the family. The practice model for early childhood interventions "needs to explicitly incorporate parent-child and child features into it."

Empirical Base

There has been extensive research on early childhood home-based services. This research falls into three general categories: longitudinal studies that track children after they exit a program, program evaluations involving pre-/post-tests on outcome variables during program enrollment, and studies that examine the process of home-visiting interventions.

Longitudinal Studies

Most studies of programs for children who are at risk use randomized control methods. The High/Scope Perry Preschool study is often cited (e.g.,

Daro 2006a; Karoly et al. 1998) as evidence of the long-term benefits of early childhood intervention. Findings in early adulthood included a higher rate of high-school graduation for the experimental group (Schweinhart 2006). At forty years of age, previous High/Scope Perry students demonstrated lower arrest rates and higher earnings from employment (Schweinhart 2006). The primary component of this program was center-based instruction for low-income three and four year olds in small groups with a specific curriculum. It is unclear how the home-visitation component contributed to program effectiveness. The Infant Health and Development Program (McCormick et al. 2006) targeted infants with the biological risk factors of low birth weight and prematurity and, like High/Scope Perry, combined center-based intervention with home visitation. Results of a longitudinal study until the children were eighteen years old were mixed. Children with the lowest birth weights and thus the highest developmental risks did not demonstrate statistically significant benefits. Those of heavier low birth weight did score significantly higher on achievement tests and showed a tendency toward lower arrest and incarceration rates than those in the comparison group. In contrast, in a study of one NFP site where home visits were the primary intervention, families with the most risk factors benefited the most (Olds et al. 1998, 1999). This study focused on parent and child outcomes. Some effects were more evident at fifteen years than they had been at two years postenrollment. For the NFP low-income single mothers, there was a significant reduction in verified child abuse reports, subsequent pregnancies, months on welfare, impairment due to substance abuse, and arrests compared to the control group. Their children showed fewer arrests and convictions, lower rates of cigarette smoking and alcohol use, and fewer parent-reported behavior problems associated with substance abuse. However, there were no significant long-term effects on child school behavior and cognitive abilities. Research on HIPPY followed program participants to the sixth grade (Bradley and Gilkey 2002). Results, unlike those for NFP, did include effects on school behavior and performance: fewer suspensions, better classroom behavior, and higher grades and achievement-test scores than the comparison group.

Farran (2000, 529) discusses the particular importance of longitudinal studies for children with disabilities that receive Part C services from infancy until age three. "What may appear to be low rates of progress or even lack of responsivity to early intervention as assessed during the first three years of life may be the foundation for much better outcomes at school age." The NEILS (Hebbeler et al. 2007) evaluated Part C program goals through phone interviews of a nationally representative sample of 3,338 parents from the time their children entered Part C services through kindergarten. Thirty-two percent of the children did not have a disability by kindergarten and another 10 percent did not need special education. Kindergarten teachers reported that a large majority of those who no longer had a disability demonstrated social skills (79 percent) and behavior (82 percent) normal for their age. Of those who were disabled and receiving special services, 36 percent exhibited normal social skills and 46 percent exhibited normal behavior.

Findings in these longitudinal studies, though largely positive, show mixed results. Interpretation is difficult, as studies track different outcomes. Results differ as to which populations benefit most, the types of benefits observed, and whether benefits increase over time.

Program Evaluations

Large-scale program-evaluation studies on early childhood home visiting have assessed the effectiveness and cost efficiency of this approach for affecting positive outcomes for children and families (Wasserman 2006). Studies particularly target child cognitive, health, and, to a lesser degree, social outcomes (Farran 2000; Gomby et al. 1999). Some comprehensive evaluations (e.g., Daro and Harding 1999) use observational measures to examine the quality of parent-child interactions as an outcome variable. More recently, program evaluations also include measures for parent outcomes that can affect the child, such as obtaining employment and adequate housing, emotional adjustment, and receiving social support (Daro and Harding 1999; Daro et al. 2005; Hebbeler et al. 2007).

Farran (2000) reviewed six studies from the late 1980s and the 1990s that used diverse research designs to examine the effectiveness of Part C home-based programs for children with various disabilities. Most of the studies focused on child development and did not measure parent outcomes. Interpretation of the results is difficult, because children with more severe disabilities receive services more intensively and over a longer time. Program effects were inconsistent, with some demonstrating no significant effects or even negative effects on specific developmental domains. The studies suggest that children with less severe impairments made more gains on standardized developmental tests. There was some tendency for children who began receiving interventions at younger ages to make more progress developmentally than those who entered the program at later ages, though still before three years of age.

Two meta-analyses of early childhood program evaluations focus specifically on programs for families of children who are at risk (Sweet and Appelbaum

2004; Geeraert et al. 2004). Both studies included evaluations that measured outcomes with pre- and post-testing and some that used random assignment, controlled for publication bias by seeking out unpublished studies, and compared effect sizes between and within studies. Sweet and Appelbaum (2004, 1448) reviewed sixty program evaluations that focused on cognitive and social-emotional outcomes for the children and on changes in attitudes, behavior, and educational achievement for the parents. They concluded that "home visiting does seem to help families with young children, but the extent to which this help is worth the cost of creating and implementing programs has yet to be determined" (see also chapter 6). A study (Geeraert et al. 2004) of forty-three program evaluations was more targeted, limiting studies to those that focused on preventing child neglect and physical abuse and with enrollment of families during pregnancy until their child was three years old. It included eighteen recent studies not reviewed by Sweet and Appelbaum (Daro 2006a, 2006b). Geeraert and colleagues found stronger effect sizes for impact on child and parent functioning. They concluded that the programs "produced a significant decrease in the manifestation of abusive and neglectful acts and a significant risk reduction on factors such as child functioning, parent-child interaction, parent functioning, family functioning, and context characteristics" (Geeraert et al. 2004, 286). Daro suggests that the differences between the results of the two meta-analyses reflect the increasing sophistication in program-evaluation methods in the last decade, enhancing the ability to measure the positive effects of these programs on children and parents.

Process Research

Literature describes moving from the first generation of early childhood program research characterized by comprehensive outcome studies to a second generation that links outcomes with the processes of program functioning (Farran 2000; Guralnick 1997). Longitudinal- and program-evaluation literature emphasizes the need for research to understand the process of home-visiting interventions (Geeraert et al. 2004; Lyons-Ruth and Easterbrooks 2006). The literature reflects a recent increase in process-oriented research and studies with qualitative components (e.g., Allen 2007a, 2007b; Hebbeler and Gerlach-Downie 2002; Korfmacher, Kitzman, and Olds 1998; LeCroy and Whitaker 2005). These studies examine specific aspects of programming to determine how best to serve families. Two important topics for this research are promoting family retention and engagement and understanding components of effective service-coordination interventions.

PROMOTING FAMILY RETENTION AND ENGAGEMENT

Attrition of families referred for home-visiting services is a major problem, particularly with families of young children who are at risk (Daro and Harding 1999; Duggan et al. 1999; Gomby et al. 1999) and those with disabilities from low-income families (Farran 2000). Evaluations indicate that number and frequency of home visits is often less than that recommended in program guidelines (Daro et al. 2005; Korfmacher et al. 1998). Child and family outcomes are better for those who are retained in programs and receive visits at the recommended frequency (Daro et al. 2005; Korfmacher et al. 1998; Raikes et al. 2006).

Findings differ on demographic characteristics that correlate with better retention. In some studies (Green, Johnson, and Rodgers 1998; McCurdy and Jones 2000; Unger et al. 2001), families with high stress, such as those living in poverty and having difficulty meeting basic family needs, participate in the programs to a greater extent than families with lower stress. However, Raikes et al. (2006) found that EHS high-risk families, particularly those with a single or teen mother and those who moved often, received fewer visits and services. For HFA sites, longer retention was predicted by the unemployed status or older age of the parent and beginning the program early in pregnancy (Daro et al. 2003).

Research has focused on "dimensions of engagement" (Wagner et al. 2003). Not all families retained in home-visit programs are fully engaged. Full engagement may be necessary for optimal program outcomes. Dimensions of engagement include program enrollment, keeping home-visit appointments, active involvement with the home visitor during sessions, working with the child and following through with referrals between visits, and participation in parent support groups. Those who were the most highly engaged during and between sessions tended to be older and financially secure. However, teen parents were most likely to seek support from sources outside the program by participating in parenting groups.

Enhanced family engagement may relate to the content of home visits and factors in the parent-provider relationship. Research indicates that a focus on child issues and parenting practices is a significant predictor of improvement in children's cognitive and language test scores, parent support for child learning and language development, and the home environment (Korfmacher et al. 1998; Raikes et al. 2006). Inversely, research on PAT suggested that program ineffectiveness was tied to a lack of focus on parent-child interactions to improve parenting practices (Hebbeler and Gerlach-Downie 2002). One study indicated that younger home visitors and those who were parents themselves obtained the most consistently positive results with families (Daro et al. 2003). Aspects of the family-provider relationship credited for promoting participation and engagement include collaboration in setting up the first visit, mutual agreement on the presenting concerns, establishing trust early in the relationship, clear communication, and perception of the provider as a friend (McCurdy and Jones 2000).

ASSESSING EFFECTIVE SERVICE COORDINATION

The 1986 Education of the Handicapped Act Amendments, Part H (PL 99-457), precipitated research on service coordination in Part C programs to monitor the transition from professional- to family-centered practices. Studies on service-coordination interventions with families of children who are at risk responded to evaluation findings that programs had limited success in linking families with community resources (Daro and Harding 1999; Duggan et al. 1999; St. Pierre and Layzer 1999). Duggan and colleagues concluded, "having a home-visiting program does not ensure effective linkage with community resources" (87). However, research (Mahoney and Filer 1996) indicates that families want service coordination and that home-visiting programs provide more "family assistance" interventions than center-based programs.

Some studies (Judge 1997; Mahoney and Filer 1996) provide evidence that the use of family-oriented approaches increased during the 1990s in Part C programs. Families receiving family-centered services feel more in control of the help-giving process and thus are more empowered (Trivette et al. 1995, 1996). Allen (2007b) found that families who characterized their home visitor's approach as highly family centered received more intensive services than others did, regardless of their level of need. However, there is no clear indication that family-oriented approaches result in improved outcomes for child development, quality of parent-child relationships, and family functioning (Mahoney and Bella 1998).

These studies, like those on family retention and engagement, support the importance of strong relationships between service providers and client families. Parents of children who are disabled and those who are at risk value relationships that are supportive and caring, build trust, respect family values, and demonstrate an interest in the child and other family members (Allen 2007a; Nownes 1998; Summers et al. 2001). These studies are also mixed on effective approaches for families with the highest needs. Research that measured need with self-report measures found that the neediest families do not necessarily receive the most intensive services (Allen 2007b; Mahoney and Filer 1996). However, a study that identified need for services by level of risk found that families "who received at least one service related to child abuse/neglect, substance abuse, or domestic violence" (Green et al. 1998, 19) often received more intensive services than other families.

Summary of Empirical Findings

Daro (2006b), in testimony to a congressional committee, summarized the following components for effective early childhood home visitation as supported by multiple studies:

- Internal consistency within programs to link program components with clearly defined outcomes
- Ability to form a relationship with a family over a sufficient period of time to effect meaningful change in the parent-child relationship and parent knowledge and skills
- Well-trained and competent staff
- High-quality supervision, including observation of the service providers
- Solid organizational capacity
- Linkages with other community resources and supports to benefit families

Although the strongest benefits to families come from interventions that begin during pregnancy or early infancy, benefits have also been shown from work that does not begin until the child is three or four years old (Bradley and Gilkey 2002; Daro 2006a, 2006b). Daro supports Weiss's (1993) observations from an earlier period in the analysis of home-visitation programs that, although home visits seem to be a necessary component of early childhood intervention, they are not sufficient in themselves to ensure positive developmental trajectories for children.

Practice Guidelines

Despite the diversity of early childhood home visitation, over time programs seem to have aligned their approaches to service delivery with the empirical evidence (Daro 2006a, 2006b). Best practices are discussed in terms of the following categories: "establishing the relationship," "setting goals and problem solving," "education," "promoting informal social support," and "creating linkage with health, education, and social service" (Kitzman et al. 1997, 29–31). An additional category is supporting and promoting the parent-child relationship.

These practice categories involve both intervention and assessment techniques. Table 5.2 provides examples of interventions in early childhood home visitation. The box highlights areas of assessment and tools used in some programs.

AREAS OF ASSESSMENT AND POSSIBLE TOOLS

Family

Home Environment—Home Observation for Measurement of the Environment (HOME; Caldwell and Bradley 1984)

Family Resources/Strengths—Family Resource Scale (Leet and Dunst 1988)

Social Support—Family Support Scale (Dunst, Jenkins, and Trivette 1998)

Family Functioning—Family Adaptability and Cohesion Evaluation Scales (FACES IV; Olson, Gorall, and Tisel 2004); Family Environment Scale (Moos and Moos 1990); McMaster Family Assessment Device (Epstein, Baldin, and Bishop 1983)

Parent-Child Interactions/Relationship—Nursing Child Assessment Satellite Training, Feeding and Teaching Scales (NCAST; Barnard 1994); Maternal Behavior Rating Scale (Revised; Mahoney 1999)

Child Development

Multiple Domains—Ages and Stages Questionnaires (ASQ; Squires, Potter, and Bricker 1995); Denver II (Frankenburg and Dodds 1990)

Social-Emotional—Ages and Stages Questionnaires: Social-Emotional (ASQ:SE; Squires, Bricker, and Twombly 2003); Deveraux Early Childhood Assessment (DECA; LeBuffe and Naglieri 2002)

Parents

Parenting Skills—Family Empowerment Scale (Koren, DeChillo, and Friesen 1992); Parenting Styles and Dimensions Questionnaire (Robinson et al. 1995)

Parenting Stress—Parenting Stress Index, 3rd ed. (PSI; Abidin 1995)

Child Abuse Risk—Child Abuse Potential Inventory (Milner 1996)

Emotional Adjustment—Beck Depression Inventory (BDI II; Beck 1996); Brief Symptom Inventory (BSI; Derogatis 1975)

Establishing the Relationship

There are special challenges to developing trust with families who may have had difficult experiences with other helpgivers and may be dealing with such life challenges as poverty, mental illness, substance abuse, and domestic violence (LeCroy and Whitaker 2005). Programs often use tools, such as those listed in the box, to assess the emotional needs of parents and the risk of child physical abuse. Early on, service providers should discuss the family's expectation for the relationship and the parameters of the home visitor's role. Service providers may need to balance their expectations with those of the family (Klass 2003). Parents often describe a close relationship with their home visitor, comparing her or him to a family member or friend (Allen 2007a; McCurdy and Jones 2000; Klass 2003). A family may also view the service provider as the child-development expert and provider of advice. The service provider's expectations in a family-centered relationship are for a mutually respectful partnership where parents are as empowered as the experts in raising their own child (Klass 2003).

Crucial to establishing the close type of relationship desired by families is empathetic listening and communication. For parents interviewed in one study, "it was also important that service coordinators demonstrate their interest in, and understanding of families' needs by asking questions and maintaining frequent contact. They described that service coordinators would often initiate topics, knowing these topics were responsive to parent desires and needs" (Allen 2007a, 277). The provider needs to pay specific attention to the young child. "When home visitors show they enjoy playing with a child or when they delight in a child's new skill, parents experience this enjoyment as affirmation of themselves" (Klass 2003, 21).

Service providers may deal with particular challenges in developing relationships with fathers and with teen parents. Scheduling visits around fathers', as well as mothers', work schedules are essential in order to emphasize the importance of father involvement in home visits and in the parenting role (Klass 2003). Some home-based services target teen parents due to evidence linking teen parents to deficits in parenting skills and poor developmental outcomes for their children (McCurdy and Jones 2000). Aggressive outreach is crucial, since adolescents may avoid seeking help in order to affirm their independence and autonomy. Efforts to engage with the teen initially may need to be more "teen-centered" than "baby-centered" (Klass 2003, 28). Service providers assume roles of "surrogate parent" and "role model" (Klass 2003, 28) as well as the usual home-visitor roles of friend, service coordinator, and counselor.

Setting Goals and Problem Solving

Multifaceted assessments of the home and family environment, child development, and parental strengths and needs provide a basis for goal setting.

Effective goal setting can lead to effective services. "Families who set a specific goal tended to receive proportionately more services in that area compared to families who did not specify that goal" (Green et al. 1998, 17). For Part C programs, the goal-setting process involves completing and updating the Individualized Family Service Plan (IFSP). Non-Part C programs that serve only children who are at risk often use a similar format (e.g., St. Pierre and Layzer 1999). The IFSP includes an assessment of family and child functioning, strengths, and needs, and it identifies goals and expected outcomes with specified time frames (IDEA 1997). All service providers involved with a family contribute to the development of the IFSP and sign the document.

Wasik and Bryant (2001) advocate a problem-solving model for home-based service delivery, as many of the parents enrolled in these programs encounter personal and parenting challenges daily. Problem-solving techniques are used once the family and home visitor form a trusting relationship and the home visitor has an understanding of the family's strengths and challenges. Home visitors facilitate the family problem-solving process through seven not necessarily sequential steps—problem definition, goal selection, generation of solutions, consideration of consequences, decision making, implementation, and evaluation.

Education

Parent education involves providing information and teaching skills. Programs such as HIPPY and PAT use curriculum materials for parent instruction to meet the child's needs at specific developmental stages. Discussion of the child's performance on developmental-assessment tools leads to educating parents about specific techniques to meet the needs of their child. Training for home visitors should focus on the following four skill areas for parent education: knowledge of the parent education concepts to be taught, ability to demonstrate the behavior with the child, ability to provide explicit information and examples of parenting behaviors, and competency in coaching parents and providing specific feedback (Mahoney et al. 1999). Helpful techniques for parent education follow behavior theory and include modeling, reinforcement, and assigning homework (Wasik and Bryant, 2001).

Supporting and Promoting the Parent-Child Relationship

A specialized component of parent education involves assessing the parent-child relationship and "enhancing parents' skills in engaging their children in play and social interaction" (Mahoney et al. 1999, 131). "Evidence from a variety of investigations suggests that the interactions of parents with children who are at risk or developmentally delayed tend to be much less optimal than parents' interactions with typically developing children" (Marfo 1992, 88). For example, infants with developmental delays provide more subtle and less frequent cues, creating challenges for parents in relating to their infants (Kelly and Barnard 2000). Interventions to support and promote parent-child relationships have followed the trend of family-centered approaches by shifting to models that emphasize strengths, collaboration, and empathetic involvement with families (Kelly and Barnard 2000). The box in this section provides examples of specific tools used to assess the relationship. Service providers seek continual feedback from parents on their perception of the relationship with their child. Thus, assessment of the parent-child relationship is cooperative, continuous, and an inseparable part of the intervention process (Kelly and Barnard 2000). Interventions to promote the relationship focus on reciprocity between the parent and child, with the parent becoming alert to and building on cues initiated by the child (Marfo 1992). Goals are to promote a "pleasurable, mutually satisfying parent-infant relationship," "foster overall competence," and "enhance specific competencies in specific domains" such as language or motor development (Marfo 1992, 100).

Promoting Informal Social Support

Difficulties producing outcomes with service-coordination interventions could reflect a need for more effective methods of integrating parents into supportive social networks (Daro and Harding 1999). "Parents' social networks can provide information, emotional and material assistance, and support and encouragement of certain child-rearing attitudes and behavior" (Klass 2003, 59). During home visits, practitioners often observe families' support networks and can assess social support in terms of its adequacy in countering isolation and in offering support rather than discouragement (Klass 2003). Service providers may refer parents to support groups or develop a group for parents enrolled in their program. There may be ways to facilitate support between clients while respecting their confidentiality. One parent described a donation program facilitated by her service coordinator, which enabled parents to give their child's used clothes to others and to receive others' used clothes for their child (Allen 2007a).

Home visitors often encounter young parents who live with or have frequent contact with extended family members. As parents discuss concerns about relationships with extended family, it can be helpful for the home visitor to remember that "her role is to strengthen the parents' role as decision makers" (Klass 2003, 61). Family members may or may not choose to be involved during home visits. Issues of confidentiality should be discussed and informed consents signed in order to respect appropriate boundaries with the parent. Childrearing practices are often an area of contention, but social workers can help family members identify areas of "common ground" to mitigate areas of difference (Klass 2003).

Creating Linkage with Health, Education, and Social Services

Research indicates that parents appreciate the service coordinator's knowledge of community resources and ability to make appropriate referrals (Allen 2007a; Nownes 1998). It seems to help if the program is visible in the community and has developed cooperative connections with other agencies (Daro and Harding 1999; Klass 2003; Summers et al. 2001) (see chapter 3, for further discussion of the administrative role of "managing relationships with the external environment"). Effective service coordination involves careful collaborative work with families to assess their needs for services, both formally with assessment tools and informally. Once referrals are made, home visitors monitor the family's success in receiving appropriate services. Role plays can be used to help parents develop skills and feel confident in advocating for their child's or family's needs with professionals (Wasik and Bryant 2001). Home visitors may participate in meetings in the community with family members or with other agencies' staff to coordinate services and advocate for family needs directly (Summers et al. 2001).

Issues of Diversity and Practice with Populations at Risk

Diversity is discussed in terms of training and self-awareness for cultural competence in home visitors and efforts to develop effective programs to serve families within their cultural context. Respecting a family's cultural context is particularly crucial in early childhood programs, due to the focus on childrearing and on serving children and families from populations at risk. Early childhood home visiting, with its focus on low-income families, specifically targets parents with cognitive delays and learning difficulties and those of minority races and cultures.

Cultural Competence

Cultural competence, defined as "the responsiveness of services to the values
and beliefs of diverse families" (Wasik and Bryant 2001, 41), is identified as a
key "principle of care" for early childhood home visiting. Home visitors need
to be aware that *developmental competence* is a culturally defined construct"
(Klass 2003, 81). Cultural-sensitivity training for staff may improve program
effectiveness (Daro et al. 2005; Slaughter-Defoe 1993). It can be a challenge
for home visitors to be culturally sensitive when assessing developmental
progress and childrearing techniques, rather than using one's own culturally
determined expectations as the benchmark. Service providers need to engage
in a dialogue with the family about their cultural norms for childrearing and
be alert to the cultural context of a family's understanding of what constitutes
a problem, the cause of the problem, and its solution (Klass 2003).

Diversity and Program Design

Studies of home-visitation programs for children at risk have noted ethnic
and racial variations in terms of engagement. African American parents may
have high rates of refusing enrollment (Wagner et al. 2003), low rates of retention once enrolled (McCurdy and Jones 2000), and receive less child-focused
content during visits (Raikes et al. 2006). A number of studies indicate that
Latino families have high rates of participation and engagement (Daro et al.
2003; McCurdy and Jones 2000; Raikes et al. 2006; Sweet and Appelbaum
2004). Reasons for ethnic and racial variations in program engagement are
not well understood. There is some indication that home visitors of the same
race/ethnicity as the families may be more effective (Daro et al. 2003).

"Program goals may be frustrated or defeated when program designers know
little of the cultural-ecological context of the families to be served" (Slaughter-
Defoe 1993, 175). Interventions may vary in order to serve a specific population.
Effective programs for parents with cognitive delays use explicit home-based
parenting-skills training characterized by "clear specification of the skills, task
analysis, and performance-based strategies" (Feldman 1997, 187). Specific cur-
ricula for preventive early intervention with American Indians "use cultural
strengths relevant to each tribe" (Michael D. Niles / Wakshe, personal communication, August 21, 2007). Family and home-based approaches are appropriate for some tribes, while community-oriented approaches work better with
others. Culturally responsive programs for African American families include
the father whenever possible, focus on identifying and mobilizing informal

support systems, emphasize parent education, and promote parenting support by extended family members (Slaughter-Defoe 1993).

Implications for Home-Based Practice

Early childhood home visitation has benefited from extensive research and support from federal, state, and private funding sources. Nevertheless, these programs face some challenges.

The enactment of the Personal Responsibility and Work Opportunity Reconciliation Act of 1996 (PRWORA) has had a dual impact on early childhood home visiting. Efforts to reduce welfare roles and promote self-sufficiency of low-income single parents may have contributed to the expansion of home-visitation programs that target family self-sufficiency. However, mandates for mothers of infants and toddlers to enter the workforce has meant scheduling and engagement challenges for home-visitation programs.

Federal and state budget cuts for social services have been a blessing and a challenge for early childhood home visitation. Legislators see home visiting for young children who are at risk as a cost saver that prevents larger expenditures on such services as special education and prison later in these children's lives (Heckman 2006). Nevertheless, it has been a challenge to preserve the effectiveness of programs, initially evaluated as pilots, which have expanded to a national scale. Expansion efforts are often underfunded and, without careful evaluation and monitoring, may lead to decreased effectiveness. The Home Visit Forum was a creative response to deal with the challenges of expanding evidence-based programs (Daro 2006a, 2006b). Initially established in 1999, it was composed of key research personnel representing six of the most widely disseminated U.S. programs for children at risk: HIPPY, NFP, HFA, PAT, EHS, and the Parent-Child Home Program. The focus of the forum has been to coordinate efforts to improve program logic and functioning and promote public policies for effective service delivery.

Despite extensive research on early childhood home visitation, there is insufficient knowledge as to which families benefit most from which home-based interventions. Findings are mixed as to whether programs serve the families most in need. Additional research is needed to establish effective strategies for engaging the most stressed and lowest-income families whose children have disabilities or are at risk. Given the predominance of several specific treatment models, such as those represented in the Home Visit Forum, it is important to promote flexibility and maintain a focus on developing the most effective home-based approaches.

Home-based services for families with young children seem clearly established after a number of decades of implementation. However, expectations for the prevention effects of home visitation need to be anchored in an understanding of the limitations of the empirical evidence (Daro 2006a). Home-based interventions do not eliminate the root causes of child maltreatment, poverty, or premature births. Continual efforts toward systemic change are needed "in the major institutions and norms that influence a parent's actions and shape a child's social environment" (Daro 2006a, 12). Home-based services are just one component, albeit a crucial one, of the community supports needed for families of young children who face special challenges. There is a need to examine and strengthen both early childhood home-based services and social, educational, and health services in the community. Effectiveness of broad community support services are crucial for families both when their children are young and as the children age, in order to support and maintain the gains promoted by early childhood home-based services.

REFERENCES

Abidin, R. R. 1995. *Parenting stress index*. 3rd ed. Odessa, Fla.: PAR.

Allen, S. F. 2007a. Parents' perceptions of intervention practices in home visiting programs. *Infants and Young Children* 20 (3): 266–281.

——. 2007b. Parents' perspectives: An evaluation of case management interventions in home visiting programs for young children. *Children and Schools* 29 (2): 75–85.

Baker, A. J. L., Piotrkowski, C. S., and Brooks-Gunn, J. 1999. The Home Instruction Program for Preschool Youngsters (HIPPY). *The Future of Children* 9 (1): 116–133.

Barnard, K. 1994. *Nursing Child Assessment Satellite Training, feeding and teaching scales (NCAST)*. Seattle, Wash.: NCAST Programs.

Beck, A. T. 1996. *BDI II*. San Antonio: Harcourt Brace and Company.

Bradley, R. H., and Gilkey, B. 2002. The impact of the Home Instructional Program for Preschool Youngsters (HIPPY) on school performance in 3rd and 6th grades. *Early Education and Development* 13 (2): 302–311.

Bronfenbrenner, U. 1974. *Is early intervention effective? A report on longitudinal evaluations of preschool programs*. Washington, D.C.: Department of Health, Education, and Welfare.

Brooks-Gunn, J., and Duncan, G. J. 1997. The effects of poverty on children. *The Future of Children* 7 (2): 55–71.

Caldwell, B., and Bradley, R. 1984. *Home Observation for the Home Environment (HOME)—Revised edition*. Little Rock: University of Arkansas.

Children's Bureau. 2007. *Child maltreatment 2005.* Available online at http://www
.acf.dhhs.gov/programs/cb/pubs/cm05/index.htm.

Daro, D. 2006a. *Home visitation: Assessing progress, managing expectations.* Chicago:
Chapin Hall Center for Children.

———. 2006b. *Perspectives on early childhood home visitation programs.* Written testimony to the Subcommittee on Education Reform of the House Committee on
Education and the Workforce, Washington, D.C.

Daro, D., and Harding, K. A. 1999. Healthy Families America: Using research to
enhance practice. *The Future of Children* 9 (1): 152–176.

Daro, D., Howard, E., Tobin, J., and Harden, A. 2005. *Welcome Home and Early
Start: An assessment of program quality and outcomes.* Chicago: Chapin Hall Center for Children.

Daro, D., McCurdy, K., Falconier, L., and Stojanovic, D. 2003. Sustaining new parents in home visitation services: Key participant and program factors. *Child
Abuse and Neglect* 27: 1101–1125.

Derogatis, L. R. 1975. *BSI Brief Symptom Inventory.* Minneapolis: NGS Pearson, Inc.

Division of Vital Statistics. 2006. Births: Final data for 2004. *National Vital Statistics Reports* 55 (1). Available online at http://www.cdc.gov/nchs/data/nvsr/
nvsr55/nvsr55_01pdf.

Dodge, K. A., Pettit, G. S., and Bates, J. E. 1994. Socialization mediators of the relation between socioeconomic status and child conduct problems. *Child Development* 65: 649–665.

Douglas-Hall, A., Chau, M., and Koball, M. 2006. *Basic facts about low-income children birth to age six.* New York: National Center for Children in Poverty.

Duggan, A. K., McFarlane, E. C., Windham, A. M., Rohde, C. A., Salkever, D. S.,
Fuddy, L., et al. 1999. Evaluation of Hawaii's Healthy Start program. *The Future
of Children* 9 (1): 66–90.

Dunst, C. J. 2000. Revisiting "rethinking early intervention." *Topics in Early Childhood Special Education* 20 (2): 95–104.

Dunst, C. J., Jenkins, V., and Trivette, C. M. 1988. Family Support Scale. In *Enabling
and empowering families: Principles and guidelines for practice,* by C. J. Dunst, C.
M. Trivette, and A. G. Deal, 157. Cambridge, Mass.: Brookline Books, Inc.

Dunst, C. J., Johanson, C., Trivette, C. M., and Hamby, D. 1991. Family-oriented
early intervention policies and practices: Family-centered or not? *Exceptional
Children* 58 (2): 115–126.

Epstein, N. B., Baldin, L. M., and Bishop, D. S. 1983. The Family Assessment Device. *Journal of Marital and Family Therapy* 9 (2): 171–180.

Farran, D. C. 2000. Another decade of intervention for children who are low income or disabled: What do we know now? In *Handbook of early childhood intervention,* 2nd ed., ed. J. P. Shonkoff and S. J. Meisels, 510–548. New York: Cambridge University Press.

Feldman, M. A. 1997. The effectiveness of early intervention for children of parents with mental retardation. In *The effectiveness of early intervention*, ed. M. J. Guralnick, 171–191. Baltimore: Paul H. Brookes Publishing Co.

Frankenburg, W., and Dodds, J. 1990. *Denver developmental screening test*. 2nd ed. Denver, Colo.: Denver Developmental Materials.

Geeraert, L., Van den Noorgate, W., Grietens, H., and Onghena, P. 2004. The effects of early prevention programs for families with young children at risk for physical child abuse and neglect: A meta-analysis. *Child Maltreatment* 9 (3): 277–291.

Gomby, D. S., Culross, P. L., and Behrman, R. E. 1999. Home visiting: Recent program evaluations: Analysis and recommendations. *The Future of Children* 9 (1): 4–26.

Green, B. L., Johnson, S. A., and Rodgers, A. 1998. Understanding patterns of service delivery and participation in community-based family support programs. *Children's Services: Social Policy, Research, and Practice* 2: 1–22.

Guralnick, M. J. 1997. Second-generation research in the field of early intervention. In *The effectiveness of early intervention*, ed. M. J. Guralnick, 3–22. Baltimore: Paul H. Brookes Publishing Co.

Guterman, N. B., and Taylor, C. A. 2005. Prevention of physical child abuse and neglect. In *Child welfare for the twenty-first century: A handbook of practices, policies, and programs*, ed. G. P. Mallon and P. McCartt Hess. New York: Columbia University Press.

Hebbeler, K. M., and Gerlach-Downie, S. G. 2002. Inside the black box of home visiting: A qualitative analysis of why intended outcomes were not achieved. *Early Childhood Research Quarterly* 17: 28–51.

Hebbeler, K. M., Spiker, D., Bailey, D., Scarborough, A., Mallik, S., Simeonsson, R., et al. 2007. *Early intervention for infants and toddlers with disabilities and their families: Participants, services, and outcomes*. Menlo Park, Calif.: SRI International. Available online at http://www.sri.com/neils/pdfs/NEILS_Report_02_07_final2.pdf.

Heckman, J. J. 2006. Catch 'em young. *Wall Street Journal*, January 10.

Herman, B. 2007. CAPTA and early childhood intervention: Policy and the role of parents. *Children and Schools* 29 (1): 17–24.

Individuals with Disabilities Education Act of 1997 (IDEA). PL 105-17. 105th Cong. 1997.

Individuals with Disabilities Education Improvement Act of 2004 (IDEA). PL 108-446. 108th Cong. 2004.

Judge, S. L. 1997. Parental perceptions of help-giving practices and control appraisal in early intervention programs. *Topics in Early Childhood Special Education* 17 (4): 457–476.

Karoly, L. A., Greenwood, P. W., Everingham, S. S., Houbé, J., Kilburn, M. R., Rydell, C. P., et al. 1998. *Investing in our children: What we know and don't know about the costs and benefits of early childhood interventions*. Santa Monica, Calif.: Rand.

Kelly, J. E., and Barnard, K. E. 2000. Assessment of parent-child interaction: Implications for early intervention. In *Handbook of early childhood intervention*, 2nd ed., ed. J. P. Shonkoff and S. J. Meisels, 258–289. New York: Cambridge University Press.

Kitzman, H., Yoos, H. L., Cole, R., Korfmacher, J., and Hanks, C. 1997. Prenatal and early child home visitation program processes: A case illustration. *Journal of Community Psychology* 25 (1): 27–45.

Klass, C. S. 2003. *The home visitor's guidebook: Promoting optimal parent and child development.* 2nd ed. Baltimore: Paul H. Brookes Publishing Co.

Korfmacher, J., Kitzman, H., and Olds, D. 1998. Intervention processes as predictors of outcomes in a preventive home-visitation program. *Journal of Community Psychology* 26 (1): 49–64.

LeBuffe, P. A., and Naglieri, J. A. 2002. *Devereux Early Childhood Assessment (DECA).* Lewisville, N.C.: Kaplan Early Learning Company.

LeCroy, C. W., and Whitaker, K. 2005. Improving the quality of home visitation: An exploratory study of difficult situations. *Child Abuse and Neglect* 29: 1003–1013.

Leet, H. E., and Dunst, C. J. 1988. Family Resource Scale. In *Enabling and empowering families: Principles and guidelines for practice*, by C. J. Dunst, C. M. Trivette, and A. G. Deal. Cambridge, Mass.: Brookline Books, Inc.

Luthar, S. 1999. *Poverty and children's adjustment.* Thousand Oaks, Calif.: Sage.

Lyons-Ruth, K., and Easterbrooks, M. A. 2006. Assessing mediated models of family change in response to infant home visiting: A two-phase longitudinal analysis. *Infant Mental Health Journal* 27 (1): 55–69.

Mahoney, G. 1999. *Maternal behavior rating scale (revised).* Tallmadge, Ohio: Family Child Learning Center.

——. 2007. Social work and early intervention. *Children and Schools* 29 (1): 3–5.

Mahoney, G., and Bella, J. M. 1998. An examination of the effects of family-centered early intervention on child and family outcomes. *Topics in Early Childhood Special Education* 18 (2): 83–94.

Mahoney, G., and Filer, J. 1996. How responsive is early intervention to the priorities and needs of families? *Topics in Early Childhood Special Education* 16 (4): 437–457.

Mahoney, G., Kaiser, A., Girolametto, L., MacDonald, J., Robinson, C., Safford, P., et al. 1999. Parent education in early intervention: A call for a renewed focus. *Topics in Early Childhood Special Education* 19 (3): 131–140.

Mahoney, G., and Wiggers, B. 2007. The role of parents in early intervention: Implications for social work. *Children and Schools* 29 (1): 7–15.

Marfo, K. 1992. Interaction-focused early intervention: Current approaches and contributions from the mediated learning experience paradigm. *International Journal of Cognitive Education and Mediated Learning* 2 (2): 85–104.

McCormick, M. C., Brooks-Gunn, J., Buka, S. L., Goldman, J., Yu, J., Salganik, M., et al. 2006. Early intervention in low birth weight premature infants: Results at eighteen years of age for the Infant Health and Development Program. *Pediatrics* 117 (3): 771–780.

McCurdy, K., and Jones, E. D. 2000. *Supporting families: Lessons from the field.* Thousand Oaks, Calif.: Sage.

Milner, J. 1994. Assessing physical child abuse risk: The Child Abuse Potential Inventory. *Clinical Psychology Review* 14 (6): 547–583.

Moos, R. H., and Moos, B. S. 1990. *Family environment scale.* Palo Alto, Calif.: Consulting Psychologists Press.

Moxley, D. P. 1989. *The practice of case management.* Newbury Park, Calif.: Sage.

Nownes, E. M. 1998. *Mothers' perceptions of family-centered early intervention service coordination.* Ph.D. diss., University of Tennessee.

Olds, D. L., Henderson, C. R., Kitzman, H., Eckenrode, J., Cole, R., and Tatelbaum, R. 1998. The promise of home visitation: Results of two randomized trials. *Journal of Community Psychology* 26 (1): 5–21.

——. 1999. Prenatal and infancy home visitation by nurses: Recent findings. *The Future of Children* 9 (1): 44–65.

Olsen, L., and DeBoise, T. 2007. Enhancing school readiness: The Early Head Start model. *Children and Schools* 29 (1): 47–50.

Olson, D. H., Portner, J., and Bell, R. 2004. *Family Adaptability and Cohesion Evaluation Scales (FACES IV).* Minneapolis, Minn.: Life Innovations, Inc.

Oser, C., and Cheatham, D. 2000. Ohio Early Start: Integrating prevention and early intervention for vulnerable infants, toddlers, and families. *Infants and Young Children* 12 (4): 89–98.

Osher, T. W., and Osher, D. M. 2002. The paradigm shift to true collaboration with families. *Journal of Child and Family Studies* 11 (1): 47–60.

Raikes, H., Green, B. L., Atwater, J., Kisker, E., Constantine, J., and Chazan-Cohen, R. 2006. Involvement in Early Head Start home visiting services: Demographic predictors and relations to child and parent outcomes. *Early Childhood Research Quarterly* 21: 2–24.

Raikes, H., and Love, J. M. 2002. Early Head Start: A dynamic new program for infants and toddlers and their families. *Infant Mental Health Journal* 23 (1/2): 1–13.

Schweinhart, L. J. 2006. The High/Scope Perry preschool study through age forty: Summary, conclusions, and frequently asked questions. Available online at http://www.highscope.org/file/Research/PerryProject/3_specialsummary%20c0/%2006%2007.pdf.

Schweinhart, L. J., and Weikart, D. P. 1983. The effects of the Perry preschool program on youths through age 15—A summary. In *As the twig is bent: Lasting effects of preschool programs,* by the Center for Longitudinal Studies, 71–102. Hillsdale, N.J.: Lawrence Erlbaum Associates.

Shearer, D. E. 1992. The Portage Project: An international home approach to early intervention of young children and their families. In *Approaches to early childhood education*, 2nd ed., ed. J. L. Roopnarine and J. J. Johnson, 97–111. New York: MacMillan.

Slaughter-Defoe, D. T. 1993. Home visiting with families in poverty: Introducing the concept of culture. *The Future of Children* 3 (3): 172–183.

Squires, J., Bricker, D., and Twombly, E. 2003. *The ASQ:SE user's guide for the Ages and Stages Questionnaires: Social-Emotional.* Baltimore: Paul H. Brookes.

Squires, J., Potter, L., and Bricker, D. 1995. *The ASQ user's guide.* Baltimore: Paul H. Brookes.

St. Pierre, R. G., and Layzer, J. I. 1999. Using home visits for multiple purposes: The Comprehensive Child Development Program. *Future of Children* 9 (1): 134–151.

Summers, J. A., Steeples, T., Peterson, C., Naig, L., McBride, S., Wall, S., et al. 2001. Policy and management supports for effective service integration in Early Head Start and Part C programs. *Topics in Early Childhood Special Education* 21 (1): 16–30.

Sweet, M. A., and Appelbaum, M. L. 2004. Is home visiting an effective strategy? A meta-analytic review of home visiting programs for families with young children. *Child Development* 75: 1435–1456.

Trivette, C. M., Dunst, C. J., Boyd, K., and Hamby, D. W. 1995. Family-oriented program models, helpgiving practices, and parental control appraisals. *Exceptional Children* 62 (3): 237–248.s

Trivette, C. M., Dunst, C. J., and Hamby, D. W. 1996. Factors associated with perceived control appraisals in a family-centered early intervention program. *Journal of Early Intervention* 20 (2): 165–178.

Unger, D. G., Jones, C. W., Park, E., and Tressell, P. A. 2001. Promoting involvement between low-income single caregivers and urban early intervention programs. *Topics in Early Childhood Special Education* 21 (4): 197–212.

Wagner, M., and Clayton, S. L. 1999. The Parents as Teachers program: Results from two demonstrations. *Future of Children* 9 (1): 91–115.

Wagner, M., Spiker, D., Linn, M. I., Gerlach-Downie, S., and Hernandez, F. 2003. Dimensions in parental engagement in home visiting programs. *Topics in Early Childhood Special Education* 32 (4): 171–181.

Wasik, B. H., and Bryant, D. M. 2001. *Home visiting: Procedures for helping families.* 2nd ed. Newbury Park, Calif.: Sage.

Wasserman, M. 2006. *Implementation of home visitation programs: Stories from the states.* Issue Brief 109. Chicago: Chapin Hall Center for Children.

Weiss, H. B. 1993. Home visits: Necessary but not sufficient. *The Future of Children* 3 (3): 113–128.

Zigler, E., and Muenchow, S. 1992. *Head Start: The inside story of America's most successful educational experiment.* New York: Basic Books.

Six

School-Based Services

CYNTHIA FRANKLIN AND CHRISTINE LAGANA-RIORDAN

Home visiting is prevalent in the history of school social work practice, and this type of intervention has seen a resurgence of applications over the past decade, being utilized in numerous programs aimed at helping high-risk children and families. A primary function of school social workers is to build partnerships with families and link community resources with the school, in order to remove barriers to academic achievement. Home visiting is a school intervention well suited for this purpose.

From the very inception of school social work practice, home visitation has had an important role for school social workers. Even though school social work tasks vary across school districts and have changed at different points in time, the role of school-family and community connector continues to be an important function of school social work practice. In the early 1900s, school social workers began their work in schools by reaching out to the home. School social workers were called "visiting teachers" and were employed by settlement homes, clinics, and community agencies to help school-aged children and their families access a variety of resources (Franklin and Gerlach 2006). In the 1950s, schools became less community focused and more socially isolated (Franklin and Streeter 1995). Costin (1969) subsequently found in a national survey of school social workers that the primary duties of school social workers had shifted toward individual clinical casework.

A national survey by Allen-Meares in 1994, however, found that school social workers had primary roles as school-community liaisons and performed
tasks such as referrals to community resources and home visits. Another survey
of 576 school social workers by Astor et al. (1998, cited in Wasik and Shaffer
2006) makes a strong case for the use of home visits by school social workers.
These researchers found that 91 percent endorsed home visits as an effective
intervention for aggressive children and that 82 percent of those surveyed reported that they had conducted home visits for this population. This suggests
that home visiting may be an integral part of a school social worker's tasks.
Further indications suggesting that school social workers might intervene with
home visits comes from data suggesting that most school social workers are
spending a large amount of time and effort working with parents. In a survey
of school social workers from twenty-four states, Kurtz and Barth (1989) found
that school social workers spend a full third of their time working with parents.

Another survey discovered that school social workers would like to spend
even more of their time in the school-home liaison role (Staudt and Powell
1996). Nelson (1990) further found that 73 percent of school social workers
in a national sample cited that working to increase parental involvement was
both a preferred and mandated task.

Of course, these surveys do not specifically answer questions regarding
the prevalence of home visits made by school social workers, but the surveys
are able to highlight the importance that school social workers place on working with families and suggest their preferred involvement with the home in
solving challenging issues.

The Population

Home visiting has a long history of use with young children, but school social
workers employ this intervention with elementary, middle, and high-school
students (Allen and Tracy 2004). It is likely that a large number of school-
aged children receive home visits from school social workers each year. However, the actual number of home visits provided by school social workers
has not been estimated. The best population data that we have on the use of
home visiting is with younger children (for the prevalence of home-visiting
interventions for young children, see chapter 5).

Frequently, school social workers and other school employees use home-
visiting interventions with students that present specific academic-related
problems in school, such as poor attendance, physical or cognitive challenges, poor academic performance, difficulty with literacy skills, or are at risk for
dropping out (Epstein and Sheldon 1995; Feiler 2003; Lehr, Hansen, and Sin-

clair 2003; Poole 1997). Students with other serious barriers to learning, such as poverty, mental health needs, child abuse, substance abuse, and behavior problems are also targeted for home visits (Coatsworth, Pantin, and Szapoc-znik 2002; Conduct Problems Prevention Research Group 2002; Franklin and Gerlach 2006; McConaughy and Kay 2000; Reddy and Richardson 2006). In addition, home visits are used to encourage teen parents to complete their education and acquire parenting skills (Fulton, Murphy, and Anderson 1991; Olds, Henderson, and Chamberlain 1998; Philliber et al. 2003; Wagner et al. 2003; Wasik and Shaffer 2006) and to assist new immigrants and English-language learners in becoming acclimated to the education system and community resources (Allen and Tracy 2004; Borenstein 1998; de Oliveira and Athanases 2007; Lopez, Scribner, and Mahitivanichcha 2001).

There has been a renewed professional interest in utilizing home-visiting programs in the past ten to twelve years to help high-risk children, adolescents, and families. As noted throughout this book, helping professionals across disciplines have employed in-home interventions as methods tailored toward high-risk populations (Borenstein 1998; Nix et al. 2005; Powell 1993; Wasik and Shaffer 2006). Research has supported an increasing use of in-home interventions by demonstrating that many risk and protective factors for children and adolescents are associated with home and community life. Home-based interventions that remedy social and mental health problems may be highly correlated with positive behavioral and academic outcomes. Factors such as mental health diagnosis, peer support, socioeconomic status, and family relationships are examples of the types of issues that may influence student outcomes in school and subsequently require the use of home visits (Berliner 2006; Blanchett, Mumford, and Beachum 2005; Lagana 2004; Lynn, McKay, and Atkins 2003; Reis, Colbert, and Hebert 2005; Repie 2005).

Educators and social workers have begun to recognize the advantages that home visiting may have in establishing home-school partnerships and in encouraging academic success. The education literature has begun to stress parental involvement and recommend home visiting as a way to engage parents and relate to students (de Oliveira and Athanases 2007; Lopez et al. 2001; Meyer 2006). Some teacher-preparation programs are also encouraging or requiring pre-service teachers to conduct home visits as part of their training (Darling-Hammond 2006; Hooks and Randolph 2004; Reglin 1995).

Increasing Mental Health and Social Challenges

The number of public-school students affected by emotional, behavioral, and mental health problems is clearly on the rise (Brown 2006). Students that underachieve also report personal or family problems and have difficulty relating to peers (Reis et al. 2005). Unfortunately, most of the children in need of mental health and family services do not receive them, causing these problems to become a major barrier to school success (Lynn et al. 2003; Repie 2005). As a result, the school often becomes a major de facto provider of mental health interventions for students, creating a greater need for the school to work with challenging home and family situations (Harris and Franklin 2004).

Similarly, social issues such as ethnic diversity and language minority status, social isolation, lack of social skills, and lack of peer support have all been linked to school dropout (Gallagher 2002; Lagana 2004). While the connection between student achievement and these social, emotional, and family factors are well known, teachers and school administrators are often poorly prepared to address these issues. Children that attend schools in areas of highly concentrated poverty, for example, tend to do poorly on academic assessments (Berliner 2006). In addition, there is a significant correlation between low income and school dropout (Lagana 2004). Although income may be more highly correlated with negative school outcomes than ethnicity, a disproportionate number of minority students also attend low-income, low-resource schools (Blanchett et al. 2005). Unfortunately, the often poor performance of these schools can prompt school administrators to "focus on blaming minority students for what are perceived as individual and cultural deficits residing in them" (Bryan 2005, 219).

Policy and Agency Context

Federal education policy has created an atmosphere that has indicated the need for home visits since as early as the 1970s. In 1971, the Elementary and Secondary Education Act of 1965 mandated that parents participate in the education of their children (Constable 1992). In 1997, the U.S. Department of Education announced seven education priorities, one of which was home-school communication (Broussard 2003). The Council of Chief State School Officials went one step further by explicitly suggesting that schools secure parents as "partners in education." To do so, they recommended that schools hire school-family liaisons and provide social work services in the schools (Constable 1992).

The No Child Left Behind Act of 2001 (NCLB) was the most influential piece of school-reform legislation in the history of public education in the United States. It was the culmination of a long trend toward educational accountability, with the goal of helping all students experience academic achievement. At the core of NCLB is the intent to close the achievement gap between low-income and minority students and their higher-income or white peers (Bryan 2005). The research on factors that influence academic success suggests that schools must address issues of diversity, family communication, and other social issues in order to increase academic gains (Constable 1992). In fact, NCLB mandates the development of school-family-community partnerships and labels these partnerships as a key to closing the achievement gap, but this clause is often overlooked (Bryan 2005). All of these policies and programs have in common a need for schools to work more closely with families to assure a student's success in school. Home-visiting interventions present a unique way to establish school-family partnerships and thus have the potential to affect the academic achievement of students.

Purposes and Goals of Social Work Home-Based Services

The major purpose of school-based home visiting varies according to student needs, but all home visits seek to provide intervention on multiple levels. Masten and Coatsworth (1998) report three main purposes of intervention suggested by the research literature on child and adolescent resilience: risk-focused intervention, resource-focused intervention, and process-focused intervention. Allen and Tracy (2004) link these three intervention purposes to school-based home visits. They suggest that school-based home visits can be used to intervene with students at each of these levels. (For a discussion of these levels of intervention, see chapter 1.)

Setting Goals for School-Based Home Visits

Some typical goals of school-based home visits include assessment of child, family, and school strengths and needs; improving family-school relationships; promoting positive family involvement; and changing certain risk issues such as poor attendance, dropout prevention, teen pregnancy, and financial problems.

IMPORTANCE OF ASSESSMENT IN HOME VISITS
One important purpose of home visits is to gather information about the child that might help to explain his or her behavior and academic achievement in school. In doing so, the social worker can help teachers and school

administrators gain a better understanding of the barriers to learning that the child faces (Broussard 2003). By helping teachers understand a student's background, social workers help them overcome their own stereotypes and make a plan to effectively serve the student in the classroom (Allen and Tracy 2004; Broussard 2003). This, in turn, can further promote parental involvement in school activities, as teacher practices are reported to be more critical in determining actual parent involvement than any family factor, including ethnicity and socioeconomic status (Dauber and Epstein 1993).

After an assessment phase, school-based home-visit interventions often seek to alleviate particular family problems. When social workers discover some difficulties with parent-child relationships, they can attempt to teach and model healthy parent-child interactions during home visits (Allen and Tracy 2004). These interventions can also be aimed at preventing child abuse and promoting child health (Gomby et al. 1993). Social workers may also help parents access educational materials for their homes to increase student opportunities for learning in the home (Feiler 2003). The presence of another responsible adult and increased communication between the school and parents may alleviate problems with attendance and help prevent dropout (Broussard 2003). When family crises occur or when students face adverse environments, social workers may use home visits to connect families to community resources (Allen and Tracy 2004; Bryan 2005).

USING HOME VISITS TO BUILD SCHOOL-FAMILY RELATIONSHIPS

Establishing positive working relationships is a major goal for school-based home visits. Meeting with someone in their home is an important strategy to build a working alliance between students, family members, and schools (Allen and Tracy 2004). Home-visit interventions seek to build relationships and overcome family-school conflict. Parents, for example, frequently perceive school officials as intimidating, and school officials often view parents as adversaries (Bryan 2005). Rather than seeking parental support or advice for a student who is struggling, schools may view parents as the root of the problem in ways that are discriminatory and counterproductive (Bryan 2005). Social workers attempt to bridge this divide by using home visitation as a method for building positive school-family relationships.

Allen and Tracy (2004) also suggest that home-visit interventions are one way to alleviate communication problems between home and school. The boundaries between the public nature of school life and the private nature of home life are often blurry in these communications and cause discomfort for parents who are embarrassed about sharing personal problems with school professionals. School-parent communication tends to be short, irregular, and focused on the immediate concerns regarding schooling. In-person exchanges are increasingly rare and often formal, causing a power imbalance between parents and school staffmembers, which can leave parents feeling intimidated (Smrekar 1994). School social workers use home visits as convenient ways to interact with families, because meeting in the home helps families overcome barriers to in-school meetings such as childcare and transportation (Wasik and Shaffer 2006). Perhaps most importantly, conducting visits in the home minimizes the power imbalance between school staffmembers and family members, since it takes place on the home "turf" (Allen and Tracy 2004).

PROMOTING POSITIVE FAMILY INVOLVEMENT

School social workers conducting home visits also set goals and create interventions to increase parents' involvement in their children's education. Recent research literature has highlighted the correlation between high levels of parent involvement and student academic achievement (Comer and Haynes 1992; Henderson and Mapp 2002; National Center for Educational Statistics 1992). Allen and Tracy (2004) point out that parent involvement does not have to be limited to attending meetings at school, volunteering at school functions, or belonging to parent-teacher organizations. Instead, parents can be encouraged to participate in their children's education by assisting them with their homework, encouraging school attendance, and offering learning activities in the home.

There is no doubt that home visits focus on goals and interventions that help schools support family involvement. Epstein (1995) identified six types of family involvement that help families and schools fulfill shared responsibilities for child learning and development. These include parenting, communicating, volunteering, learning at home, decision making, and connections with the community. Many schools use this framework to help them decide how to create family-school connections, especially regarding issues around school performance. Schools sometimes feel pressure to choose what they deem the most important methods of parent involvement, discarding methods that seem less desirable or feasible (Christenson et al. 1997). The flexible and individualized nature of school-based home visiting, however, presents a single strategy that can help promote and accomplish all six types of family involvement.

ADDRESSING RISK AREAS

School social workers are in a prime position to conduct home visits for a myriad of family and social problems. Their role as liaisons between home and school make them a natural at conducting psychosocial assessments in the home. In addition, social workers have been trained to identify and help alleviate the social and mental health problems that may become apparent during home visits. Examples of goals set to address risk areas are: to improve attendance on days when a pregnant student is not feeling well; secure safe, affordable housing for a homeless student; and enroll a student that has left the school prematurely in a continuing-education program.

Home visits also have the potential to improve the response time needed to address critical concerns and help parents build trust with the school through positive interactions with social workers (Allen and Tracy 2004). Goals for students with emotional or behavior problems can include social-skills acquisition and the development of positive communication and problem-solving skills (Conduct Problems Prevention Research Group 2002; McConaughy and Kay 2000; Reddy and Richardson 2006). Social workers can also work with parents to teach positive behavioral-intervention techniques, create action plans, and ensure consistency in behavioral expectations for home and school (McConaughy and Kay 2000).

Home-visiting programs designed for adolescent mothers have both social and educational goals. It is important to conduct home visits to help adolescent mothers return to school after giving birth and also to prevent subsequent pregnancies (Olds et al. 1998; Philliber et al. 2003). In addition, school social workers can target their interventions toward helping adolescents to improve their parenting skills (Fulton et al. 1991) and increase the chance of school readiness for their young children (Deutscher, Fewell, and Gross 2006).

All of the aforementioned goals and activities are centered around the home and can empower parents to become involved in their children's education without requiring time off from work, additional child care, or transportation, which many struggling families cannot afford. Home visits have the advantage of promoting mutual goals and cooperative behavior between families and schools. Increased cooperation between schools and families ensure a continuity of learning and behavioral expectations between home and school, enhancing positive relationships between families and school officials (Broussard 2003).

Theoretical Framework

The rationale for home visiting is grounded in the ecological and family-centered practice perspectives (Allen and Tracy 2004). The ecological perspective is a way for social workers to view the "interdependent transactions between persons and their environments" (Ungar 2002, 481). Ecological theory refers to the transactions between various parts of the system rather than to the individual components of either the person or the environment (Ungar 2002). The family-centered practice perspective focuses on including families in interventions and honoring the family as having strengths and resources to help the child succeed in school (Dunst 2002).

Ecological Perspective

Germain (1999) applies the ecological perspective directly to school social work practice. She contextualizes the dual roles of school social workers: to strengthen the coping skills of students and their families and to improve the quality of their environments. In this sense, school social workers work at the interface between the child and the school, the child and the family, the family and the school, and the community and the school. To do so, school social workers must have access to the child's home and direct attention to all aspects of the child's life, in order to examine the complex nature of both strengths and problems. It is difficult to conceive of a school social worker that is able to assess the myriad factors that influence a student without making a home visit. When school social workers have this perspective, they may help children develop appropriate social skills for the school environment and help schools become more responsive to the needs of the children.

Family-Centered Practice Perspective

School-based home visits operate in the realm of family-centered practice. Family-centered practice is a "particular set of beliefs, principles, values, and practices for supporting and strengthening family capacity to enhance and promote child development and learning" (Dunst 2002, 139). Home visits, more than any other school-based service, seek to involve a student's family as a method for increasing child academic achievement and appropriate school behaviors. In fact, it may be the only family-centered intervention utilized in today's schools. In family-centered practice, social workers focus on treating families with dignity and respect and on directing their services toward family involvement in decision-making processes. Home visits, for example, are individualized, responsive, and focused on family choice (Dunst 2002). Home visits also follow the family-centered practice perspective because they focus practitioners on directing their services to an individual family's concerns and priorities. Home visits, for example, may occur around parent schedules and negate the reasons that parents typically cite as obstacles to school participation (Allen and Tracy 2004).

Family-centered practices are familiar to most social workers, but they may be somewhat alien to some educators. Many schools continue to rely on "family-ally" approaches that are less collaborative and focus on school staffmembers as experts (Dunst 2002). When social workers forge parent-professional collaborations through home visits, they give importance to parent views, attitudes, and expectations that are otherwise ignored. Home visits provide a rare opportunity for schools to address the individual needs of a particular child as they relate to his or her family environment, rather than just viewing the child in relation to his or her classmates or to the school as a whole. In addition, home visits allow practitioners to respond to students in a more family-sensitive manner and provide opportunities to engage with families that would be otherwise difficult or impossible to reach (Wasik and Shaffer 2006). Taking a family-centered approach, home visitors develop school-related goals for children at home and school and identify family-oriented resources to help the child meet his or her school goals. Most importantly, while visiting the home, school social workers have the opportunity to gain feedback and support from hard-to-reach families (Allen and Tracy 2004).

Empirical Base

The most thoroughly researched home-visiting programs are those that focus on young children from infancy to preschool ages, as described in chapter 3. Unfortunately, there are few studies to date that review home visiting for older children. Sweet and Applebaum (2004) conducted a comprehensive meta-analysis of sixty home-visiting programs for young children from 1965 through 2004. This analysis included all programs for young children where home visiting was the primary intervention, excluding those that specifically targeted children with disabilities or chronically ill children. The programs targeted preschool children, most between the ages of birth to three years, and some included children up to the age of eight.

The overall results of the Sweet and Applebaum (2004) meta-analysis revealed that children who received home-based services fared better than children in control groups, suggesting that families do benefit from home visits. Children that received the interventions had significantly higher cognitive and socioemotional outcomes and lower risks of and actual experiences with parental abuse, for example. The magnitudes of these differences, however, while statistically significant, were quite small.

In a longitudinal study of daily student attendance and chronic absenteeism rates in elementary schools, Epstein and Sheldon (2002) found that, although the use of home visits did not affect daily attendance rates, schools that used home-visiting strategies decreased the number of students who were chronically absent. In addition, school employees rated home visiting as the most effective way to increase school attendance.

The field of maternal health offers some promising research in regards to the educational effects of home visiting programs. Olds et al. (1998) found that teen mothers who received home visits from nurses returned to school more rapidly than teen mothers in a control group. Similarly, in a review of outcomes for teen parenting programs in New Mexico from 1997 to 2000, Philliber et al. (2003) found that these programs were successful in increasing educational attainment and gains in employment. The authors found that home visits were one of the most frequently used interventions in teen-parenting programs and that two-thirds of these programs were school based. Similarly, Solomon and Liefeld (1998) found that an intervention combining home visits, parenting classes, school advocacy, and case management for urban adolescent mothers helped them delay subsequent pregnancies while they were enrolled in or completing school as compared to a control group.

Although there is a gap in the research literature regarding school-based home-visiting interventions for older children, there is a growing body of literature on multicomponent school-based intervention programs for children perceived to be at risk. These interventions combine both an in-school component and a home-visiting component. For instance, in a review of school-dropout prevention studies, Lehr et al. (2003) found that 29 percent of the interventions utilized some form of parent outreach/home visiting. Most programs combined several intervention techniques. Similarly, the Conduct Problems Prevention Research Group (2002) recently evaluated the Fast Track Project, which identified and provided intervention for children at risk for conduct disorder through parent training, home visiting, peer support, and tutoring. The study found that this intervention increased child competencies and decreased behavior problems for at-risk children in the first and third grades.

The School and Family Enrichment Project (SAFE) is a social work intervention to prevent early school failure in Garfield County, Oklahoma. A team of five social workers create family-school partnerships and provide a range of services such as mental health assessments, individual therapy sessions, group therapy sessions, parent groups, crisis interventions, and in-service trainings for both elementary and high-school students. In 1994 and

1995, social workers completed 231 home visits in addition to these other services. Poole (1997) reviewed outcomes for the SAFE project from various studies and found that students who attended a SAFE project site made larger improvements in self-esteem, grade-point averages, and test scores than students at a comparison school. In addition, after the second year of the intervention, students at the SAFE school had significantly lower absences, disciplinary referrals, and failed classes.

Finally, Coatsworth et al. (2002) completed an experimental evaluation of the Familias Unidas intervention with 167 families of sixth and seventh graders in Miami. This intervention combines intensive home visits, parent-support networks, parent-adolescent discussion, teen activity groups, peer activities, and school-counselor meetings. Results indicated that although the intervention did not seem to have an effect on academic achievement or social competence after twelve months, participants in the intervention did have more parental investment and more consistent declines in behavior problems than the control group.

Response to the Absence of Research on School-Based Home-Visiting Programs

The serious gap in the research literature regarding school-based home-visiting interventions with older children makes it difficult to compare the results of existing research on programs for young children to school-based programs. School-based home-visiting interventions, for example, often have different goals, targets, and expected outcomes than do programs for young children. As highlighted in the existing research literature, home visiting is often included alongside other interventions, which makes it difficult to determine the direct effect that the home-visiting component had on student outcomes. In addition, school-based programs are linked to the school setting, which is familiar and child focused and may therefore seem less daunting to parents than social work services in traditional office settings. Although evaluations of home-visiting programs for young children give some indication of the positive effects of home visits, the current studies are not adequate to suggest that school-based home-visiting programs are effective.

Given the absence of school-based evaluations, social workers might wish to examine the education literature on family involvement to provide a rationale for offering home-visiting programs in schools. High rates of parental involvement, for example, are correlated with a variety of positive school outcomes for children of all ages. Children whose parents are involved in their education demonstrate more academic achievement, better test scores, and more positive attitudes toward school (Broussard 2003). Increases in family involvement have also been shown to decrease dropout rates (Rumberger 1995) and the frequency of suspensions (Comer et al. 1996). In a review of the literature, Henderson and Mapp (2002) further found that children with family-member involvement in school are more likely to earn higher grades, have better attendance, go to college, and have more advanced social skills.

Practice Guidelines

While there is an absence of empirical literature on school-based home visits, there is considerable practice-based literature on the subject, and several authors provide suggestions for implementing successful home visits. Conducting successful home visits requires a range of assessment and counseling skills. First, school staffmembers conducting home visits should be highly trained (Gomby et al. 1993). Professionals carrying out home visits require exceptional clinical skills, such as active listening, empathy, and unconditional positive regard, as well as knowledge and skills related to the focus of the visit (Wasik and Shaffer 2006). Second, it is important for social workers and other professionals to have training in family therapy and ecological-systems interventions so they can respond to the family as a whole and as the main target unit of intervention. Third, social workers and other professionals should operate from a strengths-based perspective and believe that each family has competence (Allen and Tracy 2004). Fourth, social workers and other professionals conducting home visits should structure their work with the family as a collaborative effort. The social worker should not assume an expert role, for example, and cannot make an impact if he or she does not establish rapport and encourage cooperation (Wasik and Shaffer 2006). Finally, social workers must be attuned to the unique characteristics of each family and choose change strategies that are culturally and socially appropriate (Gomby et al. 1993).

Structure and Process for Home Visits

Social workers are generally flexible about the frequency and duration of home visits and allow parents to guide these decisions, which helps avoid attrition (Gomby et al. 1993). Some situations call for short-term home-visiting programs, but Feiler (2003) suggests that practitioners should complete enough visits to establish rapport with the family and have a real effect on their needs. "Joining" with the family and engaging parents in open dialogue is necessary for the intervention to be successful (Allen and Tracy 2004). To do so, social workers must be sensitive to both family culture (Feiler 2003) and family privacy (Allen and Tracy 2004).

Good school-based home-visiting programs contain three major components: assessment, goal setting, and connections to resources. Rapport building and family engagement are evident during each step of the intervention. Social workers must first assess the strengths and needs of the student, the family, the neighborhood, and the community. Included in this assessment should be the safety of the child's environment, his or her access to social activities, sources of formal and informal support, and access to resources (Allen and Tracy 2004). Assessment and evaluation do not occur solely at the beginning of a home-visiting program but continuously throughout the intervention (Wasik and Shaffer 2006).

School social workers conducting home visits help parents take the lead in setting goals for themselves and their children. This is a collaborative effort that avoids blame and focuses on strengths (Allen and Tracy 2004). Practitioners continuously teach, model, and encourage coping and problem-solving skills that are individualized for each family's unique circumstances (Wasik and Shaffer 2006). Large goals may require several intermediate steps to accomplish.

For example, a student that is pregnant, not feeling well, and having trouble coming to school some days might have to visit a doctor for some help or work out a more flexible schedule from her morning teachers before she can accomplish the intended goal of improving her attendance at school. Setting well-defined goals accompanied by small tasks with tangible reinforcements (i.e., points and gifts) for accomplishing the tasks can also be very helpful for at-risk students and a useful intervention along with goal setting. Harris and Franklin (2003, 2007) demonstrated, for example, that a goal-setting process that rewards the completion of tasks toward goals helped pregnant and parenting teens improve their attendance and grades at school.

Goals should also be perceived as a beginning and a process toward a desired outcome, not as an end in themselves. Franklin, Kim, and Tripodi (2006), for example, discuss how to use goals as a process to help students at risk for dropout change their behaviors. These authors use the goal-setting process suggested by solution-focused brief therapy. Solution-focused brief therapy utilizes student strengths and resources and student-driven goals to facilitate change. The goal-setting process used in the solution-focused approach requires social workers to listen carefully to the family's wants and needs and define concrete, behavioral goals from the perspective of the student and family members. This goal-setting process takes advantage of student and family strengths and uses what the student and family members want most as an intrinsic motivator for behavior change.

Consistent with the solution-building, goal-setting process, school-based home visits focus on assessing the strengths and needs of the child, family, school, and community in relation to school success (Allen and Tracy 2004). Social workers need to keep in mind that the problems they are helping families address are often deeply rooted, structural in nature, and involve multiple barriers (e.g., violence, poverty, stigma, and discrimination). Home visits are not a "magic cure" for these complex problems, but they may be able to help families begin to cope with them (Gomby et al. 1993).

Once the school social worker has assessed a family's needs and has helped them set goals, he or she helps link the family to resources that will assist in accomplishing them. Social workers determine the areas in which families already have support and the areas in which there are gaps in their resources (Allen and Tracy 2004). Linking families to resources help them generalize newly acquired skills to similar future situations (Wasik and Shaffer 2006).

Major Components and Helping Techniques

Wasik and Shaffer (2006) identify the major components and techniques utilized in school-based home visits. These components are discussed in the sections that follow.

PREPARATION FOR THE HOME VISIT

Social workers spend a great deal of time preparing for a home visit. They learn as much as they can about the family and the setting. It is helpful to know who lives in the student's home, for example, and who will likely be present at the time of the visit. Similarly, practitioners become knowledgeable about the family's neighborhood and may even take an exploratory drive to the neighborhood in advance of the visit to assess any safety concerns. If a previous staffmember has had interactions with the family, it might be helpful to find out which family members were most cooperative and if there were any special concerns or observations.

Before conducting a home visit, the social worker thinks about the purpose of the visit, including what he or she hopes to accomplish. It is also important to find out what the family hopes to accomplish from the visit. The social worker may ask the family, "What needs to happen today in this home visit for this session to worthwhile?" If it is an initial visit, establishing rapport and identifying goals might be the main focus. If it is a visit with a familiar family, the purpose might involve checking with the family to see if they have completed tasks toward their goals or have any new concerns since the last visit. The social worker might also consider whether it would be helpful for any other school staffmembers, such as a teacher, school nurse, or speech therapist, to attend the visit. Strategic uses of other school personnel are vital to the success of home visits. It may be important, for example, for a social worker to include another school staffperson that speaks the native language of the family. This step could be essential to assuring effective communication and rapport building.

Social workers take some basic safety precautions prior to the visit. Simple preparations such as letting co-workers know the location of the visit and the expected time of return can help ensure safety. Practitioners prepare themselves further by bringing a map of the community, carrying a cellphone in case of emergency, and parking in an area that provides easy access to an exit. (See chapter 2 for further discussion of safety precautions.)

CONDUCTING THE HOME VISIT

During the home visit, social workers apply the same effective helping skills that they would employ in any other setting. They greet the family warmly, attempt to establish rapport, and discuss the purpose of the visit with the family. Home visitors always ask about any changes since the last visit and about any recent activities or interventions. Throughout the visit, the social worker uses active listening skills to make sure that the family understands any new goals or resources that he or she suggests.

Social workers on a home visit also encourage family members to participate and give suggestions. It is essential for the home visitor to abide by family cultural norms and beliefs without judgment. Along with helping families devise plans to solve problems, home visitors assist them with following through on these plans. Prompt follow-up with families and coordination are essential in this regard. In order to help coordinate multiple services, social workers must monitor families closely and quickly link families to missing resources. Finally, each session should end with a review of the main points of the visit, the goals for the next few weeks, and the setting of the next appointment.

Issues of Diversity and Practice with Populations at Risk

The nature of home visiting, as it is applied to school settings, is to identify students who are at risk of academic or social problems. Students that struggle academically often live in urban areas, have lower socioeconomic status, and are ethnic minorities. Many of the students that school social workers might target for a home visit are considered "at risk" (Bryan 2005). Consequently, social work practitioners must be attuned to working with populations considered high risk and visiting neighborhoods that some people might consider unsafe.

Social workers model how to respond to diversity in positive ways. They consider cultural and family norms when assessing family interaction and communication patterns (Allen and Tracy 2004). Home visitors should not assume that they understand a family's culture, for example, and should ask questions and let the family define themselves. It is equally important for social workers to understand that a parent's literacy level, community expectations, and cultural norms surrounding parent-school interactions may all affect student outcomes, including how the parent chooses to interact with the school (Allen and Tracy 2004). Social workers may also help socially isolated parents and guardians (i.e., foster parents, immigrant parents, gay/lesbian parents) that feel excluded from school processes to become involved (Allen and Tracy 2004).

Social workers also assist other members of the school community in becoming more sensitive to working with diverse and at-risk students. Many school professionals are white, middle-class adults. Most education professors are also white and politically conservative (Broussard 2003). At this time, most higher-education teacher-preparation programs do not prepare new teachers to communicate with parents and children that are culturally diverse. Since they are not taught to perceive cultural differences, many teachers assume that their students' families have the same values and backgrounds as they do, and they may react negatively when families differ. This may cause teachers to interact with students that are different from themselves based on stereotypes (Broussard 2003).

School social workers can help fill the gaps created by this lack of teacher knowledge because they are explicitly trained in diversity, family systems, and ecological theories. One strategy for educating school staff is for social workers to take information that they learn on home visits and use it to educate teachers and school administrators about diverse family styles and practices and to help them understand how some children's behaviors in school may be culturally rooted. In-service trainings may be held by social workers to educate teachers and other school staff about diversity and cultural competence. Social workers may also work with the school to establish a resource center to help school staffmembers become more knowledgeable and competent about diversity issues (Broussard 2003). The resource center might house books, DVDs, treatment manuals, case studies, and other resources that help teachers learn about diversity.

Confidentiality is a major concern for all school social workers, but it is a special concern when social workers conduct home visits with students that are already at risk. Social workers often find it difficult to determine how much information to seek from families during home visits and how much information to share with an interdisciplinary team (Allen and Tracy 2004). While some information might be crucial for understanding a child's in-school behavior or achievement, the ethical principle of confidentiality is binding in the home setting, as well. Consequently, information that a social worker obtains during a home visit should remain confidential unless the parent gives permission for the social worker to share it with the school team. On the first visit, social workers should always be upfront with parents about their mandated duty to report any suspected child abuse, and they may also apprise them of policies concerning other behaviors (e.g., suicide, homicide threats, terrorist plots, and carrying weapons at school). It is important to apprise all families, especially the at-risk ones, of the limits of confidentiality because, as discussed in chapter 2, it is not unusual to encounter legal and ethical issues during home visits.

Implications for Home-Based Practice

Home visiting has a long history in social work practice and educators seem to be taking a renewed interest in the value of school-based home-visiting interventions to address a variety of problems. The lack of empirical literature regarding school-based home visits and home visits with older children suggests a need for further research in these areas. Although research regarding home visits with young children gives some indication of the positive effects that they can have, school-based home visits require further evaluation to determine whether this intervention is successful in increasing family involvement and improving student achievement. In addition, there is a need for dismantling studies to determine the specific impact that home visiting has independently and in combination with other interventions.

Recent legislation such as the NCLB stresses the importance of parental involvement and recognizes it as a major factor influencing student achievement. Consequently, social workers, who have the knowledge and skills needed to conduct successful home visits, are in a unique position to create and expand home-visiting programs to assist students and their families. This provides social workers with the opportunity to highlight the many social, cultural, and psychological factors that influence academic achievement and to help schools plan to address them.

However, the focus on high-stakes testing and accountability created by NCLB may undermine the support for parental involvement and subsequently school-based home visiting. After the third year of implementation, many school districts had not addressed NCLB parental-involvement requirements (Epstein 2005). Instead, most schools have focused their attention away from child well-being and toward raising standardized-test scores and acquiring highly qualified teachers (Prince, Pepper, and Brocato 2006). This trend highlights the importance of engaging in high-quality evaluations of school social work interventions. Evidence that school social work interventions such as home visiting can help improve academic achievement via increased parent involvement could bring renewed interest in and increased funding for this important cause.

REFERENCES

Allen, S. F., and Tracy, E. M. 2004. Revitalizing the role of home visiting by school social workers. *Children and Schools* 26 (4): 197–208.

Allen-Meares, P. 1994. Social work services in schools: A national study of entry-level tasks. *Social Work* 39 (5): 560–565.

Berliner, D. C. 2006. Our impoverished view of educational research. *Teachers College Record* 108 (6): 949–995.

Blanchett, W. J., Mumford, V., and Beachum, F. 2005. Urban school failure and disproportionality in a post-Brown era: Benign neglect of the constitutional rights of students of color. *Remedial and Special Education* 26 (2): 70–81.

Borenstein, L. R. 1998. A multidimensional approach to evaluating school-linked services: A school of social work and county public school partnership. *Social Work in Education* 20 (3): 152–164.

Broussard, C. A. 2003. Facilitating home-school partnerships for multiethnic families: School social workers collaborating for success. *Children and Schools* 24 (4): 211–222.

Brown, M. B. 2006. School-based mental health centers: Implications for counselors. *Journal of Counseling and Development* 84: 187–191.

Bryan, J. 2005. Fostering educational resilience and achievement in urban schools through school-family-community partnerships. *Professional School Counseling* 8 (3): 219–227.

Christenson, S. L., Hurley, C. M., Sheridan, S. M., and Fenstermacher, K. 1997.

Parents' and school psychologists' perspectives on parent involvement activities. *School Psychology Review* 26 (1): 111–130.

Coatsworth, J. D., Pantin, H., and Szapocznik, J. 2002. Familias Unidas: A family-centered ecodevelopmental intervention to reduce risk for problem behavior among Hispanic adolescents. *Clinical Child and Family Psychology Review* 5 (2): 87–160.

Comer, J. P., and Haynes, N. M. 1992. Parent involvement in school: An ecological approach. *The Elementary School Journal* 91 (3): 271–278.

Comer, J. P., Haynes, N. M., Joyner, E. T., and Ben-Avie, M., eds. 1996. *Rallying the whole village: The Comer process for reforming education*. New York: Teachers College Press.

Conduct Problems Prevention Research Group. 2002. The implementation of the Fast Track program: An example of a large-scale prevention science efficacy trial. *Journal of Abnormal Child Psychology* 30 (1): 1–17.

Constable, R. T. 1992. The new school reform and the school social worker. *Social Work in Education* 14 (2): 106–113.

Costin, L. B. 1969. An analysis of the tasks in school social work. *Social Service Review* 43: 274–285.

Darling-Hammond, L. 2006. Constructing twenty-first-century teacher education. *Journal of Teacher Education* 57 (3): 300–315.

Dauber, S. L., and Epstein, J. L. 1993. Parent attitudes and practices of involvement in inner-city elementary and middle schools. In *Families and schools in a pluralistic society*, ed. N. F. Chavkin, 53–72. Albany: State University of New York Press.

De Oliveira, L. C., and Athanases, S. Z. 2007. Graduates' reports of advocating for English-language learners. *Journal of Teacher Education* 58 (3): 202–215.

Deutscher, B., Fewell, R. R., and Gross, M. 2006. Enhancing the interactions of teenage mothers and their at-risk children: Effectiveness of a maternal-focused intervention. *Early Childhood Special Education* 26 (4): 194–205.

Dunst, C. J. 2002. Family-centered practices: Birth through high school. *The Journal of Special Education* 36 (3): 139–147.

Epstein, J. L. 1995. School/family/community partnerships: Caring for children we share. *Phi Delta Kappan* 76 (9): 701–712.

——. 2005. Attainable goals? The spirit and letter of No Child Left Behind Act on parental involvement. *Sociology of Education* 78 (2): 179–182.

Epstein, J. L., and Sheldon, S. B. 2002. Present and accounted for: Improving student attendance through family and community involvement. *Journal of Educational Research* 95 (5): 308–321.

Feiler, A. 2003. Early literacy and home visiting during the reception year: Supporting "difficult to reach" families. *European Journal of Special Needs Education* 18 (2): 251–261.

Franklin, C., and Gerlach, B. 2006. One hundred years of linking schools with communities: Current models and opportunities. *School Social Work, Special Issue* (Summer): 45–62.

Franklin, C., Kim, J. S., and Tripodi, S. 2006. Solution-focused, brief therapy interventions for students at-risk to drop out. In *The school services sourcebook: A guide for school-based professionals*, ed. C. Franklin, M. B. Harris, and P. Allen-Meares, 691–704. New York: Oxford University Press.

Franklin, C., and Streeter, C. 1995. School reform: Linking public schools with human services. *Social Work* 40 (6): 773–782.

Fulton, A. M., Murphy, K. R., and Anderson, S. L. 1991. Increasing adolescent knowledge of child development: An intervention program. *Adolescence* 26: 73–81.

Gallagher, C. J. 2002. Stories from the strays: What dropouts can teach us about school. *American Secondary Education* 30 (3): 36–59.

Germain, C. B. 1999. An ecological perspective on social work in the schools. In *School social work: Practice, policy, and research perspectives*, ed. R. Constable, S. McDonald, and J. P. Flynn, 33–44. Chicago: Lyceum.

Gomby, D. S., Larson, C. S., Lewit, E. M., and Behrman, R. E. 1993. Home visiting: Analysis and recommendations. *The Future of Children* 3 (3): 6–22.

Harris, M., and Franklin, C. 2003. Effectiveness of a cognitive-behavioral, school-based group intervention with Mexican American pregnant and parenting adolescents. *Social Work Research* 27 (2): 71–84.

——. 2004. The design of school social work services. In *Social work services in the school*, 4th ed., ed. P. A. Meares, 277–294. Boston: Allyn and Bacon.

——. 2007. *Taking charge: A school-based life skills program for adolescent mothers*. New York: Oxford University Press.

Henderson, A. T., and Mapp, K. L., eds. 2002. *A new wave of evidence: The impact of school, family, and community connections on student achievement*. Austin, Tex.: National Center for Family and Community Connections with Schools, Southwest Educational Development Laboratory.

Hooks, L. M., and Randolph, L. 2004. Excellence in teacher preparation: Partners for success. *Childhood Education* 80 (5): 231–237.

Kurtz, D. P., and Barth, R. P. 1989. Parent involvement: Cornerstone of school social work practice. *Social Work* 34: 407–413.

Lagana, M. 2004. Protective factors for inner-city adolescents at risk of school dropout: Family factors and social support. *Children and Schools* 26 (4): 211–220.

Lehr, C. A., Hansen, A., and Sinclair, M. F. 2003. Moving beyond dropout towards school completion: An integrative review of data-based interventions. *School Psychology Review* 32 (3): 342–364.

Lopez, G. R., Scribner, J. D., and Mahitivanichcha, K. 2001. Redefining parental involvement: Lessons from high-performing migrant-impacted schools. *American Educational Research Journal* 38 (2): 253–288.

Lynn, C. J., McKay, M. M., and Atkins, M. S. 2003. School social work: Meeting the mental health needs of students through collaboration with teachers. *Children and Schools* 25 (4): 197–209.

Masten, A. S., and Coatsworth, J. D. 1998. The development of competence in favorable and unfavorable environments: Lessons from research on successful children. *American Psychologist* 53: 205–220.

McConaughy, S. H., and Kay, P. J. 2000. How long is long enough? Outcomes for a school-based prevention program. *Exceptional Children* 67 (1): 21–35.

Meyer, J. A. 2006. Teachers' perceptions of the benefits of home visits for early elementary children. *Early Childhood Education Journal* 34 (1): 93–97. .

National Center for Educational Statistics. 1992. *Digest of education statistics.* Technical report no. NCES 90–042, U.S. Department of Education, Office of Educational Research and Improvement. Washington D.C.: U.S. Government Printing Office.

Nelson, C. 1990. *A job analysis of school social workers.* Princeton, N.J.: Educational Testing Service.

Nix, R. L., Pinderhughes, E. E., Bierman, K. L., and Maples, J. J. 2005. Decoupling the relation between risk factors for conduct problems and the receipt of intervention services: Participation across multiple components of a prevention program. *American Journal of Community Psychology* 36 (3/4): 307–325.

Olds, D., Henderson, R., and Chamberlain, R. 1998. Improving the life-course development of socially disadvantaged mothers: A randomized trial of nurse home visitation. *American Journal of Public Health* 78: 1436–1445.

Philliber, S., Brooks, L., Lehrer, L. P., Oakley, M., and Waggoner, S. 2003. Outcomes of teen parenting programs in New Mexico. *Adolescence* 88 (151): 535–553.

Poole, D. L. 1997. The Safe project: Community-driven partnerships in health, mental health, and education to prevent early school failure. *Health and Social Work* 22 (4): 282–289.

Powell, D. R. 1993. Inside home visiting programs. *The Future of Children* 3 (3): 23–38.

Prince, D. L., Pepper, K., and Brocato, K. 2006. The importance of making the well-being of children in poverty a priority. *Early Childhood Education* 34 (1): 21–28.

Reddy, L. A., and Richardson, L. 2006. School-based prevention and intervention programs for children with emotional disturbance. *Education and Treatment of Children* 29 (2): 379–404.

Reglin, G. 1995. Collaborate for school success: African American students from low income/public housing backgrounds. *Education* 116 (2): 274–280.

Reis, S. M., Colbert, R. D., and Hebert, T. P. 2005. Understanding resilience in diverse, talented students in an urban high school. *Roeper Review* 27 (2): 110–120.

Repie, M. S. 2005. A school mental health issues survey from the perspective of regular and special education teachers, school counselors, and school psychologists. *Education and Treatment of Children* 28 (3): 279–298.

Rumberger, R. W. 1995. Dropping out of middle school: A multilevel analysis of students and schools. *American Educational Research Journal* 32 (3): 583–625.

Smrekar, C. 1994. The missing link in school-linked social service programs. *Educational Evaluation and Policy Analysis* 16 (4): 422–433.

Solomon, R., and Liefeld, C. P. 1998. Effectiveness of a family support center approach to adolescent mothers: Repeat pregnancy and school drop-out rates. *Family Relations* 47 (2): 139–144.

Staudt, M., and Powell, K. K. 1996. Serving children and adolescents in the school: Can social work meet the challenges? *Sociology of Education* 69: 433–446.

Sweet, M. A., and Appelbaum, M. I. 2004. Is home visiting an effective strategy? A meta-analytic review of home visiting programs for families with young children. *Child Development* 75 (5): 1435–1456.

Ungar, M. 2002. A deeper, more social ecological social work practice. *Social Service Review* 76 (3): 480–497.

Wagner, M., Spiker, D., Linn, M. I., Gerlach-Downie, S., and Hernandez, F. 2003. Dimensions of parental engagement in home visiting programs: Exploratory study. *Topics in Early Childhood Special Education* 23 (4): 171–187.

Wasik, B. H., and Shaffer, G. L. 2006. Home visiting: Essential guidelines for home visits and engaging with families. In *The school services sourcebook*, ed. C. Franklin, M. B. Harris, and P. Allen-Meares, 745–752. New York: Oxford University Press.

Seven

Child Welfare

CATHLEEN A. LEWANDOWSKI AND KATHARINE BRIAR-LAWSON

Historically, the field of child welfare has centered primarily on the best or most appropriate home for children that would support their development. This has meant removing children from their home and family in problematic cases in which safety and related risk factors were evident. Century-old images of orphan trains stopping in communities across the country remind us that the overriding focus of practice has centered on mobilizing homes for children who either lacked them or for whom the homes were deemed problematic (Berebitsky 2000). Thus, for decades services were dominated by home-finding activities rather than providing support for at-risk families and addressing the concrete needs of families in poverty.

In more recent decades, many of the goals of home-based services in child·welfare focus on placement prevention and, whenever possible, maintaining children in their own homes. Programs such as Homebuilders have demonstrated the viability and utility of home-based services for prevention and helped develop practice strategies of engagement, empowerment, behaviorally intensive services, and provision of concrete resources. These strategies may also be applied to reunifying children with their families when placement prevention fails and to preventing adoption dissolution when parental rights are terminated and children are adopted.

Family-based assessment using an ecological perspective could be beneficial in gathering the type of information required by most state and county statutes and regulations during investigations of child abuse and neglect. Absent contextual assessments, screening for child abuse or neglect might be devoid of critical data. Expectations that investigations occur on a timely and comprehensive basis result in workers frequently conducting their investigation in the home. Often arriving unannounced, protective-service workers assess both the evidence of maltreatment and the risk and safety factors that the worker perceives must be addressed to prevent a subsequent maltreatment. For example, Texas law requires that workers should determine the (1) nature, extent, and cause of abuse or neglect; (2) identity of the person responsible; (3) names and conditions of other children in the home; (4) evaluation of parents or other persons responsible for the care of the child; (5) adequacy of the home environment; (6) relationship of the child to the persons responsible for the care, custody, or welfare of the child; and any other pertinent data (Texas State 2008). Workers may assess the amount of food in the home, heat, sleeping arrangements, and whether there are signs of domestic violence, such as a shattered bedroom door.

Just as problematic as child mistreatment is the "rescue and place" orientation of many decades of policy; more recently, practice has been rebalanced with a focus on placement prevention through an array of home-based and family-centered services. Such service strategies are based on the practice principles that the home is the best place for children to grow, that the state does not make a good parent, and that family systems can change and grow as learning communities. Moreover, helping families function more effectively is seen as a more prudent use of services and resources than solely relying on foster care and adoption strategies. Home-based services are seen as essential in child welfare. The case for home-based services has been made from a "best practice" and promising-outcomes standpoint, from a sound-ecological-assessment approach, and from an effectiveness-intervention rationale.

The Population

All children in the United States are de facto eligible to receive child welfare services, especially those services that are directly involved with the investigation of child abuse and neglect. In contrast, other child welfare services, such as family preservation, have funding caps. Thus, access to family preservation, one of the more well-known home-based child welfare services, is restricted by federal and state funding allocations. Though all children may be eligible for child welfare services, especially as the target of a child abuse or neglect investigation, the reality is that the vast majority of children who receive child welfare services are from impoverished families (Lindsey 1994; Pelton 1989). In 2006, nearly 3.6 million children received a protective-services investigation or assessment. Based on these investigations, 905,000 children were identified as victims of maltreatment. Of these, 64.1 percent were victims of neglect (U.S. DHHS 2008). National statistics on the number of children who receive family-preservation services are not readily available, because programs vary by state, in the type of programs offered, and in the amount of funding available.

The number of children entering foster care increased in both 2004 and 2005, breaking the trend of increasingly fewer children entering care between 2000 and 2003. Nonetheless, the number of children remaining in care has decreased steadily, from 552,000 in 2000 to 514,000 in 2005 (U.S. DHHS 2006). Kinship care may be formal, where children are wards of the state and are placed with extended family members, or informal, where there is an informal network of care that supports families in caring for their children (Anderson 2002). Since 1998, the number of children entering formal kinship care has been steadily decreasing, from over 162,000, or 29 percent of children in state custody in 1998 (U.S. DHHS 2005), to 124,153 (24 percent) in 2005 (U.S. DHHS 2006). It is not possible to discern an exact number of children in formal and informal kinship care, as there are no studies with national probability samples (Cuddeback 2004). The number of adoptions has increased, however, from 37,000 children adopted in 1998 to 51,323 children adopted in 2005 (U.S. DHHS 2006). However, it should be noted that 1998 adoption rates may have been underestimated. These low estimates were a result of underreporting by states, the use of inappropriate data as the basis for estimates, and real increases in the number of adoptions (Maza 1999).

Many children and families who receive child welfare services have co-occurring concerns, most notably substance abuse (Ryan et al. 2006), domestic violence (Kohl et al. 2005; English, Edleson, and Herrick 2005), and mental health concerns (Clausen et al. 1998). Poverty, community violence, lack of access to health care, homelessness, and HIV/AIDS are additional risks and vulnerabilities that often confront children who come to the attention of child welfare services (Maluccio, Pine, and Tracy 2002). Thus, child welfare workers making home visits often must take multiple factors into account during the assessment processes.

Policy and Agency Context

The discovery of battered-child syndrome in 1962 brought child maltreatment to the fore as a prominent policy and practice concern across the nation (Helfer, Kempe, and Krugman 1997). There are several factors that may have helped reinforce the development of home-based services and family-centered practice. The White House Conference on Families in 1979 brought the needs of families to the forefront. For the first time in the United States, it became possible to formulate policies that recognized that individual concerns could best be addressed in the context of the family and the wider environment (Langley 1991). Family-centered policies were also accelerated by findings from intensive services to child welfare families, through initiatives such as the Alameda Project and the permanency planning project (Yuan and Struckman-Johnson 1991). These nationally significant pilots reflected dual purposes in child welfare: promoting child safety and well-being and preserving the family whenever possible.

Because the home is where child abuse and neglect often occurs, child welfare services invariably involve some home-based practices. Such practices ensure that caseworkers can see "in vivo" family-based interactions and the physical, social, and emotional conditions that surround the child or children. Removing children from their home to place them in foster care is to be done only when necessary to protect children from subsequent abuse or related risk factors such as neglect or lack of supervision.

Based on PL 96-272, the Adoption Assistance and Child Welfare Act of 1980, states were required to demonstrate "reasonable efforts" at placement prevention to keep the family intact. The Indian Child Welfare Act of 1978 set an even higher threshold for placement prevention and required "active efforts" at promoting family intactness and placement prevention. Laws such as the Family Preservation and Support Services of the Omnibus Reconciliation Act of 1993 promoted family preservation and family supports. Even the language for this act targets children in families, including adoptive families at risk or in crisis, but it does not mention home-based services. Furthermore, family-support services in the Family Preservation and Support Services Act are defined as being community based rather than home based.

In 1997, the Adoption and Safe Families Act (ASFA) was passed, with the intention that states be required to terminate parental rights in cases of severe parental misconduct or dysfunction or when children had been in foster care for fifteen of the most recent twenty-two months. Though the intent was to assure children's rights to permanency within a reasonable amount of time, ASFA contains exceptions so that preserving the family may take precedence over children's rights to permanency. These exceptions include kinship-care placements, failure of the state to provide timely services to allow for a safe return, and when it is determined that termination of parental rights is not in the best interests of the child (Bartholet 1999).

Though ASFA increased funding for family-preservation programs, the act emphasized demonstration projects to promote innovation, rather than mandating the forms such projects might take. Thus, under the rubric of community services, home-based supports are inferred but not legislated. More recently, the U.S. Children's Bureau has regulated child welfare practice through Child and Family Service Reviews. These CFSRs measure safety, permanency, and well-being. Each state is rated on compliance with practice standards set by the U.S. Children's Bureau. Many states fail some of the compliance measures. Program Improvement Plans (PIPS) are then crafted. Several of the practice standards are designed to foster permanency and are linked to family functioning and the biological family's ability to assure the child's safety and well-being. Outcome measures include families' enhanced capacities to provide for their children and support for children's educational, mental, and physical health needs. Major facets of home-based family-centered practice are reflected in these PIPS. For example, findings from the Children's Bureau (U.S. DHHS 2004) show that safety and permanency outcomes, including timely reunification, are related to parent and child involvement in case planning and casework visits and the provision of services for the parents as well as for children and foster parents. Children's Bureau findings indicated that thirty states were doing insufficient child and family needs assessments and twenty-two states were doing insufficient risk and safety assessments. Nationwide, the two worst areas of performance were children's permanency and stability and families' enhanced capacity to meet their children's needs (U.S. DHHS 2004).

Often, these reviews and PIPs point to the need for an improved workforce capacity, including the need for trained social workers who can work effectively with biological families. If caseworkers do not have the capacity and skills needed to solve families' problems, the principles of family-centered and home-based practices may be insufficient to achieve permanency and assure children's safety, even when caseloads are reduced (Luongo 2007).

Several home-based models are readily available and can be adapted by states. Perhaps the earliest, historically relevant model was the St. Paul Project. Homebuilders, which emerged several decades later, is largely attributed with marking the beginning of the family-preservation movement and in shaping subsequent family-preservation models. Additional models are described in the practice guidelines section of this chapter.

St. Paul Project

The forerunner to more recent innovations in home-based services is the St. Paul Project. Designed in the early 1950s, this empirically based program demonstrated effectiveness with families known to multiple agencies (Birt 1956). With relentless outreach and engagement and very structured and responsive strategies to meet family needs while focusing on the child, this program demonstrated the technology of engagement and behavioral change. The "hard-to-reach, multiproblem family" was no longer seen as too difficult to serve. Evidence mounted from this nationally significant program that behavioral-change strategies such as modeling, addressing learned helplessness with task-centered strategies, and honoring the family's definition of the problem and solution were effective. Relying on systems theory and approaches, the program helped move the home-based, family-centered knowledge base forward (Horejsi 1981).

Homebuilders and Intensive Family Preservation Services

While the St. Paul Project was one of the first attempts to provide services to the family as a whole, Homebuilders is perceived as one of the first *family*-preservation programs. Underlying Homebuilders' origins in the late 1970s was the belief of two psychologists that problematic interactions with troubled youth and parents could be addressed by professionals moving in with "armored sleeping bags" to successfully change the interactions in the home and between the youth and parents (Kinney and Dittmar 1995). This home-based and behaviorally oriented service strategy shaped the well-recognized family-preservation model program in Washington State. As the originator of the "Intensive Family Preservation Services" model, Homebuilders-like programs were introduced in many states. Many remain in place today.

Public child welfare workers refer families who have a child with imminent risk of out-of-home placement to Homebuilders or programs like it. Therapists carry a caseload of two families at a time and offer intensive services, usually ten to twenty hours a week, for a period of four to eight weeks. Services are tailored to meet families' needs and may include crisis intervention, family therapy, advocacy, home management, life-skills training, and concrete assistance (Bath and Haapala 1993). The home setting is seen as providing an "in vivo" learning and teaching environment for families, especially related to parenting skills. Many families served might not have had the resources or been willing to come to an office setting (Fraser, Pecora, and Haapala 1991).

When Homebuilders was developed, the "service technology" and advancements made possible by clinically trained social workers with caseloads of two offered great and promising directions for the child welfare field. It was surmised that very few children would require out-of-home placement and, when needed, the time would be short, given the intensive and high-impact work with the family. Homebuilders' services were applied to other high-risk populations, such as homeless youth (Bronstein 1996) and juvenile justice (Borduim 1994; Fraser, Nelson, and Rivard 1997). This intensive-service technology demonstrated that parenting behaviors and parent-child interactions could be changed successfully when conditions were right.

Purposes and Goals of Social Work Home-Based Services

The field of child welfare concerns itself with children's overall well-being, including their physical, psychological, social, and emotional development. Child welfare's primary goals are to prevent, identify, and treat child abuse and neglect or child maltreatment. Home-based services address all these goals, through a range of programs and services that occur across the continuum of child welfare services. While services and programs vary across states and regions, the key child welfare services where home visits occur are family preservation, child abuse and neglect (CAN) investigations, foster care and kinship care, and when placing children for adoption. Family-preservation programs are primarily concerned with prevention of abuse and neglect and increasing the amount of time children remain in their own home. Ideally, family-preservation strategies focus on preventing an out-of-home placement. CAN investigations are also conducted in the home and are intended to identify abuse and neglect so that subsequent abuse does not occur. Over the course of the investigation, the child protection worker conducts risk and safety assessments to decide whether children would be at risk or would have their safety violated if they remained in their home. When children are removed from their home, the focus of child welfare services shifts from the biological family to children's out-of-home placement. Home visits conducted within children's family of origin monitor the risk and protective factors for subsequent abuse and determine when children may be safely reunified with their families. Foster and kinship-care families may also receive home-based services and be monitored to prevent maltreatment of children placed in their care. Ideally, reunification strategies use some of the components of family-preservation services to ensure that the same risk factors that led to out-of-home placements are reduced prior to reunification. Once children are reunified with their families, families may receive home visits to prevent the reoccurrence of maltreatment.

Parental rights are terminated and children become available for adoption if, through the investigative and legal process, it is determined that children may not be safely returned to their home. Once adoptions are finalized, families rarely hear from child welfare agencies. Adoptive parents can feel cut off and helpless once adoptions are finalized and may feel abandoned (Festinger 2002). From a best-practices perspective, all children are adopted and have a family in their life when parental rights are terminated. Unfortunately, not all children are adopted, even though parents' rights have been terminated. For those children who are of age, independent-living programs are an alternative option. However, a review of the various independent-living programs across the country suggests that home visits are not part of the services offered to youth who are participating in independent-living programs (Lemon, Hines, and Merdiner 2005). In some circumstances, parental rights are not terminated and children are raised by family members who may or may not be their legal guardians. Children in independent living, adoptive families, or being raised informally by family members could benefit from home-based services.

Underlying the struggles of family-preservation programs are a number of competing—if not retaliatory—ideologies that have surfaced in national-policy discourse, changing the landscape for policy and practice. For example, questions were raised about access to concrete services provided by home-based programs. Queries surfaced over why housekeeper assistance and parent aides were provided to low-income families when middle-income families did not have such access. Such questioning reflects the traditional ambivalence held by many members of American society regarding the appropriateness of government intervention in responding to family poverty (Heclo 1997; Halpern 1991). These concerns and the historical ambivalence toward social services complemented the public backlash over placement prevention stemming from the horrific deaths of children as a result of child abuse. In fact, child fatalities as a result of maltreatment continue to be a grave public-policy concern. Examinations of these fatalities can influence state child welfare policy. Reports of child-fatality investigations can reveal that risk and safety assessments and the responses of child protective services and other systems were inadequate (Freundlich and Bocknek 2007).

As a result of these and many other forces, the policy pendulum swung from family preservation and placement prevention to "safety first" (Gelles

2001). Such safety goals, which superseded those of keeping the family intact, were complemented by permanency timelines, limiting the time for services for parents with children in foster care and accelerating adoption. Thus, in the last decade, the primacy of the home and family for intensive child welfare services has waned.

Evidentiary and Legal Monitoring

Despite the pendulum swings in public policy, best practices, if not evidence-based strategies, warrant home-based approaches. The standards of evidence in child abuse investigations are shaped by the requirement that verifiable and reliable information and evidence be marshaled from the first report of child abuse and neglect to final permanency decisions for the child (Stavis 1987). Moreover, requirements for timely and successive court decision making and monitoring of out-of-home placement and permanency decisions add to the evidentiary and legal requisites for practice. Thus, from an investigatory, evidentiary, and monitoring standpoint, if not also a service basis, home and family variables matter in practice. In addition, a home-based assessment may help discern who helps the parent or parents, such as a neighbor serving as the extended family, a friend, or a significant other who may function as a caregiver. Since many of the risk and safety factors involve family-related variables, the home becomes one of the most comprehensive lenses through which to observe and discern the family's related strengths and risk factors (Jenson and Fraser 2006). Such assessments and findings may require continuous monitoring, especially when children are removed from their home, as parents or other caregivers must demonstrate that the very risk and safety factors that led to the out-of-home placement have been addressed before children can return home. Explicit probes of home and family functioning to inform safety and risk assessments are essential to child welfare practice.

Theoretical Framework

Charlotte Towle's *Common Human Needs* (1987) advanced the principle that beginning at infancy all humans have the same basic biological, psychological, social, and spiritual developmental needs. This argument provides an overarching framework for child welfare. Within this framework, child welfare practitioners, especially those who provide home-based services, draw upon a range of child-development theories to guide their home-based practice. One key framework derives from attachment theory. Developed primarily by Bowlby and Ainsworth, attachment theory posits that children develop different styles of attachment based on their interactions with caregivers during infancy (Bretherton 1992).

Home-based assessments and services often use an ecological framework for assessment. This may include risk and safety assessments involving drug or other safety concerns. The ecological framework is informed by the work of Brofenbrenner (1977). He argued that it is necessary to study children in their natural settings while interacting with their families over time (see also chapter 5). Within the context of this ecological framework, the intensive family-preservation movement uses cognitive behavioral strategies drawn from learning theory (Pecora 1991).

Family-systems theories and resilience perspectives, as well as risk and protective-assessment models, also inform home-based child welfare services. These theories and models may be classified as either problem oriented or strengths based. Prevention services such as family-preservation practices may use more strengths-based approaches, while social workers who conduct child abuse investigations and provide home-based treatment may be more likely to draw upon problem- or risk-based theories and models. Family-systems theories inform family- centered practices in which individual problems and needs are reframed as family issues. In fact, the family as a whole is considered when addressing children's well-being. The resilience perspective is closely related to the strengths perspective. Rather than focusing on weaknesses and problems, the resilience perspective discerns those characteristics and strategies that children and parents may use to survive and even thrive, even when experiencing adverse experiences such as abuse and neglect (Werner and Smith 1989).

Home-based service providers also rely on crisis theory to advance new behaviors and interactions in the family. Crisis theory provides a framework for explaining why individuals with nonpathological conditions may be exhibiting pathological symptoms. During a crisis, families may be more likely to be open to new ways of viewing and addressing abusive interactions and related risk factors (Gilliland and James 1997).

In sum, there is no unified theory for practice involving home-based services in child welfare. There are promising frameworks and innovations that derive from a number of theoretical perspectives, creating hybrid service models.

Empirical Base

Family preservation and risk-assessment studies are the two main empirical foundations for home-based child welfare practice. Family-preservation programs seek to maintain the integrity of the family and risk assessment guides the investigation of cases of child abuse and neglect. However, there is little consensus among child welfare researchers and practitioners on what constitutes child abuse and neglect and little understanding of how caretakers who maltreat their children can change. Without an adequate understanding of child maltreatment as well as a reliable set of measures, both family-preservation and risk-assessment research may be inconsistent, making it difficult to compare findings across studies.

Defining Child Abuse

The issue of developing an operational definition of child abuse and neglect that is empirically based is an ongoing challenge for policymakers and practitioners alike, especially when seeking an evidentiary base for risk-assessment strategies and family-preservation models. To date, child welfare lacks a logically consistent, easily operationalized, and empirically valid and reliable definition and classification system for thinking about abuse and neglect. Without such definitions, it is difficult for the field to prescribe methods for achieving a desired outcome, such as preventing subsequent abuse, and to make recommendations to policymakers on how to reduce the occurrence of abuse and neglect (Feerick et al. 2006).

Risk Assessment

Currently, there is a lack of consensus on whether risk-assessment tools and family-preservation strategies are effective. One wonders how home-based services that are designed to prevent and identify maltreatment can measure effectiveness when there is an absence of consensus on the very phenomena such services are designed to prevent. Many studies rely on administrative data to determine the presence of maltreatment, making it difficult to compare outcomes across studies, since administrative definitions vary dramatically across jurisdictions (U.S. DHHS 2003).

In child welfare, risk assessment is the process by which child welfare workers inventory variables that help determine whether child neglect or abuse has occurred. However, there is disagreement on which model of risk assessment is most effective (Ryan et al. 2005). In the absence of consensus, some suggest that workers' professional judgment may be just as effective in assessing a child's risk for abuse or neglect as using a standardized measure of risk (Baumann et al. 2005). However, a subsequent review of the research by Baumann and colleagues suggests that the study lacked internal validity because of massive case attrition (Johnson 2006). Thus, there is no consensus on the benefits of standardized risk-assessment tools or on whether workers' judgment is as effective as standardized measures of risk.

In light of the difficulties demonstrating the effectiveness of these interventions, which relied heavily on some form of a risk-assessment model, some policymakers have now concluded that risk assessment is a flawed process and should be replaced by a continuum of empirically supported decision-making tools (Hughes and Rycus 2007). Moreover, the absence of treatment-fidelity and risk-assessment standards made it difficult to evaluate outcomes of these home-based interventions. Adding to replication barriers were the mixed results reported in outcome studies (Bath and Haapala 1993; Scheurman et al. 1994).

Family Preservation

Despite a renaissance of family-centered home-based systems in the late 1980s and 1990s, child welfare programs across the United States did not replicate the intensive Homebuilder protocols faithfully. Design and measurement problems caused setbacks for the growing family-centered home-based service movement. Selection problems for those served involved a lack of standardized criteria for children facing imminent risk of out-of-home placement. There were similar questionable selection and screening issues for the use of comparison groups.

Thus, while early family-preservation studies touted the benefits of home-based services to prevent out-of-home placements, more recent studies shed some doubt on family preservation's effectiveness. For example, programs designed to address concrete needs and programs using mentoring approaches were more effective than the parenting- and child development–oriented programming usually applied in home-based family preservation. Further, center-based services were more effective than home-based services (Chaffin, Bonner, and Hill 2001). On the other hand, in their analysis of Missouri's family-centered approach to out-of-home care, Lewandowski and Pierce (2004) found that family-centered services decreased the number of days children spent in out-of-home care when compared with traditional foster care services. The improved outcomes of this family-centered approach may in part be due to the fact that family social workers addressed families' concrete needs in addition to addressing the need for improved parenting skills.

More recent studies suggest that some components of family-preservation programs can be effective. Family-strengthening skills of family-preservation programs have demonstrated cost effectiveness (Washington State Institute of Public Policy 2006). The Teaching Family Model of therapeutic group-home programming, along with elements of family-preservation programs, helped families overcome serious child behavior and child management problems that may have led to an out-of-home placement (Lewis 2005). Further, family-preservation services may be more effective under certain conditions and when specific factors are included in the intervention. Specifically, a meta-analysis of fifty-six programs (MacLeod and Nelson 2005) found that family-preservation programs with high levels of participant involvement, an empowerment/ strengths-based approach, and a component of social support had higher effect sizes than programs without these elements. The lowest effect sizes were for programs with twelve or fewer visits and durations of fewer than six months.

In addition to program components, organizational context can influence permanency outcomes. In one study of 3,883 children and thirteen networks of organizations, out-of-home placement was largely explained by variations in workers' perceptions of their work as routine, strong leadership qualities, and supervisor and co-worker support (Yoo and Brooks 2005). Innovative approaches in home-based services that would increase interagency coordination could also serve to improve desired outcomes (Nelson 2001).

Practice Guidelines

Practice Principles

As discussed previously, the purpose of the home visit in child welfare practice varies, depending on where the particular service lies on the continuum of child welfare services. As a result, families may be more receptive to home-based service providers who offer preventive and supportive services than to home-based service providers who are conducting an investigation. Practices that are adversarial, such as child protective services, often run counter to the philosophy of family-centered home-based services. Families often experience accusatory and adversarial investigative practices as hurtful and counterproductive. Both workers and families are aware that part of the reason for the visit is to gather the evidence needed to verify that maltreatment has oc-curred and that children's safety may be at risk. When cases go to court, evidence is essential for making the case that children should be removed and become wards of the state. The same is the case for foster care services. When children are placed out of the home, the caseworker is required to visit and monitor the foster home a least once a month and assess and address the well-being of the children in the context of the foster family and their new home environment. Thus, foster parents may view some caseworker visits to their homes as investigatory and as surveillance oriented rather than supportive.

Home-based family-preservation services are both programmatically innovative and philosophically different from child protective and inves-tigatory practices. For example, family-preservation workers may employ a family-centered approach, where the client may be seen as not just the child but the family. There may be a "whatever it takes" attitude to help the family parse out the problems, identify solutions, and build on sequential successes using behavioral principles. Because of such philo-sophical and skills differences between family-centered home-based ser-vices and traditional child-protection services, some programs pair fam-ily-centered home-based workers with child-protection staff to conduct joint investigations.

There is some evidence to suggest that the principles used in family-preservation services may improve outcomes across the continuum of child welfare services. Practice principles shared by home-based child welfare ser-vices include strengths-based strategies, interventions to break problems down into manageable components, intensive services, concrete resources, culturally competent practice, and service integration.

STRENGTHS-BASED

The strengths perspective seeks to mobilize clients' strengths, including their talents, knowledge, capacities, and resources, so that they may achieve their goals and visions (Rapp 1998). Home-based family-preservation strategies in child welfare largely rely on a strengths-based approach. The home is both a forum for providing service and for observing key strengths and risk and safety issues as part of the assessment process (Graybeal 2001). Thus, though assessment is an ongoing process, the goal of home-based services includes the framing and reframing of risk factors such as negative interaction patterns in goal-oriented and solution-based terms. Eliciting ideas from the family as to how they would like things to be different helps move from a problem to a solution and a focus on goals. This reduces the focus on deficits and enables family members to envision and make commitments toward achieving interim behavioral steps and working toward more desirable outcomes. Ecological assessment and interventions include the home, housing, and neighborhood environment; safety issues; and parental capacities, including supervision of children and the provision of appropriate boundaries.

BREAKING PROBLEMS DOWN

Many public-sector families have experienced helping systems as less than family friendly and often fraught with barriers and hurtful practices. To reduce the sense of what social work forbearers once called "learned helplessness," behavioral and task-centered strategies are employed. These are manageable and help move family members toward a sense of accomplishment. Thus, for example, negative interactions might be reduced from 80 to 40 percent, and a series of replacement strategies are used for what might have been problematic exchanges escalating into explosive episodes. Parent-training skills are part of the repertoire of home-based service practitioners.

INTENSIVE SERVICES

Workers have low caseloads (between two to ten cases) and can be easily accessed in a crisis (some may be available twenty-four hours a day). Interaction time with families during each week may vary, but frequent visits foster ongoing developmental improvements. Services address the family as a whole as well as the needs of individual family members, especially the child or youth at risk of placement or who has been reunified (Bath and Haapala 1993).

CONCRETE RESOURCES

Workers can help families meet some of their concrete resource needs with flexible funds. Framing needs as resource deficits may help families cope with a sense of embarrassment and anxiety over their situation (Missouri Department of Family Services 2002). Addressing families' concrete needs may be critical to their provider functions and to child safety. For example, funds may be used for a new front door in a drug-infested neighborhood or to fix the car so a single parent can go to work. Addressing concrete needs also helps families test whether their priorities will be honored by the worker. Once concrete needs are addressed, families are more likely to be open and willing to work on behavior-change issues.

CULTURAL COMPETENCE

Families have norms and bring a reservoir of culturally conditioned strategies to their child rearing and parenting. Honoring ethnic and racial differences may be the key to whether the family will accept and use services. Ensuring culturally and racially congruent service strategies is a core feature of family-centered home-based services. The culturally competent family-centered practitioner may see cultural values as strengths and incorporate them into practice. For example, Fong (2001) noted that achievement and education are valued in Chinese culture. Thus, workers may take into account the fact that traditional Chinese families may be more responsive to interventions that are educational in nature.

SERVICE INTEGRATION

Many families are involved with other service sectors, such as domestic violence, TANF, mental health, disabilities, juvenile justice, and substance abuse (Lewandowski and Hill 2008). These service providers may not have family-centered philosophies and may see such practices as potentially harmful, such as in the case of domestic violence. Thus, home-based services also become the foundation for ensuring that more coherent and integrated services are provided. A lead convener mobilizes all service providers and arranges frequent team meetings and staffings, thus facilitating service integration. Child welfare workers may perceive such collaboration to be beneficial, especially when everyone, including family members, are involved in the team process (Lewandowski and GlenMaye 2002).

Models of Service Delivery

Several child welfare models currently used in home-based services are characterized by implementing one or more of these practice principles. These models are described below.

DUAL OR MULTITRACK SYSTEMS

Some of the philosophical differences and new service technologies that have emerged from home- and family-based service traditions in the past two decades may be helping fuel the rising number of differential response, dual, or multitrack systems. These involve systemwide reforms in public child welfare, mandating differential responses for low- and moderate-risk maltreatment cases. Such families are referred for services that target needs rather than being subjected to a formal investigation. To date, preliminary research suggests improved outcomes based on the differential response strategy (Schene and Kaplan 2007).

FAMILY GROUP CONFERENCING

Family Group Conferencing has emerged in the past decades as a promising strategy to advance family and extended family problem inventories and
solutions. Adapted from the Maori in New Zealand, this strategy relies on
family members and those who support them to convene and focus on solving an array of problems. These include placement prevention and reunification strategies, kinship-care plans for children who need to be removed
from their family, and adoption plans. These family group conferences with
the service providers have become a part of numerous public and nonprofit
child welfare agencies. They may be held in the family home or in a neutral
place selected by the family (Burford and Hudson 2000; Connolly 2006; Van
Wormer 2003).

FAMILY TEAM FACILITATION

Many families whose children are brought to the attention of the child welfare system are being served by multiple systems. This is because the conditions that lead to child abuse and neglect involve co-occurring risk factors
such as substance abuse, mental health challenges, poverty, domestic violence, disabilities, and educational problems. Different funding streams and
conflicting policies may impede the development of service plans that are
coherent and relevant to family needs. Furthermore, case plans may contra-
dict or not take into account those from other systems. Workers from these
service systems often do not communicate, coordinate, or collaborate. Family
Team Facilitation has been designed to enable and empower families. Families receive support as case-planning conferences are convened to sort out
integrative and effective case plans. Supported by Foundations such as the
Annie E. Casey Foundation, this Family Team Facilitation model has been
seen to lower the length of stay in out-of-home care (Iowa Department of
Human Services 2008).

FAMILY-TO-FAMILY

Family-to-family programs have also emerged with help and leadership from
the Annie E. Casey Foundation. Program components support neighborhood-
based services. For example, children who are placed out of their home are
provided with foster care in their family's neighborhood. This is seen to ensure more continuity in cultural, community, and school ties, thus avoiding
the ruptures that can harm the child's functioning. In this model, foster families may become reunification aides. Neighborhood foster-care systems may
help children and families with more rapid returns. Many high-need families may reside in the same zip code. Thus networks of services and foster

homes may make it possible for child welfare workers to be assigned caseloads by zip code. Such experiments have led to innovative use of neighbors as peer service providers, more effective child welfare services, and coherent community-based strategies (Apple et al. 2001; Berrick 2006; Chahine, Van Straaten, and Williams-Isom 2005; Van Wagoner et al. 2001).

Issues of Diversity and Practice with Populations at Risk

Given the high rates of poverty and marginalization faced by families served by the child welfare system, it is not surprising that disproportionate numbers of racial and ethnic minority children are in the child welfare system. For example, 60 percent of children in foster care are of color, even though children of color constitute fewer than half of all children nationally (Hill 2007). Such disproportionalities have been the center of intensive and growing service innovations and some policy changes at the state level. Hill (2007) and others have laid out the blueprint for improvements. However, poverty alone may not explain such differential rates of problematic practices and outcomes for children of color (Wulczyn et al. 2005). Research has shown that, even controlling for poverty, disproportionately higher rates of children of color are involved in the child welfare system (Merkel-Holguin, Kaplan, and Kwak 2006; Wulczyn et al. 2005).

An ecological framework may be especially helpful for home-based service providers during their assessment with racial and ethnic minorities, as it allows workers to take social, cultural, and environmental factors into account. For example, low birth weight among babies may be found among African American infants and may be caused by a number of factors, including neglect. However, there is emerging evidence that, in addition to physiological factors, disproportionate rates of low birth weight as well as infant mortality and preterm delivery among African American infants may result from group differences in exposure or susceptibility to prenatal stress, including stress related to racism and discrimination (Giscombe and Lobel 2005).

Child welfare workers should take ethnicity into account when recommending family-preservation services, as African American and Latino parents report more positive outcomes on children's academic adjustment and symptomatic behavior than Caucasian parents (Ayon and Lee 2005). Service enhancements are currently being tested as means for improving access and reducing disparities (Hill 2007). At least one model has been developed to better equip child welfare workers to assess the needs of immigrant and refugee families (Pine and Drachman 2005). Using a multistage framework, child welfare personnel can better understand families' immigration and re-settlement experience, allowing for more effective prevention, protection, per-manency, and family-preservation services.

Differential response multi- or dual-track systems are also particularly rel-evant for child welfare practice with families of color and at risk. Peer-based services, employment, and income and educational ladders for parents may help move some out of economic marginalization and complement service-enhancement strategies. The use of natural helpers with jobs and career lad-ders has been fostered in numerous settings. Apple et al. (2001) found that half of services provided by professionals could be provided by natural help-ers. To this end, it is possible to envision some of the barriers to service being mediated—if not addressed—by peers.

Poverty and Child Welfare

Over the decades, the crises engulfing some families have been differentially driven by poverty and economic insecurity. Poverty, unemployment, and un-deremployment lead to a wide range of consequences, including increased risks for child abuse and neglect, depression, foster care placements, school failure and dropout problems, and juvenile crime (Briar 1988).

Home-based and family-centered services may be one of the most effec-tive methods of engaging marginalized, impoverished, and thus high-risk families. Services alone may not be sufficient, however. Poor families of-ten require concrete services to meet basic needs and as engagement and trust-building tools. Earlier models of Aid for Dependent Children (AFDC) provided special-needs grants for families. In more recent years, family-preservation services have often included flexible funds for families. This has been a core facet of home-based service strategies. In fact, for decades AFDC was to serve as the family-preservation policy for the nation by ensuring that families had subsistence funds enabling them to stay together. Innovative approaches have emerged in recent decades in a few sites in which AFDC and later Temporary Assistance for Needy Families have served as the family-preservation arm of the child welfare system. Such innovations are exempli-fied in Colorado Springs, Colorado, where TANF is becoming transformed into the child welfare system and child welfare is becoming more like an antipoverty system (Berns 2001). United by family-centered principles and practices in both TANF and child welfare, family risk factors are addressed in TANF to reduce entry into the child welfare system (Berns 2001). This work underscores the importance of income and related resources as core facets of support for family functioning and well-being (Fraser, Pecora, and Haapala 1991). Such resource-related strategies reinforce the centrality of combining economic supports with services.

Implications for Home-Based Practice

Home-based services are not mandated by federal law for families with children with abuse and neglect risk factors. Moreover, policy mandates at the federal level are less legislated than might be expected. Further, families who receive home-based services and the social workers who provide such services are affected by multiple, overlapping policies. With a few exceptions, intensive home-based services programs no longer "drive" child welfare practice.

Just as teaming has emerged as a strategy to infuse child protective services with family-preservation workers and skills, so may the principles of family-centered and home-based services require more infusion across the continuum of child welfare. For too long, the technology of intensive home-based services has been practiced at the front end of the system in placement prevention or, now, in alternative response systems. Rising numbers of children and youth are not being returned home. Some children are eventually adopted; others are launched to raise themselves without the support of any family, through independent living. Moreover, many foster homes disrupt, leaving child and youth feeling even more disconnected, unattached, self-blaming, and potentially self-destructive. The same technology of home-based family-centered practice might be more systematically applied across the continuum of services. For example, many of the same family-centered principles used with biological families can be applied to a foster home. The child and foster parent could be aided with the same home-based, family-centered service technologies that address interactions and related improvements in intensive and frequent sessions of remediation. In the same vein, reunification often fails because the risk factors that led to out-of-home placement persist. Thus, intensive reunification services that are home-based and family-centered might be more systematically applied.

Service limits of fifteen months for parents, as required by ASFA, may be insufficient to address poverty, substance abuse, mental health, and related problems. Thus ASFA is expediting the termination of parental rights and leading to accelerated adoption rates. Adoption dissolution may also be a consequence. Intensive home-based family-preservation services could reduce potential dissolutions by supporting adoptive parents. Family preservation could be provided as an entitlement across the continuum of services from placement prevention to adoption preservation. The growing focus on disparities in service access and racial disproportionalities among children who remain in care and the recognition that service access is one main barrier facing families of color might help usher in an overhaul of the system. If so, the provision of intensive home-based and family-centered services to families of color might in fact become the overriding framework to transform the entire system.

REFERENCES

Anderson, G. R. 2002. Formal and informal kinship care: Supporting the whole family. In *Balancing family-centered services and child well-being: Exploring issues in policy, practice, theory, and research*, ed. E. Walton, P. Sandau-Beckler, and M. Mannes. New York: Columbia University Press.

Apple, K., Nernstein, S., Fogg, K., Fogg, L., Haapala, D., Johnson, E., et al. 2001. Walking our talk in the neighborhoods: Going beyond lip service in service delivery improvement. In *Balancing family-centered services and child well-being: Exploring issues in policy, practice, theory, and research*, ed. E. Walton, P. Sandau-Beckler, and M. Mannes, 252–285. New York: Columbia University Press.

Ayon, C., and Lee, C. D. 2005. A comparative analysis of child welfare services through the eyes of African American, Caucasian, and Latino Parents. *Research on Social Work Practice* 15 (4): 257–266.

Bartholet, E. 1999. *ASFA: Filled with loopholes and exceptions.* Available online at http://www.pbs.org/wgbh/pages/frontline/shows/fostercare/inside/bartholet.html.

Bath, H. I., and Haapala, D. A. 1993. Intensive family preservation services with abused and neglected children: An examination of group differences. *Child Abuse and Neglect* 17 (2): 213–225.

Baumann, D. J., Law, J. R., Sheets, J., Reid, G., and Graham, J. C. 2005. Evaluating the effectiveness of actuarial risk assessment models. *Children and Youth Services Review* 27 (5): 465–490.

Berebitsky, J. 2000. *Like our very own. Adoption and the changing culture of motherhood, 1851–1950.* Lawrence: University Press of Kansas.

Berns, D. A. 2001. Addressing poverty issues in child welfare: Effective use of TANF as a prevention resource. In *Innovative practices with vulnerable children and families*, ed. A. L. Sallee, H. A. Lawson, and K. Briar-Lawson, 33–51. Dubuque, Iowa: Eddie Bowers Publishing.

Berrick, J. D. 2006. Neighborhood-based foster care: A critical examination of location-based placement criteria. *Social Service Review* 80 (4): 569–583.

Berrick, J. D., Barth, R. P., and Needell, B. 1994. A comparison of kinship foster homes and foster family homes: Implications for kinship foster care as family preservation. *Children and Youth Services Review* 16 (1/2): 33–63.

Birt, C. J. 1956. Family-centered project of St. Paul. *Social Work* 2 (October): 41–47.

Borduin, C. 1994. Innovative models of treatment and service delivery in the juvenile justice system. *Journal of Clinical Child Psychology* 23 (December): 19–25.

Bretherton, I. 1992. The origins of attachment theory: John Bowlby and Mary Ainsworth. *Developmental Psychology* 28: 759–775.

Briar, K. 1988. *Social work with the unemployed.* Silver Springs, Md.: National Association of Social Work.

Brofenbrenner, U. 1977. *Toward an ecology of human development.* Cambridge, Mass.: Harvard University Press.

Bronstein, L. R. 1996. Intervening with homeless youths: Direct practice without blaming the victim. *Child and Adolescent Social Work Journal* 13 (20): 127–138.

Burford, G., and Hudson, J. 2000. *Family group conferencing: New directions in community centered child and family practice.* New York: Walter de Gruyter.

Chaffin, M., Bonner, B. L., and Hill, R. F. 2001. Family preservation and family support programs: Child maltreatment outcomes across client risk levels and program types. *Child Abuse and Neglect* 25: 1269–1289.

Chahine, Z., Van Straaten, J., and Williams-Isom, A. 2005. The New York City neighborhood-based services strategy. *Child Welfare* 84 (2): 141–152.

Clausen, J. M., Landsverk, J., Ganger, W., Chadwick, D., and Litrownik, A. 1998. Mental health problems of children in foster care. *Journal of Child and Family Studies* 7 (3): 283–296.

Connolly, M. 2006. Fifteen years of Family Group Conferencing: Coordinators talk about their experiences in Aotearca, New Zealand. *The British Journal of Social Work* 36 (4): 523–540.

Cuddeback, G. S. 2004. Kinship foster care: A methodological and substantive synthesis of research. *Children and Youth Services Review* 26 (7): 623–639.

Dumbrill, G. C. 2006. Parental experience of child protection intervention: A qualitative study. *Child Abuse and Neglect* 30 (1): 27–37.

English, D. J., Edleson, J. L., and Herrick, M. E. 2005. Domestic violence in one state's child protective caseload: A study of differential case dispositions and outcomes. *Children and Youth Services Review* 27 (11): 1183–1201.

Feerick, M. M., Knutson, J. F., Trickett, P. K., and Flanzer, S. M., eds. 2006. *Child abuse and neglect: Definitions, classifications, and a framework for research.* Baltimore: Paul H. Brookes Publishing Co.

Festinger, T. 2002. After adoption: Dissolution or permanence? *Child Welfare* 81 (3): 515–533.

Fong, R. 2001. Cultural competency in providing family-centered services. In *Balancing family-centered services and child well-being: Exploring issues in policy, practice, theory, and research*, ed. E. Walton, P. Sandau-Beckler, and M. Mannes, 55–68. New York: Columbia University Press.

Fraser, M. W., Nelson, K. E., and Rivard, J. C. 1997. Effectiveness of family preservation services. *Social Work Research* 21 (3): 138–153.

Fraser, M. W., Pecora, P. J., and Haapala, D. A. 1991. Family preservation services to prevent out-of-home placement: The family-based intensive treatment project. In *Families in crisis*, ed. M. Fraser, P. Pecora, and D. Haapala, 1–16. New York: Walter de Gruyter.

Freundlich, M., and Bocknek, E. L. 2007. Child fatalities in New York City: An assessment of child protective service practice. *Families in Society* 88 (4): 583–594.

Gelles, R. 2001. Family preservation and reunification: How effective a social policy? In *Handbook of youth and justice*, ed. S. O. White, 367–376. Dordrecht, Netherlands: Kluwer Academic Publishers.

Gilliland, B. E., and James, R. K. 1997. *Crisis intervention strategies*. 3rd ed. New York: Brooks/Cole.

Giscombe, C. L., and Lobel, M. 2005. Explaining disproportionately high rates of adverse birth outcomes among African Americans: The impact of stress, racism, and related factors in pregnancy. *Psychological Bulletin* 131 (5): 662–683.

Graybeal, C. 2001. Strengths-based social work assessment: Transforming the dominant paradigm. *Families in Society* 82 (3): 233–242.

Halpern, R. 1991. Supportive services for families in poverty: Dilemmas of reform. *Social Service Review* 65 (3): 343–364.

Heclo, H. H. 1997. Values underpinning poverty programs for children. *The Future of Children* 7 (2): 141–148.

Hegar, R. L. 1999. The cultural roots of kinship care. In *Kinship foster care: Policy, practice, and research*, ed. R. L. Hegar and M. Scannapieco, 17–28. New York: Oxford University Press.

Helfer, R. E., Kempe, R. S., and Krugman, R. D. 1997. *The battered child*. 5th ed. Chicago: University of Chicago Press.

Hill, R. B. 2007. *Disproportionality of minorities in child welfare: Synthesis of research findings*. Race Matters Consortium. Available online at http://www.casey.org/resources/publications/disproportionalityResearch.htm.

Horejsi, C. R. 1981. The St. Paul family-centered project revisited: Exploring an old gold mine. In *Treating families in the home: An alternative to placement*, ed. M. Bryce and J. C. Lloyd, 12–23. Springfield, Ill.: Charles C. Thomas Publisher.

Hughes, R. C., and Rycus, J. S. 2007. Issues in risk assessment in child protective services. *Journal of Public Child Welfare* 1 (1): 85–116.

Iowa Department of Human Services. 2008. *Community partnerships for protecting children: Family team decision-making*. Available online at http://www.dhs.iowa. gov/cppc/family_team/index.html.

Jensen, J. M., and Fraser, M. W. 2006. *Social policy for children and families*. Thousand Oaks, Calif.: Sage.

Johnson, W. 2006. Post-battle skirmish in the risk assessment wars: Rebuttal to the response of Baumann and colleagues to criticism of their paper, "Evaluating the effectiveness of actuarial risk assessment models." *Children and Youth Services Review* 28 (9): 1124–1132.

Kinney, J., and Dittmar, K. 1995. Homebuilders: Helping families help themselves. In *Home-based services for troubled children*, ed. I. M. Schwartz and P. Auclaire, 29–54. Lincoln: University of Nebraska Press.

Kohl, P. L., Barth, R. P., Hazen, A. L., and Landsverk, J. L. 2005. Child welfare as a gateway to domestic violence services. *Children and Youth Services Review* 27: 1203–1221.

Langley, P. A. 1991. The coming of age of family policy. *Families in Society* 72 (2): 116–120.

Lemon, K., Hines, A. M., and Merdinger, J. 2005. From foster care to young adulthood: The role of independent living programs in supporting successful transitions. *Children and Youth Services Review* 27: 251–270.

Lewandowski, C. A., and GlenMaye, L. F. 2002. Teams in child welfare: Interprofessional and collaborative processes. *Families in Society* 83 (3): 245–256.

Lewandowski, C. A., and Hill, T. J. 2008. The impact of foster care and Temporary Assistance to Needy Families (TANF) on women's drug recovery outcomes. *Children and Youth Services Review* 30: 942–954.

Lewandowski, C. A., and Pierce, L. 2004. Does family-centered out-of-home care work? Differential exit rates for children in a family-centered project. *Social Work Research* 28 (3): 143–153.

Lewis, R. E. 2005. The effectiveness of Families First services: An experimental study. *Children and Youth Services Review* 27 (5): 499–509.

Lindsey, D. 1994. *The welfare of children: An inquiry into public effort on behalf of children*. New York: Oxford University Press.

Luongo, G. 2007. Re-thinking child welfare training models to achieve evidence-based practices. *Administration in Social Work* 31 (2): 87–96.

MacLeod, J., and Nelson, G. 2000. Programs for the promotion of family wellness and the prevention of child maltreatment: A meta-analytic review. *Child Abuse and Neglect* 24 (9): 1127–1149.

Maluccio, A. N., Pine, B. A., and Tracy, E. M. 2002. *Social work practice with families and children*. New York: Columbia University Press.

Maza, P. L. 1999. Recent data on the number of adoptions of foster children. *Adoption Quarterly* 3 (2): 71–81.

Merkel-Holguin, L., Kaplan, C., and Kwak, A. 2006. *National study on differential response in child welfare.* Washington, D.C.: American Humane Society and Child Welfare League of America.

National Family Preservation Network. 2008. *Family preservation.* Available online at http://www.nfpn.org/preservation/.

Nelson, K. E. 2001. Shaping the future of family-centered services: Competition or collaboration? In *Balancing family-centered services and child well-being: Exploring issues in policy, practice, theory, and research,* ed. E. Walton, P. Sandau-Beckler, and M. Mannes, 359–376. New York: Columbia University Press.

Pecora, P. J. 1991. Family-based and intensive family preservation services: a select literature review. In *Families in crisis,* ed. P. J. Pecora, 17–47. New York: Walter de Gruyter.

Pelton, L. H. 1989. *For reasons of poverty: A critical analysis of the public child welfare system in the United States.* New York: Praeger.

Pine, B. A., and Drachmann, D. 2005. Effective child welfare practice with immigrant and refugee children and their families. *Child Welfare* 84 (5): 537–562.

Rapp, C. 1998. *The strengths model.* New York: Oxford University Press.

Ryan, J. P., Marsh, J. C., Testa, M. F., and Louderman, R. 2006. Integrating substance abuse treatment and child welfare services: Findings from the Illinois alcohol and drug abuse waiver demonstration. *Social Work Research* 30 (2): 95–107.

Ryan, S., Wiles, D., Cash, S., and Siebert, C. 2005. Risk assessments: Empirically supported or value driven? *Children and Youth Services Review* 27 (2): 213–225.

Schene, P., and Kaplan, C. 2007. *Getting started with differential response: Fundamentals and first steps.* Paper presented at the Second National Conference on Differential Response, Long Beach, Calif., November.

Scheurman, J. R., Rzepnicki, T. L., and Littell, J. H. 1994. *Putting families first: An experiment in family preservation.* New York: Aldine de Gruyter.

Stavis, P. F. 1987. Standards of evidence in child abuse investigation. *Quality of Care Newsletter* 33. Available online at http://www.cqc.state.ny.us/counsels_corner/cc33.htm.

Texas State. 2008. Family code chapter 261: Investigation of report of child abuse or neglect. Available online at http://tlo2.tlc.state.tx.us/statutes/docs/FA/content/htm/fa.005.00.000261.00.htm.

Towle, C. 1987. *Common human needs.* Washington, D.C.: NASW Press.

U.S. DHHS. 2003. *National study of child protective services systems and reform efforts: Findings on local CPS practice.* Washington, D.C.: U.S. Government Printing Office.

———. 2004. *Findings from the initial child and family service reviews, 2001–2004*. Available online at http://www.acf.hhs.gov/programs/cb/cwmonitoring/results/sld005.htm.

———. 2005. Foster Care: Numbers and Trends. Available online at http://www.childwelfare.gov/pubs/factsheets/foster.cfm.

———. 2006. *The AFCARS Report: Preliminary FY 2005 Estimates as of September 2006*. Available online at http://www.acf.hhs.gov/programs/cb/stats_research/afcars/tar/report13.htm.

———. 2007. Trends in foster care and adoption: FY 2000–FY 2005. Available online at http://www.acf.hhs.gov/programs/ch/stats_research/afcars/trends.htm.

———. 2008. *Child Maltreatment 2006*. Washington, D.C.: U.S. Government Printing Office. Available online at http:www.acf.hhs.gov/programs/ch/stats_research/index.htm#can.

Van Wagoner, P., Boyer, R., Wiesen, M., Hinton, D., and Lawson, H. 2001. Introducing child welfare neighborhood teams that promote collaboration and community-based systems of care. In *Innovative practices with vulnerable children and families*, ed. A. Sallee, H. Lawson, and K. Briar-Lawson, 323–360. Dubuque, Iowa: Eddie Bowers Publishers.

Van Wormer, K. 2003. Restorative justice's model for social work practice with families. *Families in Society* 84 (3): 441–448.

Washington State Institute of Public Policy. 2006. Intensive family preservation programs: Program fidelity influences effectiveness (revised). Available online at http://www.wsipp.wa.gov/rptfiles/06-02-3901.pdf.

Werner, E., and R. Smith. 1989. *Vulnerable but invincible: A longitudinal study of resilient children and youth*. New York: Adams, Bannister, and Cox.

Wulczyn, F., Barth, R. P., Yuan,Y., Harden, B. J., and Landsverk, J. 2005. *Beyond common sense: Child welfare, child well-being, and the evidence for policy reform*. New Brunswick, Canada: Aldine Transaction.

Yoo, J., and Brooks, D. 2005. The role of organizational variables in predicting service effectiveness: An analysis of a multilevel model. *Research on Social Work Practice* 15 (4): 267–277.

Yuan, Y-Y T., and Struckman-Johnson, D. L. 1991. Placement outcomes for neglected children with prior placements in family preservation services. In *Family preservation services: Research and evaluation*, ed. K. Wells and D. E. Biegel, 92–105. New York: Sage.

Eight

Child Mental Health

MARY ARMSTRONG, ROGER BOOTHROYD, MARY E. EVANS,

AND ANNE KUPPINGER

Child mental health agencies employ social workers in various roles in the provision of home-based services to reach at-risk children and prevent hospitalization. This chapter considers the special issues of working in home- and community-based settings with children with mental health challenges and their family members, includes a brief review of the evidence base for children's mental health home-based services, and highlights social workers' roles and tasks and the effect these services have on the well-being of children with serious emotional problems and their families.

The Population

Meeting the mental health treatment needs of children and youth is a serious and growing public health concern. The Surgeon General's report on mental health described a number of risk factors that influence childhood mental health, including biological factors such as intrauterine exposure to alcohol and perinatal trauma and psychosocial risk factors including maltreatment, parental depression, and traumatic life events (U.S. Department of Health and Human Services 1999). This report estimates that over the course of a year, one out of every five children and adolescents experiences a mental health disorder and that 11 percent of children and youth experience significant functional impairments related to a mental health disorder.

A recent review of the literature (Louis de la Parte Florida Mental Health Institute 2006) highlights the substantial variations in the estimated prevalence rates of mental illness in children and adolescents. This variability is largely attributed to the age of the children studied and the method used to determine the presence of mental illness. Given the considerable discrepancy among studies associated with children's ages, lower- and upper-range estimates are presented for each age group. Prevalence rates and number of children and youth likely affected by any mental health disorder are presented in table 1.

The lower-prevalence estimate for children ages birth to four was generated by a review of studies involving ten samples of preschool children (Roberts, Attkisson, and Rosenblatt 1998). These studies varied in their sample size and methodological rigor. The upper prevalence estimate (21.4 percent) is based on a study of nearly four thousand ethnically diverse Chicago children ages two to four years (Lavigne et al. 1996). The prevalence estimates for children ages five to seventeen years are from two multisite studies of children and adolescents (Costello, Keeler, and Angold 2001; Shaffer et al. 1996) and two comprehensive reviews of prevalence studies involving children and adolescents (Costello et al. 2004; Roberts et al. 1998). The estimates are also consistent with rates from a community epidemiological study of Canadian youth ages fourteen to seventeen years (Romano et al. 2001). The prevalence estimates for young adults are based on analyses of subsamples of adults from the National Comorbidity Study (Friedman et al. 1996; Kessler et al. 1994) and data from representative national epidemiological studies carried out in other Westernized countries (Ferdinand et al. 1995; Newman et al. 1996).

TABLE 8.1

Range of Prevalence Estimates of Mental Health Disorders
for Children and Youth by Age

AGE (YEARS)	LOWER	UPPER
0–4	10.2%	21.4%
5–17	20.9%	25.0%
18–21	25.0%	37.0%

Source: Louis de la Parte Florida Mental Health Institute (2006)

The prevalence rates for young adults are higher than both previous estimates and those for younger children. As the prevalence estimates for all age groups indicate, attention must be focused on the services and supports that will respond to the needs of children with mental health problems and their families. For the past twenty years, the construct of systems of care has provided a framework for addressing the needs of these children and their families (Armstrong, Stroul, and Boothroyd 2005).

Policy and Agency Context

In 1982, a seminal study, *Unclaimed Children* (Knitzer 1982) found that two-thirds of all children with serious emotional problems were not receiving appropriate services and that there was little coordination among child-serving systems. To begin to address this need, Congress appropriated funds in 1984 for the Child and Adolescent Service System Program (CASSP), to assist states to develop comprehensive mental health systems of care for children, adolescents, and their families (Burns et al. 1995; Friedman and Kutash 1992). "System of care" was more fully defined and described as part of the CASSP initiative (Stroul and Friedman 1986). In a system of care, mental health, health, education, child welfare, juvenile justice, communities, and families work together to ensure that children with significant emotional and behavioral challenges and their families have access to the services and supports they need to succeed. These services and supports may include diagnostic and evaluation services, outpatient treatment, emergency services, case management, intensive home-based services, day treatment, respite care, therapeutic foster care, and services that will help young people make the transition to adulthood, including adult systems of care, if necessary.

As shown in the box, three core values and ten principles were articulated and guided the development of children's mental health systems of care.

As a "next step" toward operationalizing this philosophy, in 1992 the U.S. Congress established the Comprehensive Community Mental Health Services Program for Children and Their Families (Community Mental Health and Substance Abuse Services Improvement Act of 1992, U.S. Public Law 102-321 [October 1, 1992]). This program is administered by the Child, Adolescent, and Family Branch of the Center for Mental Health Services, Substance Abuse, and Mental Health Services Administration, U.S. Department of Health and Human Services. Since its inception, the program has provided over $1.16 billion to 126 grantees in fifty states, two territories, and the

VALUES AND PRINCIPLES OF A SYSTEM OF CARE

Core Values

(1) A system of care should be child centered and family focused, with the needs of the child/youth and family dictating the types and mix of services provided.

(2) A system of care should be community based, with the locus of services and management and decision-making responsibility resting at the community level.

(3) A system of care should be culturally competent, with agencies, programs, and services responsive to the cultural, racial, and ethnic differences of the populations they serve.

Guiding Principles

(1) Children/youth with emotional disturbances should have access to a comprehensive array of services that address their physical, emotional, social, and educational needs.

(2) Children/youth with emotional disturbances should receive individualized services in accordance with the unique needs and potentials of each child/youth and guided by an individualized service plan.

(3) Children/youth with emotional disturbances should receive services within the least restrictive, most normative environment that is clinically appropriate.

(4) The families and surrogate families of children/youth with emotional disturbances should be full participants in all aspects of the planning and delivery of services.

(5) Children/youth with emotional disturbances should receive services that are integrated, with linkages between child-serving agencies and programs and mechanisms for planning, developing, and coordinating services.

(6) Children/youth with emotional disturbances should be provided with case management or similar mechanisms to ensure that multiple services are delivered in a coordinated and therapeutic manner and that they can move through the system of services in accordance with their changing needs.

(7) Early identification and intervention for children/youth with emotional disturbances should be promoted by a system of care in order to enhance the likelihood of positive outcomes.

(8) Children/youth with emotional disturbances should be ensured smooth transitions to the adult service system as they reach maturity.

continued

VALUES AND PRINCIPLES OF A SYSTEM OF CARE (*continued*)

Guiding Principles

(9) The rights of children/youth with emotional disturbances should be protected, and effective advocacy efforts for children and adolescents with emotional disturbances should be promoted.

(10) Children/youth with emotional disturbances should receive services without regard to race, religion, national origin, sex, physical disability, or other characteristics, and services should be sensitive and responsive to cultural differences and special needs.

Reprinted with permission from Stroul and Friedman (1986, 17)

District of Columbia for the development of local comprehensive, coordinated, community-based, and culturally competent systems. The findings from a comprehensive evaluation (ORC Macro 2007) suggest that children, youth, and families enrolled in systems of care have reduced emotional and behavioral problems, arrests, suicide-related behaviors, school suspensions, and residential mobility compared to youth from matched non–system of care communities. Gains were also noted in family economic status, school attendance, and school performance.

Purpose and Goals of Social Work Home-Based Services

The goal of home-based services is to enable children with serious mental health problems to function in an age-appropriate manner in home, school, and community settings. One rationale for home-based rather than office-based services is that age-appropriate youth behaviors, parental skill development, and problem-resolution strategies can be addressed more effectively in the settings where these problems occur—the home and school. Stroul (1988) identified three major goals of home-based services: to preserve the family's integrity and prevent unnecessary out-of-home placements; to put adolescents and their families in touch with community agencies and individuals, thus creating an outside support system; and to strengthen the family's coping skills and capacity to function effectively in the community after crisis treatment is completed. The premise of home-based services is that outcomes would be improved by supporting and empowering families, minimizing the barriers to seeking help, and making interventions relevant to families' lives (Friesen and Koroloff 1990; McGowan 1990). The ability to tailor home-based services to the specific needs of each family is consistent with "wraparound," the preferred process for developing and monitoring strength-based, comprehensive, individualized plans of care for each child and family (Bruns et al. 2005; Walker et al. 2004; Walker and Bruns, 2006). Wraparound has been described as a planning process that results in a unique set of community services and natural supports individualized for a child and family for the purpose of achieving positive outcomes (Burns and Goldman 1999). Wraparound has a number of essential elements, including a team-driven process involving the family, child, natural supports, agencies, and community services working together to develop, implement, and evaluate an individualized service plan (Goldman 1999). (See also chapter 4.)

Intensive in-home supports for children and youth who might otherwise need restrictive placements include many types of services, such as family support and advocacy; respite care; homemaker services; behavioral consultation; concrete services such as transportation or child care; parenting training and mentoring; in-home assessment; and various forms of clinical treatment (Stroul 1988). Working with children and families at home and in the community also provides opportunities to conduct more complete assessments, teach and practice relevant skills, discover the strengths of children and family members, and incorporate community and cultural resources into the plan of care.

These goals of home-based services in children's mental health are directly related to social work's focus on enhancing the social functioning of individuals. The International Federation of Social Workers' (2000) definition of social work points out that social work intervenes "at the point where people interact with their environment." The homes of children are indeed the point where they interact with their environment of family and peers.

Theoretical Framework

Prior to the 1980s, very few children's mental health services were delivered outside of clinical settings (Petr and Spano 1990). With sustained attention of CASSP to the development of a complete array of community-based services, new approaches were introduced, including services and supports delivered in the home. Many communities that reviewed the array of existing services, from inpatient and residential care on one end of the continuum to outpatient services on the other, concluded they had a need to develop the "middle" of the continuum—particularly the intensive, community-based responses that would serve as alternatives to residential placement or hospitalization. The rationale for creating intensive home-based services was based on both the system-of-care philosophy and on several key assumptions:

- That children are best served in their own homes and with their families;
- If children cannot remain at home with their families for either brief or in some cases longer time periods, they need other family-like settings;
- Children with serious emotional disorders need intensive treatment;
- Services provided in alternative settings can be more cost effective than inpatient and residential settings.

(Stroul and Goldman 1996, 453)

Concurrent with the development of systems of care and a more complete continuum of service options, there has been an evolution in thinking about the role of parents and families (broadly defined) in their child's treatment. Over time, there has been a shift toward "family-centered" and even "family-driven" care. Parents were once held at arms' length by providers and frequently blamed for their child's problems. Now parents are increasingly included in treatment planning, provided with psychoeducation to better understand and respond to their child's needs, empowered to be strong advocates, and valued for their unique expertise regarding their child and family. At a policy level, families are also "at the table," involved in system-level design and evaluation (Flynn 2005; Osher et al. 1999). Much of the advocacy for home-based support and treatment services came from family members who argued that this would be more convenient, more grounded in reality, and would support them in keeping their children at home.

Recently the system-of-care principle regarding parents as full partners in decision making has been further refined by the construct of family-driven care. The President's New Freedom Commission on Mental Health (2003) articulated six goals of a transformed mental health system. One goal was that mental health care should be consumer and family driven. The Federation of Families for Children's Mental Health (2007), a national family-run organization dedicated to improving the lives of children with mental health needs and their families, has developed a definition of family-driven care. "Family driven" means that caregivers have a primary decision-making role in the care of their own children. This includes choosing supports, services, and providers; setting treatment goals; designing and implementing programs; and monitoring outcomes. Another characteristic of family-driven care is that child and family team meetings and service provision should happen in the home and in other settings where family and youth voices are heard, respected, and valued.

The theoretical framework also includes the notion of home-based services as mediators of involvement. Hoagwood (2005) conducted a systematic review of forty-one experimental studies of family-based services in children's health and mental health, including home-based services. The review did not focus on treatment services but on services for families such as psycho-education, family support, adjunctive services; the role families play as co-therapists in service delivery; and the core processes of involvement (e.g., therapeutic alliance, engagement, empowerment, expectancies, and choice). One of the issues explored by Hoagwood was that of mediators of involvement, for example, the factors such as engagement and empowerment that affect a family's decision to seek care and complete treatment. Home-based services, by their nature, embody some of the characteristics of approaches that could foster engagement and empowerment. The fact that social workers come to the family's home, work in partnership with families to identify concerns and solutions, and teach specific skills and problem-solving techniques mirror some of the strategies that show promise for improving retention in services and transference of skills (Bickman et al. 1998; McKay et al. 1998).

Home-based services (both supportive services such as respite and family support and treatment interventions) may reduce the strain and isolation felt by many caregivers (Messer et al. 1997; Rauktis and Miller 2002). Hoagwood's (2005) findings support the notions that empowerment occurs when strain is reduced and that knowledge (psychoeducation) and skill building likely contribute to empowerment. Hoagwood posits that provider continuity, attitudes and beliefs toward mental health services, and an expectation that services will make a difference—rather than demographic and socioeconomic factors—are predictors of service access and retention. Home-based services also hold the potential to minimize the logistical barriers (transportation, child care, etc.) and power imbalance that prevent families from accessing and continuing to receive services (Kazdin, Holland, and Crowley 1997). Because of their intensity, skill-building focus, capacity to work with the whole family, and individualized response to family-identified needs, these models may also engender greater feelings of efficacy.

Empirical Base

There are a number of evidence-based models for in-home services for children with mental health challenges and their families. Some were developed specifically for this population; others were developed in child welfare or juvenile justice settings but have been shown to be effective with the child mental health population. This section discusses these models and the research that compares different approaches to home-based services in child mental health.

Multisystemic Therapy

At the present time, there is only one intervention listed in the National Registry of Evidence-Based Programs and Practices (NREPP 2007) that would be classified as a home-based mental health treatment intervention for children: Multisystemic Therapy (MST). It was developed as a service for juvenile offenders, but many children and adolescents involved in the court system also have serious mental health and behavioral disorders. MST has been the subject of numerous randomized trials. A number of independent replications have been conducted, some of which include children at high risk for residential care or hospitalization (Littell and Schuerman 1995). An early quasi-experimental study with inner-city juvenile offenders (Henggeler et al. 1986) suggested that MST was an effective intervention. A large randomized controlled trial that compared MST with usual services in the treatment of serious juvenile offenders found that youth receiving MST had significantly reduced rates of recidivism and out-of-home placement (Henggeler, Melton, and Smith 1992). Another randomized trial compared MST to individual therapy (Borduin et al. 1995) and found decreases in arrest rates, other criminal offenses, and substance-related offenses in recipients of MST as compared to those receiving individual therapy at a four-year follow-up.

Using a randomized controlled design, MST has also been compared to psychiatric hospitalization, with evidence that MST can serve as a safe, clinical, and cost-effective alternative to hospitalization (Schoenwald et al. 2000). The youth enrolled in MST experienced a significant reduction in hospitalization and out-of-home placements as compared to youth randomized to the hospitalization condition. However, Littell, Popa, and Forsythe's (2005, 25) systematic review of MST outcome research, which included a number of unpublished studies not included in previous reviews, concluded that "MST is not consistently more effective than other alternatives for youth with social, emotional, and behavioral problems." They point out that there are "still gaps in knowledge about the widespread implementation of MST, its long-term effects, and important mechanisms of change," as well as its cost effectiveness compared to alternative treatments.

Functional Family Therapy

Functional Family Therapy (FFT) is an outcome-driven prevention/interven-
tion program that provides community-based services for youth who have
demonstrated the entire range of maladaptive acting-out behaviors and related
syndromes. The target population is youth, ages eleven to eighteen, at risk for
and/or presenting with delinquency, violence, substance use, conduct disorder, oppositional defiant disorder, or disruptive behavior disorder. Often, these
youth present with additional co-morbid challenges, such as depression. FFT
is identified by Blueprints for Violence Prevention (2007) as a prevention and
intervention program that meets strict scientific standards of program effectiveness. Clinical trials have demonstrated that FFT is capable of effectively
treating adolescents with conduct disorder, oppositional defiant disorder, disruptive behavior disorder, alcohol and other drug-abuse disorders, and who are
delinquent and/or violent (Blueprints for Violence Prevention 2007; Alexander et al. 1998, 2000; Sexton and Alexander 1999).

Intensive Family-Preservation Services

Intensive Family-Preservation Services (IFPS), such as Homebuilders, first
used in the child welfare system, have been successfully adapted for use with
children experiencing psychiatric crisis (see chapter 7 for more discussion of
IFPS and Homebuilders). Although evaluation findings for different models
of IFPS have generally been mixed in terms of placement prevention, the
Homebuilders' model has been used successfully for children and youth at
risk of placement due to serious emotional and behavioral needs (Kinney and
Haapala 1984; Miller 2006). Homebuilders was singled out as a "particularly
effective family reunification program" in a 1999 report by the United States
Surgeon General, which noted that Homebuilders has helped 75 to 90 percent of participating children avoid placement (U.S. Department of Health
and Human Services 1999).

Treatment Foster Care

Another category of home-based services for youth at risk of hospitalization
or placement in residential treatment that originated in child welfare is treatment foster care (see chapter 7). There are many versions of treatment foster
care, all of which provide higher levels of support to the foster family based

on the risk/clinical need of the child. One evidence-based model, Multi-dimensional Treatment Foster Care (MTFC), targets teenagers with histories of chronic and severe criminal behavior at risk of incarceration and those with severe mental health problems at risk for psychiatric hospitalization (Blueprints for Violence Prevention 2007; Chamberlain, Leve, and DeGarmo 2007; Chamberlain and Mihalic 1998). Evaluations of MTFC have demonstrated that program youth compared to control group youth at a twelve-month follow-up spent 60 percent fewer days incarcerated, had significantly fewer subsequent arrests, showed improved school attendance, demonstrated less drug use, and were placed from more restrictive settings (e.g., hospital, detention) more quickly into less restrictive community settings.

In-Home Case Management Services

Evans and colleagues (Armstrong and Evans 1992; Evans et al. 1996) conducted a program evaluation of the Children and Youth Intensive Case Management model (CYICM) in New York State. This model was an intensive broker model stressing linkage to services and advocacy. Case managers carried caseloads of ten high-risk children and their families, were available around the clock, and had access to flexible funds. Using a regression-discontinuity design with a matched comparison group, the evaluators found that enrollment in CYICM led to decreased hospitalization and decreased high-risk behaviors (Evans et al. 1994).

Building on the basic CYICM model, Evans, Armstrong, and Kuppinger (1996) developed a family-centered intensive case management (FCICM) model that used a team consisting of a professional case manager and a parent advocate. This team provided in-home services including parent support, parenting instruction, and service coordination, with the goal of empowering caregivers to function as case managers for their child. As with CYICM, flexible funds were available to provide for individualized services and needs. Using a randomized controlled trial, children identified for out-of-home placement by an interagency team were randomly assigned to in-home treatment (i.e., FCICM) or to a treatment foster care program called Family-Based Treatment. The children enrolled in FCICM showed better clinical and functional outcomes at significantly lower cost than those children assigned to Family-Based Treatment (Evans et al. 1998). Unfortunately, neither group of families showed improvement in family functioning at an eighteen-month follow-up.

This research team also conducted a three-year research demonstration project in the Bronx, New York, that examined the efficacy of three models of intensive in-home services as alternatives to hospitalization for children experiencing serious psychiatric crises (Evans, Boothroyd, and Armstrong 1997). An overview of the three models is presented in table 2. The first model, Home-Based Crisis Intervention (HBCI), was based on the Homebuilder's model (Fraser, Pecora, and Haapala 1991; Kinney et al. 1977). The target population for the three models was families with a child or adolescent experiencing a psychiatric crisis so severe that absent intensive community-based services, he or she would be hospitalized (New York State Office of Mental Health 2007). The second model, Enhanced Home-Based Crisis Intervention (HBCI+), followed the HBCI model with additional staff training in cultural competence, technical assistance opportunities for staff in developing and implementing intervention strategies to deal with issues of community violence, and additional support services for families. This model included a bilingual, bicultural parent advocate who established a parent support group and provided individualized parent support and advocacy. In-home and out-of-home respite care were key support service components of HBCI+ and were available on both an emergency and planned basis for families served in the program (Boothroyd et al. 1998). The third model, Crisis Case Management (CCM), was an adaptation of New York State's existing Intensive Case Management Model (ICM). CCM was distinguished from HBCI and HBCI+ primarily by the larger size of caseloads. Each case manager served four families receiving regular, long-term ICM and four families receiving short-term CCM and thus had less time to spend with each family providing skills building and counseling services.

An analysis of counselors' and case managers' self-reports regarding the types of clinical and supportive services provided highlight some important differences between the models in the delivery of these in-home services. Since the reports of counselors in both the HBCI and HBCI+ programs were similar, those two models were combined and contrasted to those of the CCM case managers. The results are summarized in table 3. HBCI counselors reported being significantly more engaged in providing services represented in seven of the eight service domains compared to crisis case managers. The one exception was that case managers reported providing concrete services to a greater percentage of families compared to HBCI counselors. Transporting children and families was the primary function in this domain.

The three models compared in the Bronx study supported the capacity of intensive in-home services to assist families during times of crisis and support children to remain at home safely (Boothroyd et al. 1998, Evans et al. 2003). Overall, 86 percent of the children served in one of the three in-home models were successfully living in the community when discharged

TABLE 8.2

A Comparison of Home-Based Crisis Intervention (HBCI), Enhanced Home-Based Crisis Intervention (HBCI+), and Crisis Case Management (CCM)

PROGRAM ATTRIBUTE	HBCI	HBCI+	CCM
Target population	Children and youth living at home who are at risk of an inpatient admission due to psychiatric crisis	Children and youth living at home who are at risk of an inpatient admission due to psychiatric crisis	Children and youth living at home who are at risk of an inpatient admission due to psychiatric crisis
Program goal	Resolve immediate crisis, teach skills, improve family relationships, link to	Similar to HBCI, with the added goal of providing long-term family needed services	Assess needs, provide concrete services, link child and family to needed services support services
Program focus	The child within the context of their family	The child within the context of their family	The child within the context of their family
Caseload per worker	Two families in crisis	Two families in crisis	Four families in crisis, four families requiring "generic" case management services.[1]
Duration of service	Four to six weeks	Four to six weeks	Four to six weeks
Respite	No respite provided	In-home and out-of-home respite available	In-home and out-of-home respite available
Staff training	HBCI training	HBCI training plus training in cultural competence and working with violence in families	Intensive case management and crisis intervention training

(continued)

TABLE 8.2
A Comparison of Home-Based Crisis Intervention (HBCI), Enhanced Home-Based Crisis Intervention (HBCI+), and Crisis Case Management (CCM) (*continued*)

PROGRAM ATTRIBUTE	HBCI	HBCI+	CCM
TPostcrisis family support services	No postcrisis family support services provided	Services available through bilingual, bicultural parent advocate who will establish a parent support group and provide individual parent advocacy	No postcrisis family support services provided
Flexible service dollars	Some flexible service dollars available through nongrant sources	An average of $100 per family is available to meet individualized needs	An average of $150 per family is available to meet individualized needs
In-home visits and supports	Provided within twenty-four hours of intake and on a regular and frequent basis throughout the crisis period	Provided within twenty-four hours of intake and on a regular and frequent basis throughout the crisis period	Provided within twenty-four hours initially, and as needed thereafter
Psychiatric services	Psychiatrist available to provide assessment and treatment services within the home	Psychiatrist available to provide assessment and treatment services within the home	Psychiatrist consultation available to crisis case managers and to families for medication review
Funding	State resources only	State resources for HBCI components and grant funds for enhancements	State resources for case managers and in-home respite and grant funds for out-of-home respite

[1] Families receiving "generic" case management services are not part of this research project.

TABLE 8.3
Percentage of Cases in Which Counselors/Case Managers
Provided Specific Services

SERVICE DOMAIN	EXAMPLES OF SERVICES	CASE MANAGEMENT (n=60)	HOME-BASED CRISIS INTERVENTION (HBCI) (n=170)
Crisis management	24/7 on call, crisis plan development	7%	86%
Behavior management	Behavior rehearsal, crisis cards	33%	99%
Emotional regulation	Depression and anger management	27%	96%
Problem solving	Parent/adolescent dispute mediation	8%	56%
Therapy	Values clarification, family counseling	47%	99%
Teaching and training	Social skills; parenting skills	22%	86%
Concrete services	Transportation; housing assistance	77%	68%
Communication	Family skills development	22%	95%

from the intervention. Ten percent of the children in the two HBCI programs were hospitalized during the intervention, compared to 5 percent of the children who received CCM. However, children in CCM were somewhat more likely to be placed out-of-home (9 percent) compared to children who were assigned to HBCI programs (4 percent).

At discharge, enrollees in all three programs showed gains in family adaptability, children's self-confidence, parental self-efficacy, and children's social competence. Enrollees in HBCI and HBCI+ showed gains in family cohesion, while only those assigned to HBCI+ showed gains in social support. At the six-month follow-up, those who had been enrolled in all three interventions showed positive gains from baseline to follow-up in family adaptability, children's self-confidence, parental self-efficacy, and children's social competence. The gains in family cohesion noted at discharge from HBCI and HBCI+ had been lost as well as the gains in social support experienced by families receiving the HBCI+ intervention (Evans et al. 2003).

Evans and colleagues (2001) examined the outcomes of children with different clinical profiles who were served in these three in-home interventions and found that the outcomes were somewhat dependent on the clinical status of the children. For example, none of the interventions were effective in promoting improved self-concept among children with psychoses or with psychotic symptoms. Additionally, among children with adjustment disorders and suicidal tendencies, social-competency skills decreased over time. In contrast, improvements in social competence were observed among children with disruptive behaviors. This analysis was important because it highlighted the types of children for whom these in-home interventions had limited impact on outcomes and revealed the generalizable or consistent effects these programs had among children with varying clinical characteristics. Social workers referring children and families to in-home interventions need to understand the varying clinical needs of children and, depending upon these needs, may need to include supplemental services to achieve optimal outcomes.

Practice Guidelines

Although social work functions can be carried out by therapists, case managers, and others located in treatment settings, in this chapter we focus on social workers whose primary setting is the child's natural environments of home, school, and community. Working in these natural settings provides the social worker with important information that cannot be obtained in an office and is useful for conducting core social work functions. These functions can be described as assessment, service planning, service implementation, service coordination, monitoring and evaluation, and advocacy (Stroul 1995). These functions and the individuals providing in-home services may be known by different titles. The functions may be referred to as care coordination, clinical case management, care management, intensive case management, service coordination, or family-centered case management, among others. The individuals performing the functions may be called family partners, care coordinators, case or intensive case managers, therapists, family associates, or other titles. Case management may be carried out by an individual case manager, by a team often comprising a professional and parent advocate, or by an interdisciplinary team that may or may not include parent advocates.

It is appropriate to differentiate here between in-home services and intensive in-home services. Winters and Terrell (2003) describe intensity of case management as being influenced by caseload size, frequency of contacts, and direct clinical responsibilities. Caseload size does not result in intensity; rather, it is a planned element in the model that allows for the intensity of contact, which is usually a 24/7 model. Intensive in-home services are typically offered by masters-level social workers and is reserved for children and families with the most salient and challenging needs for services. This includes children at risk for restrictive services such as out-of-home placement or children being reintegrated into their communities following hospitalization or residential placement. There is no gold standard for caseload size, which is dependent on the target population, ecological context, and resources available. For children with serious emotional and behavioral challenges, suggested optimal caseloads may range between five and fifteen (Katz-Leavy et al. 1992). Evans and Armstrong (2002) describe intensive models for caseloads of eight to ten, though there can be caseloads as low as two families per case manager for children in psychiatric crisis and their families (Evans et al. 1997).

It is typical for a social worker to play many roles over the course of an in-home intervention. Practitioners providing home-based services will be best equipped if their training is broad, enabling them to draw flexibly upon an eclectic repertoire of strategies and formal and informal approaches to treatment. In-home worker competencies emphasize client engagement, goal setting, and risk assessment. The basic four-day Homebuilders training curriculum (2007), for example, begins with the following components:

- Strategies for keeping family members and themselves safe
- How to engage families in the change process
- How to motivate clients to change
- How to conduct a client-centered, ecological assessment
- How to develop behaviorally specific goals
- How to identify and teach skills that will help families achieve their goals
- How to evaluate progress toward goals
- Strategies for identifying and accessing ongoing supports and resources
- How to deal with termination issues

Two of the most critical areas of expertise required for intensive in-home services are those of risk assessment and risk management. When a case is first referred for services (perhaps from a psychiatric emergency room or mobile crisis team), in-home social workers typically conduct an assessment within the first twenty-four to forty-eight hours to determine whether or not the child or adolescent can remain at home safely. Ideally, this also involves an assessment of child and family strengths and protective factors that can serve as the basis for positive change. Steps are taken to make the child's environment as safe as possible, parents are instructed in how to enhance safety, and youth are often asked to enter into contracts regarding their behavior to reduce the risk of self-injury. Risk assessment is an ongoing process and one that is enhanced by frequent, expert supervision (Henggeler et al. 1999). As important as it is to "do whatever it takes" to help children remain at home, practitioners must be prepared to respond in a timely manner when hospitalization or other placement becomes necessary.

While a central goal of the intervention is to address the psychiatric crisis that precipitated the referral and reduce the symptoms that place the child at risk of placement, most in-home practitioners take a broad view of reducing risk. Many of the services and strategies do not fit a traditional "clinical" definition, although formal services are almost always a part of a child's treatment plan. Many in-home models utilize "flexible service dollars" (Dollard et al. 1992) to pay for nonbillable services (e.g., karate lessons, car repair, bus fare to a job training program, incentives that are part of behavioral modification plans, family celebrations) considered critical pieces of the treatment plan.

In addition to having children with emotional and behavioral disorders, many of these families deal with multiple and complex challenges such as domestic violence, poverty, substance abuse, and parents who also have mental health diagnoses (Woolston, Adnopoz, and Berkowitz 2007). In these special cases, progress addressing concerns that involve the child or adolescent may be impeded unless these other issues are dealt with as well. Thus treatment plans are broadened to encompass the special needs of other family members and address how these issues affect the child with SED. For example, Woolston and colleagues describe home-based work with a boy who father was diagnosed with schizophrenia. As the clinical team prepared to terminate their work with the family, both the father and the child decompensated. The child's progress could not be sustained until the clinical team helped the family structure appropriate ways for the father to contribute as a family member and appreciated the child's need for clear information about the father's situation. Lindblad-Goldberg, Dore, and Stern (1998) also present a number of case examples where the child or adolescent's presenting concerns are complicated by family dynamics and challenges. They conclude: "There are no 'quick fixes' or simple cures. By listening to the family's story and observing the minute-to-minute feedback in every transaction during sessions, a therapist begins to formulate hypotheses about the child's symptoms and the family's organization. Working in collaboration with the parent(s), a plan is developed for treatment intervention" (Lindblad-Goldberg et al. 1998, 184).

Because most intensive in-home services are time limited, one of the key roles played by in-home service practitioners is to assure that the child and family are linked to ongoing, long-term informal supports and formal services. In-home service providers are known to say that discharge planning begins at intake. This refers both to the need to make plans in advance to ensure a smooth transition and to the problem-focused, goal-oriented, capacity-building approach that characterizes most intensive in-home models.

Due to the intensity of this work and the high needs of the youth and families, in-home workers benefit from frequent opportunities to debrief and problem-solve with their peers and supervisors. Immediate family members and other relatives or friends involved in the child's life are often provided with support and training (e.g., support groups, psychoeducation, parenting-skill development, respite, adult counseling), as their family roles are critical and often stressful. The vast majority of children served through intensive in-home services are involved in multiple systems, including juvenile justice, child welfare, and special education. To be effective, therapists must embrace and nurture collaborative approaches that involve these other systems and have substantial knowledge of the resources, eligibility requirements, and processes (e.g., dependency proceedings in family court, committees on special education) in which children and their families may be engaged.

In summary, home-based intervention is a process that involves a number of phases. The process of the evidence-based FFT model is provided as an example. Intervention is time limited, requiring as few as eight to fifteen and generally no more than twenty-six sessions with an FFT-trained therapist who works with clients in the home, clinic, school, juvenile court, community-based programs, and at the time of reentry from institutional placement. FFT focuses on enhancing protective factors and reducing risk, including the risk of treatment termination. FFT is designed to involve the following phases:

- *Engagement*, to emphasize factors that protect youth and families from early dropout
- *Motivation*, to change maladaptive emotional reactions and beliefs and increase alliance, trust, hope, and motivation for lasting change
- *Assessment*, to clarify individual, family system, and larger system relationships, especially the interpersonal functions of behavior and how they relate to change techniques
- *Behavior change*, which consists of communication training, specific tasks, technical aids, basic parenting skills, problem-solving and conflict-management skills, and contracting and response-cost techniques
- *Generalization*, during which family case management is guided by individualized family functional needs, their interface with community-based environmental constraints and resources, and the alliance with the FFT therapist/Family Case Manager

Issues of Diversity and Practice with Populations at Risk

The population of children and families receiving the various types of in-home services and supports described in this chapter is diverse in terms of demographics. One of the system-of-care principles is that service provision should happen in culturally and linguistically competent environments where family and youth voices are heard and valued, everyone is respected and trusted, and it is safe to speak honestly. Understanding the cultural, racial, and ethnic background of a family and its influence on help-seeking behaviors is especially important, given the intrusive nature of a service that is offered in the home, often for a number of hours and several days a week. Delivering services in children's homes may promote the use of culturally relevant strategies and supports. While simply changing the locus of service delivery to the home does not guarantee higher levels of cultural competence, many home-based approaches work from the premise that family and community cultural assets are an important resource (Cunningham, Foster, and Henggeler 2002). As attention is paid to expanding the evidence base to identify effective practices, there is an increased focus on the need to better understand treatment effectiveness for diverse populations (National Implementation Research Network 2003).

Many in-home models strive to identify and draw upon protective factors, including informal supports in the child and family's community that are nonstigmatizing and rooted in the family's cultural traditions. Delivering services in children's homes and in partnership with family and community members may promote the use of culturally relevant strategies and supports. One important related decision is the assignment of the in-home social worker. The assignment of a social worker from the same cultural, ethnic, or racial background as the family is recommended. However, it is important to be aware of circumstances that may counter this strategy, including the availability of culturally diverse staff; the level of cultural competence of the social worker regardless of ethnic background; and, most important, family choice in the selection of the social worker (Pumariega 2003).

Another strategy for providing culturally competent services involves employing parent/family advocates. These are specifically trained paraprofessionals hired, in part, because of their firsthand expertise in parenting a child with serious emotional or behavioral challenges and thus their ability to connect with the family based on common experiences. The job descriptions for parent advocates vary, but common activities include providing one-on-one support, guiding parents to solve practical family problems, and teaching/modeling advocacy skills. Intensive in-home providers work closely with families to identify valued outcomes and prioritize service needs from the family's perspective. Family advocates often play a central role in this process, and they may be in the best position to gain the trust of the family and identify pragmatic solutions that help families cope successfully.

Implications for Home-Based Practice

Sources of Funding

One of the challenges related to offering home-based services for this population is funding. Often, states and communities find that they must use a variety of funding strategies and sources in order to set up a comprehensive array of home and community-based services. The most common form of reimbursement for mental health services is Medicaid. Traditionally, Medicaid supports inpatient care and outpatient office-based treatment rather than home-based services. Two Medicaid funding strategies that states and communities may use for home-based services include the rehabilitation option and the Home and Community-Based Services waiver (Ires, Pires, and Lee 2006). These options differ in services and clients covered (see also chapter 4).

The rehabilitation option offers states much flexibility in the type, scope, and location for psychiatric rehabilitation services: "Any medical or remedial services . . . recommended by a physician or other licensed practitioner . . . for the maximum reduction of physical or mental disability and restoration of an individual to the best possible functional level" (Title XIX of the Social Security Act of 1965, 42 CFR Section 440.130 [d]). A variety of types of services can be covered, including behavior management–skills training, care coordination, crisis intervention, and medication management. A potential disadvantage of the rehabilitation option is a substantial increase in a state's Medicaid expenditures unless they institute management-utilization strategies such as clear eligibility criteria, certification of each child's need for intensive in-home services, and periodic reviews of a child's continuing need for these services. Once a state adds the rehabilitation option to its state Medicaid plan, these services must be available for all Medicaid-eligible children and families.

The target population for a HCBS waiver is limited to those children who otherwise would be placed in a psychiatric inpatient program or a

Medicaid-funded residential treatment program. States are able to waive parental income so that children who would not otherwise meet the income eligibility requirements for Medicaid can enroll. States can also choose to implement waiver services gradually in targeted geographic areas rather than offering them statewide. The waiver allows coverage of services that are not in a state's Medicaid plan, such as wraparound facilitation, education and support for caregivers, respite, crisis-intervention services, and daily living–skills training. A disadvantage is that the application and approval process is daunting, and waiver implementation requires substantial administrative resources for a relatively small number of children.

Gaps in Research Knowledge

There are significant opportunities for research on in-home services for children with emotional and behavioral challenges and their families. The evidence base for these interventions is just being established. Opportunities exist to study the effectiveness of in-home services with children with varying clinical profiles, the outcomes associated with models of in-home services that follow hospitalization or residential placement, and the contributions of parent advocates to child and family teams. In addition, it is important to develop and evaluate the outcomes associated with in-home interventions for culturally diverse populations. Many of the studies to date have had follow-up periods of one year or less. Because many children with emotional and behavioral challenges, especially those receiving services from multiple child-serving agencies, require extended periods of service, longer-term follow-up is indicated.

Relatively little systematic research has been conducted on the characteristics of effective practitioners of in-home services, including differences between masters-level and bachelors-level social workers. Additional research is warranted on the effectiveness of various approaches to pre-service and in-service training. It is important to examine the culture and climate of the organizations employing these human-service workers. Glisson and Hemmelgarn (1998) have demonstrated the relationship between organizational climate and culture on the quality and outcomes of services provided to children. Organizational characteristics are often not described in research studies, and their contribution to outcomes is seldom examined systematically. Finally, opportunities exist to study system-, child-, and family-level outcomes that are associated with various funding mechanisms for home-based services.

REFERENCES

Alexander, J. F., Barton, C., Gordon, D., Grotpeter, J., Hansson, K., et al. 1998. Functional family therapy. In *Blueprints for Violence Prevention, Book Three*. Boulder, Colo.: Center for the Study and Prevention of Violence, Institute of Behavioral Science, University of Colorado.

Alexander, J. F., Pugh, C., Parsons, B. V., and Sexton, T. L. 2000. Functional family therapy. In *Blueprints for Violence Prevention, Book Three*. 2nd ed. Boulder, Colo.: Center for the Study and Prevention of Violence, Institute of Behavioral Science, University of Colorado.

Armstrong, M. I., and Evans, M. E. 1992. Three intensive community-based programs for children and youth with serious emotional disturbance. *Journal of Child and Family Studies* 1: 61–74.

Armstrong, M. I., Stroul, B. A., and Boothroyd, R. A. 2005. Intercepts of resilience and systems of care. In *Handbook for working with children and youth: Pathways to resilience across cultures and context*, ed. M. Ungar, 387–404. Thousand Oaks, Calif.: Sage.

Blueprints for Violence Prevention. N.d. The Center for the Study and Prevention of Violence. Available online at http://www.colorado.edu/cspv/bluprints/index.html.

Boothroyd, R. A., Kuppinger, A. D., Evans, M. E., Armstrong, M. I., and Radigan, M. 1998. Understanding respite care use by families of children receiving short term, in-home psychiatric emergency services. *Journal of Child and Family Studies* 7: 353–376.

Borduin, C. M., Mann, B. J., Cone, L. T., Henggeler, S. W., Fucci, B. R., et al. 1995. Multisystemic treatment of serious juvenile offenders: Long-term prevention of criminology and violence. *Journal of Consulting and Clinical Psychology* 63: 569–578.

Burns, B. J., Costello, E. J., Angold, A., Stangl, D., Tweed, D. L., et al. 1995. Children's mental health service use across service sectors. *Health Affairs* 14: 147–159.

Burns, B. J., and Goldman, S. K. 1999. *Promising practices in wraparound for children with serious emotional disturbance and their families*. Washington, D.C.: Center for Effective Collaboration and Practice, American Institutes for Research.

Chamberlain, P., Leve, L., and DeGarmo, D. 2007. Multidimensional treatment foster care for girls in the juvenile justice system: Two-year follow-up of a randomized clinical trial. *Journal of Consulting and Clinical Psychology* 75(1): 187–193.

Chamberlain, P., and Mihalic, S. F. 1998. *Multidimensional treatment foster care: Blueprints for violence prevention*. Boulder, Colo.: Center for the Study and Prevention of Violence, Institute of Behavioral Science, University of Colorado.

Community Mental Health and Substance Abuse Services Improvement Act. 1992. U.S. Public Law 102-321 (October 1). *ADAMHA Reorganization Act*, Washington, D.C.: U.S. Government Printing Office.

Costello, E. J., Keeler, G. P., and Angold, A. 2001. Poverty, race/ethnicity, and psychiatric disorder: A study of rural children. *American Journal of Public Health* 91: 1494–1498.

Costello, E. J., Mustillo, S., Keeler, G., and Angold, A. 2004. Prevalence of psychiatric disorders in childhood and adolescence. In *Mental health services: A public health perspective*, ed. B. L. Levin, J. Petrila, and K. Hennessy, 111–128. New York: Oxford University Press.

Cunningham, P. B., Foster, S. L., Henggeler, S.W. 2002. The elusive concept of cultural competence. *Children's Services* 5 (3): 231–243.

Dollard, N., Evans, M. E., Lubrecht, J., and Schaeffer, D. 1994. The use of flexible service dollars in rural, community-based programs for children with serious emotional disturbance and their families. *Journal of Emotional and Behavioral Disorders* 2 (12): 117–125.

Evans, M. E., and Armstrong, M. I. 2002. What is case management? In *Community treatment for youth: Evidence based interventions for severe emotional and behavioral disorders*, ed. B. J. Burns and K. Hoagwood, 39–68. New York: Oxford University Press.

Evans, M. E., Armstrong, M. I., and Kuppinger, A. D. 1996. Family-centered intensive management: A step toward understanding individualized care. *Journal of Child and Family Studies* 5: 55–65.

Evans, M. E., Armstrong, M. I., Kuppinger, A. D., Huz, S., and Johnson, S. 1998. *A randomized trial of family-centered intensive case management and family-based treatment: Final report.* Tampa: University of South Florida.

Evans, M. E., Banks, S. M., Huz, S., and McNulty, T. L. 1994. Initial hospitalization and community tenure outcomes of intensive case management for children and youth with serious emotional and behavioral disabilities. *Journal of Child and Family Studies* 3: 225–234.

Evans, M. E., Boothroyd, R. A., and Armstrong, M. I. 1997. Development and implementation of an experimental study of the effectiveness of in-home crisis services for children and their families. *Journal of Emotional and Behavioral Disorders* 5: 93–105.

Evans, M. E., Boothroyd, R. A., Armstrong, M. I., Greenbaum, P. E., Brown, E., et al. 2003. An experimental study of the effectiveness of intensive in-home crisis services for children and their families: Program outcomes. *Journal of Emotional and Behavioral Disorders* 11 (2): 92–102.

Evans, M. E., Boothroyd, R. A., Greenbaum, P. E., Brown, E., Armstrong, M. I., et al. 2001. Outcomes associated with clinical profiles of children in psychiatric crisis enrolled in intensive, in-home interventions. *Mental Health Services Research* 3 (1): 35–44.

Evans, M. E., Huz, S., McNulty, T. L., and Banks, S. M. 1996. Child, family, and system outcomes of intensive case management in New York State. *Psychiatric Quarterly* 67: 273–286.

Federation of Families for Children's Mental Health. *Definition of family-driven care.* Available online at http://www.ffcmh.org/systems_whatis.htm.

Ferdinand, R. F., van der Reijden, M., Verhulst, F. C., Nienhuis, F. J., and Giel, R. 1995. Assessment of the prevalence of psychiatric disorder in young adults. *The British Journal of Psychiatry* 166: 480–488.

Flynn, L. 2005. Family perspectives on evidence-based practices. In *Child and adolescent psychiatry clinics of North America*, ed. B. J. Burns and K. Hoagwood, 14:217–224.

Fraser, M. W., Pecora, P. J., and Haapala, D. A. 1991. *Families in crisis: The impact of family preservation services.* New York: Aldine de Gruyter.

Friedman, R., Katz-Leavy, J., Manderscheid, R. W., and Sondheimer, D. L. 1996. Prevalence of serious emotional disturbance in children and adolescents. In *Mental health, United States, 1996,* ed. R. W. Manderscheid and M. A. Sonnenschein. DHHS Pub. No. (SMA) 96–3098. Washington, D.C.: Superintendent of Documents, United States Printing Office.

Friedman, R., and Kutash, K. 1992. Challenges for child and adolescent mental health. *Health Affairs* 11 (3): 125–136.

Friesen, B. J., and Koroloff, N. M. 1990. Family-centered services: Implications for mental health administration and research. *Journal of Mental Health Administration* 17: 13–25.

Glisson, C., and Hemmelgarn, A. 1998. The effects of organizational climate and interorganizational coordination on the quality and outcomes of children's service system. *Child Abuse and Neglect* 22: 401–421.

Goldman, S. K. 1999. The conceptual framework for wraparound: Definition, values, essential elements, and requirements for practice. In *Promising practices in wraparound for children with serious emotional disturbance and their families,* ed. B. J. Burns and S. K. Goldman, 4:9–16. Washington, D.C.: Center for Effective Collaboration and Practice, American Institutes for Research.

Henggeler, S. W., Melton, G. B., and Smith, L. A. 1992. Family preservation using multisystemic therapy: An effective alternative to incarcerating serious juvenile offenders. *Journal of Consulting and Clinical Psychology* 60: 953–961.

Henggeler, S. W., Rodick, J. D., Borduin, C. M., Hanson, C., Watson, S. M., and Urey, J. R. 1986. Multisystemic treatment of juvenile offenders: Effects on adolescent behavior and family interactions. *Developmental Psychology* 22: 132–141.

Henggeler, S. W., Rowland, M. R., Randall, J., Ward, D., Pickrel, S. G., Cunningham, P. B., et al. 1999. Home-based multisystemic therapy as an alternative to the hospitalization of youth in psychiatric crisis: Clinical outcomes. *Journal of the American Academy of Child and Adolescent Psychiatry* 38: 1331–1339.

Hoagwood, K. E. 2005. Family-based services in children's mental health: A research review and synthesis. *Journal of Child Psychology and Psychiatry* 46 (7): 690–713.

Institute for Family Development. 2007. *IFD: Training for practitioners*. Available online at http://www.institutefamily.org/training_practitioners.asp.

International Federation of Social Workers. 2000. *IFSW: Definition of social work*. Available online at http://www.ifsw.org/en/p38000017.html.

Ires, H. T., Pires, S., and Lee, M. 2006. *Public financing of home and community services for children and youth with serious emotional disturbances: Selected state strategies*. Washington, D.C.: Mathematica Policy Research, Inc.

Katz-Leavy, J., Lourie, I., Stroul, B., and Zeigler-Dendy, C. 1992. *Individualized services in a system of care*. Washington, D.C.: Georgetown University, CASSP Technical Assistance Center.

Kazdin, A. E., Holland, L., and Crowley, M. 1997. Family experiences of barriers to treatment and premature termination from child therapy. *Journal of Consulting and Clinical Psychology* 65: 453–463.

Kessler, R. C., McGonagle, K. A., Zhao, S., Nelson, C. B., Hughes, M., et al. 1994. Lifetime and twelve-month prevalence of DMS-III-R psychiatric disorders in the United States: Results from the National Comorbidity Study. *Archives of General Psychiatry* 51: 8–19.

Kinney, J. M., and Haapala, D. 1984. *First year Homebuilders mental health report*. Federal Way, Wash.: Behavioral Sciences Institute.

Kinney, J. M., Madsen, B., Flemming, T., and Haapala, D. A. 1977. Homebuilders: Keeping families together. *Journal of Consulting and Clinical Psychology* 45: 667–673.

Knitzer, J. 1982. *Unclaimed children: The failure of public responsibility to children and adolescents in need of mental health services*. Washington, D.C.: Children's Defense Fund.

Lavigne, J. V., Gibbons, R. D., Christoffel, K. K., Arend, R., Rosenbaum, D., et al. 1996. Prevalence rates and correlates of psychiatric disorders among preschool children. *Journal of the American Academy of Child and Adolescent Psychiatry* 35: 204–214.

Lindblad-Goldberg, M., Dore, M. M., and Stern, L. 1998. *Creating competence from chaos: A comprehensive guide to home-based services*. New York: W. W. Norton and Co.

Littell, J. H., Popa, M., and Forsythe, B. 2005. *Multisystemic treatment for social, emotional, and behavioral problems in children and adolescents aged 10–17* (Protocol for a Campbell Collaboration Review). Available online at http://www.campbellcollaboration.org/doc-pdf/Mst_Littell_Review.pdf.

Littell, J. H., and Schuerman, J. 1995. *A synthesis of research on family preservation and family reunification.* Washington, D.C.: U.S. Department of Health and Human Services. Available online at http://aspe.hhs.gov/hsp/cyp/fplitrev.htm.

Louis de la Parte Florida Mental Health Institute. 2006. *Rosie D. Massachusetts class size report.* Tampa: University of South Florida.

McGowan, B. 1990. Family-based services and public policy: Context and implications. In *Reaching high risk families: Intensive family preservation in human services,* ed. J. Whittaker, J. Kinney, E. Tracy, and C. Booth, 81–82. New York: Aldine de Gruyter.

McKay, M., Stoewe, J., McCadam, K., and Gonzales, J. 1998. Increasing access to child mental health services for urban children and their care givers. *Health and Social Work* 23: 9–15.

Messer, S. C., Angold, A., Costello, E. J., Burns, B. J., Framer, E. M., et al. 1997. The Child and Adolescent Burden Assessment (CABA): Measuring the family impact of emotional and behavioral problems. *International Journal of Methods in Psychiatric Research* 6: 261–284.

Miller, M. 2006. *Intensive family preservation programs: Program fidelity influences effectiveness—Revised.* Available online at http://www.wsipp.wa.gov/pub.asp?docid=06-02-3901.

National Implementation Research Network. 2003. *Consensus statement on evidence-based programs and cultural competence.* Tampa: University of South Florida, Louis de la Parte Florida Mental Health Institute.

National Registry of Evidenced-Based Programs and Practices. 2007. *Multisystemic Therapy (MST) for juvenile offenders.* Available online at http://nrepp.samhsa.gov.

New Freedom Commission on Mental Health. 2003. Achieving the promise: Transforming mental health care in America. Final report. Rockville, Md.: U.S. Department of Health and Human Services (Pub. No. SMA-03-3832).

New York State Office of Mental Health. 2007. Home-Based Crisis Intervention. Available online at http://www.omh.state.ny.us/omhweb/ebp/children_hbci.htm.

Newman, D. L., Moffitt, T. E., Caspi, A., Magdol, L., Silva, P. A., et al. 1996. Psychiatric disorder in a birth cohort of young adults: Prevalence, comorbidity, clinical significance, and new case incidence from ages eleven to twenty-one. *Journal of Consulting and Clinical Psychology* 64: 552–562.

ORC Macro. 2007. Available online at http://www.orcmacro.com/projects/cmhi/default.aspx.

Osher, T. W., deFur, E., Nava, C., Spencer, S., and Toth-Daniels, D. 1999. New roles for families in systems of care. In *System of care: Promising practices in children's mental health, 1998 Series, Vol. 1.* Washington, D.C.: Center for Effective Collaboration and Practice, American Institutes of Research.

Petr, C. G., and Spano, R. N. 1990. Evolution of social services for children with emotional disorders. *Social Work* 35 (3): 228–234.

Pumariega, A. J. 2003. Cultural competence in systems of care for children's mental health. In *The handbook of child and adolescent systems of care: The new community psychiatry*, ed. A. J. Pumariega and N. C. Winters. San Francisco: Jossey-Bass.

Rauktis, M. B., and Miller, C. 2002. Child strengths and caregiver strain: Is there a relationship? In *The fourteenth annual research conference proceedings: A system of care for children's mental health: Expanding the research base*, ed. C. Newman et al., 37–41. Tampa: University of South Florida, The Louis de la Parte Florida Mental Health Institute, Research and Training Center for Children's Mental Health.

Roberts, R. E., Attkisson, C., and Rosenblatt, A. 1998. Prevalence of psychopathology among children and adolescents. *American Journal of Psychiatry* 155: 715–725.

Romano, E., Tremblay, R. E., Vitaro, F., Zoccolillo, M., and Pagani, L. 2001. Prevalence of psychiatric diagnosis and the role of perceived impairment: Findings from an adolescent community sample. *Journal of Child Psychology and Psychiatry* 42: 451–461.

Schoenwald, S. K., Ward, D. M., Henggeler, S. W., Rowland, M. D., and Brondino, M. J. 2000. Multisystemic therapy versus hospitalization for crisis stabilization of youth: Out-of-home placement four months post-referral. *Mental Health Services Research* 2: 3–12.

Sexton, T. L., and Alexander, J. F. 1999. *Functional family therapy: Principles of clinical intervention, assessment, and implementation*. Henderson, Nev.: RCH Enterprises.

Shaffer, D., Fisher, P., Dulcan, M. K., Davies, M., Piacentini, J., et al. 1996. The NIMH diagnostic interview schedule for children version 2.3 (DISC 2.3): Description, acceptability, prevalence rates, and performance in the MECA study. *Journal of the American Academy of Child and Adolescent Psychiatry* 35: 865–877.

Stroul, B. A. 1988. *Series on community-based services for children and adolescents who are severely emotionally disturbed. Vol. 1, Home-based services*. Washington, D.C.: CASSP Technical Assistance Center, Georgetown University Child Development Center.

——. 1995. Case management in a system of care. In *From case management to service coordination for children with emotional, behavioral, or mental disorders: Building on family strengths*, ed. B. J. Friesen and J. Poertner, 3–25. Baltimore, Md.: Paul H. Brookes.

Stroul, B. A., and Friedman, R. M. 1986. *A system of care for children and youth with severe emotional disturbances*. Rev. ed. Washington, D.C.: National Technical Assistance Center for Children's Mental Health.

Stroul, B. A., and Goldman, S. 1996. Community-based service approaches: Home-based services and therapeutic foster care. In *Children's Mental Health:*

Creating Systems of Care in a Changing Society, ed. B. Stroul. Baltimore, Md.: Paul H. Brookes.

U.S. Department of Health and Human Services. 1999. *Mental health: A report of the Surgeon General.* Rockville, Md.: U.S. Department of Health and Human Services, Substance Abuse and Mental Health Services Administration, Center for Mental Health Services, National Institutes of Health, National Institute of Mental Health.

Winters, N. C., and Terrell, E. 2003. Case management: The linchpin of community-based systems of care. In *The handbook of child and adolescent systems of care: The new community psychiatry*, ed. A. J. Pumariega and N. C. Winters, 171–200. San Francisco: Jossey-Bass.

Woolston, J. L., Adnopoz, J. A, and Berkowitz, S. J. 2007. IICAPS: A home-based psychiatric treatment for children and adolescents. New Haven, Conn.: Yale University Press.

Nine

Criminal Justice

JOSÉ B. ASHFORD, KATHERINE O. STERNBACH,

AND MAUREEN BALAAM

Ordinary offenders face significant challenges returning to communities: stigma, poverty, estrangement from families and neighborhoods, limited availability of housing and jobs, and reentry to society from highly regulated institutions. Juvenile and adult offenders with special needs have even more barriers to successful reentry. Special needs is defined here as "any changeable factors associated with disorders of cognition, thought, mood, personality, development, or behavior that are linked to desired outcomes for offenders at any phase of the justice process" (Ashford, Sales, and Reid 2001a, 5). Special needs offenders include those with serious mental illness or at risk for suicide; alcohol and substance abuse disorders or co-occurring disorders (mental illness and alcohol/substance abuse); conduct, antisocial, or psychopathic personality disorders; developmental disorders and learning disabilities; violent offenders; and sex offenders. This chapter examines home-based services for ordinary offenders and those with serious mental illness or co-occurring disorders.

The Population

National estimates of adult offenders in prisons indicate that 80 percent have a substance abuse problem and 16 percent have a mental disorder (Hartwell

2004). Juvenile offenders have a high risk of mental illness and substance abuse (Ashford, Sales, and Reid 2001a; McManus et al. 1984; Melton and Pagliocca 1992; Otto et al. 1992), which does "not differ appreciably from those emotionally disturbed youth in other child service systems" (Ashford et al. 2001a, 11).

Reentry Statistics

Approximately 780,000 adult offenders reenter communities from state and federal prisons each year, and over ten million are released from jails across the country (Lanagan and Levin 2002; Sentencing Project 2004). Four out of five adult offenders are released with postrelease supervision (parole or probation) requirements (Travis 2000), and most are rearrested (Travis, Solomon, and Waul 2001). In 2005, about 50 percent of probationers had felony convictions, 49 percent had a misdemeanor, and 1 percent had other infractions (Glaze and Bonczar 2006). Furthermore, 28 percent were on probation related to a drug violation, and 15 percent drove while intoxicated. These statistics suggest there is high recidivism among offenders and that over 40 percent of all offender crimes involve drugs and alcohol (Glaze and Bonczar 2006).

The U.S. Department of Justice reported that in the year 2000, the majority of adult offenders in state prisons were violent offenders (44 percent) or drug traffickers (13 percent) and that 77 percent had a prior conviction (Durose and Langan 2004). Findings from the Serious and Violent Offender Multi-Site Evaluation (Lattimore 2007) indicate that adult male offenders are on average about twenty-nine years of age, with 40 percent reporting being married and about 60 percent having children under the age of eighteen. About 60 percent had a high-school diploma or GED. About two-thirds reported having a job six months prior to prison and about 90 percent reported they had ever worked. Two-thirds also reported drug and alcohol use in the thirty days prior to prison, and most had family and friends who used drugs and alcohol and were involved in crime.

A national census of juvenile facilities in 2003 indicates that about 97,000 juvenile offenders were detained in juvenile justice residential placements (Synder and Sickmund 2006). States are responsible for detaining juvenile offenders in residential facilities, whereas federal and state prisons and local jails hold adult offenders. The variation in policies and operating procedures of state juvenile justice programs challenges accurate data collection. Not all crimes committed by juveniles are reported. Juvenile offenders transferred to adult correctional facilities are counted in the adult facilities. Furthermore, some states may place juvenile offenders in residential treatment centers for mental illness and/or substance abuse. As a result, it is difficult to quantify the number of juveniles that are detained and released annually.

Policy and Agency Context

Over the past thirty years, there has been an unprecedented "imprisonment boom," based on a turn in criminal justice policy toward more punitive ends. The total number of prisoners serving sentences of one or more years increased from 315,000 in 1980 to 1,329,367 in 2000 (U.S. Department of Justice 2005). This increase in incarceration also coincided with shifts in policy toward determinate sentencing for adult and juvenile offenders. Determinate sentencing involves any sentencing or disposition that specifies the length of incarceration at the time of sentencing (Ashford and LeCroy 1993). Indeterminate sentencing occurs when the court specifies a minimum and maximum length of incarceration that is ultimately determined by a parole board. It is important to note that some states eliminated parole or conditional releases when the change to more punitive and determinate sentencing policies occurred.

The determinate-sentencing movement was significantly influenced by a "fairness" or "justice paradigm" that focuses on accountability for the offender's actions. Instead of emphasizing rehabilitation and accountability, criminal justice systems moved to an approach that emphasizes accountability and crime control. As a consequence, many jurisdictions moved from rehabilitative conceptions of community supervision to approaches that focused on surveillance and other accountability strategies. The result for social work practice was that policies stressing offender reintegration and rehabilitation were supplanted by policies emphasizing crime control and, in particular, use of more intensive modes of supervision for high-risk offenders (Petersilia and Turner 1993). The policy shift from rehabilitation to crime accountability in the field of corrections led to a decrease in social workers selecting corrections as a field of practice (Macht and Ashford 1991).

With these policy changes, there was a corresponding increase in the lengths of confinement for various types of offenses. Those involved in drug and violent offenses were often sentenced to longer periods of incarceration, which led to significant disruptions in relationships between offenders and members of their families. The longer sentences also produced significant gaps in the offender's employment history. These consequences were further

compounded by antirehabilitation attitudes that reduced the availability of rehabilitation services in correctional facilities. Adults and juveniles often left
prison or youth facilities without having changed key factors that contributed
to their initial incarceration. The "nothing works" assumptions about rehabilitation (Latessa, Cullen, and Gendreau 2002) resulted in the warehous-
ing of offenders in many different types of institutions. For this reason, the
postrelease process in many jurisdictions was not geared toward changing
behavior or maintaining changes that may have been addressed by correctional programming. In addition, issues of risk to the community began to
dominate sentencing policies and community supervision practices. Many
states considered offenders classified as violent as in need of intensive modes
of supervision by parole or probation officers.

Planning and policies for reentry from prison vary from state to state, regardless of the sentencing policies. Release may occur without any planning
other than assignment of a parole or probation officer in the community, provision of a minimal cash payment on release, transportation from the prison
to a train or bus station, and a set of clothing. If the correctional facility offers substance-abuse treatment or other interventions prior to release, there
may be established links to community programs such as halfway houses or
residential services and treatment for substance abuse (Ashford and Sternbach 2007a). In addition, some states have started reentry planning prior to
release. Examples include "in-reach" by community and faith-based organizations that help offenders plan for their release by identifying housing, jobs,
or training resources in the community as well as the availability of behavioral-health treatment (Ashford and Sternbach 2007a). Other efforts focus on
assessing the offender's needs through standardized assessment tools and by
identifying special parole supervision initiatives and treatment resources.

Most correctional authorities tend to focus on assessing the risk posed
by the offender upon release to the community. However, a complementary
assessment of needs inclusive of housing, employment, behavioral health,
health care, family-reunification goals, and rehabilitative supports is critical
for offenders to be successful once released. Bonta (1996, 22) has written
that widespread use of needs assessment in the justice system is a "recent
phenomena." Many correctional facilities do not use standardized assessment tools (Taxman et al. 2007). As a result, social workers must be prepared
to address the various scenarios of reentry planning using anything from
well-developed plans for implementing home-based services to no formally
developed plan at all.

State and federal laws passed by Congress and state legislatures in the
1990s as part of the "war on drugs" impose civil penalties on offenders.

These penalties apply to public housing, public assistance (including food stamps), driver's licenses, voting, student loans, and employment (Eggleston n.d.; Hirsch et al. 2002). For example, while federal law allows local public housing authorities to make individualized decisions about the eligibility of individuals with criminal records, the local authority may disallow access to parolees with histories of drug convictions or other criminal records. Registered sex offenders are also excluded from public housing by law in many jurisdictions. As a result, social workers must be prepared to assist parolees in overcoming these major barriers to reentering society.

Purpose and Goals of Social Work Home-Based Services

A pivotal goal in any reentry programming is helping offenders establish a home in the community. The definition of "home" for adult and juvenile offenders may include several housing options. Though living with family is the preferred arrangement for many offenders, this may be unrealistic due to restraining orders, unsuitability of the former family home, disrupted relationships, the need for independence, and the need for specialized treatment (Ashford and Sternbach 2007a). Housing options may include the following: licensed board and care homes that dispense medicine and provide meals and house cleaning; supported housing, which would include some staff contact at the home but not twenty-four-hour staff located at the residence; crisis housing, which would provide medical attention, dispensing of medications, and twenty-four-hour staff supervision; dedicated housing, which is a residence specifically designed for one population or identified group (e.g., offenders with co-occurring disorders) and offering a structured program with specialized staffing; and independent housing in an apartment or rooming house (Ashford, Wong, and Sternbach 2008). Also, many adults and older adolescents live with friends, return to homeless shelters, or live on the street. Thus the definition of "home" varies greatly, and social workers have to adapt their home-based interventions to different situations and risk and safety considerations.

Additional social work interventions may be required for special needs offenders in the above housing examples. Social work interventions for special needs offenders regarding medication management may include checking on psychiatric symptoms and medication compliance to confirm medication adherence, providing assistance with reordering prescribed medications, and reminding the individual and housing staff of psychiatrist appointments and assisting in transportation to the appointment. Other social work interventions may include attending to the individual's need for assistance with relationships with housing staff and other individuals, monitoring the individual's ability for self-care and knowing when to take action in psychiatric emergencies, and assisting the person in engaging with natural supports and other community resources that will facilitate their recovery and independence. Natural supports include community educational resources, faith-based organizations, and individuals or organizations that may help the offender to make pro-social friendships.

Family reunification is often a key issue that guides the structuring of home-based services. Family reunification requires involvement of the family in the reentry planning process at various stages of the offender's incarceration. This component of the home-visitation process allows practitioners and consumers to identify natural supports available for offenders. Family may include children, spouses or significant others, siblings, parents, or other extended family members. Offenders may have children in foster care or living with the other parent or family members, who may be estranged. For this reason, the practitioner must assess the offender's bonds with the family to determine if returning to the family is in the best interest of the individual and the family.

Reunification as a goal of home-based services can require distinct interventions that range in length depending on family history and dynamics. Family members that participated in recent focus groups for reentry planning in California reported that they only hear from correctional facilities or parole officers when their relative has a negative incident (Ashford and Sternbach 2007b). Many of these family members wanted to hear about the experiences of their incarcerated family member in order to remain a part of their lives and to have a better appreciation of how they are responding to incarceration. However, some offenders wanted to distance themselves from family because contact made it much more difficult to cope with the day-to-day constraints of life in prison.

Issues of housing and family reunification are not the only goals of home visitation. These programs must also take into account many of the immediate and practical problems facing offenders upon release from a correctional facility. Adult offenders often leave prison without identification, have limited funds, no designated place to call home, and few options for employment (National Governor's Association 2004). Offenders reentering the community also face discrimination in trying to cope with these challenges. For these reasons, it is important for social workers to establish goals that target immediate needs of food, shelter, clothing, and medication management during the first thirty days following the offender's release.

Findings from focus groups conducted with parolees, their family members, and other community stakeholders in California confirmed the need for intervention immediately following release (Ashford and Sternbach 2007b). Participants emphasized that both ordinary and special needs offenders are especially vulnerable to criminal recidivism during the first thirty days postrelease. Focus group participants also reported that parolees have few resources upon release. They leave the correctional facility without an ID and receive a two-hundred-dollar stipend that must cover transportation to the city or county where they committed the crime, buy clothing, and obtain food and housing. Many focus group participants reported estrangement from their families, having "burned their bridges" due to past criminal behavior. Thus they have more incentives upon their release to rely on friends involved in criminal behavior than on family members or other positive supports in the community. In fact, many focus group participants reported that criminal friends were more likely to provide resources for them to adapt to practical crises surrounding their release than were family or community agencies.

While focus group participants expressed the desire to have jobs, substance abuse treatment, and housing established before they leave prison, they reported that they had limited access to any form of planning for linking them to these services (Ashford and Sternbach 2007b). Orientation to life out of jail or prison is especially important for individuals with challenged abilities or an unstable mental condition. They require far more effort from practitioners in helping them establish linkages with the community than ordinary offenders do. Without these linkages, they are at increased risk of not having clinically meaningful levels of services to address their mental illness (Lovell, Gagliardi, and Peterson 2002).

Offenders with special needs face the stigma associated not only with their mental or substance abuse disorder but also from their criminal conviction, resulting in barriers to education and employment. For this reason, the home-supervisory program must include the goal of helping the offender earn a living. School districts and community colleges offer resources for education and training of adults, including preparation for the GED test to obtain a high-school equivalency credential. There are also resources specifically designed for ex-felons to aid with employment. Under the Tax and Trade Relief Extension Act of 1998 (PL 105-277), employers that hire ex-felons from low-income families are eligible for a tax credit of up to $2,400 (2007 allocation). Funds are also available from the federal government under the Workforce Investment Partnership Act of 1998 (PL 105-220), for states to use for a variety of services, such as on-the-job-training. Ex-offenders are specifically covered in this legislation. These latter funds are distributed through the states and individual state departments of labor have information on the services available in their state. There are also federal funds, distributed through state employment services (also known as One-Stop Career Centers), to pay for bonding for ex-felons and people in recovery from substance abuse disorders.

Additional goals of home-visitation programs are promotion of safety and recidivism prevention. In fact, these goals are an inherent component of community corrections. For this reason, social workers involved with providing home-based services cannot take for granted that criminal justice professionals understand principles of recovery from mental illness and addictions. The cultures of criminal justice and social work are very different and require extensive collaboration to understand respective goals and operating standards.

Furthermore, in the criminal justice system, the focus of reentry (probation and parole) is on control and surveillance, not rehabilitation (Ashford, Sales, and LeCroy 2001). However, research has shown that control and surveillance alone do not reduce recidivism (Petersilia and Turner 1993). In addition, recidivism by itself may not be the best measure for assessing offender reentry because, when comparing counties or states, a venue with a stronger focus on external controls may respond with more technical violations of the parolee, while another venue may place more emphasis on harm reduction and provide more intermediate sanctions than remanding the parolee to prison. "One major benefit of reentry is that it broadened the definition of success for returning inmates beyond recidivism. This change was good because recidivism was too unreliable to be a good indicator of success" (Lynch and Sabol 2004, 405–406). For these and other reasons, correctional authorities are now exploring integration of control and surveillance with rehabilitation. An emphasis on establishing partnerships with communities to address safety and broader community-reentry issues is also emerging.

Theoretical Framework

Parole supervision and aftercare for persons released from mental health institutions have different historical roots but share similarities and differences in approaching their reentry processes (Ashford, Sales, and LeCroy 2001). Both focus on trying to prevent released individuals from relapsing. In corrections, the focus is on preventing the offender from recidivating; in mental health, the focus is on preventing the reemergence of symptoms requiring hospitalization or other specialized treatment interventions. While there are different aims for postrelease supervision and aftercare, it was not until quite recently that social service and mental health professionals recognized the need for integrating principles from each of these supervisory traditions for designing reentry programming.

Risk-Needs-Responsivity Theory

Current theories of correctional rehabilitation recognize that no one correctional program will work for all offenders. The elements of each intervention must be tailored to respond to the specific needs of the offender (Taxman and Marlowe 2006). Andrews, Bonta, and their colleagues have proposed risk-needs-responsivity theory, a conceptual framework for designing and evaluating correctional programming. RNR emphasizes targeting offenders who present the most serious challenges to public safety (Taxman and Marlowe 2006). This theory connected traditional ideas about risk and need to concepts that help practitioners match needs with specific types of clinical interventions. "The corrections-based terms of risk and need were transformed into principles addressing the major clinical issues of who receives treatment (higher-risk cases), what intermediate targets are set (reduce criminogenic needs), and what treatment strategies are employed (match strategies of the learning styles and motivation of cases: the principles of general and specific responsivity)" (Andrews, Bonta, and Wormith 2006, 7).

The traditional concept of risk often included static predictors (e.g., number of convictions) that were not subject to change by correctional interventions. Criminogenic needs, on the other hand, referred to dynamic factors that were empirically linked with criminal behavior and subject to change by clinical interventions (Andrews and Bonta 1998). These two concepts revolutionized thinking about designing correctional programs because they shifted attention away from responding to the needs of offenders that were not considered criminogenic needs. Thus correctional practitioners realized that they needed to target changeable needs or factors that impact offender recidivism. Four of these factors are consistent with general personality and social-psychological explanations of crime: history of antisocial behavior, antisocial personality patterns, antisocial cognition, and antisocial associates (Andrews, Bonta, and Wormith 2006).

The first factor is primarily behavioral, involving forms of learning that can be targeted by specific behavioral interventions that offer offenders alternatives in dealing with risky situations. The second factor can be conceptualized as temperamental or involving personality characteristics associated with poor self-control or low agreeableness (Andrews, Bonta, and Wormith 2006). The third factor can be conceptualized as criminal attitudes subject to interventions that promote changes in social cognition. The fourth factor involves social experiences acquired from associations with criminal others that can be reduced by enhancing or reducing the offender's association with criminal others. In essence, each of these major predictors of crime has dynamic or changeable characteristics.

Theoretical Approaches to the Treatment of Offenders with Special Needs

Treatment of offenders with special needs often diverges from the principles identified by Andrews and his colleagues for rehabilitating ordinary offenders. In comparison to ordinary offenders, many jurisdictions do not target the criminogenic needs or dynamic risk factors in treating offenders diagnosed with serious mental disorders. In these jurisdictions, it is assumed that mentally disordered offenders are in need of case-management services that focus on the treatment of the mental illness and its associated complications without targeting criminogenic factors. Research has examined theoretical approaches to the treatment of offenders with special needs in terms of focusing on the treatment of mental illness and targeting the criminogenic needs or dynamic risk factors.

Lovell et al. (2002) have studied the use of mental health services among persons with serious mental disorders who were released from prison. Although 73 percent of the participants in their study received some form of postrelease mental health services, a sizeable proportion of these offenders (70 percent) were rearrested. However, Lovell and his colleagues also found that few of the offenders "received clinically meaningful levels of services during the first year after release" (Lovell et al. 2002, 1290). Case management is a recognized intervention of service coordination in the community for persons with serious mental disorders (Ashford et al. 2001; Lurigio, Fallon, and Dincin 2000; Ventura et al. 1998). Yet most jurisdictions do not provide case-management services for mentally ill offenders released from either jails or prisons (Lamb and Weinberger 1998; 2001).

A major turn in recent supervision policy in correctional administration directed at home visitation has been to provide case-management services for offenders with serious mental disorders. However, it is unproved whether the provision of mental health services alone is sufficient to reduce the rates of recidivism in the population of offenders diagnosed with serious mental disorders. That is, do offenders diagnosed with serious mental disorders have other attributes besides their mental illnesses that also need to be changed to reduce their recidivism?

Kunz and colleagues (2004) studied an inpatient program for the seriously mentally ill that included a cognitive intervention for persons exhibiting
aggressive or criminal behavior. The program targeted patients with a history
of repeated aggression or crime admitted to a New York City state psychiatric hospital. Their program modified an established cognitive-skills program
for criminal attitudes and showed good success in reducing rearrests in the
study's sample. Ashford, Wong, and Sternbach (forthcoming) have also tested an integrated treatment intervention that combined case-management
services with a cognitive intervention and a mental health court intervention to reduce the recidivism in a sample of offenders diagnosed with serious mental disorders. The results of this pilot study showed a correlation
between changes in the attribution biases of the offenders with mental disorders and reductions in their overall arrests and arrests for violent crimes for
the enhanced treatment group.

Inasmuch as there is preliminary evidence that criminal attitudes are appropriate targets for change with offenders diagnosed with serious mental
disorders, the jury is still out on the relationship between mental disorders
and crime (Hodgins and Janson 2002). Some scholars assume that the same
factors that predict criminal behavior in ordinary offenders predict criminal
behavior in mentally disordered offenders (Andrews et al. 2006; Monahan
and Steadman 1984). Others assume that there are distinct attributes associated with the disorders that contribute to the observed relationships between
mental disorders and crime (see Ashford et al. 2001; Hodgins and Muller-
Isberner 2000; Link, Andrews, and Cullen 1992). Clearly, these theoretical
differences regarding the relationship between mental disorders and crime
have important implications for the treatment of offenders with serious
mental disorders.

Empirical Base

A number of practice approaches have been developed for offender reentry.
This section focuses on the empirical base for each of these approaches.

Intensive Supervision Programs

Proactive Community Supervision (PCS) is a research-based strategy that focuses on "reframing supervision services for offenders" (Taxman, Yancey, and
Bilanin 2006, 2). In PCS, the parole agent emphasizes helping the offender

develop prosocial skills, uses various tools (such as motivational interviewing) and treatments to address criminogenic traits, and helps the parolee engage with families, employers, and others to support change. The PCS model was developed in response to the finding that increasing the intensity of supervision through the use of external controls (e.g., increased surveillance) has not resulted in a reduction of recidivism. Rather, using a goal-oriented approach to resocialize the offender has better results (Taxman, Yancey, and Bilanin 2006). Relying on informal supports to help individuals understand the benefits and responsibilities associated with community integration is a useful strategy. Peer support provided by successfully reintegrated ex-offenders can help with resocialization. Partnering PCS with community treatment resources to address mental illness, addiction, and criminogenic thinking are proving to have good results in improved offender self-control (Ashford et al. 2001; Ashford and Sternbach 2007a).

Forensic Assertive Community Treatment Teams

Very few communities use Assertive Community Treatment (ACT) teams with offender populations (Morrissey and Meyer 2005; Lamberti, Weisman, and Faden 2004). The Surgeon General's Report on Mental Health identified ACT as one of six evidence-based practices for treatment of adults with severe mental illness (U.S. Department of Health and Human Services 1999). ACT teams differ from other approaches to case management on several dimensions: (1) lower caseloads, (2) team rather than individual case management, (3) priority given to outreach, and (4) an orientation to having the team provide as many services as possible rather than referring individuals to others for these services. (See also chapter 10 for a discussion of ACT.)

Several experimental studies have demonstrated that ACT, compared to traditional brokered services models, significantly reduces psychiatric inpatient usage (Bond et al. 1988; Borland, McRae, and Lycan 1989; Lipton, Nutt, and Sabitini 1988; Stein and Test 1980). In addition, the results of meta-analytic studies have found ACT programs superior to clinical case management in reducing hospitalization (Ziguras and Stuart 2000). Yet the results have been mixed about whether ACT programs reduce arrests, improve symptoms, improve social functioning, and increase client satisfaction with services (Cosden et al. 2003; Marshall and Lockwood 2001; Morrissey and Meyer 2005).

Morrissey and Meyer (2005) have pointed out that ACT-like programs have emerged in many communities to help keep the seriously mentally ill out of jails and prisons. These hybrids are often called Forensic Assertive Community Treatment programs. FACT teams embed the probation officer or parole agent in the clinical team to coordinate community supervision and integrate incentives and sanctions with other treatment goals (Mohan, Slade, and Fahy 2004). The interdisciplinary FACT team includes consumers in recovery from mental illness or co-occurring disorders and behavioral health professionals including social workers, nurses, psychologists, psychiatrists, and rehabilitation and employment specialists. The team provides after-hours coverage and intensive supervision and support. Caseload sizes vary in different communities, but a one-to-ten staff-to-parolee ratio is consistent with original ACT program standards. The team uses joint decision making and works with the justice system to address community safety.

FACT teams treating offenders with serious mental disorders have been subjected to less empirical scrutiny than ACT teams (Lamberti et al. 2004). One noteworthy exception is Solomon and Draine's (1995) randomized trail of case-management approaches. Solomon and Draine assigned two hundred inmates leaving a large urban prison system to one of four conditions: the Assertive Community Treatment (ACT) team, forensic specialist case managers, mental health agencies, and the usual referral to a community mental health center. While the participants in this study who received intensive case management services did not achieve better clinical and psychosocial outcomes, more offenders under ACT were returned to jail for treatment noncompliance. Other researchers have also found that mentally disordered offenders appear to be at much greater risk of experiencing difficulties in complying with the conditions of postrelease supervision than ordinary offenders (Feder 1991; Heilbrun and Griffin 1993; Jacoby and Kozie-Peak 1997; Wilson, Tien, and Eaves 1995). For this reason, some communities have begun using mental health courts to minimize the negative effects noted by Solomon and Draine in integrating ACT teams and other forms of intensive community supervision into the criminal justice process (Cosden et al. 2003).

Specialty Courts

Specialty courts, such as reentry courts and mental health courts, emerged from the drug court model. Judge Ginger Lerner-Wren presided over the first mental health court developed in Florida. Her problem-solving court attempts to provide the treatment that mentally ill offenders need, to slow down "the revolving door of mentally ill patients who are repeatedly arrested and sent to prison when they really need treatment" (Marini 2003, 59). Judges in this type of court use their authority to integrate treatment services and forge new responses to the treatment of mentally ill offenders (Berman and Feinblatt 2003).

Designated judges in mental health and reentry courts have a separate court calendar and oversee supervision and treatment provided by correctional and behavioral-health professionals. Typically, staff positions are assigned to the specialty court (e.g., probation, the district attorney and defense counsel/public defenders, mental health treatment team). The target population for a mental health court consists of offenders having serious mental illnesses that may have contributed to their crimes. Early screening of the individual to avoid or minimize jail use and initiate timely behavioral-health treatment are elements of most mental health court programs. While there is some evidence that mental health courts reduce criminal recidivism and violence (Ashford, Wong, and Sternbach 2008; McNiel and Binder 2007), it is difficult to measure the contributing factors impacting recidivism. These contributing factors include judicial oversight and authority, use of positive incentives to motivate behavior change, treatment interventions, proactive community supervision, and other elements of court oversight.

Family Reunification Interventions

La Bodega de la Familia is a crisis center that offers family case management (FCM); it began in Manhattan's Lower East Side in 1996. The goal of this research-support program is to address the needs of families of drug offenders while demonstrating that a "supportive family is a drug user's best hope of recovery" (Shapiro 1998, 1). La Bodega de la Familia works at the neighborhood level to provide family-focused services to low-income families, many of whom are African American and Latino. Clinical and field staff engage the family and develop an action plan to help the substance-abusing family member under criminal justice supervision remain in treatment. Bilingual staff provide assessment, treatment planning, referrals, monitoring, advocacy, counseling, and social support. Field staff provide twenty-four-hour support to families that have drug-related emergencies. Typical activities include follow-up on referrals to check if the family member obtained needed services, advocacy in court or with enforcement agencies (parole or probation, child welfare), and home visits to homebound individuals. Walk-in support is available. La Bodega de la Familia also works collaboratively with parole officers and engages the family to offer support that enhances treatment compliance. This strategy is an alternative to violating the offender for drug-treatment failure. Preliminary evidence indicates that it is an effective intervention in reducing substance abuse, arrests, and convictions in offender populations (Sullivan et al. 2002).

Supported Employment

Supported employment is an evidence-based practice for individuals with co-occurring serious mental health and substance abuse disorders who have difficulties negotiating their work environment (Ashford et al. 2001; Drake et al. 1999). Individual Placement and Support (IPS) is a treatment-team model of supported employment that has dramatically increased the competitive employment and job tenure among persons with serious mental illness. Employment specialists are part of the treatment teams and share decision making. The ratio of employment specialists to consumers is one to twenty-five. In addition to treatment of mental health and co-occurring disorders by clinicians, vocational staff provide all phases of vocational services, including engagement, assessment, competitive job placement, and follow-up support (Drake et al. 1999).

Using an employment specialist or a job coach to support individuals at a job site and working with employers to address behavioral issues affected job performance may be useful strategies for offenders with significant substance abuse issues (Ashford and Sternbach 2007a). The job coach can also assist offenders and their employers with negotiating assignments and breaks, enhancing skill-development strategies, and altering workplace behavior that may threaten job stability.

Practice Guidelines

Effective reentry relies on principles and stages that, when followed, reduce recidivism, improve treatment and rehabilitation of offenders, and facilitate community reintegration (Gendreau and Ross 1979; Andrews et al. 1990; Taxman 2004). Cullen and Gendreau (2000) emphasize the following principles of rehabilitation: (1) targeting the known predictors of crime and recidivism, particularly focusing on modifiable dynamic predictors or criminogenic needs, such as antisocial values; (2) providing behavioral interventions targeted to the individual's needs, such as cognitive-behavioral programs; (3) focusing on higher-risk offenders, where the most substantial impact on recidivism can occur; and (4) emphasizing treatment effectiveness by matching styles and modes of treatment to the learning styles of offenders and engaging in effective treatment practice (staff training, sensitivity, supervision, knowledge of the particular treatment service, and provision of structured relapse prevention).

Other empirically supported principles identified by Taxman (2004) include (1) emphasizing informal social controls (family, peer, and other informal community networks and supports); (2) ensuring an sufficient duration (twelve to twenty-four months) for the intervention, to assist offenders in learning new behaviors; (3) providing sufficient dosages of the intervention, as intensity and frequency are important to help the offender make critical decisions, and matching interventions to the individuals' risk factors (of reoffending) and needs; (4) providing comprehensive, integrated, and flexible services designed to address the psychosocial needs of the offender; (5) ensuring continuity in behavior-change interventions, either in prison or in the community; and (6) providing clear communication of offender responsibility and expectations, working with the offender to establish rules, and using incentives and sanctions to support compliance.

Taxman (2004) has also written about making sure that the offender is an active participant in the reentry process. The offender's acceptance of individual responsibility and accountability for behavior is an important component of treatment and success. In Taxman's active-participant model, the offender is involved in the decision-making process for assessing risk, needs, and community factors that lead to criminal behavior. This role for the offender is an important issue for social work practitioners in defining their approach to treatment. This concept of offender responsibility somewhat parallels the concept of consumer responsibility in the recovery movement in the behavioral-health field. However, recovery emphasizes much more responsibility and control by people with mental illness in determining their treatment goals and also emphasizes the hope for recovery from mental illness (New Freedom Commission on Mental Health 2003).

One of the most important messages in these principles is that "one size fits all" programming will be inadequate to facilitate change. A reentry plan must be tailored to the individual needs of the parolee based on a thorough assessment. This principle is widely recognized in other writings on correctional programming (Taxman 2004; Ashford, Sales, and Reid 2001b; Blackburn 1996; Gendreau 1996). The plan must address the parolee's "readiness to change," his or her attitudes toward accountability and responsibility, and other risk factors and community-safety considerations (Andrews et al.

2006). Furthermore, the plan must emphasize use of informal supports to help individuals understand the benefits and responsibilities associated with community integration (Taxman 2004).

In addition to the principles of effective rehabilitation, Taxman (2004) has identified four stages for offender-reentry programs. These stages provide a framework for social work interventions with the offender. The stages are as follows:

(1) Institutional Stage (the last ninety days before release), where work begins with the offender to assess their motivation to change, develop reintegration goals, and learn about behavior patterns that affect their involvement in criminal activities

(2) Institutional/Prerelease Stage (from ninety days before release to release day), where the offender addresses basic survival issues at the time of their release, such as obtaining housing, employment, a driver's license, a Social Security card, treatment in the community, and health benefits

(3) Postrelease Stage (from release day to thirty days after release), where the offender focuses on adjustment to the community and reassesses vulnerability to criminal behavior; basic survival issues may likely be a focus if not resolved in the prerelease stage

(4) Integration Stage (from thirty days after release to up to two years), where the offender adjusts reentry plans based on experience; the focus may remain on survival skills, abstinence, treatment of special needs, developing community networks and support, maintenance of changes achieved in the prior stages, and crisis management

Case Example

The situation of Mr. X [details about Mr. X have been changed to protect his identity], a twenty-seven-year-old Hispanic male released from state prison, provides an example of limited reentry planning and highlights the procedural barriers to successful reentry described earlier in this chapter. The lack of practice guidelines that address basic needs for food and shelter, treatment and rehabilitation, work or education, and the community supervision of special needs offenders while on parole are particularly relevant.

Mr. X has a history of substance use since his mid-teens and dropped out of school. He is married and has young children but has limited work experience because his substance use interfered with his work history. His wife has been sober and in recovery from alcohol abuse for four years. Mr. X was convicted as an adult twice for drug-related robbery. In prison for three years, he joined a gang for protection and has visible tattoos on his arms and neck. He moderated his use of drugs by participating in Narcotics Anonymous (NA) and Alcoholic Anonymous (AA) programs in the prison and also began distancing himself from the gang as his release date became closer. Mr. X anticipated reuniting with his family. His wife planned to move out of the jurisdiction where Mr. X was arrested. She wanted to be near other family and to have a home for Mr. X away from his criminal friends. She also had work and educational opportunities that would enable her to better support her children.

Upon his release, Mr. X. requested a transfer of his parole supervision from one jurisdiction to the jurisdiction where his wife had moved. The transfer was denied due to extant policies that require offenders to return to the jurisdiction where the offender committed the crime. His reentry plan included assignment of a parole officer that he would see once a month or every other month, monthly drug testing, and participation in NA and AA. Now that he has lost his home and the daily support of his family, Mr. X's goals are to get his gang tattoos removed and find a job and place to live in the jurisdiction. He has been unsuccessful in removing the tattoos, as he is ineligible for public health-care benefits because he committed drug-related crimes. So far, no employer has been willing to hire him because of his criminal record, his limited skills, and his very obvious and menacing gang tattoos. His wife is especially upset, because she believes he has not developed the skills to resist using drugs without family support and being away from his circle of former friends. Mr. X would have benefited from a staged reentry process designed to connect him with his family, help him establish a residence away from his gang members, and transcend policy barriers in the community.

Issues of Diversity and Practice with Populations at Risk

Most adult offenders are poor, minority, male, and largely high-school dropouts with limited job skills (Ashford and Sternbach 2007a). Many are victims of trauma, homeless or on the verge of becoming homeless, single parents, and, if housed, live in largely poor, high-crime neighborhoods (Travis, Solomon, and Waul 2001; Lynch 2006; Ashford and Sternbach 2007a).

Women offenders constitute approximately 7.2 percent of federal and state prisoners and 12.9 percent of local jail inmates (Sabol, Minton, and Harrison 2006), and although the growth of women's incarceration is twice that of men (Sentencing Project 2005), most reentry models are based on males. A national profile of women offenders suggests the following characteristics: they are disproportionately women of color; they are in their early to mid-thirties; they are most likely to have been convicted of a drug-related offense; they have fragmented family histories, with other family members also involved with the criminal justice system; they are survivors of physical and/or sexual abuse as children and adults; they have significant substance abuse problems and multiple physical and mental health problems; they are unmarried mothers of minor children; and they hold a high-school degree/GED but have limited vocational training and sporadic work histories (Bloom, Owen, and Covington 2003). Women prisoners are more likely to be parents than men prisoners and to have had custody of their children prior to incarceration (National Governor's Association 2004). They are less likely than men to recidivate when they are provided with housing and employment assistance as designated reentry interventions (Flavin 2004; Holtfreter, Reisig, and Morash 2004; Roman 2004).

Besides addressing the gender imbalance in the design of reentry services, practitioners cannot ignore how demographic, cultural, and environmental factors will influence an offender's reentry into the community. The large numbers of offenders who are released from jails and prisons return to the same neighborhoods. Their impact on these communities must be taken into account. Efforts must be made to eliminate risks in the environments where the offenders are returning, and these efforts must include partnerships with community agencies capable of responding to these issues. To this end, practitioners need to engage the cooperation of the police and other local authorities. In addition, they need to target known injustices in the community that increase the offender's risk of recidivating, including improving access to needed services and supports.

Implications for Home-Based Practice

Advances in reentry theory and practice have moved home-based supervision approaches far beyond the earlier intensive supervision models that primarily emphasize surveillance. The RNR theory of correctional rehabilitation emphasizes assessments and interventions that target multiple risk and need and responsivity issues rather than solely the risk to community safety and criminal recidivism. However, correctional experts and social service researchers are in the initial phases of testing interventions that blend supervision and treatment models. In particular, social service practitioners need to individualize the reentry planning processes so that more attention is devoted to addressing the specific responsivity issues of each offender. More research and evaluation needs to be devoted to understanding the interactions of the individual offender and treatment characteristics. Indeed, most of the research and evaluation in the extant literature has focused on assessing risks and needs. While this research is invaluable, there are major gaps in the literature, particularly on the types of interventions that work best with specific types of risk profiles in persons with serious mental disorders.

In addition, much of the invaluable research on treatment effectiveness examined in this chapter will fall out of favor if practitioners cannot do a better job of defining and measuring the general well-being of offenders as an important outcome of offender reentry. An important future direction for social workers involved in offender reentry is to identify alternative strategies for enhancing the recovery and well-being of offenders with special needs. While the RNR theory has important implications for reducing recidivism, feminists have criticized it for bias toward the management of risks without considering correlations with "predictors of socioeconomic status, ethnicity, gender, and age" (Rigakos 1999, 145). For this reason, researchers and practitioners need to work on targets for change for special needs offenders and for women, ethnic and racial minorities, and aging offenders. In order to include quality of life as an outcome for each of these special groups of offenders, poverty, segregation, victimization, racism, and other social-structural barriers must also become important targets for change in reentry programming.

There are promising interventions for reducing recidivism and fostering the reentry of offenders, but many of these interventions are not being implemented with fidelity to the program model. Thus there are a number of correctional researchers who are calling for the development of standardized measures for monitoring the implementation quality of evidence-based practices in correctional rehabilitation (Andrews, Bonta, and Worthmith 2006). This is an important direction for future research by social workers. The field of reentry is unlikely to achieve its obvious promise without giving due diligence to developing instruments for measuring adherence to both the principles of RNR and those associated with improved quality of life for offenders. In sum, the training and specialized expertise of social workers puts them in the unique position of being able to promote models of rehabilitation that focus both on risks and on issues of quality in the lives of offenders.

REFERENCES

Andrews, D. A., and Bonta, J. 1998. *The psychology of criminal conduct*. 2nd ed. Cincinnati, Ohio: Anderson.

Andrews, D. A., Bonta, J., and Wormith, J. S. 2006. The recent past and near future of risk and/or need assessment. *Crime and Delinquency* 52: 7–27.

Andrews, D. A., Zinger, I., Hoge, R. D., Bonta, J., Gendreau, P., and Cullen, F. T. 1990. Does correctional treatment work? A clinically relevant and psychologically informed meta-analysis. *Criminology* 28 (3): 369–404.

Ashford, J. B., and LeCroy, C. W. 1993. Juvenile parole policy in the United States: Determinate versus indeterminate models. *Justice Quarterly* 10: 179–195.

Ashford, J. B., Sales, B. D., and LeCroy, C. W. 2001. Aftercare and recidivism prevention. In *Treating adult and juvenile offenders with special needs*, ed. J. B. Ashford, B. D. Sales, and W. Reid, 373–400. Washington, D.C.: American Psychological Association.

Ashford, J. B., Sales, B. D., and Reid, W. H. 2001a. Introduction. In *Treating adult and juvenile offenders with special needs*, ed. J. B. Ashford, B. D. Sales, and W. Reid, 3–27. Washington, D.C.: American Psychological Association.

———. 2001b. Political, legal, and professional challenges to treating offenders with special needs. In *Treating adult and juvenile offenders with special needs*, ed. J. B. Ashford, B. D. Sales, and W. Reid, 31–49.Washington D.C.: American Psychological Association.

Ashford, J. B., and Sternbach, K. 2007a. Best practices for parolee reentry, Monterey County, California. *Report to the Monterey County Intergovernmental Planning Committee*. Available online at http://www.onestopmonterey.org/gsipub.

———. 2007b. Monterey County parolee reentry focus group report. Salinas, Calif. Available online at http://www.onestopmonterey.org/gsipub.

Ashford, J. B., Wong, K., and Sternbach, K. 2008. Generic correctional programming for mentally ill offenders: The results of one pilot program. *Criminal Justice and Behavior* 35: 457–473.

Berman, G., and Feinblatt, J. 2003. Problem-solving courts: A brief primer. In *Judging in a therapeutic key: Therapeutic jurisprudence and the courts*, ed. B. J. Winick and D. B. Wexler, 73–86. Durham, N.C.: Carolina Academic Press.

Blackburn, R. 1996. Mentally disordered offenders. In *Working with offenders: Psychological practice in offender rehabilitation*, ed. C. R. Hollin, 119–149. Chichester: John Wiley and Sons.

Bloom, B., Owen, B., and Covington, S. 2003. Gender-responsive strategies. In *Research, Practice, and Guiding Principles for Women Offenders*. Available online at http://www.nicic.org/Library/.

Bond, G., Miller, L., Krumwied, R., and Ward, R. 1988. Assertive case management in three CMHCs: A controlled study. *Hospital and Community Psychiatry* 39: 411–418.

Bonta, J. 1996. Risk-needs assessment and treatment. In *Choosing correctional options that work: Defining demand and evaluating the supply*, ed. A. T. Harland, 18–32. Thousand Oaks, Calif.: Sage.

Borland, A., McRae, J., and Lycan, C. 1989. Outcomes of five years of continuous case management. *Hospital and Community Psychiatry* 40: 369–376.

Cosden, M., Ellens, J. K., Schnell, J. L., Yamini Diouf, Y., and Wolfe, M. M. 2003. Evaluation of a mental health treatment court with assertive community treatment. *Behavioral Sciences and the Law* 21: 415–427.

Cullen, F., and Gendreau, P. 2000. Assessing correctional rehabilitation: Policy, practice, and prospects. In *Policies, processes, and decisions of the criminal justice system*, ed. J. Horney. Washington, D.C.: National Institute of Justice.

Drake, R. E., Becker, D. R., Clark R. E., and Mueser, K. T. 1999. Research on the individual placement and support model of supported employment. *Psychiatric Quarterly* 70: 289–301.

Durose, M., and Langan, P. 2003. Felony sentences in state courts. *Bureau of Justice Statistics Bulletin*. U.S. Department of Justice, Office of Justice Programs, NCJ 198821.

Eggleston, A. N.d. Perpetual punishment: The consequences of adult convictions for youth. *Policy brief, adultification series, volume 4. Campaign for Youth Justice.* Available online at http://www.campaignforyouthjustice.org.

Feder, L. 1991. A profile of mentally ill offenders and their adjustment in the community. *Journal of Psychiatry and Law* 19: 79–98.

Flavin, J. 2004. Employment counseling, housing assistance . . . and aunt Yolanda? How strengthening families' social capital can reduce recidivism. *Criminology and Public Policy* 3: 209–216.

Gendreau, P. 1996. The principles of effective intervention with offenders. In *Choosing correctional options that work: Defining and evaluating the supply*, ed. A. T. Harland, 117–130. Newbury Park, Calif.: Sage.

Gendreau, P., and Ross, R. 1979. Effective correctional treatment: Bibliotherapy for cynics. *Crime and Delinquency* 25: 463–489.

Glaze, L. E., and Bonczar, T. P. 2007. Probation and parole in the United States, 2005. *Bureau of Justice Statistics Bulletin*. U.S. Department of Justice, Office of Justice Programs, NCJ215091.

Hartwell, S. W. 2004. Comparison of offenders with mental illness only and offenders with dual diagnosis. *Psychiatric Services* 55 (2): 145–150.

Heilbrun, K., and Griffin, P. A. 1993. Community-based forensic treatment of insanity acquittees. *International Journal of Law and Psychiatry* 16: 133–150.

Hirsch, A. E., Dietrich, S. M., Landau, R., Schneider, P. D., Ackelsberg, I., Bernstein-

Baker, J., et al. 2002. *Every door closed: Barriers facing parents with criminal record.* Washington, D.C.: Center for Law and Public Policy; Flint, Mich.: Charles Stuart Mott Foundation.

Hodgins, S., and Janson, C. G. 2002. *Criminality and violence among the mentally disordered: The Stockholm project metropolitan.* Cambridge: Cambridge University Press.

Hodgins, S., and Muller-Isberer, J. R., eds. 2000. *Violence, crime, and mentally disordered offenders: Concepts and methods for effective treatment and prevention.* Chichester: John Wiley and Sons.

Holtfreter, K., Reisig, M. D., and Morash, M. 2004. Poverty, state capital, and recidivism among women. *Criminology and Public Policy* 3: 185–208.

Jacoby, J. E., and Kozie-Peak, B. 1997. The benefits of social support for mentally ill offenders: Prison to community transitions. *Behavioral Sciences and the Law* 15: 483–501.

Kunz, M., Yates, K. F., Czobor, P., Rabinowitz, S., Lindenmayer, J. P., and Volavka, J. 2004. Course of patients with histories of aggression and crime after discharge from a cognitive-behavior program. *Psychiatric Services* 55: 654–659.

Lamb, H. R., and Weinberger, L. E. 1998. Persons with severe mental illness in jails and prisons: A review. *Psychiatric Services* 49: 483–492.

———. 2001. Adult offenders and community settings: Some case examples. In *Treating adult and juvenile offenders with special needs*, ed. J. B. Ashford, B. D. Sales, and W. H. Reid, 465–478. Washington, D.C.: American Psychological Press.

Lamberti, J. S., Weisman, R. L., and Faden, D. I. 2004. Forensic Assertive Community Treatment (FACT): An emerging model for preventing incarceration of severely mentally ill adults. *Psychiatric Services* 55: 1285–1293.

Lanagan, P., and Levin, D. 2002. Bureau of Justice statistics special report: Recidivism of prisoners released in 1994. Bureau of Justice Statistics Special Report (NCJ 193427). Washington, D.C.: U.S. Government Printing Office.

Latessa, E. J., Cullen, F. T., and Gendreau, P. 2002. Beyond correctional quackery: Professionalism and the possibility of effective treatment. *Federal Probation* 666: 43–49.

Lattimore, P. K. 2007. What we've learned: Findings from the multi-site SVORI Evaluation. NIJ Research and Evaluation Conference, July 25. Available online at http://www.svori-evaluation.org.

Link, B. G., Cullen, F., and Andrews, H. 1992. Violent and illegal behavior of current and former mental patients compared to community controls. *American Sociological Review* 57: 272–292.

Lipton, F. R., Nutt, S., and Sabatini, A. 1988. Housing the homeless mentally ill: A longitudinal study of a treatment approach. *Hospital and Community Psychiatry* 39: 40–45.

Lovell, D., Gagliardi, G. J., and Peterson, P. D. 2002. Recidivism and use of services among persons with mental illness after release from prison. *Psychiatric Services* 53: 1290–1296.

Lurigio, A. J., Fallon, J. R., and Dincin, J. 2000. Helping the mentally ill in jails adjust to community life: A description of postrelease ACT program and its clients. *International Journal of Offender Therapy and Comparative Criminology* 44: 532–548.

Lynch, J. B., and Sabol, W. J. 2004. Assessing the effects of mass incarceration on informal social control. *Criminology and Public Policy* 3: 267–294.

Lynch, J. P. 2006. Prisoner reentry: Beyond program evaluation. *Criminology and Public Policy* 5: 401–412.

Macht, M. W., and Ashford, J. B. 1991. *Introduction to social work and social welfare*. 2nd ed. New York: Macmillan.

Marini, R. A. 2003. Mental health courts focus on treatment: Criminals often overlooked in traditional systems are sentenced to hospital care. In *Judging in a therapeutic key: Therapeutic jurisprudence and the courts*, ed. B. J. Winick and D. B. Wexler, 59–62. Durham, N.C.: Carolina Academic Press.

Marshall, M., and Lockwood, A. 2001. The effectiveness of case management and assertive community treatment for people with severe mental disorders. In *The treatment of schizophrenia: Status and emerging trends*, ed. H. D. Brenner, W. Boker, and R. Genner, 181–194. Kirkland, Wash.: Hogrefe and Huber.

McManus, M., Alessi, N. E., Grapentine, W. L., and Brickman, A. 1984. Psychiatric disturbance in serious delinquents. *Journal of the American Academy of Child Psychiatry* 23: 602–615.

McNiel, D. E., and Binder, R. L. 2007. Effectiveness of a mental health court in reducing criminal recidivism and violence. *American Journal of Psychiatry* 164 (9).

Melton, G. B., and Pagliocca, P. M. 1992. Treatment in the juvenile justice system: Directions for policy and practice. In *Responding to the mental health needs of youth in the juvenile justice system*, ed. J. J. Cocozza, 107–139. Seattle, Wash.: National Coalition for the Mentally Ill in the Criminal Justice System.

Mohan, R., Slade, M., and Fahy, T. A. 2004. Clinical characteristics of community forensic mental health services. *Psychiatric Services* 55 (11): 1294–1298.

Monahan, J., and Steadman, H. J. 1984. *Crime and mental disorder*. Washington, D.C.: National Institute of Justice.

Morrissey, J., and Meyer, P. 2005. *Extending assertive community treatment to criminal justice settings*. Delmar, N.Y.: The National GAINS Center.

Morash, M., Bynum, T. S., and Koons, B. A. 1998. *Women offenders: Programming needs and promising approaches. Research in Brief*. U.S. Department of Justice, Office of Justice Programs, National Institute of Justice.

National Governor's Association. 2004. *The challenges and impacts of prisoner reen-*

try. Washington, D.C.: National Governor's Association Center for Best Practices, Social, Economic and Workforce Programs Division.

New Freedom Commission on Mental Health. 2003. *Achieving the promise: Transforming mental health care in America. Final report.* DHHS Pub. No. SMA-03–3832. Rockville, Md.

Otto, R. K., Greenstein, J. J., Johnson, M. K., and Friedman, R. M. 1992. Prevalence of mental disorders among youth in the juvenile justice system. In *Responding to the mental health needs of youth in the juvenile justice system,* ed. J. J. Cocozza, 7–48. Seattle, Wash.: National Coalition for the Mentally Ill in the Criminal Justice System.

Petersilia, J., and Turner, S. 1993. Evaluating intensive supervision probation/parole: Results of a nationwide experiment. In *Research in brief.* Washington, D.C.: National Institute of Justice.

Probation and Parole in the United States. 2005. Washington, D.C.: U.S. Department of Justice, Bureau of Justice Statistics. Available online at http://www.ojp.usdoj.gov/bjs/abstract/ppus05.htm.

Rigakos, G. S. 1999. Risk society and actuarial criminology: Prospects for a critical discourse. *Canadian Journal of Criminology* 41.

Roman, C. G. 2004. A roof is not enough: Successful prisoner reintegration requires experimentation and collaboration. *Criminology and Public Policy* 3: 161–168.

Sabol, W. J., Minton, T. D., and Harrison, P. M. 2007. *Prison and jail inmates at midyear 2006.* Washington, D.C.: U.S. Department of Justice, Office of Justice Programs.

Sentencing Project. 2005. *New incarceration figures: Thirty-three consecutive years of growth.* Available online at http://www.sentencingproject.org.

Shapiro, C. 1998. *La Bodega de la Familia: Reaching out to the forgotten victims of substance abuse.* Washington, D.C.: U.S. Department of Justice, Office of Justice Programs.

Solomon, P., and Draine, J. 1995. One-year outcomes of a randomized trail of case management with seriously mentally ill clients leaving jail. *Evaluation Review* 19: 256–273.

Stein, L., and Test, M. A. 1980. Alternatives to mental hospital treatment. *Archives of General Psychiatry* 37: 392–397.

Sullivan, E., Mino, M., Nelson, K., and Pope, J. 2002. *Families as a resource in recovery from drug abuse: An evaluation of La Bodega de la Familia.* New York: Vera Institute of Justice.

Synder, H. N., and Sickmund, M. 2006. *Juvenile offenders and victims: 2006 national report.* Washington, D.C.: U.S. Department of Justice, Office of Justice Programs, Office of Juvenile Justice and Delinquency Prevention.

Taxman, F. S. 2004. The offender and reentry: Supporting active participation in reintegration. *Federal Probation* 68 (2): 31–35.

Taxman, F. S., Cropsy, K. L., Young, D. W., and Wexler, H. 2007. Screening, assessment, and referral practices in adult correctional settings: A national perspective. *Criminal Justice and Behavior* 34 (9): 1216–1234.

Taxman, F. S., and Marlow, D. 2006. Risk, needs, responsivity: In action or inaction? *Crime and Delinquency* 52: 3–6.

Taxman, F. S., Yancey, C., and Bilanin, J. E. 2006. Proactive community supervision in Maryland: Changing offender outcomes, 2–17. Joint Research Team from the Virginia Commonwealth University and the University of Maryland. Evaluation for the Maryland Division of Parole and Probation.

Travis, J. 2000. But they all come back: Rethinking prisoner reentry. *Sentencing and corrections: Issues for the twenty-first century.* Research brief, papers from the Executive Sessions on Sentencing and Corrections. National Institute of Justice and the University of Minnesota. NCJ 181413.

Travis, T., Solomon, A. L., and Waul, M. 2001. *From prison to home: The dimensions and consequences of prisoner reentry.* Washington, D.C.: The Urban Institute.

U.S. Department of Health and Human Services. 1999. *Mental health: A report of the Surgeon General.* Rockville, Md.: U.S. Department of Health and Human Services, Substance Abuse and Mental Health Services Administration, Center for Mental Health Services, National Institute of Mental Health.

U.S. Department of Justice, Bureau of Justice Statistics. 2005. *Criminal offender statistics.* Available online at http://www.ojp.usdoj.gov/bjs/crimoff.htm#inmates.

Wilson, D., Tien, G., and Eaves, D. 1995. Increasing the community tenure of mentally disordered offenders: An assertive case management program. *International Journal of Law and Psychiatry* 18: 61–69.

Ziguras, S., and Stuart, G. 2000 A meta-analysis of the effectiveness of mental health case management over twenty years. *Psychiatric Services* 51 (11): 1410–1415.

Ten

Adult Mental Health

PATRICK SULLIVAN

The tenor of the times, fiscal policies, and key legal decisions all conspired to form the perfect storm: beginning in earnest in the second half of the 1960s, there was a dramatic depopulation of the nation's state psychiatric hospitals. This period in history, retroactively labeled the deinstitutionalization movement, has been analyzed from a myriad of angles and perspectives and simultaneously cheered and jeered. Aside from scholarly interests and an honest desire to learn from the past, the question of the primary locus of mental health care has long been decided. Indeed, as Mechanic and Rochefort (1992, 146) noted over fifteen years ago, "there is little chance of a wholesale return to the public asylum at this point."

Looking back, few would disagree that the system of community-based mental health services, prepared to serve former inpatients or those with serious mental illnesses now diverted from inpatient care, was inadequate to address the task at hand. Not only were services for the most seriously challenged lacking, but the conceptual development and articulation of specialty programs required for primary consumers and their families was at a nascent stage (Foley and Sharfstein 1983; Lamb and Bachrach 2001). As consumers tried with decidedly mixed success to navigate a complicated service network, and as families, who felt abandoned and blamed, scrambled to piece together a support network for loved ones, the gaps in care became impossible to ignore. Observing the landscape with deinstitutionalization in full swing and after community mental health centers had gained a foothold across the land, Klerman (1977) pronounced that the mentally ill were now better—but not well.

As providers and policymakers worked to close these notable gaps, new programs were devised and some old models of care revived. By the 1980s, case management emerged as having a crucial role in community mental health care. While the roles and functions of the case manager would take many forms, in time it was clear that, to be successful, providers needed to move out of the office and onto the streets (Rapp and Goscha 2004; Schmidt-Posner and Jerrell 1998).

Yet despite heroic efforts on many fronts, the mental health system is still overmatched: demand far outstrips available services. While the frustrations are many, the desire to help remains. Often, the job of creatively piecing together the formal and informal supports needed for persons to survive in the community falls on the shoulders of case managers. As a result, case management, often provided by social workers, is an essential component of contemporary community mental health. This chapter will review the role of case-management services and, in particular, services offered in the home and in the community. The advantages and challenges of "in vivo" helping will be discussed, as will many of the pressing ethical issues surrounding aggressive outreach.

The Population

Mental illness is a pervasive global problem that profoundly affects individuals and societies. Given the lack of precision in diagnosis and cultural differences in how behavior is interpreted and labeled, measures of incidence and prevalence will forever seek a moving target. The landmark U.S. Surgeon General's report on mental illness acknowledged the wide range of prevalence estimates generated by previous studies but projected that 20 percent of the population is affected by mental illnesses in any given year (U.S. Department of Health and Human Services 1999). Of prime concern to policymakers and providers is that segment of the populace who suffer from serious disorders. Current estimates suggest that 5.4 percent of the population suffer from a serious mental illness, while 2.6 percent suffer from what is now termed severe and persistent mental illness (Goldman and Grob 2006).

Severe and persistent mental illness encompasses such diagnostic categories as schizophrenia, bipolar disorder, and major depression. However, diagnosis alone tells a fraction of the story. What marks these conditions as particularly troublesome are duration and disability. The nature of these conditions portends the need for long-term if not lifelong support, and the pervasive disability that follows affects nearly every sphere of life. Adding to the challenge, the course of illnesses such as schizophrenia is not linear. For some, difficulties are episodic; others face an unrelenting foe. Good medical and psychiatric care is a necessity, and most agree that medication is key to any comprehensive care plan. Standard care, however, is insufficient, and attention must be directed to the problems in living that consumers face.

A recent study estimates that by 2003 the cost of mental health treatment in America had reached $100 billion (Mark et al. 2007). While those facing serious disorders constitute only a fraction of those diagnosed with any mental illness, the indirect and direct costs associated with conditions such as schizophrenia is staggering (Knapp, Managlore, and Simon 2004). By virtue of the use of high-end and intensive services such as inpatient care and specialized housing, high treatment costs are inevitable. When services falter or, as is often the case, available resources are outstripped by demand, these same persons can return to family or end up on the street or in jail (Cunningham, McKenzie, and Taylor 2006). Thus when policymakers turn their attention to this population, it is motivated by a mix of genuine compassion and a pragmatic concern over rising health-care costs.

Policy and Agency Context

The introduction of Medicaid and Medicare in the mid-1960s helped states reduce their fiscal burden by discharging consumers to the community, allowing them to downsize psychiatric hospitals under their control. This, and the introduction of community mental health centers, seemed to offer, as President Kennedy proposed, a bold new approach to mental illness (Foley and Sharfstein 1983). Sadly, the flaws in the plan became readily apparent. Poor coordination between hospital and community, the lack of relevant supportive services, and unreceptive communities spelled disaster for many consumers and their families. Professionals, family members, concerned citizens, and consumers demanded a midcourse correction in the mental health practice and policy landscape.

In 1978, the National Institute of Mental Health unveiled the Community Support Program (Turner and TenHoor 1978). The CSP initiative was important in several respects. First, it signaled that federal authorities recognized that a systemwide approach was needed to address the needs of those dealing with serious challenges. In addition, it served as an acknowledgment that an effective service system must focus on the medical *and* psychosocial aspects of mental illness.

Seasoned clinicians are all too familiar with the devastation caused by illnesses such as schizophrenia, major depression, and bipolar disorders. At the time when most young people are struggling with their identity and other life benchmarks such as career choice, leaving home, and starting a family, others find their lives torn asunder by mental illness. These illnesses also profoundly affect the family. At this point in history, many discharged from institutions and others who may have received inpatient care in the past were remaining at home. Without information and support—and, worse, identified as a possible source of their loved ones' difficulties—family members became isolated and demoralized. (For a historical overview, see Hatfield and Lefley 1987.) Thankfully, the combined voices of concerned family members helped spur the development and dissemination of specialty services.

The CSP concept was defined as "a network of caring and responsible people committed to assisting a vulnerable population to meet their needs and develop their potential without being unnecessarily isolated or excluded from the community" (Turner and TenHoor 1978, 329). Key components of this model included crisis-stabilization services, psychosocial rehabilitation services, and a range of practical and emotional support services for the consumer and family. Unquestionably, this program represented one salvo in an attempt to address the unintended consequences of a series of disjointed policy and legal decisions. While the excess and neglect found in some state psychiatric hospitals had been exposed and deplored, these total institutions offered twenty-four-hour care and a wide range of ancillary services needed in day-to-day life. In the absence of comprehensive services and supports, many consumers were cast adrift upon discharge, often lacking the requisite skills and resources to adjust to community life.

CSP was an important pilot project that offered the first glimpse at new models of care. In time, a new discipline emerged, alternately referred to as psychosocial or psychiatric rehabilitation. Much early work focused on skill building in areas of daily living, and various educational modules and training packages were developed, often offered in day programs attached to community mental health centers or hospitals (Pratt et al. 1999). As the field evolved, more ambitious efforts focused on independent living and vocational programming, with an eye toward full community integration for those challenged by mental illnesses.

Regardless of the soundness of these new models of care, they had little chance of widespread adoption until there were mechanisms in place to pay for them. Case management is a perfect example. Quickly identified as a needed service in a system of community-based care, the role seemed ideally suited to fill the breach between hospital and community. A case manager could serve as the point person, the identified staff member whose primary job was to locate and secure services and resources consumers were lacking. In a world that had been dominated by a largely medical view, these new services did not fit neatly into any insurance or subsidy plan. Beginning in the 1980s, a variety of incremental changes, some initiated by federal agencies such as the Department of Health and Human Services and the Social Security Administration, had a dramatic effect on community-based care (Goldman and Grob 2006). In essence, the recognition of mental illnesses as a disabling condition and the expansion of Medicaid coverage to include psychosocial rehabilitation services provided the platform needed to expand community-based mental health services, including case management. In the blink of an eye, the backbone of the mental health system became Medicaid. In fact, as Cunningham, McKenzie, and Taylor (2006, 694) note, Medicaid "has become the single largest payer of mental health services for low-income people." Significantly, various programs such as the Medicaid Rehabilitation Option provided a ready-made reimbursement mechanism to support case-management services. Savvy state officials who were searching for a way to meet demand now had an attractive tool to maximize available dollars and expand care. The end result was predictable. Expenditures began to grow (at times exponentially), and soon both federal and state budgets began to sag under the load (Boyd 2003). As we head toward the second decade of the twenty-first century, it is clear that something has to give. Managed-care programs, statewide caps on Medicaid expenditures, and a retreat to a more narrow medical orientation to care seems possible (Cunningham et al. 2006). On the other hand, in the search for effective and cost-efficient treatment methods, case management and other outreach services may survive the slash-and-burn mentality of authorities focused mainly on the bottom line.

Purposes and Goals of Social Work Home-Based Services

Case management and home-based mental health services are inherently pragmatic. As one response to deinstitutionalization and a changing treatment environment, case managers were poised to deal with the everyday realities of clients' lives. Case managers function where the rubber meets the road: jobs, food, shelter, employment, and positive leisure are a few of the areas of interest. The intent has always been to help consumers improve their quality of life and become full participants in community life.

A strict focus on mental illness has largely been beyond the purview of case managers. Nothing about the role is designed to focus *exclusively* on the symptoms and course of mental illness. However, outreach work does take services to the consumer. In that respect, case managers, when their job description includes in-home and community services, are in a prime position to observe changes in mood, attitude, and behavior. This allows for the early identification of impending difficulty and a chance to forestall relapse. Thus, a secondary focus of outreach case management is to prevent unnecessary psychiatric hospitalization or other disruptions that will affect the life of the client and others.

Other common functions of case management include offering support and information to family and friends who provide care, resource acquisition, and advocacy. These functions, critical elements of case management, are primarily geared to advance the central goal of positive community integration.

Theoretical Framework

The early models of case management affirmed the coordination or broker functions of the role. It was hoped that this one identified staff member could help piece together the items a consumer needed to successfully function in the community. This was a textbook case of the clash between theory and reality. Try as they might, case managers were not miracle workers. It was impossible to access resources that did not exist, and the community proved to be less hospitable than had been hoped. It soon became obvious that the resource coordination, or pure broker model of case management, was poorly suited for work of this nature.

Clinical models of case management also were proffered, with the notion that the person in the best position to offer case-management services was the consumer's primary therapist. While attractive in theory, clinicians by disposition and training were not inclined to focus on the community-based problems faced by clients, nor were they eager to leave the office. (See Mueser et al. 1998 for a good review of case-management models.)

Deitchman (1980, 789) recognized that the broker model of case management left much to be desired, and reaffirmed the importance of the professional relationship to good case management. In his words, those trying to adjust to life in the community needed "a traveling companion, not a travel agent." Being a traveling companion meant spending time working alongside consumers in the home and community. Case managers were asked to focus attention squarely on the psychosocial consequences of mental illness. Since they were addressing a different set of goals, reconsideration and/or exploration of the best methods to help consumers in these areas was in order.

An important and viable model of case management is the Strengths Model (Rapp 1998; Weick et al. 1989). A centerpiece of this method is an affirmation of the importance of "in vivo" helping and the centrality of the helping relationship. First labeled the Resource Acquisition model, this approach highlights the importance of identifying and building from individual and community strengths and developing a care plan largely inspired by the goals of consumers. Today, many persons and programs claim to adhere to the strengths perspective, but in the early 1980s, this approach represented a radical departure from the status quo.

More than a few eyebrows were raised at the notion of providing mental health services out of the office, particularly with those deemed most ill. Case managers were asked to perform a wide array of roles, because, as Williams and Swartz (1998, 300) suggested, "the philosophy of case management programs is to do 'whatever it takes' to support the client in the community." Consequently, as Curtis and Hodge (1994, 16) observed, "the very nature of some community support work demands shifting relationship boundaries and constant evaluation of the appropriateness of established boundaries."

Everything, it seemed, about mental health care was changing. In the world of psychotherapy, boundaries, by design, are rigidly enforced. Here, the office setting, the timing and duration of appointments, and the nature of the relationship is "the frame created by the therapist in which therapy can take place" (Williams and Swartz 1998, 300). The world of the case manager is clearly different. Instead of the office, the community becomes the frame, and case managers, far from remaining a neutral observer, work as collaborators and partners with consumers. Nonetheless, while the professional boundary is different, establishing and continually clarifying the parameters of the relationship is especially important given the irregular times and settings where services are routinely offered (Carey 1998). Early concerns aside, outreach case management, as offered by an individual or team, is now an accepted and valued role in modern community mental health. However, several questions remain. Are outreach and in-home services essential ingredients of case management in adult mental health? What tools and techniques enhance the effectiveness of outreach case management? What ethical concerns persist?

Empirical Base

Language is powerful. At one point in history, the use of the term "chronic mental illness" was widespread. Today, more hopeful concepts, such as "recovery," dot professional literature and discourse. That said, recovery can be a long and arduous journey, and the word "cure" is never used in reference to illnesses like schizophrenia. Home- and community-based services are not intended to cure or even directly affect the vexing symptoms experienced by consumers. In assessing the impact of case management, it is vitally important to recognize that the service is always shaped by context. Case managers cannot repair gaps in the system or force society to assume a more enlightened view of mental illness. When considering the daunting nature of serious and persistent mental illnesses and the resource obstacles case managers are asked to surmount, it is easy to understand why success comes in small increments.

Various reports and first-person accounts underscore that consumers value case management and their relationship with case managers. Significantly, this service is associated with overall client satisfaction (Gerber and Prince 1999; Rapp and Goscha 2004; Sullivan 1994a). Barry et al. (2003) report that Assertive Community Treatment (ACT), a team model that includes outreach case management, and strengths case management, which is an individual approach, have a positive impact on consumers' clinical profiles, with the strengths model having the edge.

Research has evaluated the effectiveness of different models of community-based treatment in adult mental health. Rapp and Wintersteen (1989) reviewed twelve replications of the strengths model of case management and noted the high level of individual goal attainment in these studies. In a similar vein, Stanard (1999) reports that the strengths model outperforms standard case management (i.e., the broker model) in the area of educational and vocational outcomes.

The most consistent findings with regard to case management and ACT are in the area of psychiatric hospitalization. Several researchers report an association between outreach case management and reduced use of the hospital, including reduction in admissions and days spent in inpatient care (Chinman, Rosenheck, and Lam 2000; Kanter 1999; Meaden et al. 2004; Schmidt-Posner and Jerrell 1998). Certainly, in today's fiscal environment there is heavy pressure to reduce high-intensity and expensive services. Simply reducing hospitalization is not an innately positive outcome and is an insufficient standalone outcome for any mental health service. Nonetheless, avoiding unnecessary hospitalization remains an important issue for consumers and policymakers.

Ziguras and Stuart (2000) conducted a meta-analysis of case-management studies published over a twenty-year period. In comparison with usual treatment, case management was associated with improved outcomes in symptoms, hospital days, dropout rates, overall level of functioning, client and family satisfaction, and family burden. The most robust findings included fewer hospital days, more contact with and longer retention in mental health services, improved social functioning, and client satisfaction.

Case management is also a vital ingredient in ACT, which is generally recognized as an evidence-based practice in mental health (Bond et al. 2001; Lehman and Steinwachs 1998). While it is difficult to determine the discrete contribution of outreach case management within this multidisciplinary team intervention, it is viewed as a critical ingredient of this widely disseminated model.

Practice Guidelines

Since case management is built on pragmatism and because so much of the job centers on resource acquisition and tasks of daily living, it is easy to minimize the importance of or undervalue the skill required to perform the role. Consumers tell a different story. Case managers often become important and influential persons in the lives of those facing serious mental illnesses. Isolation and loneliness are pervasive among consumers, and case managers can be the one constant positive presence. Case managers perform their tasks differently than psychotherapists. Carey (1998, 315) argues, in contrast to classic therapy, "relationship variables are not seen as *sources* of change but rather as essential factors that *facilitate* change."

Engaging with Consumers and Developing a Working Alliance

Engaging consumers is not an easy task, particularly when they have had long treatment histories, unsatisfying experiences with professionals, and have struggled with illnesses that portend difficulties in interpersonal relationships. Bordin (1979) offered three key components to forming a therapeutic alliance: goals, shared tasks, and an attachment bond. In many ways, the nature of outreach case management enhances the opportunity to forge a productive working alliance. In particular, consumers appear to appreciate the practical nature of case management, in part because they receive assistance in matters vitally important to their success and survival (Chue 2006; Priebe et al. 2005; Sullivan 1994a). Seemingly simple things like getting help with transportation, shopping together, and going to lunch are important to consumers. Not surprisingly, consumers value having someone who listens to them, takes them seriously, and who treats them with respect and dignity

(Gerber and Prince 1999; Ware, Tugenberg, and Dickey 2004). These expressions of interest and concern are consistent with expectations of professional conduct, and they are also the cornerstone of effective practice. Borg and Kristiansen (2004) admit that some professionals view this aspect of care as superfluous but argue that a reciprocal relationship signals that helpers look beyond illness and see a fellow human being who is both capable and resourceful. Menikoff (1999, 43), going one step further, notes that "although psychiatry has developed a number of technologies that minimize the worst symptoms, help prevent relapses, and support rehabilitation, the oldest clinical intervention—the relationship—has not lost its importance. . . . Given the fragmented communities and disjointed health care system in the United States, the relationship may be coming into its own as a therapeutic agent."

Home- and community-based work is the ideal forum for such a relationship to flourish. First and foremost, engagement appears to be a function of regular contacts and time spent with the client (McCabe and Priebe 2004; Priebe et al. 2005; Rapp and Goscha 2004). By taking services to the consumer, the case manager can tend to crisis and upsets, help consumers with specific tasks, and even revive the old social work concept of friendly visiting. While it is important to underscore that not all consumers are comfortable with in-home services, many are. When conversations occur in a living room, a car, or a local diner, people often are more at ease.

Ware et al. (2004) sought consumer perspectives on those aspects of their relationship with professionals that were most valued. A review of the priority areas that emerged from this work highlights key aspects of good outreach case management. Consumers enjoyed practitioners who would share a personal story, give them a needed ride, or do something perceived to be "a little extra." In essence, good helpers are able, when appropriate, to shed their professional skin. Similarly, consumers enjoyed interactions that seemed to focus on the common ground between them. This could involve recognition of similar personal traits and beliefs or shared activities like working together to accomplish an identified goal. Feeling like the helper knew them beyond a superficial level, that there was adequate time to talk about a variety of things, and that they were treated like individuals instead of just another person with mental illness were also cited. Other tangible aspects of the relationship that consumers appreciated included the availability and accessibility of the professional, flexibility in appointment times, and the opportunity to participate in care planning.

Forming a solid working alliance is vital because it translates into actual client outcomes, either directly or as a mediating variable (Angell, Mahoney, and Martines 2006; Chinman et al. 2000; Chue 2006; McCabe and Priebe 2004; Meaden et al. 2004). Because frequent contact is a key ingredient to the process of engagement, outreach services are particularly important when working with those with serious and persistent mental illnesses. Some challenges, like major depression, naturally hinder office-based treatment attendance. Clinical features like paranoia leads to distrust, and some consumers fear that contact with professionals will lead to a return to the hospital. Unfortunately, isolation exacerbates the problems these same people face. In part, services such as case management and initiatives such as Program for Assertive Community Treatment (PACT) or ACT were predicated on aggressive outreach to ensure that consumers would not get lost in the system and to provide support and respite for families (Bond et al. 2001; Stein and Test 1980).

Engaged clients tend to participate and adhere to a care plan, including a medication regime, and to perceive services to be useful (Angell et al. 2006; Chue 2006; Meaden et al. 2004). Making contact with consumers in the home and community may be important perquisites to establishing a working alliance, but what other aspects of case management make a difference once a relationship has been established?

Strengths-Based Assessment

Like all mental health interventions, strength-based case management begins with an assessment. Graybeal (2001, 235) astutely observes that "it is critically important to understand that there is not and cannot be a distinct demarcation between assessment and intervention in social work practice." The process of conducting a strengths-based assessment signals a different set of expectations to the consumer and demonstrates that the professional hopes to understand the whole person. These expectations are especially important for a client population that has routinely experienced professionals who hold low expectations for their life chances (Blundo 2001). Strengths-based assessment is a process that unfolds as the relationship develops. Because it is believed that recovery requires positive transactions with the social environment, the strengths discovery process explores healthy aspects of the person and the world around them (Cowger, Anderson, and Snively 2006; Sullivan and Rapp 2006).

Individual strengths are not captured well on simple checklists, and environmental strengths are rooted in context. Strengths are best deciphered in action and observation—not through words alone. All people perform differently in different social contexts. Accurate assessment, particularly when information is to be used in the service of goals germane to daily living, must commence in the worlds where consumers live, work, and play (Rapp and Goscha 2004).

In fact, Kanter (1999) posits that one of the distinct advantages of home-based mental health services lies in the ability to conduct "in vivo" assessments.

Good assessment begins with listening. Cowger et al. (2006) articulate the importance of gathering and documenting the client's story, giving preeminence to the story and discovering uniqueness. This also means listening to peoples' problems and sorrows. Many are overwhelmed, and their own capacities to cope and adjust have been overrun. It is likely that a standard diagnostic workup will be part of the assessment process. This standard information can obviously be useful to an outreach case manager. However, given the goals of case management, different data are needed, and, at some point, an assessment must move toward strengths. Timing is important, for as McQuaide and Ehrenreich (1997, 207) suggest, "in making this transition the client must not feel the worker is abandoning the client self that feels too vulnerable to solve his or her problem or that the worker views the client's problem as easy to solve."

Nonetheless, individual, family, and community strengths are building blocks in the recovery process. Anthony (1993, 15) defines recovery as "a deeply personal, unique process of changing one's attitudes, values, feeling, goals, skills and/or roles. It is a way of living a satisfying, hopeful, and contributing life even with the limitations caused by illness." Survival and resilience are mainstays in the lexicon of the strengths perspective, as are ideas and words such as "hopes," "dreams," and "goals." Recovery narratives speak to the importance of these concepts, which have often been stripped from the hearts and minds of those facing mental illness. A diagnosis is formed in the mind of the professional; a strength assessment belongs to the consumer. Where a deficits assessment asks what is wrong, a strengths assessment asks what is right. In traditional mental health, problematic behaviors, thoughts, and beliefs are attacked, often rightfully so. In strengths-based practice, individual and community assets are identified and amplified. It is argued here that strengths are rarely adequately assessed in the office.

A central premise of the strengths model is that behavior is a function of the resources available to people (Davidson and Rapp 1976). Accordingly, case managers must draw upon the assessment of individual, family, and community strengths to shape a relevant care plan. Expressly to be avoided is the tendency to match an identified need with a specialized professional service. Such resources segregate consumers from community life and are limited and expensive. Natural community resources are limitless and potentially expansive.

Case examples, illustrating these principles in action, abound. Note that the strengths and interests identified can be relatively simple items that are often passed over in standard assessments and care plans, if they are ever noted at all.

Bryan and Jenny Clauson met each other at a mental health program and were married one year later. Both were diagnosed with schizophrenia. While they had done well in the early days of their marriage, over the past year they had become withdrawn and quit taking their prescribed medication. A return to inpatient care appeared imminent. Intensive case-management services were offered and, while skeptical, the couple agreed to meet. Over the course of the assessment, the case manager learned that they had once enjoyed playing cards at the clubhouse program sponsored by the mental health center and that they had held leadership positions at the program. The case manager began by setting up times to play cards with them as a way keep them active, and then casually mentioned that another couple nearby also enjoyed playing cards. A meeting was arranged between the two parties, which went well. Before long, Bryan and Jenny returned to the clubhouse, followed their respective care plans more closely, and began to consider looking for volunteer opportunities in the community.

As in other fields of practice, there is much to be learned by meeting with a consumer in their home and community. Often the landscape is surveyed for things gone awry—toxic elements in the proximal personal and social environment. Such things cannot be ignored, because they truly have a negative effect on behavior. However, the pioneering work of Kretzmann and McKnight (1993, 9) offered another view of communities, even the most impoverished. Their model of community development pivots on the identification and mapping of community assets. The work "starts with what is present in the community, the capacities of its residents and workers, the associational and institutional base of the area—not what is absent and problematic, or what the community needs." To illustrate:

Alison MacLeod suffered from bipolar disorder. Diagnosed at age twenty, she spent most of a decade in and out of inpatient care. Her attendance at the day-treatment program was sporadic, and she often commented that her failure to attend was due to boredom. In the course of the strengths assessment, Alison noted that her career goal was to become a hairdresser, but she didn't know where to start. Alison's case manager did some investigating and located a popular neighborhood hairdresser. Soon it was agreed that Alison could job shadow and do a few odd jobs around the shop. From this, she learned more about the field and decided to pursue the career in earnest. The hairdresser agreed to continue to mentor her through the process. During this period, Alison followed her medication plan and met regularly with her therapist and case manager.

Goal Setting

Individually tailored goals become the lynchpin of case-management practice. Good goals are observable and measurable and, in case management, largely behaviorally anchored. The goals desired by mental health consumers mirror those held by nearly everyone: a home, a job, meaningful personal relationships, and enjoyable leisure activities. A common feature of comprehensive community mental health services are programs geared to improve the functional skills of consumers or transitional services that aim to move participants toward independence. The persistent problem with these programs is that it is difficult for people to transfer skills learned in such programs to real community settings (Harding, Zubin, and Strauss 1987). A contributing factor to the downfall of traditional educational and training programs is that they are rarely individualized. By seeking uniqueness, strengths-based practice strives to identify the natural community resources that facilitate goal accomplishment or represent end targets and, with the consumer, develop an individually tailored work plan.

Professionals may take a dim view of the goals consumers identify, deeming them unrealistic given their current predicaments. Strengths-based practitioners see the issue differently. There are few goals viewed as out of bounds, in part because it is believed that all goals can be broken down into manageable steps. Even small steps are important accomplishments in the recovery journey. In this partnership model, case managers who leave the office are particularly indispensable. Understimulating environments, medication effects, the illness process, and fear are enemies of activity. In the end, many consumers are reluctant to leave the home. At times, it is important for them to regroup, but at other points encouragement is needed. Goals can provide a measure of motivation, particularly when they are client-directed and not prescribed by others. Learning to cook, ride the bus, or visit the library can be a significant stride forward for many, representing small steps toward a larger goal and serving as an opportunity to master skills and behaviors necessary for community life.

Three decades ago, Turner and TenHoor (1978) wrote that CSPs were designed to be not just a system of services but also a system of opportunities. The intent was to stimulate the expansion of programs that provided more opportunities for consumers to assume valued social roles. One sequelae of major mental illness is a reduction in the size and strength of ties in an individual's social support network (Sullivan and Poertner 1989). An important role for case-management services is to rebuild such networks by identifying people and places that are willing to assist and befriend others. This is an important aspect of community integration and reduces the burden faced by families, who often go it alone. Good case managers put themselves out of business by locating others who replace functions provided by professionals and formal services.

The more consumers can do on their own to improve their lot, the better. Yet while the public may be better informed about mental illness than in the past, forces of stigma and discrimination are still at work. Case managers often serve as advocates at the individual, program, and policy level (Rapp 1998). The more these advocacy efforts are conducted face to face in the community, the better the outcomes will be.

Safety Considerations

There are many benefits to offering mental health services in the home and community, but there are also some practical considerations when leaving the office. Not only are case managers entrusted to positively engage with and provide care for consumers; they are also expected to ensure public safety. Not all clients receive care voluntarily, and some have committed serious crimes. While violence is an overstated and sensationalized aspect of mental illness, it also cannot be dismissed. Providing services at irregular times and in environments where crime is common is also a pressing concern for providers.

Weisman and Lambert (2002) argue that some violent behavior is predictable, often when prompted by irrational beliefs and perceptions. Violence is also more likely when consumers fail to take prescribed medication, use and abuse alcohol and drugs, and have a history of violent behavior. With these known threats in mind, it behooves case managers to thoroughly review a consumer's chart before work begins.

All are rightfully concerned when consumers are in a downward spiral. Home-based services can be a useful way to respond to and prevent relapse and perhaps reduce the likelihood of criminal behavior. There are times when consumers deteriorate rapidly. This can be a function of drug use, trauma and stress, or the effect of discontinuing a medication that impacts behavior quickly (e.g., lithium). However, it is more common for deterioration to follow a slow and gradual course, which underscores the utility of regular contact, including telephone calls or brief visits. Vigilant case managers recognize that a fundamental sign of impending problems is reclusive behavior and a failure to keep appointments. Case managers should work with consumers and family members so all can recognize common and idiosyncratic indicators of relapse and devise strategies to respond quickly. Recovery narratives indicate that symptom management is a skill that can be learned over time and that some relapses can be prevented (Ritsher et al. 2004; Sullivan 1994a). An important step toward recovery for consumers is to learn to recognize and respond to indicators of relapse. Sometimes medications need adjusting; sometimes better sleep and diet will turn things around. In the throes of a major crisis, a brief stay in an inpatient or crisis-respite program can be useful, but rarely is this more useful than helping consumers learn to deal effectively with the challenges presented by mental illness and the world around them (Sullivan 1994a).

There are some practical guidelines to consider when making home visits, and particular care is needed in a crisis situation. It is important that someone knows the whereabouts of case managers at all times and that they have a cellphone handy. Before making the first visit to a client, it is often useful to visit the location in advance and note any special concerns about the area, including the best places to park. Weisman and Lambert (2002) suggest that it is best to team up for an initial visit, know who is in the house, and position oneself to have a direct route to a door or window. Case managers should leave the home quickly if the consumer is intoxicated or in an extremely disorganized state and contact their immediate supervisor. Instincts should always be trusted. (See chapter 2 for further discussion of safety issues.)

Issues of Diversity and Practice with Populations at Risk

The Surgeon General's report on mental illness confirmed that the existing system of care was failing minority populations in a variety of ways (U.S. Department of Health and Human Services 1999). At the most basic level, noticeable discrepancies in access to service, availability of quality services, and poor treatment retention have been identified. Other clinical concerns focus on cultural bias in diagnosis, differential patterns in the prescription and use of medication, and the overrepresentation of minority populations in inpatient psychiatric settings (Pi and Simpson 2005; Snowden 2003). Considering these trends, Snowden (2003, 239) notes it is impossible to determine the independent impact of bias but argues "to *ignore* racial and ethnic differences reflects a kind of bias."

"Race," "culture," and "ethnicity" are all slippery terms (Escobar and Vega 2006; Kleinman and Benson 2006), and an elucidation of these debates is beyond the scope of this chapter. Yet culture, however defined, affects every facet of mental health treatment. An individual's culture of reference and the dominant culture in which they are embedded influences how symptoms are manifested, understood, interpreted, and responded to (Bernal and Saez-Santiago 2006).

Also at play are key life circumstances that cause significant stress, such as language barriers, poverty, discrimination and, with recent immigrants, the loss of a valued support network. The opportunities for misunderstanding and misdiagnoses are rife, especially where common mental health nomenclature cannot be viably translated across cultures. These issues are particularly salient for those in case management and other outreach mental health services in the public sector. How can these services be designed and delivered to effectively address the needs of an increasingly diverse population? At the structural level, assertive outreach teams can specifically target services to diverse groups, and efforts can be made to match consumers with clinicians with similar backgrounds. Additionally, Lefley and Bestman (1991) describe the use of cultural brokers. Here, staff or consultants who possess useful knowledge about a population of concern can offer insights that can improve the effectiveness and relevance of services.

However, it is important to recognize that not all members of a given racial or ethnic group are the same. Stereotyping is to be avoided, particularly what Kleinman and Benson (2006, 1674) refer to as the trait-list approach, which "understands culture as a set of already known factors." Similarly, Escobar and Vega (2006, 42) observe that commonly used terms such as "Hispanic" and "Latino" are too broad and heterogeneous to be meaningful. In fact, they assert that country of origin and immigrant status may be the most important issues to consider, even as many ethnic and racial categories used in the United States "are growing more inaccurate with the passage of time."

Understanding the uniqueness of each individual is central to good social work practice. Home-based practice allows the professional to learn about the culture of the family they serve and, where appropriate, bring members of the extended family, fictive kin, and other relevant community members to the table (Slaughter-Defoe 1993). To this end, an acculturation assessment may be particularly useful (Sue 2006; Ziguras et al. 2003). This assessment can provide a sharper understanding of how an individual or family understands mental illness, what they believe is an acceptable response to illness, and their expectations for services. In this work, professionals may encounter the range of indigenous labels some use to describe and understand mental illness. While one natural response is to counter these depictions with seemingly more modern and scientific data, in fact, these labels may normalize the experience for individuals and families and provide a more optimistic view of the future (Sullivan 1994b). Similarly, Fang and Schinke (2007) report a high use of complementary alternative medicine among Chinese Americans and suggest that psychiatrists should evaluate the efficacy of traditional remedies and perhaps integrate them with traditional treatments. Acculturation assessments may also suggest the extent to which extended family members expect to be participants in the process and point to the resources and assets in a person's support network.

Sue (2006) touts the benefits of a pretherapy phase to help clarify the nature of the intervention and what to expect in the process of helping. This is especially important where an intervention lacks "ascribed credibility" and is not routinely valued by a particular culture as important. Sue feels that to gain "achieved credibility" the consumer and family should quickly experience a direct benefit from helping, such as reduced anxiety or the accomplishment of a small goal or task.

Kleinman and Benson (2006, 1674), using tenets of ethnography, offer the "explanatory models approach" as a useful tool in working with diverse populations. Ethnography represents an effort to understand what life is like for a person and "emphasizes intensive and imaginative empathy." An important step is to explore ethnic identity and understand how central it is to a client's overall sense of self. From there, a skilled helper discovers what illness means to a person, how they explain it, what stresses result, and what supports exist for them.

Implications for Home-Based Practice

Most would agree that the development of community-support programs, including ACT, and the addition of outreach case management to standard community mental health offerings have been positive developments. And as these programs have expanded, more has been asked of them. The public commitment to community mental health and those with mental illness is at best lukewarm, and even with improvements in medication management and direct service offerings, only so much can be accomplished.

In this context, new methods of leverage and control have become omnipresent in community practice (Davis 2002). For example, outpatient-commitment laws are now in place in the majority of states, and representative payee programs and tying treatment compliance to housing are commonplace (Monahan et al. 2001; Swartz et al. 2006). These developments have prompted any number of questions about the ethics of assertive community treatment and aggressive outreach services (Bonnie and Monahan 2005; Gomory 2005; Stovall 2001). Egan and Kadushin (1999), in a look at the field of home care, report that a majority of workers acknowledge that ethical issues are endemic to their work.

The outreach worker is always on the horns of a dilemma. The issues of leverage and assertive outreach cannot be dismissed lightly. Neale and Rosenheck (2000) highlight the constant tension between the desire for client self-direction and therapeutic limit setting. Stovall (2001, 140) asks: "is treatment that won't go away ethical?" This is a particularly penetrating question if resources are tied to program participation. Additionally, when consumers discontinue participation in traditional mental health programming, outreach activities are likely to intensify. Gomory (2005) argues that ACT and other similar programs are not only coercive and paternalistic but are also less effective than commonly reported.

Bonnie and Monahan (2005) feel the debate around forced treatment and coercion has become stale, and they offer a new perspective. They direct attention away from debates about coercion and toward the notion of the "relational contract." The idea of a relational contract emphasizes the issue of bargaining and negotiation, and here, "the quality of the relationship between the 'contracting parties' is a key variable, as the dynamic process of negotiation during the period of treatment" (488). The contract paradigm "focuses attention on the interactive process of negotiation that typically precedes and accompanies the use of therapeutic mandates and on characteristics of the relationship among service providers, patients, and leveraging agencies that implement these arrangements" (501). Here one asks if the contract allows for choice and if there is a goodness of fit with standard benchmarks for ethical practice, including respect for autonomy, doing no harm, offering a benefit, and reflecting a fair distribution of resources (Stovall 2001).

In times of fiscal conservatism, human services become less and less a public-policy priority. When the fallout from such choices is translated into human outcomes, the impetus is to control and contain the outsider, the deviant, and those deemed inconvenient. Fiscal policy will ultimately determine the future of home- and community-based mental health services. Case management was a dormant service until funding streams were found to support it. What has been given can easily be taken way. Concerns about the rise in Medicaid rolls and, concomitantly, the fiscal burden on states can lead to the return to restrictive definitions of medical necessity and a retreat from ancillary mental health services. Managed-care arrangements tend to favor less expensive and intensive services, and this can prove to be a stay of execution for case management, but how deeply will review processes restrict the range of services case managers perform? As described here, effective case management requires reasonable caseloads, the ability to work with key community allies, and creatively built care plans based on the unique goals of each consumer. Ideal conditions for case managers rarely exist today, and the future looks precarious at best.

This chapter has also underscored the importance of the treatment alliance between the consumer and professional. In the early days of strengths-based case management, the service was embraced by an enthusiastic cadre of committed individuals who had a passion for the role. This passion extended to the people with whom they worked. As case management has exploded, has this been lost? Saleebey (1991) cautioned that an emphasis on technology and technique could lead social work astray. In a world driven by the bottom line, and given the human service preoccupation with evidence-based practice, it is important to remember that the most important ingredient for good social work practice is to care. The voice of consumers consistently reminds us that this is the most important practice standard of all.

REFERENCES

Angell, B., Mahoney, C., and Martines, N. 2006. Promoting treatment adherence in assertive community treatment. *Social Service Review* 80 (3): 485–526.

Anthony, W. 1993. Recovery from mental illness: The guiding vision of the mental health system in the 1990s. *Psychosocial Rehabilitation Journal* 16 (4): 11–23.

Barry, K., Zeber, J., Blow, F., and Valenstein, M. 2003. Effect of strengths model versus assertive community treatment model on participant outcomes and utilization: Two-year follow-up. *Psychiatric Rehabilitation Journal* 26 (3): 268–277.

Bernal, G., and Saez-Santiago, E. 2006. Culturally centered psychosocial interventions. *Journal of Community Psychology* 34 (2): 121–132.

Blundo, R. 2001. Learning strengths-based practice: Challenging our personal and professional frames. *Families in Society* 82 (3): 297–304.

Bond, G., Drake, R., Mueser, K., and Latimer, E. 2001. Assertive community treatment for people with severe mental illness: Critical ingredients and impact on patients. *Disease Management and Health Outcomes* 9 (3): 141–159.

Bonnie, R., and Monahan, J. 2005. From coercion to contract: Reframing the debate on mandated community treatment for people with mental disorders. *Law and Human Behavior* 29 (4): 485–503.

Bordin, E. 1979. The generalization of the psychoanalytic concept of the working alliance. *Psychotherapy: Theory, Research, and Practice* 16 (3): 252–260.

Borg, M., and Kristiansen, K. 2004. Recovery-oriented professionals: Helping relationships in mental health services. *Journal of Mental Health* 13 (5): 493–505.

Boyd, D. 2003. The bursting state fiscal bubble and state Medicaid budgets. *Health Affairs* 22 (1): 46–61.

Carey, K. 1998. Treatment boundaries in the case management relationship: A behavioral perspective. *Community Mental Health Journal* 34 (3): 313–317.

Chinman, M., Rosenheck, R., and Lam, J. 2000. The case management relationship and outcomes of homeless persons with serious mental illness. *Psychiatric Services* 51 (9): 1142–1147.

Chue, P. 2006. The relationship between patient satisfaction and treatment outcomes in schizophrenia. *Journal of Psychopharmacology* 20 (6): 38–56.

Cowger, C., Anderson, K., and Snively, C. 2006. In *The strengths perspective in social work practice*, 4th ed., ed. D. Saleebey, 93–115. Boston: Pearson Education, Inc.

Cunningham, P., McKenzie, K., and Taylor, E. 2006. The struggle to provide community-based care to people with serious mental illness. *Health Affairs* 25 (3): 694–705.

Curtis, L., and Hodge, M. 1994. Old standards, new dilemmas: Ethics and boundaries in community support services. *Psychosocial Rehabilitation Journal* 18 (2): 13–33.

Davidson, W., and Rapp, C. A. 1976. Child advocacy in the justice system. *Social Work* 21 (3): 225–232.

Davis, S. 2002. Autonomy versus coercion: Reconciling competing perspectives in community mental health. *Community Mental Health Journal* 38 (3): 239–250.

Deitchman, R. 1980. How many case managers does it take to screw in a light bulb? *Hospital and Community Psychiatry* 31: 788–789.

Egan, M., and Kadushin, G. 1999. The social worker in the emerging field of home care: Professional activities and ethical concerns. *Health and Social Work* 24 (1): 43–55.

Escobar, J., and Vega, W. 2006. Cultural issues and psychiatric diagnosis: Providing a general background for considering substance use diagnosis. *Addiction* 101 (Suppl. 1): 40–47.

Fang, L., and Schinke, S. 2007. Complementary alternative medicine use among Chinese Americans: Findings from a community mental health population. *Psychiatric Services* 58 (3): 402–404.

Foley, H., and Sharfstein, S. 1983. *Madness and government: Who cares for the mentally ill?* Washington, D.C.: American Psychiatric Press.

Gerber, G., and Prince, P. 1999. Measuring client satisfaction with assertive community treatment. *Psychiatric Services* 50 (4): 546–550.

Goldman, H., and Grob, G. 2006. Defining "mental illness" in mental health policy. *Health Affairs* 25 (3): 737–749.

Gomory, T. 2005. Assertive community treatment (ACT): The case against the "best-tested" evidence-based community treatment for severe mental illness. In *Mental disorders in the social environment*, ed. S. Kirk, 165–189. New York: Columbia University Press.

Graybeal, C. 2001. Strengths-based social work assessment: Transforming the dominant paradigm. *Families in Society* 82 (3): 233–242.

Harding, C., Zubin, J., and Strauss, J. S. 1987. Chronicity in schizophrenia: Fact, partial fact, or artifact? *Hospital and Community Psychiatry* 38 (5): 477–486.

Hatfield, A., and Lefley, H, eds. 1987. *Families of the mentally ill.* New York: Guilford Press.

Kanter, J. 1999. Clinical issues in delivering home-based psychiatric services. In *Psychiatric home care: Clinical and economic dimensions*, ed. A. Menikoff, 19–37. San Diego, Calif.: Academic Press.

Kleinman, A., and Benson, P. 2006. Anthropology in the clinic: The problem of cultural competency and how to fix it. *PLoS Medicine* 3 (10): 1673–1676.

Klerman, G. 1977. Better but not well: Social and ethical issues in the deinstitutionalization of the mentally ill. *Schizophrenia Bulletin* 3: 617–631.

Knapp, M., Mangalore, R., and Simon, J. 2004. The global costs of schizophrenia. *Schizophrenia Bulletin* 30 (2): 279–293.

Kretzmann, J., and McKnight, J. 1993. *Building communities from the inside out: A path towards finding and mobilizing community assets.* Evanston, Ill.: Center for Urban Affairs and Policy Research, Neighborhood Innovations Network, Northwestern University.

Lamb, R., and Bachrach, L. 2001. Some perspectives on deinstitutionalization. *Psychiatric Services* 52 (8): 1039–1145.

Leffley, H., and Bestman, E. 1991. Public-academic linkages for culturally sensitive community mental health. *Community Mental Health Journal* 27 (6): 473–488.

Lehman, A., and Steinwachs, D. 1998. Translating research into practice: The schizophrenia Patient Outcomes Research Team (PORT) treatment recommendations. *Schizophrenia Bulletin* 24 (1): 1–10.

Mark, T., Levit, K., Buck, J., Coffey, R., and Vandivort-Warren, R. 2007. Mental health treatment expenditure trends, 1986–2003. *Psychiatric Services* 58 (7): 1041–1048.

McCabe, R., and Priebe, S. 2004. The therapeutic relationship in the treatment of severe mental illness: A review of methods and findings. *International Journal of Social Psychiatry* 50 (2): 115–128.

McQuaide, S., and Ehrenreich, J. 1997. Assessing client strengths. *Families in Society* 78 (2): 201–212.

Meaden, A., Nithsdale, V., Rose, C., Smith, J., and Jones, C. 2004. Is engagement associated with outcome in assertive outreach? *Journal of Mental Health* 13 (4): 415–424.

Mechanic, D., and Rochefort, D. 1992. A policy of inclusion for the mentally ill. *Health Affairs* 11 (2): 128–150.

Menikoff, A. 1999. The goals and principles of psychiatric home care. In *Psychiatric home care: Clinical and economic dimensions*, ed. A. Menikoff, 39–57. San Diego, Calif.: Academic Press.

Monahan, J., Bonnie, R., Appelbaum, P., Hyde, P., Steadman, H., and Swartz, M. 2001. Mandated community treatment: Beyond outpatient commitment. *Psychiatric Services* 52 (9): 1198–1205.

Mueser, K., Bond, G., Drake, R., and Resnick, S. 1998. Models of community care for severe mental illness: A review of research on case management. *Schizophrenia Bulletin* 24 (1): 37–74.

Neale, M., and Rosenheck, R. 2000. Therapeutic limit setting in an assertive community treatment program. *Psychiatric Services* 51 (4): 499–505.

Pi, E., and Simpson, G. 2005. Cross-cultural pharmacology: A current clinical perspective. *Psychiatric Services* 56 (1): 31–33.

Pratt, C., Gill, K., Barrett, N., and Roberts, M. 1999. *Psychiatric Rehabilitation*. San Diego, Calif.: Academic Press.

Priebe, S., Watts, J., Chase, M., and Matanov, A. 2005. Process of disengagement and engagement in assertive outreach patients: A qualitative study. *British Journal of Psychiatry* 187: 438–443.

Rapp, C. 1998. *The strengths model.* New York: Oxford University Press.

Rapp. C., and Goscha, R. 2004. The principles of effective case management in mental health services. *Psychiatric Rehabilitation Journal* 27 (4): 319–333.

Rapp, C., and Wintersteen, R. 1989. The strengths model of case management: Results from twelve demonstrations. *Psychosocial Rehabilitation Journal* 13 (1): 23–32.

Ritsher, J., Lucksted, A., Otilingam, P., and Grajales, M. 2004. Hearing voices: Explanations and implications. *Psychosocial Rehabilitation Journal* 27 (3): 219–227.

Saleebey, D. 1991. Technological fix: Altering the consciousness of the social work profession. *The Journal of Sociology and Social Welfare* 18 (4): 51–67.

Schmidt-Posner, J., and Jerrell, J. 1998. Qualitative analysis of three case management programs. *Community Mental Health Journal* 34 (4): 381–392.

Slaughter-Defoe, D. 1993. Home visiting with families in poverty: Introducing the concept of culture. *Home Visiting* 3 (3): 172–183.

Snowden, L. 2003. Bias and mental health assessment and intervention: Theory and evidence. *American Journal of Public Health* 9 (2): 239–243.

Stanard, R. P. 1999. The effect of training in a strengths model of case management on client outcomes in a community mental health center. *Community Mental Health Journal* 35 (2): 169–179.

Stein, L., and Test, M. A. 1980. Alternative to mental hospital treatment: I. Conceptual model, treatment program, and clinical evaluation. *Archives of General Psychiatry* 37 (4): 392–397.

Stovall, J. 2001. Is assertive community treatment ethical care? *Harvard Review of Psychiatry* 9: 139–143.

Sue, S. 2006. Cultural competency: From philosophy to research and practice. *Journal of Community Psychology* 34 (2): 237–245.

Sullivan, W. P. 1994a. A long and winding road: The process of recovery from severe mental illness. *Innovations and Research* 3 (1): 19–27.

———. 1994b. Recovery from schizophrenia: What we can learn from the developing nations. *Innovations and Research* 3 (2): 7–15.

Sullivan, W. P., and Poertner, J. 1989. Social support and life stress: A mental health consumer's perspective. *Community Mental Health Journal* 25 (1): 327–336.

Sullivan, W. P., and Rapp, C. A. 2006. Honoring philosophical traditions: The strengths model and the social environment. In *The strengths perspective and social work practice*, 4th ed., ed. D. Saleebey, 261–278. Boston: Pearson Education, Inc.

Swartz, M., Swanson, J., Kim, M., and Petrila, J. 2006. Use of outpatient commitment or related civil court treatment orders in five U.S. communities. *Psychiatric Services* 57 (3): 343–349.

Turner, J., and TenHoor, W. 1978. The NIMH Community Support Program: Pilot approach to needed reform. *Schizophrenia Bulletin* 4: 319–348.

U.S. Department of Health and Human Services. 1999. *Mental health: A report of the Surgeon General—Executive Summary*. Rockville, Md.: U.S. Department of Health and Human Services, Substance Abuse and Mental Health Services Administration, Center for Mental Health Services, National Institutes of Health, National Institute of Mental Health.

Ware, N., Tugenberg, T., and Dickey, B. 2004. Practitioner relationships and quality of care for low-income persons with serious mental illness. *Psychiatric Services* 55 (5): 555–559.

Weick, A., Rapp, C., Sullivan, W. P., and Kisthardt, W. 1989. A strengths model for social work practice. *Social Work* 89 (4): 350–354.

Weisman, R., and Lambert, J. S. 2002. Violence prevention and safety training for case-management services. *Community Mental Health Journal* 38 (4): 339–348.

Williams, J., and Swartz, M. 1998. Treatment boundaries in the case-management relationship: A clinical case and discussion. *Community Mental Health Journal* 34 (3): 299–311.

Ziguras, S., Klimidis, S., Lewis, J., and Stuart, G. 2003. Ethnic matching of clients and clinicians and use of mental health services by ethnic minority clients. *Psychiatric Services* 54 (4): 535–542.

Ziguras, S., and Stuart, G. 2000. A meta-analysis of the effectiveness of case management over twenty years. *Psychiatric Services* 51 (11): 1410–1421.

Eleven

Older Adult Services

KATHRYN BETTS ADAMS

The Population

The United States is aging, in part thanks to improvements in health care preventing deaths from cancers, heart attacks, strokes, and other common serious conditions of late life. As the oldest of the Baby Boomer generation hits the age of sixty, another influx of older adults is just around the corner. The group over age sixty-five is projected to increase from its current 12.4 percent of the population to 20.7 percent by 2050. And the "oldest old," those aged eighty-five and over, are projected to increase the most rapidly, more than tripling their proportion of the population over the next few decades (Administration on Aging 2007a).

Longer life spans mean many older people live longer with chronic conditions and impairments; many undergo surgery and other medical procedures that require recovery time. According to the 2000 Census, approximately 42 percent of all people aged sixty-five or older reported having some sort of physical or mental disability. Over three million citizens in this age group reported having a disability that required them to have assistance with self-care, and nearly seven million in this group reported having a disability that made it difficult to leave their homes to shop or visit a doctor's office (Administration on Aging 2007a). The likelihood of having one or more disabling conditions increases with advancing age (Kropf 2000). Many older adults in urban, suburban, and rural areas prefer to remain in their homes, "aging in place," despite the onset of functional limitations and the increasing inconvenience of stairs, yards, or neighborhoods without adequate public transportation (Adams 2006). Moreover, hospital stays are brief under managed care, and older patients are often discharged to home well before they are ready to function at their presurgery or preillness level, making home-based health care a necessity (Dunkle, Roberts, and Haug 2001). Home-based health and psychosocial services give these older adults the support they require to recover at home, in familiar surroundings. Whether older adults are recovering from illness or surgery or experience more chronic functional limitations, psychiatric disorders, or frailty of advanced old age, home-based services may be used to hasten a return home, to prolong the time remaining at home, or to avoid the need for institutional care altogether.

For the client and family, there are several important benefits to receiving in-home services. Foremost, older adults with mobility and transportation limitations can be seen in the relative comfort and security of their homes without the burden to them or their families that an outpatient office visit might involve. For some individuals, home-based services are the only alternative to no service or to moving to an institutional setting. Second, ongoing provision of in-home social work and related psychosocial services allows the older adult to continue to live in familiar surroundings, perhaps with family, pets, familiar neighbors, and beloved possessions. According to Kropf (2000, 170), "an important part of psychosocial adjustment to receiving services is the value that older people attach to their home environment. Most older people desire to remain in their own homes and communities—places which have real and symbolic value." In addition, for the geriatric service provider, home-based assessment and treatment or case management offers the optimal means of observing the person within his or her physical and social environment, in real time and under real conditions. Thus there is a great need for subacute health and psychosocial services for older adults, augmented by consumer and family preferences and expectations for remaining in the home and receiving individualized care, which points to the increased popularity and importance of home-based services.

Policy and Agency Context

Long-term care is no longer synonymous with nursing home care, but it is descriptive of a great variety of community-based services offered for older adults, including home-based services, which constitute the "least restrictive" level of care for frail or disabled older adults (Kropf 2000; Applebaum 2006). Many older adults who may have required institutional care in previous generations can now have their health and psychosocial needs accommodated primarily in their homes. Private geriatric care-management agencies and public and private hospital-affiliated home health-care agencies provide a large proportion of the home-based services to older people. Agencies for low-income elders are another major source of these services. There are four main routes to receipt of psychosocial home care services:

- *Fee for service through a home health-care agency or geriatric-care manager.* These services are increasingly available in urban and suburban communities. Private-home health agencies cater to older adults and their grown children who have the means to pay for services that might enable the elder to live independently and have a higher quality of life. These agencies, whose geriatric-care manager may be a social worker, can provide or arrange for both medical services (some of which may be covered by insurance, particularly following a hospital stay) and a variety of nonmedical services from aides, homemakers, or companions. These services offer the security of someone to "check on" the elder, who may be physically frail, mildly cognitively impaired, or impaired by vision or mobility limitations. Older adults or their families contacting a private-home care agency may seek companionship or supervision for someone who lives alone, assistance with personal care (washing, dressing, and grooming), meal preparation, and with tasks such as letter writing, making phone calls, or running errands.

- *Medicare and private health insurance.* Medicare and supplements purchased to extend Medicare's coverage will pay for home-based services that are considered medically necessary, often following discharge from an acute-care hospital. One of the needed services must be intermittent skilled nursing care, physical therapy, speech-language pathology services, or occupational therapy. If one of those is prescribed by a physician, then Medicare and most private health insurance will also cover part-time or intermittent home health aide services, social services such as counseling by a social worker, and medical equipment and supplies needed to offer these services in the home (Medicare 2007). Since October 2000, Medicare operates through a Prospective Payment System (PPS) to fund home health care for eligible adults aged sixty-five and over, giving incentive to providers to control costs (Lee and Gutheil 2003).

- *Medicaid waiver services.* Whereas Medicaid traditionally covered only institutional long-term care, usually nursing homes, many states have initiated a waiver program for Medicaid to cover home- and community-based long-term care. To be eligible for these programs, individuals generally need to have the same low income and limited financial assets that would qualify them for Medicaid coverage in a nursing home. These waiver programs result in an increasing number of low-income older adults receiving services in their homes, with the goal of keeping them out of institutional settings. They are also cost savers for the states, because part of the requirement is that the home-based services must cost less than a full-time nursing home stay.

■ *Older Americans Act Services.* Title III of the Older Americans Act (OAA) of 1965 included provisions for home-based services to be offered to anyone aged sixty or over. Amendments to the act have added Alzheimer's disease as a covered condition (in 1987) and case management as a recommended service (in 1992; Gelfand 2006). These OAA services, usually administered through local Area Agencies on Aging, include basic in-home assessment for service needs, home-delivered meals ("Meals on Wheels"), visiting nurses and home health aides, friendly visiting, homemaker and chore services, telephone reassurance, and an array of caregiver support services that were added in 2000 (Richardson and Barusch 2006). In different geographic areas, services may be coordinated and administered in different ways—sometimes along with Medicaid waiver services, sometimes separately. Eligibility for services may also vary. The services are supposed to be targeted to older Americans in rural areas; those with greatest economic need or greatest social need (particularly low-income minority elders); those with severe impairments, Alzheimer's disease, or related disorders; and elders who do not speak English (Gelfand 2006).

TWO EXAMPLES OF SOURCES OF HOME CARE

Aging Network Services (www.agingnets.com) is a home-care agency in Bethesda, Maryland, founded and run by two social workers each having over thirty years of geriatric experience. Aging Network Services provides family consultation, in-home psychosocial and medical assessments, service planning and arrangement of in-home services, and counseling or psychotherapy for both midlife and older adults. Some services are covered by Medicare or supplemental insurance; others are fee for service, offered on a sliding scale. The social workers who own Aging Network Services specialize in helping families make the adjustments needed when an older parent is failing but may be refusing help or when there are complicated family relationships. In addition, like many geriatric care-management agencies, they link families concerned about an aging family member to geriatric social workers in communities all around the country, so that families living at a distance from the older parent may arrange for assessment and service provision in the older person's home from a trusted service provider.

In Ohio, the larger of two state Medicaid waiver programs for people over sixty is PASSPORT (Pre-Admission Screening System Providing Options and Resources Today). For Medicaid-eligible adults at least sixty years of age who need personal care or assistance in order to remain at home, this program covers the following services: personal care; adult day care; environmental accessibility and adaptations; transportation to medical appointments; specialized medical, adaptive, and assistive equipment and supplies; homemaker or chore services; social work and counseling; nutritional consultation; and home-delivered meals. A case manager (either a social worker or registered nurse) develops the care plan cooperatively with the client and/or a family representative. A telephone screening for eligibility is followed by a thorough in-person assessment in the home setting, arrangement of needed services, and ongoing monitoring and management of the client's service needs (Ohio Department of Aging 2007).

There are many other examples of proprietary and nonprofit agencies providing home-based services to older adults, some of them part of large chains and some independent or associated with public or private hospitals. Many of these agencies are Medicare and/or Medicaid certified, so they can provide services reimbursable by these programs; they may also accept other insurance and direct payment of fees. The need for home-based services such as mental health and case management has never been greater, but, at times and in some areas, a lack of availability and funding constraints prevent adequate service delivery. Wodarski and Williams-Hayes (2002) write of the increasing numbers of older adults in the community with needs for assistance. They stress that geriatric institutionalization can be avoided with the provision of adequate resources and that older adults thrive in an environment suited to their social and functional needs, making dependency on family less of an issue. These authors assert that well-funded social work case management can help ensure that elderly clients receive appropriate services in order to maintain them adequately in the community, providing benefits both to caregiving families, who need relief and support, and to society, given the lower costs of care.

Rural areas face particular challenges in providing home-based services, chief among them large, sparsely populated geographic areas. Cassity and Huber (2003) describe the status of community-based programs and services for rural older adults. They conclude that successful strategies for maintaining rural elders in their homes must be innovative and collaborative. They suggest that social workers who deliver and coordinate home-based services in rural areas should recognize the heterogeneity of the population, obtain the clients' input in service planning, stay current on local and regional resources, and focus on educating the community about client needs.

In-home geriatric mental health services pose unique challenges for service delivery (Kohn et al. 2004). Those who can benefit from in-home mental health services are either homebound for psychiatric reasons, medical reasons, or both, or they are simply noncompliant with the prescribed medical regimen. Because of the limited availability of in-home mental health services, such as medication reviews, counseling, and psychotherapy for older adults with mental illness, and strict eligibility requirements for these services to be paid through Medicare, many older people with chronic mental illness are placed in nursing homes for lack of a better solution (Kohn et al. 2004) These authors recommend pooling sources of funds that currently exist to create comprehensive, mobile, interdisciplinary psychiatric teams to assess and treat older adults in their homes. In addition, they see the need for homemaker and chore services to accompany the psychiatric services, enabling these clients to live independently and in relative comfort.

Purposes and Goals of Social Work Home-Based Services

Many geriatric in-home services are performed, coordinated, or supervised by social workers. They are key members of interdisciplinary home health and mental health teams who participate in geriatric assessments and care management for older adults living in the community. Social workers have an important role in the assessment and monitoring of the older person's psychosocial needs and may be the "first responder" to evaluate the situation (Yagoda 2004). The holistic systems-and-strengths perspectives utilized by social workers are appropriate to the assessment of the individual within his or her home environment. Yet, as is the case in many health institutions, it is not uncommon for social work to be considered a secondary profession in home health agencies and funding contexts, where psychosocial outcomes are not as highly valued as medical outcomes. Because of this, in the current era of cost containment, social workers must be vigilant about demonstrating the positive, efficient outcomes of services provided to older adults in their homes and must communicate clearly to other disciplines about social work areas of expertise (Lee and Gutheil 2003).

In case-management situations, social workers typically counsel the older person and family as they adjust to chronic conditions or new impairments, helping clients and families understand and adapt to issues surrounding illness or disability. Furthermore, although home-based psychiatric services for older adults are limited in a number of states (Kohn et al. 2004), social workers frequently provide direct mental health treatment or psychotherapy in the home, sometimes to clients with depression or anxiety secondary to medical conditions. Determining eligibility for various services and coordinating care can be overwhelming for families and older clients (Dunkle et al. 2001). Social workers also possess expertise in brokering community resources and can offer instrumental help, such as explaining available service options, assistance with financial paperwork, and making specific referrals and arrangements for service. Social workers frequently coordinate formal and informal care, serving as the liaison with care providers on behalf of the client and family (McInnes-Dittrich 2005).

Clinical skills are important to home-based social work case managers (Yagoda 2004). For instance, a somewhat subtle but extremely important aspect of the social worker's role in home-based services for older adults is negotiating the delicate balance between the older person's independence and dependence (McInnes-Dittrich 2005). Commonly, the physical and functional changes that can occur quickly from events such as a stroke or broken hip are difficult for clients to process emotionally. In other situations, slow-onset conditions erode functioning gradually, and the elder fights the notion of asking for assistance despite obvious declining abilities and emotional stress. In these and similar situations, the social worker is in a position to support the client and family as they redefine their own roles and identities, wrestle with how much help is appropriate, and consider whether a move to a more restrictive environment such as assisted living may be preferable. Ethical issues often arise in the course of working out these arrangements: who is the client for the social worker when families disagree with the older person on matters of safety versus autonomy (McInnes-Dittrich 2005)? Although some older adults react to functional impairment by assuming a more dependent role and gratefully accept services or even initiate a move to an age-segregated setting, it is not unusual for the elder to wish to retain more independence even in the face of increased risks or deprivations. Families, on the other hand, may wish to place more restrictions on their loved one in order to assure his or her safety. These are very important issues for the families involved. Social work knowledge and skills can be invaluable in helping them understand one another and negotiate solutions.

Dyeson (2005) discusses additional roles for social workers in home care: those of advocate for clients, community organizer for groups of elders who may need home care in a given setting or geographic area, and team consultant to other members of the interdisciplinary treatment team. Social workers providing assessment and other services in older peoples' homes maintain an awareness of the potential for abuse or neglect as they interview and observe these clients. Social work case managers or adult protective services workers have the sometimes difficult task of assessing the presence of abuse or neglect, determining whether the older person may be in danger, and what steps should be taken to protect the client and ameliorate the situation (see case vignette in chapter 2).

Theoretical Framework

The theoretical literature pertaining to home-based geriatric social work begins with theories about why older people want to stay in their homes and how they manage. Continuity theory (Atchley 1989), corroborated by findings from longitudinal studies of aging (Costa, Metter, and McCrae 1994), suggests that people's basic personality structure, style, and preferences remain relatively stable throughout life, including old age. According to Atchley and Barusch (2004, 354), therefore, "one way that people cope with changes in their physical and mental capacities is to concentrate time and attention on long-standing patterns of activity. And a large measure of this continuity comes from having lived in the same dwelling for a long time." The gerontologist M. Powell Lawton (1975) used a stress and coping framework to understand how older adults handle stresses from aging, such as deteriorating health and the toll of caregiving. From this perspective, he developed the idea of "environmental press," which suggests that there is an optimal level of challenge, stimulation, and support in an individual's environment, based on his or her capabilities and resources. When older adults experience a change in functional status—cognitive impairment, mobility limitations, sensory loss—they may sense an imbalance of this challenge and stimulation. At this point, the older person may need increased assistance to cope effectively, or the environment may need to be altered.

Another key theoretical perspective informing contemporary geriatric social work home-based services is the strengths perspective. This perspective, along with the closely related empowerment approach, translates social-justice ideals into direct social work practice. It was developed to help underprivileged, oppressed, or disenfranchised clients, as a way to avoid focus on deficits and problems but instead to identify and capitalize on the strengths these individuals possess but may not recognize or use effectively (Saleeby 1992). The strengths and empowerment perspectives have been applied and adapted to work with frail elders, recognizing the importance of maximizing personal mastery and control for all individuals, even those with disabilities and impairments (Chapin and Cox 2001). Strengths-based practice with elders in home-based services focuses on identifying the strengths and abilities of the elder, as well as those of the family and community (Fast and Chapin 2000). A hallmark of strengths-based practice with frail elders is supporting the client's autonomy to the greatest extent possible, particularly by engaging the client's participation in defining their needs and determining goals, as well as by identifying strategies to meet those goals. Strengths-based and empowerment practice with older adults does not imply that problems or deficits are ignored. Indeed, encouraging the older client and family to identify and express feelings about disability, dependency, and the need for services should be a part of the process (Fast and Chapin 2000). However, as Chapin and Cox (2001, 173) assert, "resiliency, resources, promise, and dreams are to be given center stage."

Empirical Base

Although home-based services are increasing in prominence and availability as community-based long-term care begins to supplant institutional care, there have been few studies dedicated to home-based social work practice with older adults. One is a qualitative study by Naleppa and Hash (2001) that reports on the "challenges and opportunities" presented by home-based social work practice with older adults. These authors interviewed social workers to examine both what practitioners think makes home-based practice with older clients unique and their experiences of key events that encompass either positives or challenges. Naleppa and Hash categorized their findings into "intervention context" and "intervention process" issues. Some of the challenges within the intervention context include practitioners' reports of concerns with cleanliness, aggressive animals, hazardous conditions for entering the home, and dangerous environments, such as drug dealing in the older person's home by other relatives. In terms of opportunities within the context of home-based interventions, practitioners reported that most clients appreciate being seen in the home. However, some clients may be suspicious or uncomfortable allowing a social worker into the home.

Intervention-process challenges, which were highlighted in the study, included scheduling mix-ups—both conflicts with other service providers or daily activities or arriving and having the client not answer the door. Another major challenge mentioned by the interviewees in this study was the blurring of boundaries in home-based practice. Older clients frequently offer food or drink and may tend to see the social worker as a friendly visitor rather than a professional, sometimes offering gifts or asking for the social worker to run routine errands. Other challenges mentioned included distractions from a television or from others present in the home. The biggest intervention-process opportunities with home-based practice were the ability to do thorough assessments and to see the older person in their environment move around and interact. Participants in the study valued the ability to view family photos and art, observe medication bottles and food supplies, and detect problems with incontinence or alcohol abuse over the course of home visits to their clients.

A number of studies relevant to home-based geriatric social work demonstrate positive outcomes of specific home-based psychosocial interventions or programs. Some of these interventions are highly innovative, and many offer possibilities for serving socially isolated and frail elders and their caregivers. Discussions of the studies on a number of these interventions follow.

Task-centered case management is a promising intervention approach for frail elders living in the community. Kaufman et al. (2000) report the results of a study that tested the effectiveness of providing home-delivered task-centered mental health services to seventy-eight elderly patients of a rural home health-care agency. The task-centered model is based on the work of the late social work educator and researcher William Reid and has been modified for use with older home-care clients (Naleppa and Reid 1998). Task-centered practice takes a structured approach that focuses on the client's current goals and the tasks to achieve the goals. Related to empowerment practice and problem-solving approaches, this method is appropriate for work with frail elders in their homes. Clients who completed the brief task-centered psychotherapeutic intervention reported improvements in their emotional well-being and indicated significant reduction of the problems associated with the target complaints raised by the senior (Kaufman et al. 2000).

In one of the few studies offering home-based mental health treatment to people with early-stage Alzheimer's disease, Brierley and colleagues (2003) piloted a home-based, six-session psychodynamic-interpersonal approach that focused on identifying feelings and interpersonal problem solving. The model was adapted for people with early-stage Alzheimer's disease by adding time at each session to confer with the caregiver, and one of the goals was to "open up a dialogue" with the person about their problem of memory loss. Other components of the brief model were helping the person focus on personal qualities that revealed their individual strengths, making links from the past to the present and future, using emotional expression within the here and now of the sessions, and helping resolve past conflicts. The authors noted that although the twenty people they treated had marked memory loss, they were very receptive to the treatment and were able to remember the therapist and use the sessions to tell their stories and explore and express their feelings appropriately.

In another home-based intervention study, Stevens (2001) identified older women as a group susceptible to loneliness and reported on a "friendship enrichment" program designed to combat the loneliness of this population. Stevens' study, like that of Brierley, took place in England. The program was educational in nature, helping the women analyze their current social networks, set goals for developing friendships and social activities, and devise strategies to make those changes. The ultimate goal was empowerment. Participants were followed for one year after the program to determine the status of their relationships. According to Stevens, many women who participated in the program developed new relationships, improved old ones, and experienced reduced loneliness.

In the past two decades, many programs have been developed using technologies to connect isolated or home-bound elders and caregivers to service providers. Buckwalter and colleagues (2002) reviewed innovative telehealth programs for older adults and their caregivers living in rural areas. They found promising programs, including telephone-based caregiver skill training, a computer network to meet the educational and support needs of in-home caregivers of persons with dementia, an automated voice-response technology telephone system to provide brief respite care for caregivers, a multi-component anger-management intervention for home-based caregivers, and an Internet-based information and support system for family caregivers.

A telephone support-group model for family caregivers was designed to overcome problems arising from geographic isolation and physical or social constraints that prevent caregivers from attending in-person support groups. The model reported by Smith et al. (2004) consists of twelve sessions of about seventy-five minutes each, with a somewhat preset agenda consisting of three major components: emotion-focused coping, problem-solving coping, and support. The group leader would individually call each member first, greet them, and get them connected to the conference call, using an Internet-conferencing service provider. The first half of the meeting includes checking in and a brief didactic session by the social worker about emotion-focused coping strategies such as cognitive restructuring, perspective taking, and relaxation training. The second half of the meeting consists of problem solving for members who wish to share specific pressing problems. Encouragement to give vent to feelings and give one another empathic support occurs throughout the sessions. The researchers found that the leader must be more active in a telephone support group, be totally comfortable with the technology, and use more structure than in an in-person group. The telephone support group was found to be applicable to caregivers with different ethnicities and levels of socioeconomic status.

Finally, a frail elderly community-based case management project (Duke 2005) in a rural North Carolina county combined traditional social work and nursing case management with "telehealth," using small units that allowed two-way audio and visual interface. For medically frail clients, the telehealth aspect appeared to head off trips to the emergency room, reduced hospital stays and costs, and offered needed reassurance. Clients with more than mild dementia, however, found the telehealth units difficult and frustrating to use.

Several current or recent studies have shown promise for brief, structured, in-home therapy approaches for older adults with depression or anxiety. A brief problem-solving intervention is being tested in a randomized controlled trial funded since 2005 by the National Institute of Mental Health. The problem-solving approach is being used to treat minor depression in older home-care patients by Zvi Gellis and colleagues (2007, 2008). Another approach, the Program to Encourage Active, Rewarding Lives for Seniors (PEARLS), is found in SAMSHA's national registry for evidence-based programs and practices, having shown a low-cost, effective means for improving minor depression or dysthymia in older adults receiving home-based services (SAMSHA 2007). And the Medicaid Institute at the United Hospital Fund, a New York City organization, is working to demonstrate the effectiveness of a screening and coordination-planning effort to reach and treat depression in home-bound older adults, particularly members of minority groups with limited incomes (Medicaid Institute 2007).

The few studies conducted on home-based social work services and intervention approaches to date have shown the promise of both structured and brief interpersonal approaches. Technological innovations such as telephone support and telehealth monitoring for home-bound elders and caregivers have also been shown to be feasible and effective, with certain limitations, to supplement or replace in-person case-management services. New studies are underway that will add to the evidence base for home-based geriatric social work, particularly in the areas of screening and brief treatment for depression and anxiety. In the current era of cost containment and emphasis on evidence-based programs and practices, the development and evaluation of innovative approaches to provide screening, case management, mental health treatment, and family support for frail elders in their homes is likely to remain an important focus for the social work profession.

Practice Guidelines

There is limited descriptive and prescriptive writing about providing home-based social work services to older adults. In the practice literature, the strengths-based approach to case management (Chapin and Cox 2001; Fast and Chapin 2002) has received much attention, and its influence is seen in many practice textbooks. In addition, several authors have delineated guidelines for the management of elder abuse (Anetzberger 2005; Brandl 2000). Still others have outlined general practice issues specific to working with elders in their homes (e.g., Naleppa and Hash 2001; Knight 2004; Emlet, Crabtree, and Condon 2007; McInnes-Dittrich 2005). The remainder of this chapter draws on these authors and several practice texts to offer a summary of current best practices and guidelines.

Assessment

"The ideal place for an assessment to be done is the elder's home. This places the elder on his or her own turf, reducing the distractions and anxieties inevitable in an unfamiliar setting. The home setting also provides the social worker with invaluable information to corroborate or challenge what the elder says about the ability to function" (McInnes-Dittrich 2005, 91). Visiting older adults in the home is the ideal way to assess the suitability of the environment for their needs (Emlet et al. 2007). Many important questions can be answered through observation. Do the immediate neighborhood, yard, and entrances from outside appear to provide a safe and secure living environment? Is the home interior clean and tidy, or does it appear dirty or cluttered? Are things in need of repair? Does the older person appear to have the ability to manage within that environment, with or without assistance or special modifications? For example, can she navigate between the sleeping, bathroom, sitting, and kitchen areas? Can she reach what she needs and operate equipment safely? Is there an area for bathing that she can get to and get into and out of? Is the space where she lives hazard free? What sorts of food and drinks are in stock in the home? Do you smell alcohol or see signs that the client or family has been drinking excessively?

One or more home visits are also very helpful for the assessment of the older person's social environment. Are family members or other individuals present in the home, and do they appear to be helpful and supportive of the older adult? How is the interaction between the older person and the spouse, family members, or others in the household? Is there too much commotion or isolation? Do neighbors or friends call or come by during the visit? Does the client mention any family, friends, or neighbors during the interview? What sorts of photos or mementos are visible in the home? Does the client appear to be well-groomed, bathed, and cared for, or is there the possibility that the older person is being neglected, exploited, or mistreated?

In addition to the physical and social environment, the social worker will want to assess the areas of health and functioning (medical needs, mobility issues, nutrition, transportation to physicians' appointments), mental status (cognitive impairment, thought disorders, confusion or memory loss), emotional status (grieving, anxieties or fears, depression, paranoia, discouragement versus hopefulness), and financial questions or concerns.

In some ways, engaging in home-based social work with older clients is much like any other social work practice. The assessment may be focused on certain needs (for example, discharge from the hospital following hip surgery). Or the assessment may need to be more comprehensive. In either case, the primary tasks of home-based geriatric assessment are to establish a relationship with the client (and family, if applicable) and to identify the concerns and goals for the work. With older people, this may require more time for the worker. Frail elders may have hearing or vision loss, tend to communicate more slowly than younger adults, tire more easily, and may be somewhat confused about details, particularly if they are recently discharged from a hospital. Some may have a condition that causes cognitive impairment, such as Alzheimer's disease. Add to this that family members with their own concerns and anxieties may also be present, and it becomes challenging to take the time necessary to form a working relationship with the older adult. Some general recommendations for first visits to an older client's home are listed below.

RECOMMENDATIONS FOR IN-HOME ASSESSMENTS WITH OLDER ADULTS

- Try to schedule appointments when the older person is not likely to be receiving personal care or eating a meal
- Confirm the appointment by telephone on the day before you go
- Arrange a place to sit where the older person can see and hear you
- Ask to turn off the TV or radio
- Allow enough time for the assessment—it may require a return visit
- Explain the purpose of your visit and establish your role as a helpful professional early on; distinguish social chit-chat from the work of interviewing and decision making

- Ask for permission to speak with family members and any other close friends or neighbors likely to be involved with the client's care
- Spend some time interviewing the older person and any family members present separately as well as together
- Ask to see all of the living areas that the older person inhabits
- Try to get to know the interests, strengths, and coping strategies of the older person—use photos and other displayed objects in the home to talk about the person's relationships and history
- Ask about the client's experiences and preferences; although part of your value to the client and family will be your knowledge of available services that may be appropriate, do not rush to explain service options before they have had the opportunity to voice their concerns and perceptions of the needs for service
- Try not to make assumptions prematurely about whether the person should or should not remain in the home
- Use brief assessment instruments to assess mental and emotional status, bearing in mind that soon after a major illness or surgery the older person is more likely to be confused, apathetic, and possibly depressed; readminister these instruments at a follow-up visit
- The client may be actively grieving for the loss of functioning or independence; offer support and any realistic hopes for improvement or adaptations that can be made
- Other professionals, such as physical and occupational therapists, may be involved with the case or may need to be brought in to complete specialized assessments

Ongoing Treatment and Monitoring

While good assessment is the heart of the social work process in home-based services, there are also important considerations for the ongoing work that follows. Bowers and Jacobson (2002) researched how excellent geriatric care managers do their jobs. They found that the best of these professionals nurtured relationships with clients, listened well, used creative rather than formulaic strategies, and attended to their supervisory relationships to enhance their work. Social workers may conduct a number of types of psychotherapy in the home, from reminiscence or life review to problem-solving therapy or cognitive-behavioral work, all of which have shown promise in research studies with depressed or anxious older adults.

Knight (2004) advises the worker who wishes to conduct psychotherapy in the older client's home to be somewhat more structured with sessions. For instance, social workers can establish a regular appointment time and place in the home for the session, ask the client to minimize outside distractions, and state that it is time to begin and end to signal the session's parameters.

Exposure to the many disabling conditions older clients face can be emotionally draining to professionals who work with them and may evoke the worker's own fears or concerns about aging, cognitive loss, disability, or death (McInnes-Dittrich 2005). Countertransference in work with older adults refers to the worker's experience of feelings about the client or the work that are based on experiences with other people, usually from the past. Thus, in working with older people, providers may respond to aspects of the person that are similar to a parent or a grandparent, with some of the emotions inherent in those relationships, which may be inappropriate for the professional situation (Knight 2004). This can be problematic if the worker has strong opinions about how a case should go that are based on unexamined feelings from past or current family situations. For instance, a social worker may find herself arguing that a client's family should sacrifice a great deal to maintain her at home, when in fact her opinion partly stems from the complex feelings she has about her own parents and responsibilities toward them (Knight 2004). This is only one example that highlights the importance of reflective use of self and the need for sensitive social work supervision in home-based practice with older adults.

Determining service needs, eligibility, availability, and costs may make up much of the work of ongoing case management. The coordination of services will be subject to many constraints of the local marketplace, policy context, and the client's and family's attitudes toward each service and individual providers. There are two important guidelines for this phase of home-based social work with older people. First, always follow up on every referral with the client system and the service or resource provider. Second, address barriers to compliance or satisfaction with services. It is not unusual for older people to be quite agreeable when service options are being discussed, but then when it is time to partake or participate, they do not find the services to be appropriate or satisfactory and either actively or passively refuse (McInnes-Dittrich 2005). This is a time for more exploration of the client's goals and their feelings about dependency.

Home-Based Services for Elder Maltreatment

Elder abuse and neglect are more likely to occur when the older person is dependent in several activities of daily living, socially isolated, or cognitively impaired (McInnes-Dittrich 2005). Most elder abuse and neglect is perpetrated by family members or relatives (Administration on Aging 2007b). Thus it makes sense that home-based social workers will be exposed to situations of elder maltreatment in their work. Social workers must be alert to potential signs of maltreatment, such as poor hygiene, poor nutrition, excessive fearfulness, family discord, untreated conditions, or unexplained injuries (Adams 2006; McInnes-Dittrich 2005). If abuse or neglect is suspected, the social worker should ask to interview the older person separately (Richardson and Barusch 2006). Very sensitive questioning and empathic listening are necessary to gain the elder's trust and obtain information about what has been occurring (Brandl 2000).

Although elder abuse and neglect cases may begin with a home-based assessment, frequently services need to be extended to the older adult, the caregiver, and family members, and they may involve a number of professionals and programs. Following a review and analysis of 473 strategies for intervention in elder-abuse cases, Nahmiash and Reis (2000) compiled a list of the most accepted and successful strategies: nursing and other medical care, homemaking assistance, empowerment strategies with the older adult, support groups for abused older adults, information about rights and resources, and volunteer buddy/advocates. For abusive caregivers, the most successful interventions involve individual supportive counseling to reduce anxiety, stress, or depression, as well as education and training (Nahmiash and Reis 2000). Anetzberger (2005) has developed an integrative framework for treatment of elder abuse that consists of protection, empowerment, and advocacy; working within the family system where possible; and providing emergency support as needed to treat the victim and prevent further abuse. Safety planning may be necessary: the victim should have a role in evaluating options (such as moving to another relative's home or pressing charges), and the abuser should be held responsible for his or her actions (Brandl 2000).

Issues of Diversity and Practice with Populations at Risk

Older people of color and those who are recent immigrants from outside the United States are increasing in numbers and proportion (Pandya 2005). Because of continuing health disparities for minority elders, rates of disability are higher among African Americans than among white older adults. A 2000 survey found that African Americans aged sixty-five and over used home health care services at a higher rate (.382 percent) than whites of the same age group (.246 percent; Pandya 2005). The physical and mental health challenges to older African Americans are numerous and often interconnected (Ford and Hatchett 2001).

At the same time, a new group of elder immigrants from Hispanic and Asian cultures have moved to the United States, many living in multigeneration households and relying on adult children when they require care (Pandya 2005). The incidence of informal caregiving is higher among Hispanic, Asian, and African American families with older adults than among whites (McInnes-Dittrich 2005). In general, minority elders are more disadvantaged financially and educationally than majority white elders (Torres-Gil and Moga 2001) and thus may rely on public health and social service systems at higher rates. Social work geriatric case managers play a crucial role in helping these elders and their families integrate formal and informal care and promote independence for the elders to the greatest extent possible (Ford and Hatchett 2001). With the current and anticipated increase in diversity among elders who may require long-term care services, in-home practice requires social workers to possess cultural competence, which is defined as the ability to understand and relate effectively to people of different cultures and backgrounds.

Some of the ways geriatric social workers can demonstrate cultural competence include coordinating services with workers and representatives of the cultural group and native speakers of the language and attempting to be sensitive to the values and traditions of clients from these diverse cultures (Adams 2006). Culturally relevant programs such as On Lok Senior Health (www.onlok.org), which integrates home-care services along a continuum of care for older Asian Americans in the San Francisco Bay Area, demonstrate the value of indigenous and native-speaking workers who work alongside other providers to serve elders from outside the majority, white American culture. However, individual social workers can also adopt the skills and attitudes of cultural competence through education and deliberate actions. For instance, a strengths perspective suggests that the provider try to see the situation of a particular elder from an insider's perspective. Although this can be difficult across cultures, some basic knowledge of cultural mores and traditions, open-mindedness, and taking adequate time to develop a relationship are important.

When making home visits with older adults of different racial or cultural backgrounds, culturally competent social workers use the home environment to guide their approach, show respect for the elder and family, follow cues from the family, and allow them to ask for what they would like before offering services or advice. Although it is not appropriate to stereotype members of other cultures, it is also helpful to remember that the values held by some cultures may differ from those of the social worker's own, particularly regarding filial responsibility to parents and expectations for caregiving. Listening for the client's and family's values when they discuss the elder's situation will go a long way toward achieving cultural competence as a home-based practitioner.

Implications for Home-Based Practice

Home-based practice for older adults will continue to be an important social work modality as the number and proportion of older people increases, a managed health-care environment limits hospitalization, and families expect to find help to maintain their elder members in the community. The transitions frail elders and their families face, the need to balance the interests of several parties, and the sometimes limited resources available can make this both a very challenging field of practice and a very valuable one to the clients and families who are served.

Social workers making home assessments and providing home-based services to older adults deal with obstacles and surprises that institution- or office-based social workers do not generally face. They may encounter dirty or chaotic home settings, barking dogs, and icy walkways. Inside the elders' homes, they may be witness to heartbreaking scenes of poverty, social isolation, or self-neglect. Home-based geriatric social workers regularly interact with a number of other health and mental health disciplines, from psychiatrists to minimum-wage home health aides, along with family members who may be stressed and overwhelmed. At times, the family may be the primary client, as the older person may be very ill or cognitively impaired. Even when the older client is able to participate in decision making, he or she may be unaware of the level of difficulties, confused, depressed, angry, or uncooperative. Other times, elders may be very grateful and form a real attachment to the care providers who visit. Thus these home-based social work practitioners must be prepared with a strong knowledge base about health and the mental health and social functioning of older people, strong clinical skills, and the ability to regularly engage in self-reflection and self-care.

The research literature on home-based social work services is still in an early stage. Development and testing of brief screening and assessment measures and intervention approaches to maximize the effectiveness of home visits with older clients are an ongoing priority. A promising area is in the efforts to better recognize and treat the subclinical depressive and anxiety symptoms that are very common in home-bound and frail elders (e.g., Gellis et al. 2007, 2008). Judging from the recent literature, an area in which progress is rapidly being made is in the use of technology in the home to monitor and assist home-bound older adults. There will always be limitations to these technological approaches and there will always be a need for in-person service providers, but in both rural and urban areas, a number of demonstration projects have shown some success. There are a number of areas to address in future research—unanswered questions about the appropriate application of psychosocial home care and home-based case management. Examples of these questions are how to optimally support frail elders in their own homes with minimal family availability and how to help families decide when to consider a more restrictive home environment for the older adult.

Little recent research has specifically evaluated the effects of social work services in the home with older adults—for example, comparing outcomes in case management with and without social workers on the interdisciplinary team or comparing the approaches and outcomes for geriatric in-home care of social work providers with nurses. In this era of cost containment, payment for in-home social work services for older adults is limited and sometimes inadequate (Lee and Gutheil 2003). The situation in many areas of the country is particularly dire in the area of home-based geriatric mental health services (Kohn et al. 2004). This health and mental health environment suggests that more studies demonstrating the importance of professional social workers in geriatric home care are needed. Alongside formal research efforts, both individual social workers and professional groups need to be confident and vocal about the worth of this important work and the needs of these clients and their families (Lee and Gutheil 2003).

REFERENCES

Adams, K. B. 2006. Late adulthood. In *Human Behavior in the Social Environment: A Multidisciplinary Perspective*, 3rd ed., ed. J. A. Ashford, C. W. LeCroy, and K. Lortie, 568–625. Belmont, Calif.: Thomson-Brooks/Cole.

Administration on Aging. 2007a. *A profile of older Americans 2006*. Available online at http://www.aoa.gov/prof/Statistics/profile/2006.

———. 2007b. *Elder abuse*. Available online at http://www.aoa.gov/eldfam.

Anetzberger, G. J. 2005. Clinical management of elder abuse: Some general considerations. *Clinical Gerontologist* 28 (1/2): 27–41.

Applebaum, R. 2006. Managing long-term care, herding cats, and other twenty-first century mysteries. *The Gerontologist* 46: 698–700.

Atchley, R. C. 1989. A continuity theory of normal aging. *The Gerontologist* 29: 183–190.

Atchley, R. C., and Barusch, A. S. 2004. *Social forces and aging: An introduction to social gerontology.* 10th ed. Belmont, Calif.: Thomson/Wadsworth.

Bowers, B. J., and Jacobson, N. 2002. Best practice in long-term care case management: How excellent case managers do their jobs. *Journal of Social Work in Long-Term Care* 1 (3): 55–72.

Brandl, B. 2000. Power and control: Understanding domestic abuse in later life. *Generations* 24 (11): 39–45.

Buckwalter, K. C., Davis, L. L., Wakefield, B. J., Kienzle, M. G., and Murray, M. A. 2002. Telehealth for elders and their caregivers in rural communities. *Family and Community Health* 25 (3): 31–40.

Cassity, C. W., and Huber, R. 2003. Rural older adults at home. *Journal of Gerontological Social Work* 41 (3/4): 229–245.

Chapin, R. and Cox, E. O. 2001. Changing the paradigm: Strengths-based and empowerment-oriented social work with frail elders. *Journal of Gerontological Social Work* 36 (3/4): 165–179.

Costa, P., Metter, E., and McCrae, R. 1994. Personality stability and its contribution to successful aging. *Journal of Geriatric Psychiatry* 27: 41–59.

Duke, C. 2005. The frail elderly community-based case management project. *Geriatric Nursing* 26 (2): 122–127.

Dunkle, R., Roberts, B., and Haug, M. 2001. *The oldest old in everyday life: Self-perception, coping with change, and stress.* New York: Springer.

Dyeson, T. B. 2005. The myriad roles of the home care social worker. *Home Health Care Management and Practice* 17: 398–400.

Emlet, C. A., Crabtree, J. L., and Condon, V. A. 2007. *In-home assessment of older adults: An interdisciplinary approach.* 2nd ed. Gaithersburg, Md.: Aspen.

Fast, B., and Chapin, R. 2000. *Strengths-based care management for older adults.* Baltimore, Md.: Health Professions Press.

Ford, M. E., and Hatchett, B. 2001. Gerontological social work with older African Americans. In *Gerontological social work practice: Issues, challenges, and potential,* ed. E. O. Cox, E. S. Kelchner, and R. Chapin, 141–155. Binghamton, N.Y.: Haworth.

Gelfand, D. E. 2006. *The aging network: Programs and services.* 6th ed. New York: Springer.

Gellis, Z. D., McGinty, J., Horowitz, A., Bruce, M. and Misener, E. 2007. Problem-solving therapy for late life depression in home care elderly: A randomized controlled trial. *American Journal of Geriatric Psychiatry* 15: 968–978

Gellis, Z. D., McGinty, J., Tierney, L., Burton, J. Jordan, C. Misener, E., et al. 2008. Randomized controlled trial of problem-solving therapy for minor depression in home care. *Research on Social Work Practice* 18 (6): 596–608.

Kaufman, A. V., Scogin, F. R., MaloneBeach, E. E., Baumhover, L. A., McKendree-Smith, N. 2000. Home-delivered mental health services for aged rural home health-care recipients. *Journal of Applied Gerontology* 19 (4): 460–475.

Knight, B. G. 2004. *Psychotherapy with older adults.* 3rd ed. Thousand Oaks, Calif.: Sage.

Kohn, R., Goldsmith, E., Sedgwick, T. W., and Markowitz, S. 2004. In-home mental health services for the elderly. *Clinical Gerontologist* 27 (1/2): 71–85.

Kropf, N. P. 2000. Home health and community services. In *Gerontological social work: Knowledge, service settings, and special populations,* 2nd ed., ed. R. L. Schneider, N. P. Kropf, and A. J. Kisor, 167–190. N.p.: Brooks Cole, 2000.

Lawton, M. P. 1975. Competence, environmental press, and the adaptation of older people. In *Theory development in environment and aging,* ed. P. C. Windley and G. Ernst. Washington, D.C.: Gerontological Society of America.

Lee, J. S., and Gutheil, I. A. 2003. The older patient at home: Social work services and home health care. *Care Management Journals* 4 (2): 101–109.

McInnes-Dittrich, K. 2005. *Social work with elders: A biopsychosocial approach to assessment and intervention.* 2nd ed. Boston: Allyn and Bacon.

Medicaid Institute. 2007. *Connecting care systems: Dealing with depression in a home care population.* Available online at http://www.medicaidinstitute.org/ccs.htm.

Medicare. 2007. Home health compare—Medicare coverage of home health care. Available online at http://medicare.gov/HHcompare/Home.

Nahmiash, D., and Reis, M. 2000. Most successful intervention strategies for abused older adults. *Journal of Elder Abuse and Neglect* 12 (3/4): 53–70.

Naleppa, M. J., and Hash, K. M. 2001. Home-based practice with older adults: Challenges and opportunities in the home environment. *Journal of Gerontological Social Work* 35: 71–88.

Naleppa, M. J., and Reid, W. J. 1998. Task-centered case management for the elderly: Developing a practice model. *Research on Social Work Practice* 8: 63–85.

Ohio Department of Aging. 2007. *Program profile: PASSPORT Medicaid waiver program.* Available online at www.goldenbuckeye.com.

Pandya, S. M. 2005. *Racial and ethnic differences among older adults in long-term care service use.* AARP Public Policy Institute. Available online at http://www.aarp.org/research/longtermcare/trends/fs119_ltc.html.

Richardson, V. E., and Barusch, A. S. 2006. *Gerontological practice for the twenty-first century: A social work perspective.* New York: Columbia University Press.

Saleeby, D. 1992. *The strengths perspective in social work practice.* New York: Longman.

SAMHSA. 2007. *Intervention summary: Program to encourage active, rewarding lives for seniors (PEARLS).* Available online at http://nrepp.samhsa.gov/programfulldetails.asp?program_id=107.

Smith, T. L., Toseland, R. W., Rizzo, V. M., and Zinoman, M. A. 2004. Telephone caregiver support groups. *Journal of Gerontological Social Work* 44 (1/2): 151–172.

Stevens, N. 2001. Combating loneliness: A friendship enrichment programme for older women. *Ageing and Society* 21: 183–202.

Torres-Gil, F., and Moga, K. B. 2001. Multiculturalism, social policy, and the new aging. In *Gerontological social work practice: Issues, challenges, and potential*, ed. E. O. Cox, E. S. Kelchner, and R. Chapin, 13–32. Binghamton, N.Y.: Haworth.

Wodarski, J. S., and Williams-Hayes, M. M. 2002. Utilizing case management to maintain the elderly in the community. *Journal of Gerontological Social Work* 39: 19–38.

Yagoda, L. 2004. *Aging practice update: Case management with older adults, a social work perspective.* Available online at www.socialworkers.org/practice/aging/aging0504.pdf.

Twelve

Hospice and End-of-Life Care

ELLEN CSIKAI

Care of the dying at home is certainly not a new phenomenon. However, with the rise of hospital systems and advances in medical treatments that can prolong life almost indefinitely, the site of death has undergone a dramatic shift. Even though most people prefer to die at home, in the general population of the United States, about one-half of all individuals that die do so in an acute care setting (Teno et al. 2004).

The provision of hospice care services in the home relative to other aspects of the health care system is a recent development. The option of Medicare hospice benefits was first authorized in 1982. This is seen as the watershed event in the hospice movement. Since then, there has been a proliferation of hospice care organizations. According to the National Hospice and Palliative Care Organization (NHPCO), as of 2005 there were more than 4,100 hospice programs, and most (93.6 percent) were certified Medicare providers (NHPCO 2007a).

The term "hospice" goes back to medieval times. It referred to a place of shelter and rest for weary or ill travelers on a long journey. Dame Cicely Saunders founded the first modern hospice in 1967, St. Christopher's Hospice, in a residential suburb of London. She was the first to apply the name "hospice" to specialized care for dying patients. The first modern hospices in the United States began to appear in the late 1960s and 1970s, patterned after St. Christopher's Hospice. Many hospices of this era were run exclusively by volunteers, as there was no insurance payment available to support this type of care. Initially, many hospices were inpatient facilities where patients could receive care until they died. Services were also provided for patients who could be cared for in the home. These services allowed them to remain and die in their home. Currently, British and European models of hospice care primarily utilize inpatient hospice care, while the United States (by following the Medicare benefit) focuses primarily on home hospice care. Inpatient hospice units are reserved for brief stays for pain management and control, respite care, and for those in the last stages of dying.

The primary site for social work hospice intervention is the home. Perhaps at no other time in life are people most vulnerable as when they are dying. This vulnerability can be extremely difficult, or it can provide an opportunity for growth for the individuals who are dying, their family, and their caregivers. The highest level of respect and professionalism is required when entering a situation of such high vulnerability. Seeing hospice patients in the home provides the best opportunity to accurately assess and intervene in their life situations and environment. One of the primary roles of the hospice social worker is to ensure individuals' self-determination as they make end-of-life decisions.

The Population

In 2005, about one-third of all those who died in the United States, over 1.2 million individuals, received hospice services. Three-quarters of hospice recipients died in a place that they considered "home": a private residence, nursing home, or other residential facility. The majority of hospice users are women. Although four out of five hospice patients were over the age of sixty-five and one-third were over the age of eighty-five, the population served by hospice agencies covers the entire lifespan (NHPCO 2007a). The rate of children with complex chronic conditions dying at home has increased significantly from 1989 to 2003 (Feudtner et al. 2007).

Diagnoses for which patients are admitted to hospice care are becoming more varied and include those of a more chronic nature. Cancer diagnoses account for 46 percent of all hospice admissions. In 1998, for those electing the Medicare hospice benefit (over sixty-five years of age), five of the top ten diagnoses were cancer related (lung, prostate, breast, colon, and pancreatic). In 2005, three of the top ten diagnoses were cancer related (lung, prostate, and breast). The fastest growing non-cancer-related diagnoses are Alzheimer's disease, debility not otherwise specified, adult failure to thrive, and senile dementia. Hospice use tends to increase with age for most causes of death. Hospice use was higher among individuals with diseases that tend to impose a high burden on caregivers and among those with diseases that had a more predictable prognosis leading to death (Connor et al. 2007).

Because of the extended trajectory of dying for non-cancer-related diagnoses, the length of hospice service has increased. In 2006, the average length of hospice service for a person with a diagnosis of Alzheimer's was 108 days (U.S. Department of Health and Human Services 2007). This has contributed to the increasing average overall length of service (LOS) in hospice care. In 2005, the average LOS was fifty-nine days. The median LOS also increased to twenty-six days, which statistic is more accurate than the average for describing the experiences of typical hospice recipients. Along with an increase in the number of recipients receiving services for greater than six months, a decrease in the number of recipients receiving services for fewer than seven days has also affected the overall LOS (NHPCO 2007a).

Policy and Agency Context

Federal Policy

The first federal legislation passed in support of hospice care came in the early 1980s. Congress included a provision to create a Medicare hospice benefit in the Tax Equity and Fiscal Responsibility Act of 1982. In 1986, Congress made the Medicare Hospice Benefit permanent. Also at that time, states were given the option of including hospice care in their Medicaid programs and hospice care was made available to terminally ill nursing home residents.

The standards set forth under the Medicare hospice benefit defined how hospice care should be delivered in order to receive medical-insurance reimbursement, including a mandate for the availability of social work services. Current requirements are for social workers to have a minimum of a bachelor's degree in social work from an accredited program. There was an attempt made several years ago to be able to substitute a licensed professional counselor for a social worker; however, due to social work advocacy, this was not accepted by the Center for Medicare and Medicaid Services (CMS), and a social work degree is still required. Core services that must be provided according to Medicare regulations include nursing services, medical social services, and counseling services. Nursing and medical services are certainly the core of hospice care, but it is significant that the Medicare regulations recognized the importance of services that can enhance the quality of the dying process and provide for a dying individual and their family a holistic approach to death.

The hospice benefit is available under Medicare Part A (hospital insurance). When beneficiaries choose the Medicare hospice benefit, they choose to receive aggressive pain and symptom management for their terminal illness and thus waive standard Medicare benefits for treatment of that illness. They can continue to receive standard Medicare benefits for treatment of other illnesses not related to the terminal diagnosis for which they are receiving hospice care. There are three conditions for eligibility for the Medicare hospice benefit: (1) Two physicians, typically the primary-care physician and the hospice physician, must certify that the individual has a prognosis of six months or less until death; (2) the beneficiary must sign a statement stating that he or she chooses the Medicare benefit, thereby forgoing curative treatments for the terminal diagnosis; and (3) the beneficiary must enroll in a Medicare-certified hospice program. Medicare pays hospice programs a "per diem" rate for the care of each individual enrolled. The coverage is typically the same for the Medicaid Hospice Benefit, which was patterned after the Medicare regulations. Coverage for hospice services by private insurance companies vary according to the insurance plan. Currently, the per diem coverage is as follows (USHHS 2007):

- 100% for routine care – to ensure symptom control and that patient is comfortable. This care is to be provided through scheduled visits by hospice team (nurse, CNA, social worker, chaplain, physician)
- 100% for general inpatient care – short-term management for out-of-control symptoms provided in an inpatient facility
- 100% for continuous care – short-term crisis care at home or in an assisted living facility with twenty-four-hour care provided by the hospice team
- 100% for equipment and supplies – needed for the life-limiting illness and provided by hospice-approved contractors
- 100% for twenty-four-hour on-call access to hospice staff support for patients and families; grief support and complementary therapies
- 95% for respite care – five-day maximum patient stay in a nursing facility to give the caregiver rest so he or she can continue to provide care in the home
- For medications needed for the life-limiting illness, the patient pays no more than five dollars for each pain-relief and symptom-control medication.

Structure of Hospice Agencies

Both small and large hospice agencies exist and serve individuals and families in both rural and urban locations throughout the country. In addition, these agencies may be either nonprofit or for profit. Nonprofit hospice agencies continue to be in the majority (67.7 percent), dominating the field. For-profit agencies account for 27.7 percent of the existing organizations. The remainder (5.2 percent) are government-run programs (NHPCO 2007a). Both nonprofit and for-profit hospice agencies subscribe to a palliative care, thus holistic, approach to providing care, but many believe there is a difference in management philosophy. One key aspect that distinguishes these two types of agencies is that nonprofit agencies are free to accept and actively solicit donations to augment the income from Medicare, Medicaid, and private insurances. In essence, nonprofit hospice agencies may have the ability to provide "extra" services that for-profit agencies may not be willing to provide because of watching the "bottom line."

Service delivery. Hospice services are delivered in whatever setting the individual considers "home." This includes individuals' own homes or family caregivers' homes and residential facilities such as assisted living facilities and nursing homes. Ideally, individuals will have a family caregiver in the home to care for them throughout the dying process. Hospice agencies are reluctant to admit patients without a clear identification of a primary caregiver or plan that will provide twenty-four-hour supervision for an individual, particularly in the last stages of dying. A formal paid caregiver is another alternative when there is no family available. There may also be any combination of formal and informal care arrangements to meet the individual's daily needs.

To begin provision of services, an initial admission visit is conducted with the new hospice enrollee and their identified primary caregiver. The purpose of this visit is to gather comprehensive information regarding biological, psychological, social, and spiritual issues that may be important in the situation. Each hospice agency has an assessment protocol. Often a nurse, alone, will conduct this visit and assess the physical aspects and, in particular, pain-management needs of the individual. The nurse may also gain a sense of psychological or social issues that need further attention. This information is shared with the hospice medical director and other team members who may then get involved. A social worker will also do an initial assessment within two days of the individual's admission. Some agency protocols dictate that a nurse and a social worker make a joint visit to the home. This is the ideal model, because all aspects of an individual's situation can be assessed at the beginning of service, and any psychological (depression or anxiety), social (caregiving or financial), or spiritual (religious or existential) issues can be identified and addressed early. This model may prevent possible crisis situations during the provision of hospice care.

A care plan for the patient and the patient's family is then developed with input from all involved disciplines, including social work, within two days of admission, as per Medicare regulations (USHHS 2007). The admission assessments are reviewed within each domain (biological, psychological, social, and spiritual) in order to determine the appropriate courses of action.

The interdisciplinary team (IDT) is important, as no one discipline has the expertise to meet the wide range of issues and needs patients may have at the end of life. The core of these teams normally consists of physicians, nurses, social workers, chaplains, certified nursing assistants (CNAs), and volunteers. Other disciplines may be brought in as needed and may be available for consultation by the team. Each individual and their family is assigned a core team with which they interact. The core team communicates regularly with one another through formal IDT meetings and informally at other times in order to modify the patient's plan of care as the illness progresses. According to Medicare regulations, each patient's care plan must be reviewed and updated at least once every two weeks. Coordination and leadership of the IDT meetings vary according to agency policy and protocol and normally take place in the agency office. Although typically designated as a nursing responsibility, the hospice medical director or a social work supervisor could also be responsible for leading the discussion of case care plans. The expectation is that all personnel on the care team, including volunteers, will be present to provide input regarding the case. Each discipline provides input regarding their assessments and observations. The medical director reviews, with nursing input, aspects of medical management, primarily pain control. Because the nurse sees the patient and family more frequently than any other member of the IDT, nurses play a major role in providing information about psychosocial issues and risk factors that may emerge as time goes on. The same is true for any CNAs involved in a case. Because they provide very intimate care of the patients (personal hygiene, bathing), they may become aware of issues that no one else on the IDT may have seen. Social workers provide information about psychosocial issues, particularly those involving the patients' caregivers.

Nurses make at least weekly visits to individuals in the home. A nurse will typically be the professional called when a patient has died to pronounce the death. Other disciplines are involved with individuals and families as needed to address various care needs. Agencies may have policies or protocols that specify a minimum number of visits by various members of the team. It is more typical that staffing protocols specify a maximum number of visits per week, such as for a CNA to assist with bathing or other hygiene needs. Volunteers in hospice agencies are an available and necessary part of the team. They perform a range of direct-care services that can augment care provided by the professional staff. For example, volunteers may be called on to "sit" with individuals and provide a respite for caregivers while the caregivers do needed shopping or go out with a friend to have a break. Agencies offer bereavement services after death occurs, most commonly in the form of periodic letters to the bereaved caregiver that describe the normal grief/bereavement process. Depending on the assessed needs, social workers may also intervene one on one, in family meetings, or in group settings.

All hospice services are available and provided to hospice patients living in nursing homes and other types of residential care facilities. These services are an invaluable resource to nursing home staff with little time to give individual attention to any one person, let alone to someone who is dying. A major issue for hospice nurses and other hospice staff with patients in residential facilities is appropriate pain control and management. Social workers routinely visit these individuals to assess psychosocial issues of the individuals or family members and intervene as necessary.

Roughly one in five hospice agencies operate an inpatient hospice facility. These agencies are usually larger agencies with an average daily census of more than two hundred patients (NHPCO 2007a). Other agencies may contract with hospitals or other residential facilities to provide inpatient care as needed. Inpatient care can be utilized for short stays (less than two weeks). Inpatient care may be desirable in situations such as: (1) if pain cannot be controlled in the home setting, (2) if death is predicted to be close and the family is not comfortable with the individual dying at home (e.g., they may have small children and not want them to view the final stages of death), (3) if death is imminent after discharge from a hospital or other acute care setting and the family is not able to care for the individual at home, or (4) if a short respite is needed for caregivers who may be overwhelmed by daily care needs or have medical issues of their own.

Purposes and Goals of Social Work Home-Based Services

Goals of Hospice Care

According to Cicely Saunders (1998, viii), founder of the hospice movement in the United States, the work of the interdisciplinary team in providing palliative care is aimed toward enabling the dying person "to live until he dies, at his own maximum potential, performing to the limit of his physical activity and mental capacity with control and independence whenever possible. . . . If he is recognized as the unique person he is and helped to live as part of his family and in other relationships, he can still reach out to his hopes and expectations and to what has deepest meaning for him and end his life with a sense of completion."

One of the most distinguishing features of hospice care corresponds to the core value of social work self-determination. It was designed to be driven by the individual and the family. The interdisciplinary team's responsibility is to support dying individuals in the manner they have chosen to live out the rest of their lives (Raymer 2004). The emphasis is on psychosocial care, a holistic perspective of care, and so sets itself apart from the medical model. The team works together to focus on the dying person's physical, emotional, and spiritual needs.

Role of Social Work

In the hospice setting, social workers' skills and knowledge are essential. Social work values and principles have influenced hospice theory and practice (MacDonald 1991). Cicely Saunders was a nurse, medical social worker, and physician, and she included aspects and values of these disciplines in her conceptualization of the modern hospice (Kulys and Davis 1986). Social workers form relationships with patients and families to maximize the quality of what life remains and to resolve any ethical issues that may arise. Social workers are an integral part of the hospice team in providing care to those with terminal illnesses and their families.

Initial assessment and care plans. Although social work participation in the initial admission visit contributes to positive outcomes (Reese and Raymer 2004), this is dependent on individual agency policy and protocol. A nurse member of the team assesses the medical aspects of the situation and may identify other areas where coordination with other team members is needed. If not at the admission visit, the social worker will make a home visit to complete a comprehensive psycho-social-spiritual assessment. The unit of care consists of both the patient and family (including other close significant others). Areas to be addressed in assessment are individual, family, physical, and social resources, including support from family, friends, and church. The social worker contributes in developing the care plan as part of the interdisciplinary team assigned to the family.

IDTs. During IDT meetings, social workers update the team on interventions undertaken or currently engaged in to resolve psychosocial problems identified through their own assessment or from issues brought up by team members regarding the patient and family. The IDT meeting may also be an opportunity for the social worker to educate the team about family dynamics, cultural sensitivity, or other topics pertinent to patient and family care.

Teamwork in meeting nonmedical needs is essential. Members of the IDT in hospice care often have overlapping roles. Medical needs are to be met only by the medical disciplines; nonmedical needs may be addressed by anyone on the team. When doing so, in essence fulfilling part of the social work role, patients and families should expect "a consistent, careful, and effective approach to be adopted by all of them" (Monroe 1998, 867), an approach that can be taught, modeled, and used in interactions between social workers and the other team members. All members of the team are involved in listening, talking, and sharing information with patients and families. Members of the team expect that social workers will act as a "safety net" for those social work tasks that are particularly difficult for other team members to fulfill (Monroe 1998). At times, however, this role overlap may create tension and turf issues among team members. In one study (Reese, Raymer, and Richardson 2000), social workers believed that they were influential in helping the team resolve turf issues, differences in professional boundaries, differences in approach to self-determination, and lack of knowledge of the expertise of other disciplines.

Social work intervention. Ferrell (1998) identified eleven issues of concern for families caring for patients with cancer that can be seen in the provision of hospice care: emotional strain, physical demands, uncertainty, fear of the patient dying, altered rules and lifestyles, finances, ways to comfort the patient, perceived inadequacies of services, existential concern, sexuality, and nonconvergent needs among household members. One of the most common interventions used by social workers in hospice care is the provision of information and referral to community resources for practical assistance. These basic needs must be met before other more complex emotional needs can be addressed. After basic needs are met and when the family and individual are ready, social work interventions address the dying process and what it means to that individual and family. This can be in the form of reminiscing, engaging in life reviews and legacy projects, and discussing the meaning and value of an individual's life (Reese and Raymer 2004). Other activities that hospice social workers report performing most often are counseling with patients and families and interdisciplinary planning. They report that the activities in which they are least involved include research and volunteer training (Csikai 2004).

Theoretical Framework

Hospice Philosophy

The hospice philosophy is to affirm with patients and families that death is a natural part of the life cycle. This is accomplished by understanding and addressing all aspects of having a life-limiting illness, particularly the multiple aspects of suffering on physical, social, spiritual, and emotional levels.

The central concept in the provision of hospice care services is palliative care provided by an interdisciplinary care team. Palliative care focuses on caring for patients' total needs, not on curing or eliminating disease. Palliative care has been defined by the World Health Organization (WHO 1990) as follows: "The active total care of patients whose disease is not responsive to curative treatment. Control of pain, of other symptoms, and of psychological, social and spiritual problems, is paramount. The goal of palliative care is the achievement of the best quality of life for patients and their families."

Further, palliative care

- Affirms life and regards dying as a normal process
- Intends neither to hasten nor postpone death
- Integrates the psychological and spiritual aspects of patient care
- Offers a support system to help patients live as actively as possible until death
- Offers a support system to help the family cope during the patient's illness and in their own bereavement
- Uses a team approach to address the needs of patients and their families, including bereavement counseling, if indicated
- Will enhance quality of life and may also positively influence the course of illness
- Is applicable early in the course of illness, in conjunction with other therapies intended to prolong life, such as chemotherapy or radiation therapy, and includes those investigations needed to better understand and manage distressing clinical complications

(WHO 1990)

Empirical Base

The hospice movement began with a strong psychosocial emphasis. However, over time this has seemed to erode with the cost consciousness created by the limits of the Medicare hospice benefit and of other insurers who follow Medicare's lead in determining benefits. Because of this, some hospice administrators view social work as a nonessential service, one that can be handled on an "as needed" basis. Other disciplines involved in patient care see themselves as capable of providing the "same" care as social workers. Thus the role of social workers in some hospice agencies has diminished primarily to involvement in assessment, and caseloads are on the rise (Reese and Raymer 2004).

In response to this phenomenon, there have been several attempts in recent years to assess the activities and effectiveness of social work practice in hospice care. In 2000, Raymer, Reese, and Richardson conducted the National Hospice Social Work Study with the support of the NHPCO (at the time, the National Hospice Organization). Social workers and hospice directors completed questionnaires for this research (Reese et al. 2000). The social workers, representing seventy-six hospice agencies, reported that they provided input regarding psychosocial issues of patients and families and emotional support and counseling to other team members. These social workers also provided input in terms of advocating for patient self-determination (92.8 percent) and understanding issues of cultural diversity (83.2 percent), the systems perspective (73.6 percent), and spirituality (76 percent).

Social workers in this study (Reese et al. 2000; Reese and Raymer 2004) completed chart reviews for the last five patients that had been discharged by their agency. A model of social work effectiveness was tested based on the chart review data. This study revealed a number of significant results. First, there were lower overall hospice costs if social workers participated in the intake interview and if social workers had more experience since obtaining their social work degree. Despite this finding, only 38 percent of the respondents reported participation in the initial intake. A higher ratio of social workers to patients was associated with fewer nights of costly inpatient care. If a social worker was able to intervene early, the crisis that might lead to the inpatient stay could be prevented by problem solving with the family. Also, increased social work involvement predicted higher patient quality of life, improved client satisfaction, improved staff satisfaction, decrease in staff turnover, fewer nights of continuous care, and a lower severity of cases (Reese and Raymer 2004).

In another empirical effort to document the work of social workers, Reese and colleagues (2006) replicated an early study (Kulys and Davis 1987) that examined hospice agency directors' views of the roles of social workers. The sample included two hospice directors from each state and Washington, D.C. There were respondents from thirty-four states. In the direct provision of service, the directors believed that social workers were the most qualified member of the IDT to handle financial counseling, make community referrals, assess psychosocial problems, facilitate social support, and provide crisis intervention and counseling regarding issues of suicide, denial, and anticipatory grief. The agency directors also perceived that social workers were the most qualified team members to promote cultural competence and lead community-outreach efforts.

More research is needed to document the activities of hospice social workers and to link these activities to overall effectiveness. The social work profession has been slow to document the effectiveness of their interventions and to disseminate these results for the benefit of dying individuals and their families.

Practice Guidelines

National Association of Social Workers Standards

In recognition of the growing number of social workers practicing in fields related to end-of-life care, the National Association of Social Workers developed the "NASW Standards for Palliative and End-of-Life Care" (NASW 2004). This document describes the background of the field, including definitions, and enumerates standards of professional practice and for professional preparation and development. The standards for practice cover the following aspects: ethics and values, knowledge, assessment, intervention/ treatment planning, attitudes/self-awareness, empowerment and advocacy, documentation, interdisciplinary teamwork, cultural competence, continuing education, and supervision, leadership, and training. These standards provide guidance to professionals and to agency administrators as to the appropriate and expected role of social workers in end-of-life care.

NHPCO Social Work Practice Guidelines

The NHPCO, with the assistance and leadership of the Social Work Section, composed of social worker members of the National Council of Hospice and Palliative Professionals (NCHPP), has developed a set of guidelines for the organization and delivery of social work services in hospice care. The guidelines cover all aspects of practice, including the areas of the scope of social work services, education, salary, workloads, supervision, social work assessment, care plans, team collaboration, documentation, quality, ethics, culture, communication/language, Medicare/Medicaid/private insurance, local/state/national organization, and research. Hospice organizations and individuals have access to these guidelines, which could be utilized, for example, to organize, reorganize, or enhance hospice services or to develop training on the role of the hospice social worker (NHPCO 2007b). The key areas for social work services are described in more detail in the sections that follow.

Availability and scope of social work services. The NHPCO Social Work Guidelines (NHPCO, 2007b) specify that, first and foremost, each patient, family, or significant other will have access to social work services, including:

- Completion of a social work assessment at the time of admission and ongoing assessments
- Development of a care plan that stems from the initial assessment
- Coordination of care among the patient/family and the interdisciplinary team
- Provision of ongoing social work services in a timely manner
- Organization and provision of social work services/supervision
- Availability of direct services including counseling, crisis intervention, patient/family education, identification of financial and other resources, and referral, advocacy, and bereavement care
- Discharge planning
- Availability of indirect services including education, administration, and participation in interdisciplinary team meetings

Workloads. In order for social workers to provide services effectively, a reasonable caseload is necessary. The guidelines recommend that "caseload should be a size that allows the social worker to provide early, frequent, consistent, and timely follow-up services to clients" (NHPCO, 2007b). NHPCO recommends a caseload of twenty to thirty patient/family cases at any one time. At this writing, a caseload of thirty exceeds the national average for a full-time hospice social worker.

There are a number of factors to be considered in determining caseload size. Factors that indicate the need for more intensive social work services and thus a caseload reduction would include the following: high-risk factors that affect family functioning, such as suicidal ideation, domestic violence, addiction, and mental illness; acuteness of clients' needs, for example with pediatric patients or adults with multiple needs for assistance; concerns regarding the individual's physical setting, as in cases of substandard housing or poor sanitation; family size and complexity of family dynamics;

cultural and linguistic differences; legal issues; multiple agencies/systems involved; or historical discrimination that causes trust issues and a need for team education.

Another factor in determining the size of a social work caseload is the roles of each social worker in the agency. Social workers may have roles at three levels: administrative, community, and organizational. Responsibilities at the administrative level can include supervisory or coordinator activities, documentation beyond direct patient care, community outreach, development of community resources, organization of special events, referral and admission, intake, follow-up and bereavement services, evaluation and research, and team support. On the community level, travel time related to the geographic area served, travel conditions, and resource infrastructure issues need to be considered. At the organizational level, social workers may be asked for input regarding issues of agency solvency, rapid changes in patient level of care, patient length of stay, and data gathering for quality assurance and other research projects.

Social Work Assessment. According to the Social Work Guidelines (NHPCO 2007b), the initial comprehensive assessment should be completed by a qualified social worker, which is defined as those holding a BSW or MSW from an accredited university. The assessment should be completed at the time of admission or as soon after as possible. Particular attention should be paid to assessing specific risks, strengths, needs, and resources. This includes, for example, patient and family understanding of prognosis, diagnosis, and end-of-life goals; understanding of the disease process, dying, and death event; care and symptom management; caregiving approaches; and anticipatory grief.

There has been no standardized assessment for social workers in the field of hospice care. Each agency develops an assessment tool or documentation requirements for the initial psychosocial assessment. Usually agencies have a separate tool or use progress notes for ongoing assessments. Social workers, adhering to the ecological perspective and a belief in the uniqueness of each individual, have been slow to accept that there may be a need for a standardized assessment tool. While it does raise questions about client empowerment, such an instrument could be used to create a national database that could then be a resource for the documentation of social work outcomes, development of standards, and identification of best practices (Reese et al. 2006).

One standardized assessment instrument, the Social Work Assessment Tool (SWAT), was recently developed to be used at each social work visit with hospice patients and families (Reese et al. 2006). It was developed by the Social Work Outcomes Task Force of the Social Work Section, NHP-CO, NCHPP. A copy of this tool is included at the end of this chapter. The tool was developed through pilot studies and has been evaluated with 101 patients and eighty-one primary caregivers in a study of practicing hospice social workers. The psychosocial domains addressed in the SWAT include spirituality, death anxiety, social support, denial, end-of-life care decisions, cultural group, safety, comfort, suicidal ideation, preferences about environment, assistance with financial resources, and complicated anticipatory grief. Social workers that used the SWAT found that it reminded them of areas that should be addressed and helped with the assessment of outcomes. They thought it was comprehensive, covered key areas, and was easy to use. They believed it could be used in conjunction with agency assessment forms. Some drawbacks included readiness of the field to assess outcomes, discomfort in addressing some of the issues with patients, and the inability to use it with patients who are unresponsive or have dementia. It was also pointed out that further training regarding assessment of each of the domains may be needed (Reese et al. 2006).

Care Plans. Social work assessments directly contribute to care plans. Care planning is a deliberate, rational, and ongoing process that reflects the interdisciplinary nature of hospice care. Care plans serve the following purposes: to prioritize a set of issues/problems to be addressed, direct specific interventions that will be utilized, provide a means for evaluating effectiveness of interventions and measuring outcomes, and enhance continuity of care. Care plans should include the identification of needs and strengths, measurable goals/objectives for each need, specific interventions, time frames for implementing interventions, methods for monitoring progress, and frequency of visits required to meet the goals. They should be individualized, reflect the inclusion of patient and family goals of care, and be reviewed and updated regularly.

Issues of Diversity and Practice with Populations at Risk

Culture and Social Work in End-of-Life Care

Social work has a longstanding tradition at its core of working to advance the rights of underserved and unrepresented groups in all areas of practice. Hospice social workers must commit themselves to identifying and addressing issues that may compromise access, equity, and quality of care at the end of life. Those who are culturally or linguistically diverse are more likely to suffer inequities in the health care system. Culture refers to "the patterns of human behavior that include the language, thoughts, communications, actions, customs, beliefs, values, and institutions of racial, religious, and social groups" (NHPCO 2007b). In end-of-life care, social workers should be guided by this broad definition of culture based on the following assumptions (NHPCO, 2007b):

- End-of-life experience is deeply personal although potentially influenced by social context and historical era
- All clinical encounters are cross-cultural, relational, and affected by imbalances in power in which control is vested in health-care workers
- Western culture and institution-based end-of-life care represent distinct cultures and thereby hold the potential for creating cross-cultural tension
- The experiences of symptoms, including pain, can have different meanings based on culture
- Culture is not limited to ethnicity and may include categories such as age, gender, spirituality/faith/religion, ablement, sexual orientation, race, national origin, linguistic tradition, and socioeconomic status

Utilization and Access to Hospice Services

Racial/cultural disparities. Hospice services are disproportionately used by European American, middle-class individuals and families. Several studies have been conducted in the last ten to fifteen years to ascertain the rate of hospice utilization/access among the three largest racial groups in the United States, European Americans, African Americans, and Hispanics/Latinos (Colon 2003; Harper 1995; O'Mara 2001). In one study (Colon 2003) of close to two thousand descendents involved with hospice services from 1995 to 2001, 82.8 percent were European American, 13.9 percent African American (compared to 18 percent in the general population), and 1.6 percent Hispanic/Latino (compared to 12 percent in the general population).

African Americans have been found to be more likely to choose more aggressive medical treatments and less likely to be enrolled in hospice care at the end of life (Hopp 2000). More than one-half of the African American participants (family members of decedents) in one study (Rhodes, Teno, and Welch 2006) reported that they were not informed about hospice services, and 12 percent were informed but chose not to enroll. Those with a cancer diagnosis were more likely to have received information about hospice care. Underutilization of hospice services among African Americans has been a longstanding issue and still is not fully understood. In addition to lack of knowledge about hospice care, other factors that may contribute to underutilization are mistrust of the health-care system, cultural beliefs, and socioeconomic status (Reese et al. 1999; Rhodes et al. 2006).

For the Hispanic community, barriers to hospice use may include lack of insurance, language barriers, acculturation, difficulty navigating and distrust of the health-care system, and beliefs about health (Colon 2005; Randall 2003). A belief in fatalism is common among Hispanics and may account for some disparity in hospice use. According to this concept, exterior forces control the universe and an individual's destiny. An acceptance of illness exists because God allowed it to happen (Campos 1990; Colon 2005). Mexican Americans were least likely to believe that a person should be informed of imminent death (Gelfand et al. 2001).

Suggestions to combat the lack of education about and access to hospice care by diverse groups include active community outreach. Agencies should focus attention on recruiting a diverse staff and board members and making services culturally amenable (Gordon 1996; Lyke 2004) in order to build trust in the services.

Rural/urban disparity. Both population density and geographic location have been found to be important in the use of hospice services by Medicare recipients. Lower rates of hospice usage were associated with lower population density and greater distance from an urban area (Virnig et al. 2004). Rate of hospice use prior to death for residents of urban counties were 22.2 per hundred deaths, 17.0 deaths for rural counties adjacent to urban areas, and 15.2 for rural areas not adjacent to an urban area (Virnig et al. 2002). One recent study found that 2,900 ZIP codes in the United States are not served by hospice services. The availability of hospice services was strongly correlated with an urban influence. Ninety percent of the ZIP codes in rural areas adjacent to urban areas are served by hospice; only 76 percent of the ZIP codes in rural areas nonadjacent to urban areas are (Virnig et al. 2006).

Along with barriers such as lack of education about hospice care, low socioeconomic status, and racial/cultural issues, another challenge to providing access to services for rural residents is that the agencies often are not physically located within the rural community. Therefore, an additional barrier may be the distrust of "outsiders." In addition, when an individual does choose to enroll in hospice services, often staff must travel a great distance to reach the rural residents. This geographic distance may influence or compromise the timeliness and frequency of services provided due to the costs involved.

Implications for Home-Based Practice

Although there has been a tremendous rate of growth in the use and accessibility of hospice services, it is not believed to have reached a "steady state" with respect to "market penetration." (individuals/families served by hospice providers). Currently, 33 percent of decedents have received hospice care prior to death (Connor et al. 2007). It is yet unknown what the optimal level of individuals/families served should be, although some have suggested a percentage as high as 67 percent. This means that there is still ample room for continued expansion of hospice services so more individuals and families can benefit (Connor et al. 2007). A primary strategy is education and outreach aimed at increasing access to hospice services among underserved populations.

The potential for social work in hospice care is yet to be fully realized. The value of working with individuals and families in the home setting has long been established in the social work profession and will likely remain a preferred strategy for intervention, particularly in hospice care. Social workers can seize this opportunity by furthering efforts to document the effectiveness of interventions, to show that the beliefs and values of the profession can not only support individuals and families in their quest toward a "good" death experience but also help agencies be more efficient. It is incumbent on social workers in hospice care to keep current on best practices in the field and to engage in continuing education.

REFERENCES

Campos, A. P., ed. 1990. *Social work practice with Puerto Rican terminally ill clients and their families.* Springfield, Ill.: Charles C. Thomas.

Colon, M. 2005. Hospice and Latinos: A review of the literature. *Journal of Social Work in End-of-Life and Palliative Care* 1 (2): 27–43.

——. 2003. Comparison of hospice use and demographics among European Americans, African Americans, and Latinos. *American Journal of Hospice Care and Palliative Care* 20 (3): 182–190.

Connor, S. R., Elwert, F., Spence, C., and Christakis, N. A. 2007. Geographic variation in hospice use in the United States in 2002. *Journal of Pain and Symptom
Management* 34 (3): 277–285.

Csikai, E. L. 2004. Social workers' participation in the resolution of ethical dilemmas in hospice care. *Health and Social Work* 29(1): 67–76.

Ferrell, B. R. 1998. The family. In *Oxford textbook of palliative medicine*, ed. D. Doyle,
G. Hanks, and N. MacDonald, 909–917. Oxford: Oxford University Press.

Feudtner, C., Feinstein, J. A., Satchell, M., and Zhao, H. 2007. Shifting place of
death among children with complex chronic conditions in the United States,
1989–2003. *JAMA* 297 (24): 2725–2732.

Gelfand, D. E., Balcazar, H., Parzuchowski, J., and Lenox, S. 2001. Mexicans and
care for the terminally ill: Family, hospice, and the church. *American Journal of
Hospice and Palliative Care* 18 (6): 391–396.

Gordon, A. K. 1996. Hospice and minorities: A national study of organizational access and practice. *The Hospice Journal* 11 (1): 49–70.

Harper, B. C. 1995. Report from the National Task Force on access to hospice care
by minority groups. *The Hospice Journal* 10 (2): 1–9.

Hopp, F. P. D. 2000. Racial variations in end-of-life care. *Journal of the American
Geriatrics Society* 48: 658–663.

Kulys, R., and Davis, M. 1986. An analysis of social services in hospices. *Social
Work* 31: 448–456.

——. 1987. Nurses and social workers: Rivals in the provision of social services?
Health and Social Work 12 (1): 101–112.

Lyke, J. C. 2004. Practical recommendations for ethnically and racially sensitive
hospice services. *Journal of Hospice and Palliative Medicine* 21 (2): 131–133.

MacDonald, D. 1991. Hospice social work: A search for identity. *Health and Social
Work* 16 (4): 274–280.

Monroe, B. 1998. Social work in palliative care. In *Oxford textbook of palliative medicine*, ed. G. H. D. Doyle and N. MacDonald, 867–882. Oxford: Oxford University
Press.

NASW. 2004. *Standards for palliative and end-of-life care*. Washington, D.C.: NASW.

NHPCO. 2007a. NHPCO facts and figures—2005 findings. Available online at
http://www.nhpco.org.

——. 2007b. *Social work guidelines*. Alexandria, Va.: NHPCO.

O'Mara, A. M. 2001. Minority representation, prevalence of symptoms, and utilization of services in a large metropolitan hospice. *Journal of Pain and Symptom
Management* 21 (4): 290–297.

Randall, H. C. 2003. Issues affecting utilization of hospice services by rural Hispanics. *Journal of Ethnic and Cultural Diversity in Social Work* 12 (2): 79–94.

Raymer, M. R. 2004. The history of social work in hospice. In *Living with dying: A handbook for end-of-life healthcare practitioners*, ed. J. S. Berzoff, 150–160. New York: Columbia University Press.

Reese, D. J., and Raymer, M. 2004. Relationships between social work involvement and hospice outcomes: Results of the national hospice social work survey. *Social Work* 49 (3): 415–422.

Reese, D. J., Raymer, M., and Richardson, J. 2000. *National Hospice Social Work Survey: Summary of Final Results*. Alexandria, Va.

Reese, D. J., Raymer, M., Orloff, S. F., Gerbino, S., Valade, R., Dawson, S., et al. 2006. The social work assessment tool (SWAT). *Journal of Social Work in End-of-Life and Palliative Care* 2 (1): 65–95.

Reese, D. J., Ahern, R. E., Nair, S., O'Faire, J. D., and Warren, C. 1999. Hospice access and use by African Americans: Addressing cultural and institutional barriers through participatory action research. *Social Work* 44 (6): 549–559.

Rhodes, R. L., Teno, J. M., and Welch, L. C. 2006. Access to hospice for African Americans: Are they informed about the option of hospice? *Journal of Palliative Medicine* 9 (2): 268–272.

Saunders, C. 1998. Foreword. *In Oxford textbook of palliative medicine*, ed. G. H. D. Doyle and N. MacDonald, v–ix. Oxford: Oxford University Press.

Teno, J. M., Clarridge, B. R., Casey, V., Welch, L. C., Wetle, T., Shield, R., et al. 2004. Family perspectives on end-of-life care at the last place of care. *JAMA* 291 (1): 88–93.

U.S. Department of Health and Human Services (USHHS). 2007. *Centers for Medicare and Medicaid services*. Available online at http://www.cms.hhs.gov/home/medicare.asp.

Virnig, B. A., Ma, H., Hartman, L. K., Moscovice, I., and Carlin, B. 2006. Access to home-based hospice care for rural populations: Identification of areas lacking service. *Journal of Palliative Medicine* 9 (6): 1292–1299.

Virnig, B. A., McBean, A. M., Kind, S., and Dholakia, R. 2002. Hospice use before death: Variability across cancer diagnoses. *Medical Care* 40: 73–78.

Virnig, B. A., Moscovice, I., Kind, S., and Casey, M. 2004. Do rural beneficiaries have limited access to the Medicare hospice benefit? *Journal of the American Geriatric Society* 52: 731–735.

WHO. 1990. Definition of "palliative care." Available online at http://www.who.int/cancer/palliative/en.

Social Work Assessment Tool (SWAT)

Complete after each social work visit. Rate the patient on how well (s)he is doing on concerns regarding each issue. Rate the primary caregiver on how well (s)he is doing on each issue, OR on how well (s)he is coping with patient concerns regarding the issue. If there are no concerns in an area, circle 5 ("extremely well"). Each issue should be assessed during each client contact.

Date of social work visit: _____

HOW WELL ARE PATIENT AND PRIMARY CAREGIVER DOING?

ISSUE:	PATIENT					PRIMARY CAREGIVER				
	1 Not well at all	2 Not too well	3 Neutral	4 Reasonably well	5 Extremely well	1 Not well at all	2 Not too well	3 Neutral	4 Reasonably well	5 Extremely well
1. End-of-life decisions consistent with their religious and cultural norms	1	2	3	4	5	1	2	3	4	5
2. Patient has thoughts of suicide or wanting to hasten death	1	2	3	4	5	1	2	3	4	5
3. Anxiety about death	1	2	3	4	5	1	2	3	4	5
4. Preferences about environment (e.g., pets, own bed, etc.)	1	2	3	4	5	1	2	3	4	5
5. Social support	1	2	3	4	5	1	2	3	4	5

(continued)

Social Work Assessment Tool (SWAT) *(continued)*

HOW WELL ARE PATIENT AND PRIMARY CAREGIVER DOING?

ISSUE:	PATIENT					PRIMARY CAREGIVER				
	1 Not well at all	2 Not too well	3 Neutral	4 Reasonably well	5 Extremely well	1 Not well at all	2 Not too well	3 Neutral	4 Reasonably well	5 Extremely well
6. Financial resources	1	2	3	4	5	1	2	3	4	5
7. Safety issues	1	2	3	4	5	1	2	3	4	5
8. Comfort issues	1	2	3	4	5	1	2	3	4	5
9. Complicated anticipatory grief (e.g., guilt, depression, etc.)	1	2	3	4	5	1	2	3	4	5
10. Awareness of prognosis	1	2	3	4	5	1	2	3	4	5
11. Spirituality (e.g., higher purpose in life, sense of connection with all)	1	2	3	4	5	1	2	3	4	5

The Social Work Assessment Tool was developed by the Social Work Outcomes Task Force of the Social Work Section, National Hospice and Palliative Care Organization, National Council of Hospice and Palliative Professionals. Members of the Task Force included Mary Raymer, ACSW, Dona Reese, Ph.D., MSW, Ruth Huber, Ph.D., MSW, Stacy Orloff, Ed. D., LCSW, and Susan Gerbino, Ph.D., MSW. Further information can be obtained from Dona Reese, Social Work Section Leader, NHPCO (dona.reese@gmail.com).

PART III

Conclusion

Thirteen

Conclusions and Considerations
for the Future

ELIZABETH M. TRACY AND SUSAN F. ALLEN

Service delivery in the home is a vital aspect of care across many service-delivery systems and client populations. Home-based services are evident across the lifespan—from early childhood programs to hospice and end-of-life care. As stated in chapter 1, authors contributing to this book have presented the "who, what, when, and where" of home visiting within contemporary social work practice. Chapters identify different target audiences for home-based services (the who) and describe the type and scope of such services (the what) within the dimensions of the lifespan period to which the services are directed (the when) and the larger service-delivery system (the where). The purpose of this volume was to present a comprehensive overview of home-based services to clients in a range of social work fields of practice, focusing on the current context of services from a practice and policy perspective. Taken as a whole, the chapters in this book allow us to examine a variety of models for the delivery of home-based services and to identify key factors and issues crucial to effective home-based practice with the range of clients served in social work fields of practice. This final chapter will compare and contrast the models presented in the preceding chapters with the goal of outlining an overall conceptual framework and future directions for home-based social work.

Home-based services and home visiting within social work practice are best understood within the contexts in which they are delivered. Figure 13.1

depicts such a contextual understanding of home-based services. Each concentric circle represents a separate, yet often overlapping, context that shapes the focus and structure of home-based practice. These contexts include client/consumer, professional, and ethical issues, which are common to all forms of social work practice but which may be heightened when services are delivered in a home setting. Within the context of a focus on evidence-based practices, home-based services must draw from research on effective interventions and contribute to the research base on social work interventions. Each home-based program is shaped by the service-delivery system in which it is a part and the particular funding streams, accountability reporting systems, and administrative structures adopted by those systems. In turn, service-delivery systems are shaped and informed by the larger social welfare policy context, which includes social welfare legislation and regulations affecting practice. Naturally, there is interplay between each context; for example, social policies shape service-delivery systems, which in turn shape the practices carried out within the home setting, by whom and for how long. In addition, home-based services are but one of many forms of social work practice, and the place of home-based vis-à-vis other services or types of interventions, such as sessions in an office or school, is an important consideration as well. The remainder of this chapter will identify and discuss cross-cutting themes within each of these contexts, highlighting areas of commonality and distinction among the various client populations and fields of practice included in this volume.

Client/Consumer Issues

A unique contribution made by the chapter topics included this book is the voice they give to the consumer experience of home visiting. Across all fields of practice and developmental life phases, the client's experience of home-based services is different and, in many ways, may be more positive than office-based services. This perspective is most evident in the chapters on ethical practice, early childhood programs, school-based services, criminal justice, and older-adult services. Home-based practice brings social work back to its roots, in that the value of the relationship between the worker and client is made more visible and potent. The home visitors' use of self in the helping relationship appears to be an important element of home-based practice; research confirms that consumers value the relationship with the home visitor (see for example, chapters 5 and 10).

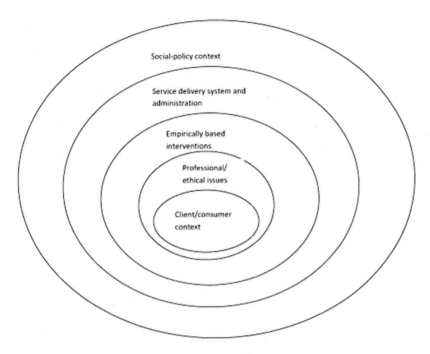

FIGURE 13.1 Home-Based Social Work Practice in Context

Related to the value placed on relationship are the very real challenges of engagement with clients in home settings, which becomes apparent across all fields of practice. Because home-based services are often put in place to enhance continuity of care or to access difficult-to-reach clients with multiple complex problems, the initial practice tasks of forming a working relationship or alliance will be more difficult yet all the more essential. For example, chapter 5 mentions the challenges of using home-based programs to reach teen parents, and chapters 9 and 10 discuss outreach to adults with serious mental health and/or criminal histories that may be living in board and care homes. Often, home-based services are delivered to one targeted client, yet other family members in the home have complex service needs as well. For example, family caregivers of older adults may experience depression or physical health problems related to their caregiving tasks, and thus work with older adults must take the needs of other family members into consideration. In child welfare, parents' needs in terms of their own previous abuse or substance use often must be addressed if the care of the child is to improve.

As discussed in many of the chapters in this book, disability issues and health concerns are evident throughout the lifespan, which may pose considerable barriers to the home-based worker. For example, early childhood home-based services and the role of the home-based provider must adapt to fit the needs of a parent with a health problem such as multiple sclerosis.

In addition, establishing who the client is may be more complex in the home setting. Although determining who the client is (the target of change) is an element in all forms of social work practice, completion of this basic practice task is often more complex in the home setting. Several chapters discuss the issues involved in balancing the needs of more than one household member, for example, the child's needs versus the parents' needs in child mental health interventions or the family's needs versus those of the member with mental illness or dementia. Many fields of practice define the client as the family jointly; this is common in early childhood home visiting and home-based hospice care, where the needs and concerns of both the targeted client and the family (including extended family) are incorporated in the service plan. The ability to discover and make use of informal helping resources appears as a common factor across home visiting in many contexts; home-based social workers seek to mobilize social networks on behalf of their clients. Personal social networks can be direct sources of support and help for the identified client but also may be helpful indirectly to reduce the burden on the client's family members.

Professional and Ethical Issues

As described in chapter 2, home-based service delivery across all settings present characteristic professional and ethical issues. This is because the home-based social worker has increased exposure to information about the client and greater autonomy in clinical decision making but at the same time diminished control over the work setting (the client's home). While there is no specialized code of ethics for home-based practice, professional supervision and consultation serve important functions for home-based workers. The need for these and other programmatic supports for workers are outlined in chapter 3.

Because the home-based service provider typically assumes multiple roles in their work with a client/family (e.g., counselor, advocate, skills trainer, broker, educator, concrete services provider) within the less formal context of the home, establishing and maintaining appropriate boundaries may be a particular practice issue of concern. The home-based worker is often charged with roles and tasks beyond practice as usual in an office setting. For example, home-based social workers provide a wide variety of concrete services and supports (e.g., teaching transportation or shopping skills as part of mental health case management). Several chapters discuss the issues of being perceived as a "friend" and the blurring of boundaries that may result.

Related to boundary and role issues is the professional identity of those employed as home-based workers. Social workers in home-based services may belong to the profession of social work or to the more nebulous occupation of home-based worker. For example, some case managers who provide services to older adults may be individuals without any formal social work training but who have the title of social worker. Similarly, in child welfare, social workers may be employed from a wide variety of backgrounds and yet be viewed as social workers. An overarching concept deriving from many of the chapters in this book is the problem of a professional definition of the role of the social workers in delivering home-based services. As presented in this volume, social worker training and preparation appear to be uniquely suited to home-based work and have much to offer in terms of assessment perspective, interventions, and brokering of resources, yet an understudied area is the relationship between worker training and client outcomes from home-based work.

A final professional issue addressed across all chapters is worker safety. While safety has been sensationalized in the media, it is a genuine concern for workers and agencies. Throughout this book, many practical guidelines have been offered for both workers and supervisors to ensure safety in home visits. Some guidelines, such as having the agency know the worker's whereabouts at all times and having access to a cellphone, involve program resources and adequate supervision. Other guidelines are dependent upon good assessment and engagement skills on the part of the worker and solid pre-service and in-service preparation and training for home- and community-based work. The appropriate use of technology has been cited as a means to not only improve safety but facilitate practice as well. The availability of cellphones, laptops, and teleconferencing can facilitate quick access to needed resources and team consultation. Telephone communication has also been used to monitor and support the health and well-being of clients in the home (see, for example, chapter 11).

Empirically Based Interventions

The chapters as a whole bring up issues of the place of home-based services in the context of evidence-based practice. To what extent are home-based services considered to be empirically based? What is the type and quality of evidence?

Are there particular models that are more effective than others? With which clients? With which interventions or service components? For how long? What is the cost-benefit analyses of home-based versus other forms of practice? The chapter authors highlight the challenges of conducting research on home-based services, including the particular difficulty of maintaining fidelity to treatment models when workers are dispersed across a wide geographic area and working largely on their own. The need for more research from a social work perspective on home-based practice is evident in nearly all fields of practice. The empirical base for home-based services is stronger in some fields of practice than others; for example, while there has been considerable research in home-based services within early childhood, child welfare, and child and adult mental health services, less research has been conducted in school-based and criminal justice contexts. However, in no field of practice are the questions posed above answered to a satisfactory extent. While home-based work draws from a wide range of theoretical frameworks, more research is needed on how particular models or approaches are adapted to home-based work. For example, chapter 11 discusses research studies of home-based work with older adults using task-centered, psychodynamic, psychoeducational, and brief-structured approaches. Home visits are often a component of interventions that are generally considered "evidence based," such as Assertive Community Treatment or Multisystemic Therapy; however, it can be difficult to discern the unique contribution of the home-visit component itself. More research is needed on which models are most effective with which client populations.

Service-Delivery Systems and Administration

Home-based programs are situated in a particular service-delivery system (e.g., child welfare) and agency context (e.g., public versus private nonprofit), which shape the format and structure of the program. Depending on the context, the definition of "home" may differ. In many contexts, the home is the physical structure in which the client and his or her family reside, but some programs provide home-based services to clients without homes, living in shelters, or in alternative homes such as nursing homes, group homes, and boarding houses. In such circumstances, home-based services are delivered in the setting that constitutes the psychological home and immediate social environment of the client. The common denominator is that these services are brought to the client, rather than the client having to go the services, and that the home-based worker makes full use of the environment in assessment and intervention, incorporating a strengths-based approach to practice. It is noted frequently in this book that home-based services serve the function of reaching out to clients who might not otherwise access or use more traditional services in office settings. Several chapters note differences between rural and urban settings in terms of the availability of home-based services, which professions are available to provide home-based services, and the fact that home-based services in some rural settings may serve multiple functions and purposes due to the relative lack of accessible services. Finally, the importance of the cultural context in the home and thus cultural competency of the home-based social worker is stressed in each chapter in this book. Culturally responsive home- based programs hire a racially and ethnically diverse group of home-based service providers and maintain cultural competency skills through in-service training and supervision.

Service delivery in the home means that the traditional ways in which agencies have administered social services must be altered. As noted by the authors of chapter 3 (on administrative practices), the weekly supervision hour and office-based team meetings, for example, must give way to ready access to supervision seven days a week and electronic forms of communication between staff and supervisors. Teamwork takes on different meanings in home-based work. Team members provide backup support for each other and take consultative roles. Since many clients have multiple problems that cross cut service-delivery systems (e.g., mental health and substance abuse), interdisciplinary teams can be crucial to home-based work. Administrators of home-based service programs must help workers manage interagency connections and foster interdisciplinary work. Because of the complexity of many situations that home-based workers face, maintaining reasonable caseloads even in the wake of reduced funding and increased productivity requirements is essential. It is also critical to ensure that adequate funding is available so that professionally trained social workers can be hired to deal with the complex situations faced in home-based work.

Social-Policy Context

Nearly all the authors in this book call for advocacy to increase the availability of home-based services along with research that can demonstrate the worth and value of home-based service delivery. Research is needed both to improve practice and to build a knowledge base for advocacy efforts. Social workers must articulate the need and rationale for home-based services and the contribution of home-based services to service effectiveness. From a policy perspective, many chapters note that home-based services are not available in all localities (e.g., in-home geriatric mental health services) and are underfunded in many parts of the country. Funding sources, both public and private, have been slow to cover out-of-office services like home-based care. Chapters mention the creativity needed to combine public and private sources to fund home-based services or the savvy use of public funding options, such as the Medicaid waivers discussed in chapter 8. The authors of chapter 4, in their review of social policies that may facilitate or act as a barrier to home-based service delivery, note that home-based care is not similarly "robust" in each service-delivery system. They note that overall family-centered services are not well integrated in our social welfare policies and legislation.

Many chapter authors call for reclaiming home-based services as social work's own. For example, as chapter 12 points out, the research conducted in hospice and end-of-care services highlights the advantages of social work involvement. Some authors fear that the social work role and contribution is undervalued by service-delivery systems. This undervaluing is revealed in low levels of funding and reimbursement for social work services, the hiring of human-service workers who do not have social work degrees as a less costly alternative, and inadequate supports made available for home-based workers. In some fields of practice, such as special and early childhood education, social work is a mandated discipline in the team approach to home-based services, but this is not the case in many of the systems covered in this text.

One final point from a social-policy perspective, which is repeated throughout this book, is that home visiting is not a panacea for larger societal ills. Home-based social workers will come face to face with the social and environmental problems confronting service recipients: poverty, social isolation, poor housing, neighborhood violence, inadequate health care, and lack of educational and/or recreational resources, among others. Language barriers, discrimination, and immigration laws may affect access to and availability of services. It can be difficult to implement home-based services in a social and political climate that is not responsive to the multiple and complex needs of vulnerable members of society. For example, chapter 10 discussed how negative community attitudes and lack of community resources were problematic for home-based adult mental health case managers. A resource-rich environment facilitates effective home-based services. Clients and workers deserve policies, funding, and staffing patterns that support effective service delivery in the home.

Concluding Thoughts

Home visiting, with its historical legacy in social work and important place in the current trend of community-based services, is positioned to be a vital part of social work practice for the future. It is crucial to provide training that prepares social workers for home-based practice by emphasizing culturally sensitive, family-centered approaches to help-giving, work in multidisciplinary teams, assessments and interventions that enhance client and community strengths and resources, and strategies that promote the safety of workers and clients. Future directions for social work research involve strengthening the evidence base for in-home services. Finally, as social advocates and policymakers, social workers can play a vital role in developing and reinforcing policies that support services delivered where individuals and families live, relate, and face daily challenges and triumphs: their homes.

Organizations Associated with Home-Based Programs, Research, or Policies

Ethical Issues and Guidelines

Association for Practical and Professional
    Ethics (Indiana University)
Indiana University
618 East Third Street
Bloomington, IN 47405-3602
http://www.indiana.edu/~appe/
(812) 855-6450

Institute for Global Ethics
11 Main Street
P.O. Box 563
Camden, ME 04843
http://www.globalethics.org
(207) 236-6658; (800) 729-2615 (U.S. only)

The Parr Center for Ethics
Department of Philosophy
University of North Carolina at Chapel Hill
Caldwell Hall
Campus Box Number 3125
Chapel Hill, NC 27599-3125
http://parrcenter.unc.edu
(919) 843-5641

Early Childhood Programs

Chapin Hall Center for Children
1313 East Sixtieth Street
Chicago, IL 60637
http://www.chapinhall.org
(773) 753-5900

Healthy Families America
500 N. Michigan Avenue, Suite 200
Chicago, IL 60611
http://www.healthyfamiliesamerica.org/home/index.shtml
(312) 663-3520

High Scope/Perry Preschool project
600 North River Street
Ypsilanti, MI 48198-2898
http://www.highscope.org/index.asp
(734) 485-2000

Indigenous Early Intervention Alliance
411 North Central Avenue #880M
Phoenix, AZ 85004
http://indigenous-early-intervention.com
(602) 496-0102

Invest in Children, Cleveland, Ohio
Center on Urban Poverty
11235 Bellflower Road
Cleveland, OH 44106
http://povertycenter.cwru.edu
(216) 368-6946

National Early Intervention Longitudinal Study
SRI International
333 Ravenswood Avenue, BS129
Menlo Park, CA 94025
http://www.sri.com/neils
(800) 682-9319

Nurse Family Partnership Program
1900 Grant Street, Suite 400
Denver, CO 80203
http://www.nursefamilypartnership.org
(866) 864-5226

Parents as Teachers
Parents as Teachers National Center
Attn: Public Information Specialist
2228 Ball Drive
St. Louis, MO 63146
http://www.parentsasteachers.org
(314) 432-4330

Research and Training Center on Service Coordination
UConn Health Center
A. J. Pappanikou Center for Excellence in Developmental Disabilities
263 Farmington Avenue, MC 6222
Farmington, CT 06030
http://www.uconnucedd.org/Projects/RTC/
(860) 679-1500; (866) 623-1315

School-Based Services

Fast Track Project
Fast Track Child Study Center
Pennsylvania State University, USB1
University Park, PA 16802
http://www.fasttrackproject.org/

Harvard Family Involvement Project
3 Garden Street
Cambridge, MA 02138
http://www.gse.harvard.edu/hfrp/projects/fine/resources/guide
(617) 495-9108

Child Welfare

Child Welfare League of America
440 First Street NW, 3rd Floor
Washington, DC 20001-2085
http:///www.cwla.org
(202) 638-4004

"Friends" National Resource Center for Community-Based
    Family Resource and Support Programs
Chapel Hill Training-Outreach Project
800 Eastowne Drive, Suite 105
Chapel Hill, NC 27514
http://www.friendsnrc.org
(800) 888-7970

Healthy Families America
(See Early Childhood Programs)

Homebuilders
34004 Sixteenth Avenue South, Suite 200
Federal Way, WA 98003-8903
http://www.institutefamily.org
(253) 874-3630 (Seattle); (253) 927-1550 (Tacoma)

National Child Welfare Resource Center
    for Family-Centered Practice
Learning Systems Group
1150 Connecticut Avenue NW, Suite 1100
Washington, DC 20036
http://www.cwresource.org
(202) 638-3812

National Clearinghouse on Child Abuse and Neglect
330 C Street SW
Washington, DC 20447
http://cbexpress.acf.hhs.gov
(800) 394-3366

National Family Preservation Network
3971 North 1400 East
Buhl, ID 83116
http://www.nfpn.org
(888) 498-9047

National Resource Center on Child Maltreatment
1349 West Peachtree Street NE, Suite 900
Atlanta, GA 30309-2956
http://gocwi.org/nrccm
(404) 881-0707

National Resource Center for Foster Care and Permanency Planning
Hunter College School of Social Work
129 East Seventy-ninth Street, Room 802
New York, NY 10021
http://guthrie.hunter.cuny.edu/socwork/nrcfcpp
(212) 452-7053

Child Mental Health

Blueprints for Violence Prevention
Center for the Study and Prevention of Violence
Institute of Behavioral Science
University of Colorado at Boulder
1877 Broadway, Suite 601
Boulder, CO 80302
http://www.colorado.edu/cspv/blueprints/index.html
(303) 492-1032

Federation of Families for Children's Mental Health
9605 Medical Center Drive, Suite 280
Rockville, MD 20850
http://www.ffcmh.org/systems_whatis.htm
(240) 403-1901

Louis de la Parte Florida Mental Health Institute
University of South Florida
13301 Bruce B. Downs Blvd.
Tampa, FL 33612
http://home.fmhi.usf.edu
(813) 974-4602

National Association for Family-Based Services
6824 Fifth Street NW
Washington, DC 20012
http://www.nafbs.org
(202) 291-7587

National Center on Family Group Decision Making
American Humane Association
63 Inverness Drive
East Englewood, CO 80112
http://www.fgdm.org
(303) 925-9421

National Registry of Evidenced-Based Programs
    and Practices (NREPP), Substance Abuse
    and Mental Health Services Administration
1 Choke Cherry Road
Rockville, MD 20857
http://nrepp.samhsa.gov
(866) 436-7377

Research and Training Center on Family Support
and Children's Mental Health
Regional Research Institute for Human Services
Portland State University
Portland, OR 97207-0751
http://www.rtc.pdx.edu
(503) 725-4175

Criminal Justice

Campaign for Youth Justice
1012 Fourteenth Street NW, Suite 610
Washington, DC 20005
http://www.campaignforyouthjustice.org
(202) 558-3580

Monterey County, California, Prisoner Reentry
Program and Research
Salinas One Stop Career Center
730 La Guardia Street
Salinas, CA 93902
http://www.onestopmonterey.org/gsipub
(831) 796-3363

Multidimensional Treatment Foster Care
OSLC Community Programs
315 West Broadway
Eugene, OR 97401
http://www.mtfc.com/
(541) 343-2388 x204

Multisystemic Therapy for Juvenile Offenders
710 J. Dodds Blvd., Suite 200
Mt. Pleasant, SC 29464
http://www.mstservices.com
(843) 856-8226

National Institute of Corrections
791 N. Chambers Rd.
Aurora, CO 80011
http://www.nicic.org
(800) 877-1461

Office of Juvenile Justice and Delinquency Prevention
(OJJDP), Model Programs
810 Seventh Street NW
Washington, DC 20531
http://ojjdp.ncjrs.org/Programs/mpg.html
(202) 307-5911

Serious and Violent Offender Reentry Initiative,
Multisite Evaluation
Office of Justice Programs
810 Seventh Street NW
Washington, DC 20531
http://www.svori-evaluation.org
(202) 305-1367

Adult Mental Health

Assertive Community Treatment Association
810 East Grand River Avenue, Suite 102
Brighton, MI 48116
http://www.actassociation.org
(810) 227-1859

Center for Psychiatric Rehabilitation
940 Commonwealth Avenue, West
Boston, MA 02215
http://www.bu.edu/cpr
(617) 353-3549

National Association of Case Management
The National Association of Case Management (NACM)
37 Coconut Lane
Ocean Ridge, FL 33435
http://www.yournacm.addr.com
(561) 364-1349

The University of Kansas Strengths Institute
University of Kansas, School of Social Welfare
1545 Lilac Lane
Twente Hall
Lawrence, KS 66044-3184
http://www.socwel.ku.edu/Strengths
(785) 864-4720

Older Adult Services

Aging Network Services
Topaz House
4400 East-West Highway, Suite 907
Bethesda, MD 20814
http://www.agingnets.com
(301) 657-4329

Aging Practice Update
National Association of Social Workers
750 First Street NE, Suite 700
Washington, DC 20002-4241
http://www.socialworkers.org
(202) 408-8600

American Association of Service Coordination
521 Village Park Drive
Powell, OH 43065
http://www.servicecoordinator.org
(614) 848-5958

Medicaid Institute, Connecting Care Systems
Medicaid Institute at United Hospital Fund
Empire State Building
350 Fifth Avenue, Floor 23
New York, NY 10118
http://www.medicaidinstitute.org
(212) 494-0700

On Lok Senior Health
On Lok Development Department
1333 Bush Street
San Francisco, CA 94109
http://www.onlok.org
(415) 292-8768

Hospice and End-of-Life Care

Center for Medicare and Medicaid Services (CMS)
7500 Security Boulevard
Baltimore, MD 21244
http://www.cms.hhs.gov
(800) 633-4227

National Hospice and Palliative Care Organization (NHPCO)
1700 Diagonal Road, Suite 625
Alexandria, VA 22314
http://www.nhpco.org
(703) 837-1500

Administrative Supports and Practices

Addiction Technology Transfer Center
National Office
University of Missouri–Kansas City
5100 Rockhill Road
Kansas City, MO 64110
http://www.nattc.org/index.html
(816) 235-6888

Promising Practices
RAND Corporation
1776 Main Street
Santa Monica, CA 90401
http://www.promisingpractices.net/default.asp
(310) 393-0411, x7172

The authors are indebted to Suzanne Brown, MSW, LICSW, for her assistance in compiling the electronic resources in this appendix.

Contributors

Kathryn Betts Adams is assistant professor of social work at the Mandel School of Applied Social Sciences, Case Western Reserve University, in Cleveland, Ohio, where she teaches the course in social work practice with older adults. Her major research interests are the measurement of geriatric depression, the intersection of normal aging and depression in late life, and the emotional experiences and mental health of dementia patients and their family caregivers. She received her Ph.D. from the University of Maryland at Baltimore.

Susan F. Allen, assistant professor of social work at the University of South Florida, St. Petersburg, has over twenty years of clinical experience working with children, families, and adults in both home-based and center-based settings. Her research interests are prevention programs for young children and their families, the effect of home and family environment on child outcomes, and child-care policy and practice. She received a Ph.D. in social welfare from the Mandel School of Applied Social Sciences, Case Western Reserve University.

Mary Armstrong is assistant professor and director of the Division of State and Local Support, Department of Child and Family Studies, at the Louis de la Parte Florida Mental Health Institute, University of South Florida. Her current research focuses on financing of effective children's mental health systems, the effects of public-sector managed care on children with serious emotional problems, the effects of child welfare privatization and IV-E waivers, mental health literacy among caregivers and providers, and resilience of children in multiple countries. She has a Ph.D. in social work from Memorial University of Newfoundland, Canada.

José B. Ashford is a professor and associate director in the School of Social Work in the College of Public Programs at Arizona State University. He is also the director of the Office of Forensic Social Work and an affiliate professor in the School of Criminology and Criminal Justice and the School of Justice and Social Inquiry. Dr. Ashford has published widely in the areas of forensic and correctional mental health and is the associate editor of the forensic social work section of the second edition of the *Social Workers' Desk Reference*. Dr. Ashford has a Ph.D. in sociology, specializing in criminology and deviant behavior, from Bowling Green State University, Ohio.

Maureen F. Balaam is a licensed marriage and family therapist with twenty-seven years experience in California's mental health system working with children and adults with serious mental illness. She implemented Monterey County's Mentally Ill Offender Crime Reduction grant in 2001 and designed the clinical program that complemented their mental health court. Currently she is in private practice in Monterey, California. She received her M.S. in counseling from San Francisco State University.

Roger Boothroyd is a professor and the associate chair in the Department of Mental Health Law and Policy at the Louis de la Parte Florida Mental Health Institute, University of South Florida. He is currently the principal investigator on a state-funded study to evaluate Florida's Medicaid managed care mental health programs and the principal investigator on an NIH-funded study of research methods. Dr. Boothroyd has a Ph.D. in educational psychology from the State University of New York at Albany.

Katharine Briar-Lawson is dean and professor at the School of Social Welfare, State University of New York at Albany. She is a national expert on family-focused practice and child and family policy. Among her books are *Family-Centered Policies and Practices: International Implications* (coauthored), *Innovative Practices with Vulnerable Children and Families* (coedited), and two volumes on *Evaluation Research in Child Welfare* (coedited). She is the president of the National Association of Deans and Directors of Schools of Social Work. She received her Ph.D. from the University of California, Berkeley.

Katharine Cahn is the executive director of the Child Welfare Partnership at Portland State University's Graduate School of Social Work. Her areas of interest focus on improving the child welfare system and include dynamics of systems change and the adoption and sustaining of innovation; leadership roles of managers and supervisors; collaborative, family-driven, strengths-based practice; promoting youth and family voice; kinship care; and racial/ethnic justice. She coedited *Children Can't Wait*, a book on permanency planning and court collaboration. Dr. Cahn earned a Ph.D. in social work and social welfare research from Portland State University.

Ellen L. Csikai is associate professor in the School of Social Work at the University of Alabama. Her areas of teaching and research are focused on social work practice in health care, end-of-life care and decision making, aging, and crisis intervention. Dr. Csikai is the editor of the *Journal of Social Work in End-of-Life and Palliative Care*. She has coauthored two textbooks: *Ethics in End-of-Life Decisions for Social Work Practice* and *Teaching Resources for End-of-Life and Palliative Care Courses*. Dr. Csikai received her Ph.D. from the University of Pittsburgh.

Mary E. Evans is a distinguished university health professor and the associate dean for research and doctoral study at the College of Nursing, University of South Florida. She is a child mental health services researcher with interests in interventions for children with emotional and behavioral problems and their families and in system-level issues such as collaboration and conflict in interorganizational efforts to serve this population. Dr. Evans has a Ph.D. in sociology from the State University of New York at Albany.

Cynthia Franklin is professor and holder of the Stiernberg/Spencer Family Professorship in Mental Health at the University of Texas at Austin, School of Social Work. She is an internationally known leader in school-based mental health practice, with over one hundred publications in the professional literature and several books, including *The School Services Sourcebook: A Guide for School-Based Professionals*, *Family Treatment: Evidence-Based Practice with Populations at Risk*, and *Clinical Assessment for Social Workers*, now in its second edition. She earned her Ph.D. at the University of Texas at Arlington.

Mindy Holliday is an assistant professor at Portland State University, School of Social Work. She has experience as a practitioner and program director for home-services programs: the VESTA program for adjudicated youth, Detroit, Michigan; Families First in Macomb County, Michigan; and the HOME-BUILDERS program in Clark County, Washington. Her research focuses on barriers to services for indigenous groups in Mexico, communities of color in the U.S. juvenile justice system, and lesbians and their families. She earned an M.S.W. from the University of Michigan and an M.A. in cultural anthropology and sociology from Oakland University in Rochester, Michigan.

Anne Kuppinger is an independent consultant with over twenty years of experience facilitating the development of effective, integrated systems of care for children. She has worked with state and local governments, youth and family advocacy organizations, and private providers to conduct strategic planning, policy reform, implementation management, evaluation, and resource development. She was responsible for the administration of home-based crisis-intervention services, family-based treatment, and federally funded demonstration projects at the New York State Office of Mental Health. She received her M.Ed. from the University of Maryland at College Park

Christine Lagana-Riordan is a Ph.D. student at the University of Texas at Austin's School of Social Work, with experience as a school social worker serving students with special cognitive and mental health needs. Her research interests include school social work, developmental disabilities, and education policy. She is currently the co-principal investigator on a study examining school social workers' perceptions about educational accountability in Texas. She earned an M.S.W. from the University of Maryland at Baltimore.

Cathleen A. Lewandowski is an associate professor at the School of Social Welfare, State University of New York at Albany, and director of the Center of Human Services Research. Her recent research has focused on drug-treatment outcomes for women who are receiving child welfare, welfare, and drug-treatment services. She has also studied the needs of social workers who work in public agencies such as child welfare. She is a clinical social worker in the U.S. Army Reserves and consults with military leaders on how to best support military families. Her Ph.D. is from the University of Kansas.

Kristine Nelson is dean and professor at the School of Social Work at Portland State University in Oregon. She has been the principal investigator on six federally funded studies of family preservation services and child neglect and has participated in several national symposia and expert panels on research and research methodology in these areas. Dr. Nelson is coauthor of *Reinventing Human Services: Community- and Family-Centered Practice, Evaluating Family-Based Services*, and *Alternative Models of Family Preservation: Family-Based Services in Context*. Dr. Nelson earned her doctoral degree at the University of California, Berkeley.

Katherine Sternbach is a principal with Mercer Government Human Services Consulting at Mercer Health & Benefits LLC. She specializes in the design, implementation, and management of behavioral-health service systems. She has experience at the national, state, and local levels with behavioral-health programs, developmental-disabilities systems, and jails and criminal justice agencies. She also has expertise in government sector–managed behavioral health care. She received her M.Ed. from Northeastern University and an M.B.A. from Boston University.

Kim Strom-Gottfried is the Smith P. Theimann Jr. Distinguished Professor of Ethics and Professional Practice at the University of North Carolina, Chapel Hill. Dr. Strom-Gottfried is an active scholar, trainer, and consultant in the field of ethics. She has written numerous articles, monographs, and chapters on the ethics of practice. She is the author of *Straight Talk About Professional Ethics* and *The Ethics of Practice with Minors* and the coauthor of *Direct Social Work Practice* and *Teaching Social Work Values and Ethics: A Curriculum Resource*. She received her Ph.D. from the Mandel School of Applied Social Sciences, Case Western Reserve University.

Patrick Sullivan serves as professor at the Indiana University School of Social Work. He helped develop the strengths model of social work practice and has extended the model to mental health and addictions treatment. He has over sixty professional publications on a diverse range of topics. He received the Distinguished Hoosier Award from Governor Frank O'Bannon in 1997 and earned the Sagamore of the Wabash, the highest civilian honor awarded in Indiana, from Governor Joseph Kernan in 2004. Dr. Sullivan has a Ph.D. from the University of Kansas.

Elizabeth M. Tracy is a professor at the Mandel School of Applied Social Sciences, Case Western Reserve University, and is chair of the Ph.D. program there. Her research on the development and evaluation of social work practice methods that support families and make use of natural helping networks has been applied by other researchers to family-preservation programs, residential settings for youth, early intervention, and community mental health case management. She has coauthored a number of books, including *Person-Environment Practice: The Social Ecology of Interpersonal Helping* and *Social Work Practice with Children and Families*. Dr. Tracy received her Ph.D. from the University of Washington.

Index

concrete needs, 145–46, 148, 152, 291
Conduct Problems Prevention Research Group, 121
confidentiality, 8, 14, 24–25, 31, 102, 128. *See also* privacy
consultation, 21, 23, 28
continuity of care, 4, 37, 289
continuity theory, 247
coping skills: of family, 164; framework for older adults, 247; of students/families, 119
Council of Chief State School Officials, 57, 114
countertransference, 28, 255
criminal justice, 11, 61–64, 189–214; adult offenders, 61–63; diversity issues/populations at risk and, 206–7; electronic monitoring and, 62–63, 73; empirical base for, 199–203; focus groups for, 195; GPS technology and, 62; home-based practice implications for, 193–96, 207–8; juvenile offender and, 63–64; needs assessment in, 192; policy/agency context of, 191–93; population, 189–91; practice guidelines for, 203–6; purpose/goals of home-based service and, 193–96; RNR theory of, 197–98, 207–8; substance abuse and, 196–97; theoretical framework for, 196–99
Crisis Case Management (CCM), 171, 172–73, 174
cross-sector collaboration, 73, 74
CSP. *See* Community Support Program
cultural competence, 31, 49, 60, 86, 103, 127, 148–49, 293; of geriatric social workers, 257; parent/family advocates and, 179
culture, 231, 277–78
CYICM. *See* Children and Youth Intensive Case Management model

DECA. *See* Deveraux Early Childhood Assessment
Denver II, *98*
Department of Health and Human Services, 219
depression, 216, 218, 225, 246, 251
Deveraux Early Childhood Assessment (DECA), *98*
diversity: adult mental health and, 230–32; child mental health and, 179–80; criminal justice and, 206–7; early childhood services issues of, 102–4; hospice services and, 277–80; older adult services and, 256–58; program design and, 103–4; school-based services issues of, 126–28
domestic violence, 69, 149, 177; assessment of, 135; offenders, 62

Early and Periodic Screening, Diagnosis, and Treatment Provision, of Title XIX, of Social Security Act, 61
early childhood programs, 56–57, 81–110, 290, 294; challenges for, 104–5; for children with disabilities/poor developmental outcomes, 81; diversity/populations at risk and, 102–4; ecological perspective of, 88, 90, 143; effective home visiting components and, 97; empirical base for, 91–102; family-centered practice for, 81–82; federal/state budget cuts for, 104; parent education for, 84; policy/agency context for, 84–86; population for, 82–85; populations at risk for, 102–4; practice guidelines for, 97–102; pregnancy to age 5, 81; program evaluation for, 93–94; theoretical framework for, 88, 90–91; training/funding for, 85–86. *See also* early intervention services
Early Head Start (EHS), 56, 87, 104; family retention and, 95